For Margaret, Matthew, and Penelope

Acknowledgments

Many of our ideas have been developed in the course of conversations with Carolyn Cooper and Michael Raber, our colleagues and collaborators in numerous industrial archaeology projects. Robert Vogel, one of the first practitioners of industrial archaeology in the United States, has generously shared his extensive experience and insights, helped us with machine-tool studies, and allowed us to use his collections of photographs and documents.

Charles Hyde read the first draft of the manuscript and helped us with many valuable suggestions. He also shared his extensive knowledge of the industrial archaeology of Detroit and northern Michigan. Peter Liebhold assisted in our experiments with historic machine tools and helped us locate many illustrations.

A number of scholars have discussed interpretation in industrial archaeology with us, including Richard Anderson, Martin Blatt, John Bowditch, John Bowie, Pierre Bureau, James Celenza, Bruce Clouette, John Cotter, Victor Darnell, Susan Douglas, Edward Ezell, the late Michael Folsom, Robert Friedel, Greg Galer, Richard Greenwood, Laurence Gross, Richard Hills, Donald Hoke, David Hounshell, Donald Jackson, Emory Kemp, David Killick, Larry Lankton, Thomas Leary, Svante Lindqvist, Carter Litchfield, Steven Lubar, Judith McGaw, Patrick Martin, Peter Molloy, Sandra Norman, Charles Parrott, Theodore Penn, Edward Pershey, Frederic Quivik, Terry Reynolds, Matthew Roth, Theodore Sande, Bruce Sinclair, Merritt Roe Smith, Myron Stachiw, David Starbuck, Robert Weible, David Weitzman, Dennis Zembala, and Michael Zuckerman.

Scholars who have shared unpublished manuscripts, reports, and research findings with us include Robert Asher, Betsy Bahr, Paul Bigelow, Lindy Biggs, Julia Bonham, Anne Booth, Nancy Cleary, Edward Connors,

James Conrad, Kim Dawson, Mary Donahue, Emma Dyson, Robert Frame, Kingston Heath, Michael Herbert, Demian Hess, Louis Hutchins, Steven Kasierski, Ginny Leslie, John Light, John Lozier, William Mass, John McGrain, Mark Newell, Scott Nixon, Douglas Reynolds, Victor Rolando, Edward Rutsch, Roch Samson, Helen Schenck, George Sellmer, Peter Stott, Alan Steiner, and Bonnie Stepenoff.

Institutions and individuals who allowed us to use specific illustrations are acknowledged in the figure captions, but there are others who deserve special credit for taking photographs, creating maps, or producing drawings. Lyn Malone used her cartographic skills to produce four of our figures. Charles Parrott drew the Wilkinson waterwheel and provided copies of other illustrations. Bill Sacco, Greg Galer, Charles Hyde, Matthew Roth, Brooke Hammerle, and Charles Francis did photography at our request. David Weitzman, who provided a number of photographs from his personal collection, made a special trip to photograph a California mining site for us.

Many colleagues at Yale have helped us with discussions and counsel, including Michael Coe, William Nordhaus, Turan Onat, Brian Skinner, and William Smith. William Cronon, Leo Hickey, and the other members of the faculty seminar on the environment have given us new insights, as have Abbott Cummings, Frank Hole, Howard Lamar, Jules Prown, and other members of the Yale American Art and Material Culture discussion group. Arthur Goodhue has given us an oral history of toolmaking. We have received help from Barbara McCorkle at the Sterling Memorial Library map room, Aida Rodriguez at the Kline Geology Laboratory, William Sacco of the Peabody Museum, Renee Kra, Barbara Narendra, and Stephen Victor.

Colleagues at Brown have been equally helpful. Joseph Steim read the petroleum sections, provided important sources and suggestions, and analyzed historic photographs. Susan Smulyan, Barrett Hazeltine, Hunter Dupree, and the late Carl Bridenbaugh were very generous with counsel and support. Richard Gould, Patricia Rubertone, and Larry Murphy provided anthropological insights. Peter Heywood helped with ecological theory. Paul Kahn and Cooper Abbott used the Intermedia computer program to model some of our ideas on wood technology. Kathy Franz assisted in research and with captions. Ned Connors proofread galleys. Carol Frost assisted in the preparation of the indexes. The American Civilization Department and the university administration provided a most welcome sabbatical leave at a critical point in this project.

The Smithsonian Institution has important collections of artifacts, drawings, and photographs. We have benefited from access to these collections and from assistance given by many members of the Smithsonian staff, including Nanci Edwards, Edward Ezell, Bernard Finn, Harry Hunter, Peggy

Kidwell, Gary Kulik, Peter Liebhold, Steven Lubar, Arthur Molella, Robert Post, Jim Rowan, Terry Sharrer, Carlene Stephens, Jeffrey Stine, Susan Tolbert, Deborah Warner, John White, William Worthington, and Helena Wright. A Regents' fellowship at the Smithsonian provided time for completion of the manuscript.

Eric Delony, Ellen Minnich, and Gray Fitzsimons helped us with access to the Historic American Engineering Record (HAER) collections of the National Park Service. Stephen Ostrow expedited the duplication of photographs from the HAER collections at the Library of Congress.

At the Slater Mill Historic Site, Holly Begley, William Johnson, and Gail Mohanty cooperated with enthusiasm. In addition, we got valuable help from former curatorial staff (Gary Kulik, Sandra Norman, Thomas Leary, Stephen Victor, Priscilla Brewer, John Johnson, and Robert Macieski) and from trustees such as Walter Pulawski, David Macaulay, Judith Benedict, and Dana Newbrook.

At the Museum of American Textile History, Laurence Gross read several sections of the manuscript, generously shared the results of his research on the textile industry, and found important documents, artifacts, and photographs for us. Clare Sheridan and her staff provided wonderful access to the library and graphics collections. Diane Affleck supplied information on fabrics. Directors Thomas Leavitt and Paul Rivard were highly supportive, and the museum awarded a generous Sullivan fellowship for research on incremental innovation in the textile industry.

Members of the Old Sturbridge Village research and curatorial staff who have given us new ideas on the transformation of American life from agricultural to industrial and helped us locate sources and photographs include Jack Larkin, John Worrell, Myron Stachiw, Caroline Sloat, Tom Kelleher, and Frank White.

At the Hugh Moore Museum, Lance Metz and Mike Knies helped us examine photographs. At the Henry Ford Museum and Greenfield Village, John Bowditch gave us a tour of the machinery collections, and archivists provided access to Ford Motor Company photographs. At the Hagley Museum, we were assisted by Frank McKelvey and Robert Howard. Stuart Frank, Mary Malloy, and Gare Reid at the Kendall Whaling Museum let us participate in several whale-oil renderings and provided data on the results of these imitative experiments. Greg Galer and James Parkinson showed us artifacts and videotapes at the Valentine Museum and helped us examine the site of the Tredegar Iron Works.

At the Springfield Armory National Historic Site, John McCabe, William Meuse, Richard Harkins, Larry Lowenthal, and Stuart Vogt answered many questions and located artifacts for us.

At the Rhode Island Historical Society, Denise Bastien and Joyce Botelho located photographs and maps, and Harold Kemble and Cynthia Bendroth showed us business records. Director Albert Klyberg was always supportive.

Director James Pepper and historian Douglas Reynolds of the Blackstone River Valley National Heritage Corridor Commission encouraged our work in the valley. Robert Giebner, Louis Hutchins, and Emma Dyson showed us in-progress reports and drawings of the HAER Slater Mill survey.

In Lowell, we received help from the Lowell Historic Preservation Commission, the Lowell National Historical Park, the Lowell Historical Society, the Proprietors of Locks and Canals, the University of Lowell, the Tsongas Industrial History Center, the Lowell Museum, the Lowell State Heritage Park, and the Mogan Center. The Baker Library at Harvard also made Lowell materials available to us.

In Danville, Pennsylvania, we had help from many people, including Mollie Harter, Ethel Hinkel, Judith Andrews, Eugene Shipe, and Thomas Magill. For news of the mine fire in nearby Centralia, we relied on George Schad, who sent us a stream of clippings. Also in Pennsylvania, Douglas Miller showed us Curtin Furnace.

The Pennsylvania Historical and Museum Commission has assisted us in numerous site tours and in searches for historical photographs. We are particularly grateful to director Brent Glass, to William Sisson and Brenda Barrett at the Bureau for Historic Preservation, to Vance Packard for helping us at various sites, to David Salay at the Anthracite Museum Complex, to Dan Perry at the Scranton Iron Furnaces, to Joyce Inman at the Drake Well Museum, and to Dolores Buchsen at the Pennsylvania Lumber Museum.

At the Rhode Island Historical Preservation Commission, we depended on Richard Greenwood, Paul Robinson, Edward Sanderson, W. McKenzie Woodward, and others. The Connecticut Historical Commission was also highly cooperative; Mary Donohue, David Poirier, and the late Herbert Darbee assisted us in many ways.

At the Rhode Island Department of Environmental Management, Judith Benedict and Ginny Leslie were particularly helpful.

Because the research for this book took us to many industrial sites with which we were not familiar, we have depended on people with expert knowledge of specific locales. In many cases, they not only shared information with us but also led field trips for us. Ross Allen, James Dawson, Morris Glenn, and Richard Ward took us to sites in the Adirondacks. Michael Folsom showed us the Waltham Watch Factory and the Ely smelter ruins. Michael Hughes guided us to the Methuen Mill. Susan and Dennis Frye and Paul Shackel took us on field trips to Harpers Ferry and Virginius Island. David Harvey arranged a trip to his experimental bloomery and to the smithy at Colonial Williamsburg. M. C. Korb brought us to the open-pit anthracite mine operated by Bethlehem mines. Peter Molloy and Kingston Heath led expeditions to mines and gold mills in the Rocky Mountains. James Kellett flew us over the Mississippi River in flood. Frank O'Hare and Donald Stevens introduced us to the Muskingum Canal and took us to locks and dams on the Ohio River. Rob Clapper paddled us in his canoe through the Enfield Canal. Matthew Roth and Peter Stott were our waterborne guides on several New England streams. Alex Barbour led us to a graveyard of steamboats on the Yukon River. Chuck Powell set up a scuba dive in the Bonne Terre Lead Mine. Thomas Leary and Marlene Nicoll showed us industry in western New York. Claire Mousseau brought us to the forges of Saint-Maurice in Canada. Karl Borgh explained the workings of the Knight foundry. John Staicer and Keith Bott arranged an inspection of the Hanford Mills Museum. Charles Hyde took us around Detroit's industrial areas and, with Larry Lankton and Patrick Martin, showed us the Michigan copper district as well. Mark Newell and John Shields led us around the Augusta Canal. Richard K. Anderson met us in South Carolina to provide a special tour of Columbia's industrial architecture.

Many of the sites mentioned in this book were examined on tours arranged by the Society for Industrial Archeology, the International Committee for the Conservation of the Industrial Heritage, the Society for Commercial Archeology, the Association for Preservation Technology, the Tsongas Industrial History Center, or the Society for the History of Technology. We are grateful to all volunteer organizers and guides of such tours and to the many operators of museums and businesses who opened their sites for study.

Finally, we want to thank our editors at Oxford University Press: Joyce Berry, Irene Pavitt, and Susan Denny deserve great credit for helping us turn our manuscript into a book.

New Haven, Conn.   R.B.G.
Providence, R.I.   P.M.M.
August 1992

Contents

THE TEXTURE
OF INDUSTRY

Introduction

As people in northern Europe and North America[1] industrialized their societies, they transformed the scale and the social setting of work and created opportunities for the use of new skills. They consumed forest and mineral resources, diverted rivers, and discarded wastes on a scale previously unknown. They placed rural and urban workplaces and transportation networks on the face of the land and increasingly detached patterns of daily life from their agricultural roots. With their new transportation and communication systems, Europeans, joined later by Americans, spread the influence of Western industry worldwide, first in the exploitation of distant, natural resources for use by the industrial nations and, later, by the delivery of industrial products to traditional societies.[2]

Until about A.D. 1000, Europeans used technology in much the same way as peoples in other parts of the world, but their adoption of water power for industry was a harbinger of change. In 1086, the Domesday survey of England revealed one water-powered grain mill for every fifty households.[3] Europeans began using mechanical power in tasks that included beer-making, fulling, tanning,[4] and ironmaking.[5] A conjunction of conveniently available natural resources, weak national governments, and religious beliefs that assigned dignity to work and that did not hinder technological enterprise helped Europeans to nucleate industrialization.[6] They subsequently brought their industrial heritage to North America. In the early decades of the republic, Americans began the stage of industrialization that soon came to dominate much of the landscape and most people's lives.

The rate at which Americans created an industrial society was slow compared with the rapidity with which they are now dismantling it. Already young Americans have lost most of their opportunities to see or experience the transformation of materials into finished products or to learn about the properties of wood and steel or about the handling of tools through personal experience. During the years of industrial growth, the village smithy often stood under a spreading chestnut tree, a place where

> . . . *children coming home from school*
> *Look in at the open door;*
> *They love to see the flaming forge,*
> *And hear the bellows roar,*
> *And catch the burning sparks that fly*
> *Like chaff from a threshing-floor.*[7]

Today young people are rarely allowed to enter workplaces for fear of lawsuit. The tactile experiences of making and shaping materials are being replaced by manipulation of images on video screens and by work in the so-called service or leisure industries. Symbolic of this change is our use of the word *works,* originally a factory but now a trendy way of designating a boutique.

The industrial experience, incredibly complex, touched deeply the values, art, and relation to the land of North Americans. But the popular and scholarly presentation of our industrial heritage has been largely framed in the narrow context of heroic inventors or, more commonly today, of the conflict between "labor" and "capital" established as a social issue in nineteenth-century Britain. These approaches are incomplete, and they deal with limited aspects of the texture of industrial life. Some of this texture is preserved in museums (much less in North America than in Europe, where interest in the industrial heritage has been stronger) and photographs, but this material is often displayed through the selective filter of nostalgia. Watching the crowds that pass through the industrial sections of the National Museum of American History in Washington, D.C., or the Henry Ford Museum in Dearborn, Michigan, will show an observer that Americans have much curiosity about their industrial heritage. A better understanding of past industrial experience can help us see the conditions necessary for the creation of wealth and the extent of its costs; it can help us understand the social consequences of replacing old industries with new ones and allow us to make informed decisions about the use of abandoned industrial sites. It can provide perspective for people coping with these changes.

Any attempt to study the industrial experience in North America through the documentary record alone faces immediate difficulties. Participants in past industries left few written records and only fragments of oral histories describing their work experiences. Business records yield information about finance and sales, but rarely about how work was carried out. Most descriptions of what went on in factories, mines, and mills were written by nonparticipants, who were often advocates rather than objective reporters.

Industrial archaeology is the study of historic industrial activity through analysis of both material and documentary evidence. It relies on the physical remains of industry to fill gaps in the documentary record and to provide information that is not easily conveyed in words or pictures. Material evidence—sites, structures, and artifacts—as well as the documentary record are interpreted by industrial archaeologists with methods drawn from archaeometry (the study of artifacts in the laboratory), field archaeology, art history, architectural recording, cartography, and other disciplines to supplement the historical record and reconstruct the texture of industry.[8]

In this book, we draw on evidence from artifacts and landscape features as well as documents to explore the industrial experience in North America, particularly the years up to 1930, when people were making industry and its products a dominant part of their lives. We cover both the broad landscape of industrial activity and the specific workplaces in which people labored.

Plan of the Book

In Part I, Chapter 1 introduces industrial archaeology, and Chapter 2 discusses the components of industry, which include the natural and human resources that are used and the social and environmental consequences that result. Part II deals with the landscapes of industry; Part III, with workplaces.

The industrial landscape includes the sites of mines, mills, and factories as well as the communities in which the participants in industrial activities lived. In drawing on resources such as forests and water, or in releasing effluents from stacks or drains, some industries influenced areas much greater than their immediate sites. These areas were also part of the industrial landscape. Our discussion of landscapes in Part II is organized around natural resources. The industries examined in Chapter 3 drew energy from wood and flowing water to make products out of wood, natural fibers, and iron. Iron ore was abundant and widely available. Mechanical power from flowing water was a renewable resource, and woodland could be managed to provide a sustained yield, but mechanical power from water and wood fuel was economically useful only near their sources. Consequently, industries dependent on wood fuel and water power could not easily be concentrated in cities; most of them were dispersed across the countryside.

Once the proprietors of canals and railways had opened continuous routes, they could often bring coal to consumers at a cost competitive with that of its energy equivalent in locally available wood or water. Chapter 4 shows how Americans changed the landscape as they removed the constraints on the size and location of industrial works by using cheap coal and cheap iron made with coal fuel. Coal was a nonrenewable energy resource; however, long before there was any question of scarcity, Americans turned to petroleum, a less abundant but more convenient fuel. The high energy content and the convenience of liquid fuel made from petroleum helped factory proprietors escape the constraints on location imposed by the fixed routes of canals and railways. At the same time, entrepreneurs were transforming electrical technology into a means of transmitting power over long distances, thereby enhancing the relative importance of nonferrous metals such as copper and tungsten. In Chapter 5 we examine the landscape of nonferrous-metal mining and petroleum production. Unlike wood and water, which could be managed as renewable resources, and coal, which was abundant, petroleum was nonrenewable and scarce enough that unmistakable signs of resource exhaustion were evident within a hundred years of its first industrial use. Another reorganization of the industrial landscape will occur in future decades as this scarcity increases. The transitions between different energy sources have been gradual and have occurred at different times in different parts of North America. Although Chapters 3 to 5 discuss a progression in time, they also overlap and do not represent a strict chronological development.

Part III is organized around "microgeography," spatial and functional relations within workplaces. The wood-and-water resource base supported small, dispersed units of production that are discussed in Chapter 6. With the advent of canals and railways, coal mines and metallurgical mills assumed major importance. Chapter 7 shows how they were generally larger than the workplaces that used the renewable resource base but less organized at the level of the worker than was the case in factories, where the closest supervision and organization of work were possible. Factory space and the mechanization of manufacturing in factories are discussed in Chapters 8 and 9.

Among the alternative words that might be used for the participants in industry who handle tools and materials with some degree of skill, we use *artisan* or, sometimes, *artificer* to avoid the connotations that come with other choices. *Craftsman* sometimes implies an individual who is responsible for the production of an entire object, perhaps as a proprietor of a shop, or one whose craft includes a substantial aesthetic component. *Mechanic* is a perfectly good term for a wide range of nineteenth-century industrial artisans, but it now suggests someone who repairs machines or engines, such as a garage mechanic. The terms *workers* and *laborers* were often used to draw a class distinction with capitalists. We use *artisan* to mean a person who manipulates materials in a job that requires both physical and mental skills.

Unskilled laborers and operatives who run very simple machines would not qualify as artisans, but we do not reserve the term (as many do) for the highly skilled elite of the workplace. We believe that those who work with tools usually have more skill than accepted job descriptions imply.

We do not attempt either comprehensive or representative geographical coverage of industrial remains in North America. Instead, we have selected artifacts and sites that we found most useful in the interpretation of the industrial experience. To keep the book to a reasonable length, we had to limit the number of topics we could cover; a number of significant industries, such as shoemaking and food processing, are not discussed at all. Wherever possible, we have chosen sites and artifacts that are accessible to the public in museums or parks so that readers can easily view them for themselves.

Notes

1. In this book, "North America" refers to all the land north of Mexico.

2. An example is the adoption of the snowmobile in Alaska and Lapland (Pertti Pelto, *The Snowmobile Revolution: Technology and Social Change in the Arctic* [Menlo Park, Calif.: Cummings, 1973]).

3. M. T. Hodgen, "Domesday Water Mills," *Antiquity* 13 (1939): 261–279.

4. Terry S. Reynolds, *Stronger Than a Hundred Men: A History of the Vertical Water Wheel* (Baltimore: Johns Hopkins University Press, 1983).

5. Ronald F. Tylecote, *The Prehistory of Metallurgy in the British Isles* (London: Institute of Metals, 1986), chaps. 9, 10; Robert B. Gordon and T. S. Reynolds, "Medieval Iron in Society," *Technology and Culture* 27 (1986): 110–117.

6. Nathan Rosenberg and L. E. Birdzell, Jr., *How the West Grew Rich* (New York: Basic Books, 1986).

7. Henry Wadsworth Longfellow, "The Village Blacksmith," in *The Poetical Works of Henry Wadsworth Longfellow* (Boston: Houghton Mifflin, 1889), p. 37.

8. Industrial archaeology began in Britain, and British authors have produced both general books and regional guides to the material remains of their industries. Two general books are Brian Bracegirdle, *The Archaeology of the Industrial Revolution* (London: Heinemann, 1973), and Neil Cossons, *The B P Book of Industrial Archaeology* (Newton Abbott: David & Charles, 1975). The use of industrial archaeology in the interpretation of industrialization is shown in Barrie Trinder, *The Making of the Industrial Landscape* (London: Dent, 1982). An excellent book on the industrial archaeology of the province of Ontario is Dianne Newell and Ralph Greenhill, *Survivals: Aspects of the Industrial Archaeology of Ontario* (Evin, Ont.: Boston Mills Press, 1989).

I
INDUSTRIAL ARCHAEOLOGY

1

Industrial Archaeology

The prominence of industry in the culture of the North Atlantic nations has provoked thoughtful people to ask penetrating questions about the roots of innovation and the social and environmental consequences of industrial technology. One cluster of questions, long of interest to scholars, focuses on how and by whom new technologies were created and how their selection, use, or rejection has been influenced by cultural values.[1] In the past quarter century, the impact of technologies and industries on the environment has become a widespread concern among citizens of the industrialized nations. People are raising questions about the past and present uses of natural resources and how their availability influences economic growth. They are concerned about the consequences of releasing industrial wastes and effluents into the air and water. They are also exploring their personal experiences with mechanisms and technological devices—how these artifacts enter work, play, and art, and how they express cultural values.

Because the field of the history of technology is relatively new, scholars have approached it within the framework of established disciplines. The work of historians with the written record and of economists with numerical data is securely established in the academic world. We would add to these the material record, the domain of the industrial archaeologist (Fig. 1.1). Evidence from artifacts is particularly important for the study of workers (because the written record is sparse), of inventors (because much of the secondary literature simplifies the complexities of invention),[2] and of the industrial landscape. To discover the texture of industry, we need to examine both the documentary and the material record; artifacts as well as documents must speak for the experiences of past workers. An artifact, in the

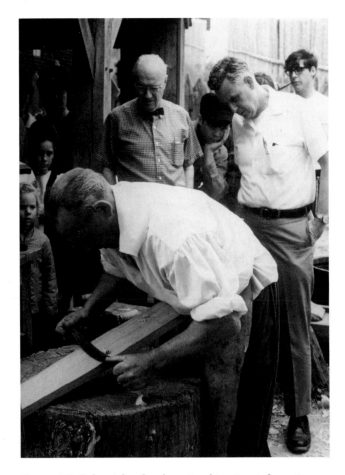

FIGURE 1.1. Industrial archaeology gives historians information not easily determined or missing from the written record. Professors Hunter Dupree and Carl Bridenbaugh of Brown University observe material evidence of an artisan's work at Plimoth Plantation, Massachusetts. Bridenbaugh studies the way coopered barrels could be taken apart, shipped as compact bundles of parts, and then reassembled at destination. Dupree examines the cooper's ability to make visual judgments of size and symmetry without resorting to scales, calipers, or gages.

words of historian Brooke Hindle, is "a solid piece of the past in a way that no quotation can ever be."[3] Students of industry must rely heavily on material evidence because few participants in industry left written records of their experiences and because some aspects of technology cannot be expressed effectively in words.

Industrial workers had neither leisure nor incentive to write because literary accomplishments were not often a part of the culture of work and were rarely among the skills that led to advancement. British historian W.K.V. Gale observed of the iron puddlers he knew in the 1920s that "a new man in the trade started to learn in earnest, the hard way, by doing, not talking and he developed a taciturnity which lasted all his life."[4] Those who did write about their work were likely to be exceptional individuals[5] who wrote reminiscences intended to air a grievance or to advance a cause or political philosophy.[6]

The written record of industrial life is also sparse because artisans were usually reluctant to reveal information about their skills. The French inspector of industry LePlay noted in the early nineteenth century that "the artists of all classes and in all countries are, in general, little disposed to communicate to others the results of their experience." He observed that proprietors of works or scholars who might have wished to communicate a technology to others were largely unable to do so because the technology resided with the workmen rather than the managers and that there "is barely a common language between the workman and the savant"; thus it is "extremely difficult to determine what qualities a workman means when he says that an iron has 'body' . . . [a property] that [is] perfectly clear to the workman handling the iron." LePlay also noted that deception was by no means uncommon in the accounts of industrial processes given to inquiring visitors.[7]

Deception or misrepresentation in written descriptions and technical illustrations of industrial processes can appear for any number of reasons. We should not be surprised when artisans and companies, seeking to retain a competitive advantage, provide deliberately misleading accounts of their methods. There is also the human tendency to portray one's own achievements in the best possible light and thereby to embellish reality. This tendency, often unconscious, also affects the way people describe the work of rivals, on whom a much dimmer light is cast. Another related source of inaccuracy is the natural reluctance to admit errors or corrections on the way to an eventual solution. Triumph over adversity is considered admirable in our culture, but it is difficult to admit one's failings and shortcomings. Experienced historians recognize that witnesses may have selective memories and that documents must be read with caution. Biased testimony, if accepted as truth, can become history with a hidden agenda.

Although written language, with its nuances and complexities of expression may be more informative than inanimate objects, there are fewer biases in artifacts. These material products may occasionally be misleading, but they were rarely designed to deceive, to cover up the truth, or to promote a particular opinion. The authority of physical evidence refutes the data found in many documentary or graphic records, particularly in the area of engineering construction and machine design. Artifacts do show how something was done, not how someone said something was done.[8] Acts of omission and carelessness can be as damaging to the historical record as intentional deception. Anyone who has worked from construction plans or mechanical drawings knows that changes are common in the field or at the workbench. Last-minute modifications and responses to unexpected problems can mean the difference between success or failure. If those critical changes are not entered on the drawings and specifications, surviving documents may mislead future historians. Many historic drawings are records of intention or early planning, but not of execution. The best evidence of execution is in the product.

Even when authors took pains to describe industrial processes and work, written language was not equal to the task. Mechanical techniques involve a large component of nonverbal thinking that is not easily recorded in words or even in drawings.[9] Artisans who operate furnaces and machines respond to many sensory clues about their equipment, reaching decisions on grounds they would find difficult to explain to outsiders. That much technology can be understood without the aid of writing is shown by the mechanical and metallurgical accomplishments of nonliterate people, such as the working of metals by the Inca of Peru in the sixteenth century and the smelting of iron in the African Iron Age.[10] Modern engineers often find it difficult to duplicate these processes.

Artifacts are a particularly stimulating link with the past. Most of us have at some time experienced the evocative effect of historic objects and built environments. For many of us, just to see a scarred blacksmith's anvil at close hand is to watch the sparks fly with our mind's eye. We heft an artisan's hammer and develop a better appreciation of the skill and strength required to use it. A historical description of a manufacturing operation begins to make sense for the first time when we stand before the actual machine and see the spatial arrangement of controls, feed mechanisms, and belt drives. Watching and hearing a skilled operator run a machine can be a revelation. When we enter an early workplace with most of its manufacturing equipment still in place, the experience is almost like stepping from a time machine.

An industrial landscape can give us a unique sense of place and an awareness of scale. We can study maps and descriptions of an industrial site until we build a detailed picture in our mind, only to go there and find our mental image grossly deficient. Walking the historic terrain and examining structures that survive, we can assess the achievement of harnessing the river, spanning the gorge, erecting the mill, transporting the ore. The ruins and missing elements are equally revealing, for they inform us of disasters, technical failures, and the crueler aspects of market economies.

While industrial archaeology informs us about the past, it can also contribute to better use of human resources in industry today. Technology may change rapidly, but the interactions of people with tools, machinery, and other workers have enduring components that are best understood from past experience. We allocate resources for research and development in technology according to a paradigm of industrial history containing a large admixture of socially constructed reinterpretation that enlarges the importance of inventors and scientists. As a consequence, we have neglected the education of artisans and the practice of manufacturing technology.[11]

By studying artifacts, workplaces, and landscapes, as well as the documentary sources familiar to historians of technology, industrial archaeologists reach conclusions about how work was carried on, what natural and economic resources were used, and what skills were required of workers and managers. No reputable industrial archaeologist believes that we should study material evidence alone when documentary records are available. Our objective is to expand the body of information on which historical conclusions are based.

Case studies become the basis for generalizations about the character of work, the effectiveness of different technologies, or the reasons behind industrial successes and failures. The links between generalizations and actual industrial processes are explicit. Aggregated data on profits, for example, can demonstrate the degree of success of a technology; industrial archaeology can help uncover the reasons.

Principles of Interpretation

Although industrial archaeology shares with its sister branches of archaeology many problems in the interpretation of artifacts and material culture, it is too new a field to have been much influenced by recent attempts to make archaeology more "objective" or "scientific."[12] Thus it has been relatively free of disputes about methods of interpretation.[13] Another difference is that industrial archaeology deals with processes governed explicitly by principles of engineering and science, principles that limit the possible interpretations. Thus bounds set by physiology on the amount of physical work a person can do in carrying out a task can be used to evaluate other kinds of evidence about the labor required in an industrial process. Science and engineering provide guidelines against which historical interpretations can be tested.

Evidence of the work of individual artisans is preserved in the shapes, internal structures, and surficial markings of artifacts. The study of this evidence, known as "personalization," has become a recognized technique in archaeology within the past decade.[14] However, industrial work rarely is carried out by persons working alone, and it should be possible to use material evidence to discover how social interactions influenced the way tasks were undertaken. One guide in generalization, less restrictive than the principles of science and engineering, is the notion that there is a way to do a task that is superior to all others in terms of the physical and mental effort required.[15] We expect that the easiest way to do a task would be discovered and used by artisans who were allowed full play of experimentation in their work. If, however, we find that an alternative was chosen, it is a signal to look for cultural factors that affected the approach to work. These factors can reveal aspects of technology that are governed by cultural preferences, constraints, or even whimsy—the decoration of machinery by its designer or user, customary ceremonies among seamen on ships, or rules that restrict the participation of women in mining and smelting in some societies.

Reconstruction

The reconstruction of ancient tools, equipment, and buildings is an established way to explore people's past experiences with technology.[16] At Butser in England, archaeologists built an Iron Age community so that they could experience the life of those times. Gerald Forty navigated a small sailing vessel with replicas of the astrolabes, cross-staffs, and backstaffs used by navigators on the great voyages of exploration to find both the limitations of the instruments and the skills needed to operate them.[17] In industrial archaeology, reconstruction may take the form of rebuilding and operating machinery no longer in use, as in the reconstruction of the waterwheel at the Slater Mill Historic Site, in Pawtucket, Rhode Island.

When resources are not available for reconstruction of actual machinery or industrial sites, thought experiments are a useful alternative. By thinking through the sequence of decisions a machine operator might make, we can infer where things might go wrong at each stage. Ultimately, we want to test the conclusions drawn from imaginative reconstructions against actual experience; sometimes this can be done with surviving machinery, such as the Howe pin machine now on display at the National Museum of American History, but the chances to operate larger industrial apparatus, such as an open-hearth steel furnace, will be rare. Occasionally, restored and reconstructed machinery, such as the narrow-fabric loom at the Slater Mill Historic Site, can be made to earn revenue and be partially self-sustaining, but today no one can afford to operate, for example, a charcoal-fired blast furnace.

Because some types of machinery have been particularly attractive to persons interested in restoration and reconstruction, the selection of technologies studied by reconstruction has not necessarily reflected historical significance. Steam locomotives have been particularly popular, and gristmills, sawmills, smithies, canal boats, and sailing vessels have also attracted

FIGURE 1.2. The Wilkinson (left) and Slater (right) mills on the Blackstone River. The Wilkinsons, a family of metalworkers, built their stone factory in 1810 as a combination textile mill and machine shop. It contained a steam engine as well as a waterwheel. Sometime between 1826 and 1829, the Wilkinsons replaced their original midbreast wheel with a wider one, a re-creation of which is at the Slater Mill Historic Site. The "Great Flume" runs under the Slater Mill to bring water to the arched entry of the wheel pit, visible at one end of the Wilkinson building. In the river wall, the rectangular opening is the outlet of the covered tailrace from the Wilkinson wheel pit; the Slater Mill tailrace discharges through the large arch. (Drawing by P. D. Malone. Courtesy of Slater Mill Historic Site)

attention. But other important elements of our industrial heritage—tanneries, finery forges, and slaughterhouses—have not.

The re-creation of the waterwheel at the Wilkinson Mill (now part of the Slater Mill Historic Site [Fig. 1.2]), is an example of research by reconstruction. The wheel had been sold at auction in 1829, but the wheel pit survived in the mill building. Excavation and measurement showed that the pit once held a midbreast wheel 12 feet in diameter and just over 12 feet wide. The re-creation of the wheel was based on evidence gleaned from the pit, from other water-power sites where parts of breast wheels had survived, and from documents.

Many waterwheels in Rhode Island operated in "backwater" for much of the year because when streams were high, the wheel pits were partially flooded (Fig. 1.3). At the Wilkinson Mill, the bottom of the wheel was at or just below the normal water level in the pit. When the Blackstone River was high, the buckets of the wheel would dip beneath the surface of the water as the wheel rotated.

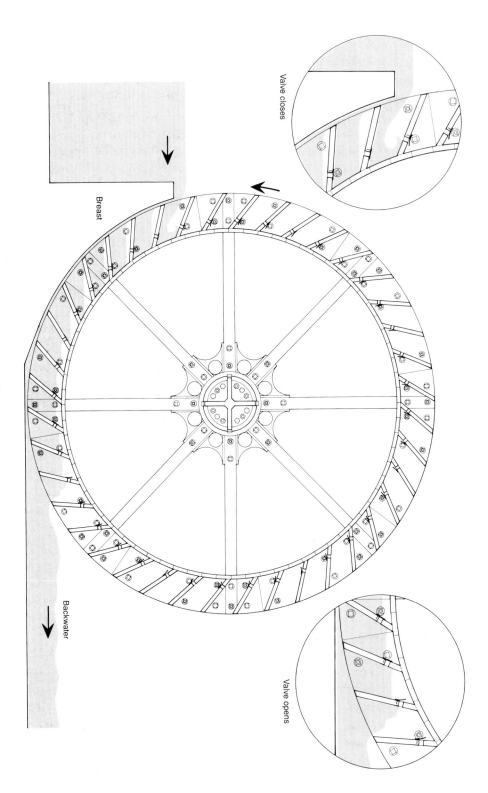

Valve closes

Breast

Backwater

Valve opens

The designers of the new wheel knew that nineteenth-century breast wheels had operated successfully when partially submerged. They chose a design that incorporated straight buckets, the form that Zachariah Allen, author of a book on mill engineering and mechanics in 1829,[18] considered best for wheels frequently in backwater. Allen mentioned valves in the buckets, but the modern designers, failing to appreciate the importance of these valves, decided to build the wheel without them.

The re-created waterwheel was made of both wood and iron. Once installed, it ran smoothly with a small flow of water, the only apparent problem being that the wooden parts leaked profusely. The wheel turned without obvious resistance, its bottom submerged in about 6 inches of water. The designers had assumed that the wooden parts, as they soaked up water, would swell and that the wheel would run even better when the joints tightened. No one could understand why Zachariah Allen wanted valves in the buckets. The wheel worked beautifully without them.

But within hours, the wheel's steady rotation began to falter. The huge machine slowed, laboring through a small arc and then stopping briefly before moving again. It filled a bucket, paused, and then turned slowly to fill another. Each time it paused, there was a loud hissing sound. Next came a splash in the pit as a wave of water emerged from beneath the wheel. With each splash, the wheel turned a fraction of a rotation, an arc equal to the space between the buckets. The wheel was no longer leaking, but that was little consolation to the dismayed and baffled designers.

Why wasn't the wheel working smoothly? After some hours of observation, the designers realized that the buckets were trapping water. The wet wood had swelled, preventing both air and water from leaking through joints. When a full bucket of water began to rise from the pool in the wheel pit, water could not drain out because there was no way for air to get in. The wheel could not turn while carrying the full bucket upward, and the water could not drop until the vacuum above it was relieved.

The hissing noise was air forcing its way through the bucket's tight joints. When enough air had entered, the water dropped out with a splash. A rereading of Zachariah Allen's book showed that he was concerned about water being held too long in the buckets, thus impeding the rotation of the wheel. The designers had not realized the need for valves, as Allen explained it, "which close when filled with water, but open when inverted, whereby the air is admitted freely to displace the water without causing it to be lifted above the level of water in the millrace."[19] It was only when the wheel itself gave this vivid demonstration of the effects of backwater that the operators of the reconstructed wheel knew what to do; they made one-way valves by drilling holes in the buckets and covering these holes with flexible leather flaps that open when inverted (with a little assistance from atmospheric pressure). The wheel now runs smoothly and can, in fact, operate in several feet of backwater. The designers have rediscovered what was once common knowledge among American millwrights.

Context

Artifacts studied as isolated objects may be misinterpreted if we do not also look at the context in which they were made and used. One component of context is the setting in which an artifact is placed. A machine taken from a factory, cleaned up and repainted, and displayed in a clean, quiet, brightly illuminated museum conveys an incomplete, and possibly misleading, message about what it was like to work with or around it. A museum display is unlikely to show the amount of light that was available to the operator, the intensity of noise, and the extremes of heat or cold that might accompany its operation. The cold Bessemer converter, sitting like an immense piece of public sculpture in a plaza in Pittsburgh, is an impressive sight, but it conveys little of the experience of seeing a converter in action. Nor does a power-loom display in a museum gallery reveal the deafening noise of a weave room.[20]

Part of the context of any device involved in manufacturing is the flow of materials to and from it. Few industrial tasks are done in isolation, and materials often are received from a preceding operation and passed on to a subsequent one. In a production line with operations arranged in series, materials must be moved steadily along the line in such a way that the rate of work at each station stays in balance. Outside the workplace, the networks that describe the extraction of raw materials and their transfer to other sites for conversion to products and wastes are part of the context of each individual site.

In addition to materials, industrial processes use energy, and many are among the most energy intensive of human activities. Part of the context of an industrial site or mechanism is the means by which power is supplied to it, as through the flow of water, mineral fuel, oil, or electricity. Equally significant is the removal of the effluents of power production, such as smoke and ash. The way that power reaches individual workplaces also influences the environment there. For example, belts driving machines from overhead shafting are more noisy and dangerous than individual electric motors.

In industrial societies, work is carried out in an economic context, and in capitalist industrial communities, entrepreneurs include the relative cost of equipment and labor in their calculations of expenses. They are unlikely to use a machine or an industrial plant for long without modification if it does not produce enough revenue to cover at least its operating costs. Successful technologies are often modified (and sometimes made less sophisticated) to accommodate changes in economic conditions rather than to respond to inventions or advances in engineering or cultural preferences. When railway managers decided it was economically necessary to allow more than one crew to operate a given locomotive, they found that their relations with the railway workers and the performance of the equipment were changed in ways they had not anticipated.

The relation of artisans to their machines and workplace is another component of the context of industrial work. It includes the skills and strength required as well as the degree of cooperation needed among workers. It also involves the formal and informal social structures that grow around their joint efforts.

Individuals who do not participate in an industrial activity but who are exposed to it are another component of context. The designers of factories or machines may add elements that are not directly functional but that convey messages to nonparticipants. One historian has interpreted the elaborate decoration of American machinery in the nineteenth century as an attempt to convey confidence in the merits of these mechanisms to persons unable to judge their technical characteristics.[21] Some people, such as home owners located downwind of a factory smokestack, are involuntary observers of technology. Often ignored in the past, today they are sometimes able to force significant changes on the conduct of industrial processes.

People with authority in industrial organizations have used technological change as a way of gaining control over artisans on the shop floor. This pattern is often reflected in individual machines redesigned by engineers to eliminate the special knowledge that had been necessary to run them. It is also apparent in managerial modifications of processes and entire systems of production. Uniformity and standardization of specific tasks in a workplace may signal the imposition of the preferences of managers or union officials over those of individual artificers. Rules that restrict artisans to work in particular trades, or narrowly define their jobs in other ways, may also take away their opportunity to develop a broad range of skills.[22]

Finally, industrial artifacts should also be considered in the wider context of the society in which they are placed. This context may be expressed in regional or ethnic preferences in architecture, styles of working, tools, or products. The axe, a tool used widely during the nineteenth century, was often identified by such names as "New Orleans pattern" or "Michigan pattern," in recognition of regional styles.

Practice of Industrial Archaeology

The field of industrial archaeology is particularly well placed to help us discover how the industrial past has shaped our culture. Interest is fostered if parents and grandparents participated in industry and strengthened when community historical societies or other interest groups get involved in research projects. It is unlikely that industrial archaeologists will ever have resources for professional study of all the significant industrial sites in North America. Recruiting nonprofessionals to help with fieldwork is one way to cope with limited resources. Investigation of an industrial site does not necessarily require knowledge of the finer points of archaeological field procedure, and older persons with industrial experience can bring personal knowledge to industrial archaeology projects that would be difficult to get in other ways.

Today, study of the remains of our industrial past often falls in the domain of public archaeology or is undertaken to meet legal requirements when old industrial sites are reused. These projects can create new opportunities for research, but since the sites are selected for study on the basis of current needs and land values, the choices may not reflect historical significance. Often the data collected from such studies are simply deposited in the files of a sponsoring agency, making it difficult for scholars and students to know what sites have been studied and obtain access to the reports.

Preservation

Preserving industrial remains is a special problem in public archaeology because of the size and complexity of most industrial sites. The survival of some historical artifacts is dependent on the survival of the industrial arts needed to maintain them. For example, the particular skills and techniques used in making the complex, curved structural members of a wooden ship's hull have no modern application and would vanish without institutions such as the shipyard at the Mystic Seaport Museum in Mystic, Connecticut. This is one of the few places where large wooden hulls can still be repaired and where young people are trained in the craft. Iron puddling is another art that can be learned only by experience. When the last commercially operated puddling furnace, located at the Atlas Forge in Bolton, England, closed, the equipment was removed to the Blists Hill Open Air Museum in Iron Bridge, where staff members are learning the art of puddling so that the furnace, steam hammer, and roll train can be operated in view of visitors.[23]

In recent years, some members of Congress have used preservation of an industrial heritage as a device for providing financial aid to communities in their districts that have lost economically viable industries. These efforts raise especially difficult problems of interpretation and may create romantic, nostalgic representations of a past that never existed or proxy restatements of current social problems. One characteristic of industry is that new technology is continually replacing old. If industrial heritage is interpreted in a display that artificially arrests change (as by subsidizing an industry that is no longer economically viable), a basic characteristic of industry is misrepresented and, because it celebrates fantasy rather than reality, is less likely to be of lasting value to a community than aid in developing new industries. The best place for the display of obsolete industrial processes may be in a museum or professionally managed historic site, where their appropriate contexts can be re-created and interpreted. However, it is often possible, and even advantageous, for industrial companies to make necessary technological changes while preserving significant features of their (and our) industrial heritage on their own property. It is neither affordable nor desirable to place everything of historic value in a museum setting. Companies that develop their own programs for intelligent preservation and reuse can boost employee pride, create interesting and effective work spaces, and enhance their public images.[24]

Fieldwork

Industrial archaeologists examine both standing structures and sites that must be studied by excavation. Formal recording procedures for structures and large artifacts (but not for excavations) have been established by the Historic American Engineering Record (HAER), a unit of the National Park Service. HAER survey teams usually record sites with a combination of measured engineering and architectural drawings, written reports, and large-format photographs. Unfortunately, only a small fraction of HAER historical reports have been published. Historians of technology would make much more use of archaeological information from HAER if its reports were readily available in published form and thus subject to scholarly reviews in journals such as *Technology and Culture*.

Relatively few excavations have been undertaken on industrial sites. Procedures established for digging prehistoric sites are applicable to industrial sites, but practical modifications, such as the use of power equipment, are sometimes needed to cope with the scale and character of many of the remains. Excavators need to take special precautions at sites where hazardous materials, such as mercury, have been used.[25] Obviously, principal investigators must know industrial history and be familiar with the analysis of industrial artifacts to conduct their work successfully.

Archaeometry

Archaeometry, the application of modern investigative technologies to the study of artifacts, is particularly useful in industrial archaeology. The techniques used include engineering analysis, study of surficial markings on artifacts, materials analysis, reconstruction, and experimental archaeology.

ENGINEERING ANALYSIS

By applying engineering principles to an artifact, an archaeologist can often determine its function and show how it worked or evaluate the sophistication of its design in relation to its function.[26] In a study of a block mill set up in 1801 in the Portsmouth, England, naval dockyard, historian Carolyn Cooper showed how the block-making machines functioned together as one of the earliest mechanized industrial production lines.[27] Her method was to determine the arrangement of the machines and to calculate the production capacity of each machine. Some of the individual block-making machines are displayed in museums, but out of context so that their interdependence is not evident.

Another technique is the study of the uniformity of dimensions among parts of mechanisms supposed to have been mass-produced in order to be interchangeable. Using this technique, historian Donald Hoke showed that the parts of wooden-works clocks made for Eli Terry were fully interchangeable after 1807.[28] The mechanisms of military firearms made from the early years of the nineteenth century onward illustrate well the development of interchangeable manufacture in the United States. Measurements of the sizes and shapes of lock parts from military small arms show that the precision attained by American armory artisans in hand filing, for example, improved tenfold between 1810 and 1850.[29]

Engineering analysis is applicable to sites as well as to artifacts. We can often determine the amount of water power available for manufacturing, the difficulties of mining at a particular locality, or the suitability of a transport system at a particular place. An example is the computation of water-power potential based on the size of a drainage basin and historical data on stream flow and climate.[30] Such an analysis may be based on methods or data that were not available when the site was in use and may tell why a water-powered factory succeeded or failed.

SURFICIAL MARKINGS

Surficial markings can be used to examine the work of individual artisans or to obtain information about how an object was used.[31] Wear patterns on workplace floors and the polish on handles of machines are records of work procedures. Marks left by artisans' tools are usually best preserved on the

FIGURE 1.4. Cavity for the lock mechanism in the stock of a U.S. M1816 musket made at the shop of Lemuel Pomeroy in 1824. The center of an auger bit left the small holes; after boring with the bit, the cavity was shaped with chisels and gouges that left a characteristic undulating texture on the bottom surface. (Photographed at the Springfield Armory National Historic Site)

interior surfaces of artifacts, areas not usually finished to enhance appearance. Historian Edwin Battison was one of the first to solve a problem in industrial archaeology using surficial evidence; he interpreted markings found on the lock mechanism of a musket made at Eli Whitney's armory in Hamden, Connecticut, to show that, contrary to the accepted story, Whitney's muskets were not made with machine-milled parts.[32] Since Battison's work, analysis of surficial markings has been used to study how artisans made objects ranging from Neolithic ceramic vessels to sixteenth-century wheel locks and astrolabes to nineteenth-century roll-forged axes.[33]

Tools used to shape wood or metal leave distinctive markings. Archaeologists can apply the results of recent research on the mechanics of cutting wood to deduce from surficial markings the kind of tool that was used on an artifact and the working style of its maker.[34] We can easily distinguish surfaces cut by hand from those cut by machine tools. Figure 1.4 shows the recess cut into the wooden stock of a musket made in the shop of New England arms maker Lemuel Pomeroy in 1824. The stocker used a brace and bit to make the circular hole and to start the deeper recess (leaving the small hole at the right end); the rest of the cavity was then cut with hand chisels and gouges, leaving a gently undulating surface. By 1854, armorers were using machinery to inlet stocks at the Whitney Armory, and the cutters of

FIGURE 1.5. Part of the recess in the stock of a U.S. M1841 rifle made at the Whitney Armory in 1854. The circular marks, which were made by the cutting tool of a lock bedding machine, show that stock making had been mechanized at the Whitney Armory by 1854. (Photographed at the Springfield Armory National Historic Site)

these machines left characteristic circular marks in the recess that are easy to identify (Fig. 1.5).[35]

With the growing interest in the evolution of the landscape, it is not surprising to see the same type of analysis applied to the marks of man and his machinery on the surface of the earth. Scars left by surface mining or dredging, for instance, can provide information on the mining equipment involved and the processes of extraction.

MATERIALS ANALYSIS

Laboratory techniques can be used to examine the interior structure of an artifact to obtain information about how it was made and used.[36] Industrial archaeologists find two techniques developed in the nineteenth century by Henry C. Sorby, an amateur microscopist in Sheffield, England, particularly useful. Sorby showed how to examine internal structures under an optical microscope by using thin sections for ceramic and organic materials, or polished and etched surfaces for metals.[37] We can distinguish a cast-metal artifact from one forged or hammered to shape. When a casting cools and solidifies, a distinctive pattern of crystallization is left in the metal (Fig. 1.6). Deforming the metal—as by forging, hammering, or rolling—distorts the cast structure (Fig. 1.7). The texture shows the direction that the metal flowed during working and may be used to deduce the forming processes.

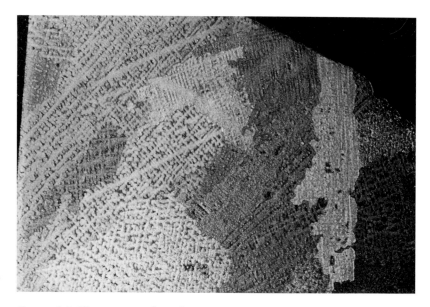

FIGURE 1.6. The structure of cast brass seen under a reflected-light microscope. The specimen has been polished and etched to reveal the structure. Different grains have different colors. Within each grain is a gridlike dendritic pattern formed on solidification.

FIGURE 1.7. A polished and etched section of a brass cartridge case seen under a reflected-light microscope. The grains have been distorted and contain deformation markings, dark, intersecting bands developed by the plastic flow of the brass while the case was being drawn.

FIGURE 1.8. A polished and etched section of a brass cartridge case after it has been annealed at 600°C. The deformed grains shown in Figure 1.7 have been replaced by grains free of distortion (recrystallization), and the metal has been softened.

We can recognize annealing after forming because when heated, the distorted structure re-forms, producing a characteristic "recrystallized" pattern (Fig. 1.8).

Archaeologists often use the electron microprobe to find the compositions of the different components in an artifact. The microscopist directs a narrow beam of electrons on the component to be analyzed and determines its composition from the characteristics of the X-rays that are excited by the electrons. Archaeologists were able to identify how crucibles found at the site of Eli Whitney's armory and dated by context to the 1850s were used by making microprobe analyses of drops of metal within the slag adhering to the crucibles. Droplets of brass were found in some of the crucibles, while others contained bits of an iron–carbon–silicon alloy suitable for casting. With this clue, the investigators discovered that Eli Whitney, Jr., had developed a technique for casting revolver frames as an alternative to the forging process used by Samuel Colt and other arms makers.[38]

One measure of the attainment of technological maturity is a society's capacity to make reliable and serviceable materials. We want to know the strength properties of historic building materials, either to evaluate how well they were made or to determine how safe they are in a structure today. Inferences about strength can sometimes be drawn from composition and microstructure, but the only reliable way is by mechanical testing. Engineer A. P. Mills of Cornell University tested the strength and ductility of iron links from the chains of the suspension bridge over the Merrimack River in Newburyport, Massachusetts, built in 1810, rebuilt after it collapsed in 1827, and replaced by a new bridge in 1913. His data show that the quality of the links was variable and that some were completely brittle and, therefore, likely to fail without warning. These and similar tests on other artifacts demonstrate that scarcity of dependable iron was a major difficulty faced by engineers in the United States throughout the first half of the nineteenth century.[39]

EXPERIMENTAL ARCHAEOLOGY

When records of processes or machinery are incomplete or vague and lack the detail needed for reconstruction, experimental archaeology sometimes may be used to "rediscover" them.[40] Yet both physical and intellectual risks are inherent in such experiments. Trying to operate unfamiliar machinery can cause injuries, and there is a real possibility of misinterpreting the working experience. Showing that something is possible with a tool or machine does not, in itself, prove that earlier artisans did it that way. Conversely, the failure of an imitative experiment may tell us more about our own incompetence than it does about the limitations of past artisans and their tools. Problems can arise when those who try to re-create historic work processes lack the skills of the original workers and cannot approximate their performance.

Finding the right tools and materials is the first step; the next is to use the tools with enough skill to make something that closely matches a historic product. The third step is to reach the rate of production achieved in the past, a goal often difficult to attain. If we fail to work at the pace of earlier workers, we may misunderstand the demands of their jobs or the way they actually performed them. For example, smithing demonstrations at open-air museums rarely demonstrate the intensity of a practicing smith's work. _

Experimental archaeology is applicable to a wide range of problems in industrial archaeology. Archaeologist John Worrell of Old Sturbridge Village rediscovered the technology used by early-nineteenth-century rural potters in New England with the aid of a kiln constructed as one of the working exhibits at Sturbridge.[41] David Harvey, a conservator at Colonial Williamsburg, has recovered lost metallurgical skills in bloom smelting, the extraction of wrought iron directly from ore. This was an important industrial process in North America from earliest colonial times until the early twentieth century. But the last bloomery in the United States closed more than eighty years ago. No experienced practitioners of the art of bloom smelting survive today, nor have bloomery sites in North America been excavated to provide physical data on the equipment used. In order to demonstrate the art of bloom smelting at Colonial Williamsburg, Harvey had to

FIGURE 1.9. David Harvey at his experimental bloomery in Colonial Williamsburg. The hearth in which iron is formed by reduction of ore with charcoal is in the center of the brickwork structure. An overhead lever operates the bellows at the back. (Courtesy of the Colonial Williamsburg Foundation)

build a bloomery hearth and relearn the process by trial and error. He constructed a hearth (Fig. 1.9) and found supplies of iron ore nearby. Eventually, he was able to make small pieces of iron, some of it good enough to be forged into nails.[42]

Experimental archaeology can also be used to learn about the operation of machinery. The Wilder spool and bobbin lathe now in the Wilkinson Machine Shop of the Slater Mill Historic Site had been run for decades at the Atwood, Crawford Company by wood turner George McComiskey (Fig. 1.10). Since acquiring this machine, staff members at the museum have used it successfully to turn out dozens of thread spools from white-birch bars of square cross section, but no one has ever been able to match Mc-

FIGURE 1.10. George McComiskey making spools on the Wilder bobbin lathe at the
Slater Mill Historic Site. Shavings peel rapidly away as McComiskey's knee (not visible
in the picture) presses the forming cutter of the lathe into a rotating bar of birch.
Further knee action will engage the cutoff knife to separate a finished spool.
He is withdrawing the drill with his right hand, while preparing to move the lathe
carriage farther down the wooden bar with his left hand. So far, he has drilled,
turned, and cut off two spools from this bar; others will follow in rapid succession.
Once he has used up the bar, McComiskey will knock out the stub end and jam
another piece into the spinning chuck (shown at the right edge of the photograph).

Comiskey's pace of production. McComiskey provided demonstrations and
explanations that clarified true methods of operation. What would staff
members have concluded about the jobs of spool makers if they had simply
tried to run the machine by themselves? It is doubtful that they would have
understood the correct operation of this multifunction lathe, even after a
study of artifacts, patent history (the 1874, 1881, and 1882 Wilder patents),

and published descriptions. From the material evidence, they might have assumed correctly that both McComiskey and his father forged and ground their cutting tools, made sheet-metal gauges for the hundreds of different spools produced, and developed their own modifications of the basic lathe. The members of the museum staff were, however, unlikely to guess the secret of the incredible rate of production attributed to this type of machine. The census of 1880 claimed that an operator of a similar lathe could make 10,000 druggist's boxes a day, and McComiskey claimed the same rate for small spools.[43]

Watching McComiskey run the lathe in his first demonstration for the museum staff was a revelation in more ways than one. He worked much more smoothly than anyone had envisioned, perfectly coordinating intricate actions with both hands and one knee. (A knee-activated lever controls two operations of the lathe.) His workpiece was a sawn birch bar 2 feet long and 2 inches square. In seconds, he turned one end of the bar to a cylindrical form, drilled a hole through it, shaped it to the form of a spool, cut it off, and threw it into a bin. Turning spool after spool from the bar, McComiskey was a blur of motions. As he cut off the last spool and knocked the stub of the bar out of the chuck, everyone waited for him to throw the overhead lever that would stop the machine and allow him to insert a new bar. What he did was completely unexpected. He did not turn off the lathe before inserting a new workpiece.

The threaded bell chuck of a Wilder lathe turns at more than 1,200 revolutions a minute. The bar of wood that McComiskey jammed into that chuck had sharp, rough edges. Using his left hand, he stuck the bar into the spinning chuck, released his grip almost instantaneously, and caught the other end of the bar in the sliding, trumpet-shaped carriage that held the first cutting tool. His right hand pressed the carriage toward the chuck at the headstock end of the lathe, forcing the bar firmly into the threads of the chuck. With his perfect timing, McComiskey avoided injuring his hand while inserting the bar.

No matter how quickly an operator turned, drilled, and cut, making 10,000 spools a day would be impossible if the lathe was stopped when each new piece of wood was inserted. Before seeing McComiskey at work, no one at the museum imagined reloading stock with the lathe running; it was seemingly impossible and too dangerous to consider. A botched insertion could even send a bar flying out of the lathe at an operator's head. In demonstrating the Wilder lathe, the staff still uses the interrupted loading process for safety reasons; it is far easier to give a verbal explanation of the correct method than it is to acquire George McComiskey's skill.

Notes

1. These questions have been addressed in George Basalla, *The Evolution of Technology* (New York: Cambridge University Press, 1988).

2. The social construction of invention is explained in Carolyn C. Cooper, "The Evolution of American Patent Management: The Blanchard Lathe as a Case Study," *Prologue* 19 (1987): 245–259.

3. Brooke Hindle, "The American Industrial Revolution Through Its Survivals," in *Science and Society in Early America,* ed. R. S. Klein (Philadelphia: American Philosophical Society, 1986), pp. 271–310.

4. W.K.V. Gale, "Wrought Iron: A Valediction," *Transactions of the Newcomen Society* 36 (1963–1964): 8–9.

5. One of the few nonpolitical accounts of industrial work by a participant is Patrick McGeown, *Heat the Furnace Seven Times More* (London: Hutchinson, 1967), which traces McGeown's career in an open-hearth melting shop of the early twentieth century.

6. An example of this type of industrial history is James J. Davis, *The Iron Puddler* (Indianapolis: Bobbs-Merrill, 1922). Davis was the Secretary of Labor from 1921 to 1930 and subsequently a U.S. senator from Pennsylvania.

7. Quoted in J. R. Harris, "Skills, Coal, and British Industry in the Eighteenth Century," *History* 61 (1976): 167–182.

8. Patrick M. Malone, "Museums and the History of Technology," *The Weaver of Information and Perspectives on Technological Literacy* 3, no. 1 (1984): 2. For an example of an industrial artifact refuting both documentary and graphic evidence, see Svante Lindqvist, *Technology on Trial: The Introduction of Steam Power Technology into Sweden, 1715–1736* (Uppsala: Almqvist & Wiksell International, 1984), pp. 283–290.

9. Eugene S. Ferguson, "The Mind's Eye: Nonverbal Thought in Technology," *Science* 197 (1977): 827–836; Janet W. D. Dougherty and Charles M. Keller, "Taskonomy: A Practical Approach to Knowledge Structures," in *Directions in Cognitive Anthropology,* ed. Janet W. D. Dougherty (Urbana: University of Illinois Press, 1985), pp. 161–174, which discusses the conceptualization of blacksmiths' work.

10. See, for example, Heather Lechtman, "Andean Value Systems and the Development of Prehistoric Metallurgy," *Technology and Culture* 25 (1984): 1–36; J. W. Rutledge and R. B. Gordon, "The Work of Metallurgical Artificers at Machu Picchu," *American Antiquity* 52 (1987): 578–594; and David J. Killick, "Technology in Its Social Setting: Bloomery Iron Smelting at Kasungu, Malawi, 1860–1940" (Ph.D. diss., Yale University, 1990).

11. For an example, see Max Holland, *When the Machines Stopped* (Boston: Harvard Business School Press, 1989).

12. The debate about archaeological method is examined in Guy Gibbon, *Explanation in Archaeology* (Oxford: Blackwell, 1989). See also Frank Hole, "Changing Directions in Archaeological Thought," in *Ancient South Americans,* ed. J. D. Jennings (San Francisco: Freeman, 1983), pp. 1–23, and Ian Hodder, *Reading the Past: Current Approaches to Interpretation in Archaeology* (Cambridge: Cambridge University Press, 1986).

13. In the United States, little has been said about methods and theory in industrial archaeology since 1978. At a symposium held that year, Dianne Newell

argued the importance of establishing a research design before setting up plans for recording industrial sites, and Theodore Penn pointed out the difficulties of extracting more than mere technical information from specific artifacts (Newell, "Industrial Archeology as a Scholarly Discipline," in *Industrial Archeology and the Human Sciences,* Occasional Publication No. 3, ed. Dianne Newell (Washington, D.C.: Society for Industrial Archeology, 1978), pp. 2–4; Penn, "Archeological Evidence and the Study of Historical Industry," in *Industrial Archeology and the Human Sciences,* ed. Newell, pp. 6–8). Recently, concerns about the adequacy of interpretation in industrial archaeology have been raised by some British practitioners; see, for example, C. M. Clark, "Trouble at t'Mill: Industrial Archaeology in the 1980s," *Antiquity* 61 (1987): 169–179, and Marilyn Palmer, "Industrial Archaeology as Historical Archaeology," *AIA Bulletin* 15 (1988): 1–3. A critique of the presentation of the results of archaeology in British open-air industrial museums is in M. Shanks and C. Tilley, *Re-Constructing Archaeology: Theory and Practice* (Cambridge: Cambridge University Press, 1987). Robert Hewison, in *The Heritage Industry* (London: Methuen, 1987), shows how museums have been used to create an imaginary industrial heritage that, while commercially valuable and politically useful, is inherently anti-industrial.

14. Hole, "Changing Directions in Archaeological Thought," p. 16.

15. A critique of the use of optimization methods in prehistoric archaeology is found in Arthur S. Keene, "Biology, Behavior and Borrowing: A Critical Examination of Optimal Foraging Theory in Archaeology," in *Archaeological Hammers and Theories,* ed. James A. Moore and Arthur S. Keene (New York: Academic Press, 1983), pp. 135–155, and Michael Jochim, "Optimization Models in Context," in *Archaeological Hammers and Theories,* ed. Moore and Keene, pp. 157–172.

16. Overviews of reconstructions in archaeology are given in John Coles, *Experimental Archaeology* (London: Academic Press, 1979), and Jay Anderson, *Time Machines: The World of Living History* (Nashville, Tenn.: American Association for State and Local History, 1984).

17. Peter Reynolds, *Iron Age Farm—The Butser Experiment* (London: British Museum, 1979); Gerald Forty, "Sources of Latitude Error in English 16th Century Navigation," *Journal of the Institute of Navigation* 36 (1983): 388–403; Forty, "The Backstaff and the Determination of Latitude at Sea in the 17th Century," *Journal of the Institute of Navigation* 39 (1986): 259.

18. Zachariah Allen, *The Science of Mechanics* (Providence, R.I.: Hutchens & Cory, 1829). For his description of backwater problems and breast-wheel design, see p. 216.

19. Ibid.

20. The Lowell National Historical Park has just opened a full weave room, with operating machinery. For discussion of the problem of context in industrial exhibits see John Bowditch, "The Big, the Bad, and the Ugly: Collecting Industrial Artifacts for History Museums," *Pittsburgh History* 72 (1989): 88–95.

21. John F. Kasson, *Civilizing the Machine* (New York: Grossman, 1976), chap. 4.

22. See, for example, Nathan Rosenberg, *Perspectives on Technology* (Cambridge: Cambridge University Press, 1976), p. 117, and David Montgomery, *Workers' Control in America* (New York: Cambridge University Press, 1979).

23. An illustrated account of the operation of the Atlas Forge was written just before it closed (Joseph Brough, *Wrought Iron: The End of an Era at Atlas Forge* [Bolton: Bolton Metropolitan Arts Department, n.d.]).

24. A review of the problems and opportunities in the museum exposition of past

work experiences is in Thomas E. Leary, "Shadows in the Cave: Industrial Ecology and Museum Practice," *Public Historian* 11 (1989): 39–60.

25. An example of an excavation of an industrial site is David R. Starbuck's study of the New England Glassworks ("The New England Glassworks," *New Hampshire Archaeologist* 27 [1986]). This enterprise operated between 1780 and 1782, and the site in southern New Hampshire remained unused thereafter. By 1970, few above-ground traces of the works were visible, but excavation revealed the furnace foundation and other features of the glasshouse and permitted interpretation of the operation of the enterprise.

26. Engineering analysis is also a useful technique in prehistoric archaeology (David P. Braun, "Pots as Tools," in *Archaeological Hammers and Theories,* ed. Moore and Keene, pp. 108, 111).

27. Carolyn C. Cooper, "The Production Line at Portsmouth Blockmill," *Industrial Archaeology Review* 6 (1981–1982): 28–44; Cooper, "The Portsmouth System of Manufacture," *Technology and Culture* 25 (1984): 182–225. Further applications are given in her book, *Shaping Invention: Thomas Blanchard's Machinery and Patent Management in Nineteenth-Century America* (New York: Columbia University Press, 1991).

28. Donald Hoke, *Ingenious Yankees: The Rise of the American System of Manufactures in the Private Sector* (New York: Columbia University Press, 1990), chap. 2.

29. Robert B. Gordon, "Who Turned the Mechanical Ideal into Mechanical Reality?" *Technology and Culture* 29 (1988): 744–788.

. 30. Robert B. Gordon, "Cost and Use of Water Power During Industrialization in New England and Great Britain: A Geological Interpretation," *Economic History Review* 36 (1983): 240–259; Gordon, "Hydrological Science and the Development of Water Power for Manufacturing," *Technology and Culture* 26 (1985): 204–235.

31. Brian Hayden, ed., *Lithic Use-Wear Analysis* (New York: Academic Press, 1979); Robert B. Gordon, "Laboratory Evidence of the Use of Metal Tools in Machu Picchu and Environs," *Journal of Archaeological Science* 12 (1985): 311–327. Studies of markings on stone tools have been used to identify the products of individual prehistoric artificers (John R. Cross, "Twigs, Branches, Trees and Forests: The Problem of Scale in Lithic Analysis," in *Archaeological Hammers and Theories,* ed. Moore and Keene, pp. 88–106).

32. Edwin A. Battison, "Eli Whitney and the Milling Machine," *Smithsonian Journal of History* 1 (1966): 9–34.

33. Pamela Vandiver, "The Implications of Variation in Ceramic Technology: The Forming of Neolithic Storage Vessels in China and the Near East," *Archeomaterials* 2 (1988): 130–174; Vernard Foley and others, "Leonardo, the Wheel Lock, and the Milling Machine," *Technology and Culture* 24 (1983): 399–427; Robert B. Gordon, "Sixteenth-Century Metalworking Technology Used in the Manufacture of Two German Astrolabes," *Annals of Science* 44 (1987): 71–84; Gordon, "Material Evidence of the Development of Metal Working Technology at the Collins Axe Factory," *IA, Journal of the Society for Industrial Archeology* 9 (1983): 19–28.

34. Robert B. Gordon, "Material Evidence of the Manufacturing Methods Used in 'Armory Practice,'" *IA, Journal of the Society for Industrial Archeology* 14 (1988): 23–35; Patrick M. Malone, "Little Kinks and Devices at Springfield Armory," *IA, Journal of the Society for Industrial Archeology* 14 (1988): 59–76.

35. One of these machines is preserved at the American Precision Museum, Windsor, Vermont. Another is described in K. R. Gilbert, "The Ames Recessing

Machine: A Survivor of the Original Enfield Machinery," *Technology and Culture* 4 (1963): 207–211. Pomeroy had dropped out of arms-making by 1854 for want of capital to retool his factory.

36. A summary of methods of physical examination of artifacts is M. S. Tite, *Methods of Physical Examination in Archaeology* (London: Seminar Press, 1972).

37. Cyril Stanley Smith, *A History of Metallography* (Chicago: University of Chicago Press, 1960). For a full explanation of the technique, see George F. Vander Voort, *Metallographic Principles and Practice* (New York: McGraw-Hill, 1984), and Vander Voort, ed., *Applied Metallography* (New York: Van Nostrand Reinhold, 1986).

38. Carolyn C. Cooper, R. B. Gordon, and H. V. Merrick, "Archeological Evidence of Metallurgical Innovation at the Eli Whitney Armory," *IA, Journal of the Society for Industrial Archeology* 8 (1982): 1–12.

39. Robert B. Gordon, "Strength and Structure of Wrought Iron," *Archeomaterials* 2 (1988): 109–137; A. P. Mills, "The Old Essex–Merrimack Suspension Bridge at Newburyport, Massachusetts, and Tests of Its Wrought Iron Links after 100 Years' Service," *Engineering News* 66 (1911): 129–132.

40. Coles, *Experimental Archaeology.*

41. John Worrell, "Re-creating Ceramic Production and Tradition in a Living History Laboratory," in *Domestic Pottery of the Northeastern United States, 1625–1850,* ed. Sarah P. Turnbaugh (New York: Academic Press, 1985), pp. 81–97.

42. David Harvey, "Reconstructing the American Bloomery Process," *Historic Trades* 1 (1988): 19–37. Another experimental bloomery has been built by Dan Perry at the Scranton iron furnaces, Scranton, Pennsylvania.

43. For discussion of bobbin-making machinery and worker skills, see Carolyn C. Cooper and Patrick Malone, "The Mechanical Woodworker in Early Nineteenth-Century New England as a Spin-off from Textile Industrialization" (Paper presented at the Old Sturbridge Village Colloquium, 17 March 1990).

2
Components of Industry

Industry uses technical and organizational skills, engineering knowledge, and energy to transform natural resources into useful products. (Our definition of industry excludes such late-twentieth-century coinages as "banking industry," "leisure industry," and "culture industry.") When we carry on industry, we alter the landscape by using natural resources, by releasing wastes, and by building workplaces, industrial communities, and transportation systems. The components of industry include the skills and technical knowledge of the participants as well as the landscape and natural resources devoted to industrial activity. We cover the industrial landscape in Part II; in this chapter, we introduce the human and natural resources used by industry.

Human Resources

The work skills of artisans, the organizational skills of managers and entrepreneurs, and the engineering skills of designers and innovators have always been as essential as natural resources to industrial success. Although scientific skills had relatively little place in most industrial enterprises until the late nineteenth century, they are now essential to the success of many industries.[1] The skills in consideration here are the mental and physical capacities of individuals to do difficult tasks. These "genuine" skills are not necessarily the same as the "socially constructed" skills that are defined by job descriptions or established as barriers to control entry into a trade or profession.[2] Among work skills, those of artisans are the most poorly recorded and are, consequently, the most difficult for historians to interpret; additionally, artisan's skills are sometimes ignored, or even denigrated, by authors seeking to describe industrial work in terms of exploitation of workers or to inflate the accomplishments of inventors or entrepreneurs. Some skills that were essential in industrialization, such as those used in mining and burning coal, are hardly described in the historical record because they developed gradually and were difficult for observers to perceive. Firing a furnace with coal seems to be a simple, physically demanding task, but it requires judgment and experience to do well in a locomotive, a crucible steelworks, a glasshouse, or other heat-using industries. The stoker's skill often went unrecognized until attempts were made to transfer technology dependent on burning coal elsewhere. In the eighteenth century, the best French scientific talent was unable to guide the transition of glassmaking from wood to coal fuel because the French did not have access to the skills of British strokers.[3]

Work Skills

Few subjects in industrial history have been so surrounded by theories based on scanty facts as the place of artisans' skills in industrial life.[4] The role of artisans in innovation, in the development of new manufacturing and metallurgical processes, and in the solution of the day-to-day problems of production can be obscured by the interpretation of industrial experience in terms of conflict between "labor" and "capital" and by the representation of innovation in manufacturing technology as simply a device that entrepreneurs and managers used for asserting control over the workplace. Such simplistic descriptions overlook the complex texture of industrial work. We will show that the exercise of skills by artisans has always been an essential component of industrial success. One cause of the declining role of American manufacturing technology in world markets today is our neglect of this principle.

Often we fail to recognize the contribution of artisans' skills because the sum of the incremental improvements in technique made by many individuals becomes identified with one person in the historical record through the social reconstruction of invention in the patent system[5] or through efforts to simplify and organize history. We will see that, contrary to the folklore of innovation, industrial technologies advance primarily by many successive, incremental improvements made by artisans, managers, and engineers and that an important part of bringing new techniques to maturity is the development of new skills among the participating artisans. Transfer of the skills so learned can be the most difficult step in the subsequent diffusion of new techniques,[6] while organized resistance to the acquisition of new skills can cause industries to relocate. Although the history of manufacturing technique written in terms of the accomplishments of individual inventors obscures the contributions of artisans—almost all of whom remain anonymous—archaeological evidence can be used to discover the work of these unnamed individuals.

A central part of artisans' skill is the capacity to carry out complex industrial processes in the face of incomplete understanding and incomplete information on which to base decisions. In puddling iron (the principal nineteenth-century method of converting pig iron to wrought iron), decisions had to be made about the temperatures to be used, the rate of charging the pig iron into the furnace, the type and amount of fettling (oxidizing agent), and the amount of slag to be drawn off. The puddler had no instruments to read and no analyses of the raw materials; the progress of the process and the quality of the product had to be judged through subtle indications conveyed by sight, sound, smell, and touch.

Artisans' work skills can be thought of as a mix of different proportions of four components: dexterity, judgment, planning, and resourcefulness.[7] In addition to the ability to manipulate objects, as measured in standard psychological tests, artisans' dexterity skills include the capacity, learned by practice and experience, to manipulate tools and machines so that they will produce work of superior quality. The dexterity achieved by the artisans who shape materials is directly visible in the artifacts they make through features such as smooth, continuous curves, flat surfaces, right angles at corners, and good finish. While such features may be aesthetically pleasing, there is also a functional basis for the standards of workmanship used to judge mechanical dexterity; smooth curves and the absence of deep tool marks reduce the stress concentrations that are a common cause of cracks in the metal parts of mechanisms. Superior workmanship is a manifestation of an understanding of the properties of materials that was shared by artisans and artists but not achieved by materials scientists until well into the twentieth century.[8] It is curious that this deeper understanding of craftsmanship has been widely rejected by many practitioners of the fine arts today.

A measure of the level of judgment skill needed by an artisan is the number of variables that must be dealt with in completing a task relative to the amount of explicit information about these variables that can be acquired in the time available to reach a decision. Little judgment is needed if an artisan knows exactly the requirements to be met and the state of the work at every stage, as when the size of an object being machined is gauged with a digital readout and compared with specified numerical limits. A high level of judgment skill is called on when many decisions have to be made, but only limited information is supplied by the designers of the product or by the instrumentation available to monitor the progress of the task.

Planning the sequence of work is important, for example, when all the parts of a mechanism have to be made and fitted together without guidance from gauges or when a series of operations must be carried out in the correct sequence, as in iron smelting.[9] Both documentary and material evidence show that opportunities for artisans to exercise their planning skills were reduced during the nineteenth century. Finer division of labor meant that designers or managers rather than artisans planned more of the production process. With improved communication, the "right" way of doing particular tasks was widely accepted among artisans, making it less likely that an individual would deviate from the usual way of working. The increasing use of mechanical appliances such as filing jigs or fixtures on machine tools meant that someone else had planned how the main aspects of an artisan's task should be done. Many artisans found that they had to make one part of a mechanism, or carry on one aspect of a process, to increasingly higher standards of precision and reliability. The work was not necessarily repetitious or routine. It called for skill because inhomogeneities in the materials used, faults in parts received from others, and wear of tools created contingencies to be dealt with through an artisan's resourcefulness. All these elements of skill are used by artisans, but their relative importance changed as industrial techniques matured.[10]

Since the exercise of skill often depends on the ability to detect subtle clues without the benefit of instruments or measurement, artisans may face unresolvable difficulties when these clues are unavailable or ambiguous. Artisans' skills may be inadequate when the signals "sent" by a process fall outside the range of direct sensory perception or when the process is of such complexity that similar signals can result from different conditions within it. During American industrialization, artisans were most successful with processes that offered rich patterns of clues about their progress, such as machine-tool operation and precision gauging. In the cutting of wood or metal with a machine tool, the success or failure of the operation is shown by the noise made by the machine and the appearance of the chips and the surface being cut. If the performance is unsatisfactory, the artisan can make corrections and observe the results of the change promptly. The success of precise gauging methods that were developed in the nineteenth century to ensure interchangeability of components in mechanisms depended on the sensitivity of artisans' judgments of the fit of parts into gauges. For example, precision to within two-thousandths of an inch in routine production was attained with the mechanical gauging system developed at the Springfield Armory by 1870 and based on artisans' judgments of precision of fit (Chapter 9).[11]

One reason for uneven progress in American industrial growth was the ineffectiveness of artisans' skills in dealing with some areas of critical importance. The chronic inability of nineteenth-century ironmasters to exercise adequate control over the quality of the metal they made was a continuing source of difficulty for manufacturers and a danger to passengers on railways and steamships. In the manufacture of small arms, the greatest quality-control problem was the nonuniformity of the iron available. By about 1850, the unreliability of the wrought iron sold in the United States drove most arms makers to begin substituting steel imported from England, which was much more expensive to buy and to work. The reason that the quality of wrought iron was so difficult to control was that poor properties could result from several causes, none of which is clearly distinguishable in visual clues during the ironmaking process.[12] Consequently, even highly skilled metallurgical artisans were often unable to ensure the uniformity of their product.

When artisans' skills are an essential component of manufacturing technology, their transfer usually can be effected only through the transfer of persons with those skills. There are many examples. Two well-known success stories from the 1850s illustrate such exportation across the Atlantic: American James Burton set up production machinery made in the United States at the Enfield Armory in England, and Englishman William Onions was instrumental in bringing to Springfield Armory the technology of welding musket barrels in a rolling mill from England.[13] Yet examples of failed transfers arising from ineffective skills are also abundant. One was the attempt, in 1864, to introduce the Styrian steelmaking process to the United States with the aid of imported artisans and some of the best American scientific talent.[14]

Organizational Skills

Organizational skills—marshaling the materials, personnel, and financial support needed to undertake an industrial enterprise and to sell the finished products—are as essential to industrial success as the skills of artisans. We give just one example because organizational skills are so well covered in business histories.[15] Samuel Slater, who is famous for transferring textile technology from England to America, should be given as much credit for his organizational abilities as for his purely technical skills. Slater's apprenticeship with the British industrialist Jedediah Strutt prepared him for the responsibilities of management and showed him the economic potential of mechanized production. Despite his familiarity with cotton textile mills and machinery, he was not a trained mechanic and could not have set up his manufacturing system in Pawtucket, Rhode Island, without the assistance of local artisans, including such technically gifted men as Sylvanus Brown and David Wilkinson. He was a successful, although not always popular, manager of artisans and operatives (including children) and a first-class entrepreneur. Most of all, he knew how to run a factory. His confidence, business acumen, technical understanding, and promotional flair kept alive a risky industrial experiment that had begun in 1789. With his astute business partners and investors—William Almy, Moses Brown, Smith Brown, and Obadiah Brown—Slater established a profitable factory operation and promoted the widespread marketing of mass-produced goods.[16]

Engineering and Scientific Skills

Technology is not applied science, even though scientists have sometimes applied themselves to the design of engineering works and engineers have made use of scientific theories.[17] The objective of science is the organization of observations of natural phenomena in a framework of theory; the scientific method is reductionist, and results are judged in terms of elegance and ingenuity. The phenomena selected for study are those that appear to practicing scientists to be susceptible to theoretical explanation; other subjects may be designated as unimportant or uninteresting and cast aside by the social hierarchies through which power and resources are awarded to scientists. The objectives of engineering are quite different. Engineering is the design and operation of technical systems to achieve specific goals. It includes the application of science, economics, and aesthetics to these ends. Among the criteria for success, effective performance of a system is more important than abstract elegance.

Scientific principles are an essential component of engineering because structures built or processes operated in violation of these principles will surely fail. As Thomas Telford astutely observed, "Nature to be commanded must be obeyed." But, unlike science, engineering cannot succeed by reductionist methods because aspects of technology that are not adequately explained by the current state of science must often be used in the completion of an engineering task. It is this necessity to carry on in the face of incomplete scientific understanding that makes engineering appear less elegant or less intellectual than science to many observers, particularly members of the academy.

Natural Resources

Nonrenewable resources can be used but once, and, as they are used up, we can sustain the services they provide only by finding new sources or substituting alternatives. Minerals, mineral fuels, and much of the groundwater in the arid parts of North America are nonrenewable resources. Renewable resources regenerate, and we can use them indefinitely, provided that our rate of consumption is slower than their renewal rate. Wood and surface water can be used as renewable resources, as when woodland is managed for sustained yield by balancing the rate of harvesting with the rate of tree growth.

Water

Most of the cost of a water supply or power system arises from the initial investment in engineering works required to develop the resource; the topography of the site used is a major factor in determining that cost. Sites particularly suitable for the development of power are usually referred to as "water privileges" in North America, reflecting English riparian law. On a given river, water privileges can be ranked in order of the unit cost of generating power at each site.[18] The number of water privileges that are economically useful along a river depends on the prevailing price of power: when the price increases, it may become feasible to develop privileges with higher unit costs, thereby expanding the power resource. For almost all natural resources, availability depends on both economic and physical factors. Often the economic bounds are much more important than the physical ones. The physical upper bound of a river's water power would be reached if all its flow and fall were harnessed for mechanical work. Yet the actual utilization of the potential of streams, even in heavily industrialized regions, has almost always fallen well short of this limit because power from alternative sources, such as animals or mineral fuels, has been cheaper than power from the more expensive water privileges. The water power in the United States that could be developed if cost were no object is about 161,000 megawatts; only about 20 percent of this has been worth using at today's prices.[19]

Although water continues to flow in rivers and streams indefinitely (unless a watershed is destroyed or a stream diverted), industrial installations that collect river water in ponds or reservoirs are not necessarily using a truly renewable resource. Rivers also carry sediment eroded from the surrounding land or from their banks; this accumulates as deposits when river water enters ponds or reservoirs (an example is discussed in Chapter 3). The storage capacity of a reservoir is reduced as it fills with sediment. Since it is often impractical to remove this material because of cost and environmental consequences, the sedimentation rate limits the useful life of a reservoir or a water-power installation, which can be as short as a decade.

Wood

Forests are a renewable resource when managed to produce a sustained yield of wood. Management of woodland for continual production was usually undertaken in Europe and North America only when the cost of cutting and

FIGURE 2.1. Much of the slate taken from this quarry near Slatington, Pennsylvania, was of poor quality or in pieces too small to be sold. Workers dumped it next to the quarry pit. It will be many years before this rock weathers enough to form soil that will support vegetation; in the meantime, it will continue to look like wasteland.

transporting wood from virgin forests became prohibitive. An early example of managing forests for sustained yield was the adoption of coppicing in sixteenth-century England to provide a continual fuel supply for ironworks in the Weald. In coppicing, the new shoots put up by the roots of cut trees were protected from browsing animals and allowed to grow for fifteen to twenty years, when they would be large enough for charcoaling. An ironworks had to acquire enough land so that when it was divided into twenty parts, each resulting parcel was large enough to provide the fuel for a year's production.[20] The system provided a sustained supply of fuel but did not allow for expansion unless more forest could be acquired. Because their virgin forest resources were so large, Americans used coppicing only well into the nineteenth century.

Ores and Minerals

Ores are mineral deposits in which metals have been concentrated well above their average abundance at the earth's surface. The grade of ore (the proportion of valuable mineral contained) that can be mined economically depends on the price of the metal. In recent years, the price of copper has been high enough to make mining ore containing less than 0.5 percent metal worthwhile. In other words, more than 99.5 percent of the copper ore taken from the ground is waste and must be discarded. Large piles of waste are often conspicuous remains of past mining activity (Fig. 5.1). As lower grades of ore are used in the future, the cost of dealing with mine waste will increase. Quarrying abundant minerals such as lime, cement stone, slate, and dimension stone also scars the land with pits and waste. For example, only part of the slate brought out of quarries is good enough to be sold; the rest may be left in waste piles covering many acres (Fig. 2.1). There is less waste in granite quarrying, but the pits are large, conspicuous cavities (Fig. 2.2).

Mining is an uncertain, often short-lived enterprise. It is particularly sensitive to changes in market conditions, and it sometimes requires participants to gamble on the extent of underground deposits. Because mining

FIGURE 2.2. In the Fletcher Quarry in northeastern Massachusetts, granite blocks are removed by cutting the stone with torches and wire saws and then hoisting out the blocks with the quarry crane. If the stone is free of defects and the work is carefully planned and skillfully executed, the quarried blocks will be close to the desired size and there will be little waste. Granite often occurs as large pods in surrounding rocks. As the entire pod of granite is removed, the quarry becomes a large cavity like this one.

frequently takes place in remote areas, the remains of mine structures and communities may survive longer than the remains of other kinds of industry. The alteration of the surrounding landscape is often long-lived as well.

Fuels

All the fossil fuels—coal, oil, and gas—are formed from organic material that has been buried in the earth. Although fossil fuels are still being formed, the rate of formation is so slow that they are nonrenewable resources. Years of geological exploration have provided information about the amount of coal that remains in North America; in the United States, the ratio of measured coal reserves to annual production is 670 years, and we usually think of coal as an abundant resource.[21] In North America, we have been using oil and gas at a higher rate than we have been discovering new reserves for the past two decades.[22] We will see in the following chapters how shifts in the relative prices of different energy sources have caused major changes in the texture of industry in the past. Understanding these can help us cope with the changes that will inevitably come in the future as a result of environmental concerns and resource consumption.

Costs of Wealth

The components of industry are used to create wealth, but their costs must be balanced against the benefits gained. It is important for historians and archaeologists to discover and make known the costs of wealth, particularly those that have been obscured or have become so commonplace as to be widely accepted as inevitable.

The owners of an industry must pay certain costs directly. They charge these expenses against income, and the balance determines whether or not there is a profit. Because no industrial venture that operates at a loss can survive for very long (unless it receives a subvention supplied for political reasons), cost accounting is an important management skill. Although it has gradually become both widespread and sophisticated, this method of accounting has only recently begun to attract the attention of historians of technology.[23]

Industrial activity also involves costs that are not charged directly to the company and may not appear in any company account books or financial statements. In economic theory, such costs are called "negative externalities." They are the unfortunate side effects caused by the production of goods and services. There are two scenarios that have made negative externalities a persistent problem in our culture. In the first, neither the manufacturer nor the consumer is asked to pay all the costs involved in making a product. For instance, effluents discharged into a river from a dyeworks cause damages downstream, but those who own the offending plant and those who wear its colorful cloth do not pay compensation for the damages. In the second scenario, there is no reward for the individual or company that assumes the cost of eliminating an offensive side effect. The voluntary installation of a system for filtration and chemical treatment of effluents at the dyeworks would halt pollution but would provide no direct benefit for the owners. (It would, in fact, cost them money to install and operate the system.) The cheapest way to do something is not often the way that will provide the broadest public benefits.[24] Making adequate provision for externalities is a particularly vexing question in democratic, industrialized societies. Although governments have begun to offer rewards (such as tax credits) for positive actions, punishment in the form of fines or imprisonment is still a common way to halt unacceptable behavior and to affect future decisions. Of all the externalities associated with industry, the one that has attracted most attention in recent decades is the alteration of the environment.

A historical and archaeological perspective is essential in studying the costs of wealth because many of these costs become evident only over a long period of time. We will see in Chapter 4 that some of the environmental consequences of mining coal continue for hundreds of years after a mine stops producing. Many other examples could be chosen. Throughout this book, we will try to point out archaeological evidence of as yet unpaid costs of wealth.

Depletion of Natural Resources

Concern about the depletion of natural resources has accompanied the development of industry from early times. Alleged depletion of forests by the iron industry attracted the attention of the British government in the sixteenth century and again became an issue in the seventeenth century, when it gave rise to one of the first conservation movements.[25] The issue of the depletion of nonrenewable resources was raised to the level of national debate by William S. Jevons when his book, *The Coal Question,* was published in 1866. Jevons argued that the continued development of the export market for British manufactured goods would deplete the coal reserves needed to sustain the domestic economy and so should be discouraged. Jevons's work became one of the intellectual roots of the interest in conservation that developed toward the end of the nineteenth century.[26]

The existence of abundant natural resources in North America tended to promote complacency. Few were concerned about conservation until, in the

1870s, John Muir began to publicize the continuing loss of wilderness areas. Muir was determined to set aside unaltered wilderness for future generations, but he soon faced powerful opposition from those who favored full exploitation of natural assets. A federal law passed in 1891 allowing "forest reserves" departed from the conservation ethic that Muir had helped establish through the creation of Yosemite National Park in the previous year. Forestry interests promoted the harvesting of trees in what became the national forests, and the struggling conservation movement split over the issue of the proper government role in land management. Gifford Pinchot, who became chief forester of the United States Forest Service, led the campaign to conserve while still making economic use of available resources. Public demands for government regulation of resources increased after Frederick Jackson Turner focused attention on the disappearance of the frontier and thereby raised the possibility that the nation's natural wealth was being exhausted.[27] Mining, lumbering, and grazing have continued in the public domain with varying degrees of governmental restriction throughout the twentieth century.

Jevons's argument has been repeated in many forms, and there have been numerous predictions of unfortunate economic consequences arising from exhausting particular resources; among them are the reports by the Paley Commission in 1952 and the Club of Rome in 1970.[28] Whenever it has been possible to test such predictions, they have been found wanting for two reasons. The first is that improvements in technology have resulted in the more efficient use of natural resources. These improvements continued to be made even in fully mature industries such as smelting pig iron, where the amount of fuel used per ton of iron smelted was reduced by 20 percent in the decade 1958 to 1968. The second reason is that new technology has been used to substitute more abundant resources for scarce ones, as when fiber-optic cable replaced copper wire in telecommunications. The drag on economic growth due to scarcity of natural resources has proved to be small as long as there is a capacity to innovate and replace old technologies.[29]

Degradation of the Environment

Most industry produces wastes—materials that have such small economic value that their further use is not profitable. In the absence of regulation for the public good, the cheapest way of disposing of fluid and gaseous wastes has been to disperse them by releasing gases and particulates into the atmosphere and liquids to a river, a lake, or the ocean. Solid wastes usually accumulate in rubbish piles, which sometimes, through changing economic conditions, become valuable enough to be considered resources useful for recycling. The fine coal in the culm piles in the anthracite coal region of

Pennsylvania had no value a hundred years ago because it could not be burned in existing grates, but it can now be profitably reclaimed because new combustion technology has made it a useful fuel.

Extraction and consumption of natural resources are sources of environmental change that may also accompany industrialization. Throughout much of the nineteenth century, it was thought by many in America that deforestation caused changes in climate on both a local and a regional (but not global) scale. Belief in a relationship between forest cover and local climate can be documented from the time of Columbus, who commented on the effect of deforestation on the climate of the Azores. American writers in the nineteenth century often reported anecdotal evidence of such change, observing, for example, that a particular variety of fruit tree would no longer grow at a given location after the forests in the region were cut. These claims were sometimes cited as evidence by those who for other reasons wished to see forests preserved. After Charles Schott used an extended series of instrumental observations compiled by the Smithsonian Institution to argue in 1872 that deforestation had no detectable, large-scale effects on the climate of the United States, interest in the subject dwindled. Better data and heightened awareness of the environment have led people to reopen this question as a global issue in recent decades. [30]

Cases of environmental degradation due to the release of wastes can be found from ancient times onward, but widespread popular attention was first focused on it in the first third of the nineteenth century as a result of pollution caused by the use of steam engines in factories and the effluents released by the textile finishing trades in the manufacturing cities of Great Britain. That the popular view of industrial effluents was mixed is shown by nineteenth-century drawings of industrial works that illustrated prosperity by showing plumes of smoke trailing from factory stacks. Nevertheless, public concern about pollution was expressed by an early-nineteenth-century law requiring locomotives to "consume their own smoke" and by lawsuits over smoke emissions in cities. This concern contributed to initiation of the "condition of England" debate of the 1840s. [31] As a result, there was much public inspection of industry as partisans searched for evidence to support their views on the benefits and evils of industrialization. Many of our currently held beliefs about industry originated in the positions then advanced by the friends and foes of industry. [32]

The efforts made by nineteenth-century Europeans and Americans at waste disposal were incomplete, since they gave little attention to the ultimate fate of the effluents that they collected and transported by sewers or released by stacks. The untreated contents of the sewers were discharged directly into rivers or the sea; often this practice has continued to the present day. Additionally, nineteenth-century reformers were almost entirely concerned with smokes and stinks, nuisances that could be detected directly by the senses of sight and smell. Only in recent decades have components without such obvious evidence, such as lead in paint, been recognized as health hazards. Many deposits of wastes from old manufacturing operations contain materials that are only now being recognized as dangerous. (These can pose special problems to industrial archaeologists carrying out excavations.) The costs of dealing with these materials are a part of the cost of wealth that has been left for future generations to pay.

In the twentieth century, environmental effects that cannot be traced to specific sources with the aid of the human senses alone are being recognized. Chemists have shown that the invisible and nearly odorless emissions from automobiles and refineries are the primary cause of the smog that is both a nuisance and a health hazard in many communities. Ameliorating these sources of pollution in democratic societies depends on widespread acceptance of scientific evidence on causes and effects that most persons must take on faith, since they cannot confirm them by their own direct observation.

Accident and Injury

The risk of accidental injury accompanies everything we do, but some types of industrial work carry unusually great risks for workers. One reason Bronze Age metalsmiths substituted tin for arsenic as the alloying element they used in copper was to avoid the debilitating effect of arsenic fumes. The risks that accompany the use of mercury in felting are expressed by the phrase "mad as a hatter." Some trades that became very important in the nineteenth century, such as cutlery grinding, file cutting, and coal mining, have long had well-deserved reputations as unhealthful; others, such as lumbering, rail-car switching, and running farm machinery, had a high potential for accidental injury; and some, such as coal mining, were both unhealthful and subject to a high frequency of accidents. In 1904, the rate of accidental deaths for railroad workers was 28 per 10,000, prompting one critic to comment, "War is safe compared to railroading in this country." Two years later, the American rate of fatal coal-mining accidents reached 48 for every 10,000 miners. From 1900 to 1906, this annual rate averaged 33, much worse than for the British mines (13) or the French (9).[33]

There is much anecdotal evidence of the frequency of industrial accidents. Dr. Alice Hamilton, whose powerful 1943 autobiography, *Exploring the Dangerous Trades,* described her crusading efforts for safety in the workplace, focused most of her attention on lead poisoning, silicosis, and the hazards of manufacturing explosive munitions. In the notes of her federal survey of the lead trades in 1911, she recorded the following statement by a black man who worked in a particularly dangerous "white-lead factory" in St. Louis: "It is better paid than any other work a Negro can get, but it sure does break your health." From Pittsburgh in the same year, she wrote to her mother:

> One of the great Carnegie Steel Mills is just below [the hospital] and as I sat by the window I could watch the ambulances crawl up the hill to the accident entrance with a new victim inside. Three came while I was there. So many cases are sent from the mills that evidently the clerk got tired writing the name of the Company and had a rubber stamp made which, appropriately enough, he uses with red ink. All down the pages there are red blotches, just like drops of blood.[34]

Earl J. Malone, Jr., recorded in his diary the dangers of work at his father's Missouri woodworking mill in 1911:

> We heard today that the foreman of one of the working crews at the Holly-Matthews Mfg. Co.'s plant got caught in a belt and bruised with a broken rib besides yesterday, also a sawyer got a thumb almost severed there same day. Today a fellow got his foot badly scalded in one of the vats down there. It seems like the factory gets a turn at them all sooner or later for many men are hurt or killed there.[35]

Our perception of the risk from accident is strongly conditioned by social factors that are only now being explored by scholars. Through much of the nineteenth century, public perception of industrial accidents was much like the mid-twentieth-century perception of automobile accidents. They were accepted as the price of benefits thought to be worth this cost. By the latter half of the nineteenth century, however, railway accidents were no longer regarded as inevitable, and, consequently, resources were devoted to the development of safety brakes and interlocking block signals. Some of the unhealthful occupations, such as grinding axes and cutting files by hand, were eliminated by mechanization, but these were primarily benefits derived from efforts to increase productivity and have to be balanced against increased health hazards such as those caused by the introduction of pneumatic drills in mining.[36] Widespread concern about industrial health and accidents is a twentieth-century development.

Notes

1. The connection between science and industrial development is discussed in Nathan Rosenberg and L. E. Birdzell, Jr., *How the West Grew Rich* (New York: Basic Books, 1986), chap. 8, and Edwin T. Layton, Jr., "Scientific Technology, 1845–

1900: The Hydraulic Turbine and the Origins of American Industrial Research," *Technology and Culture* 20 (1979): 64–89. Scientific skills did contribute significantly to the success of textile printing and dyeing in the 1820s and, through the work of James Francis and Uriah Boyden, to the development of hydraulic turbines in the 1840s and 1850s.

2. Charles More, *Skill and the English Working Class, 1870–1914* (London: Croom Helm, 1980), chap. 1.

3. J. R. Harris, "Skills, Coal, and British Industry in the Eighteenth Century," *History* 61 (1976): 167–182.

4. Patrick Joyce, ed., *The Historical Meanings of Work* (Cambridge: Cambridge University Press, 1987), chap. 1.

5. The social construction of invention through the patent system is explained in Carolyn C. Cooper, "The Evolution of American Patent Management: The Blanchard Lathe as a Case Study," *Prologue* 19 (1987): 245–259.

6. The important role of skills in the transfer of technology is discussed in Nathan Rosenberg, *Perspectives on Technology* (Cambridge: Cambridge University Press, 1976), pp. 93–102. See also Patrick M. Malone, "Little Kinks and Devices at Springfield Armory, 1892–1918," *IA, Journal of the Society for Industrial Archeology* 14 (1988): 59–76.

7. These components of skill are illustrated in Robert B. Gordon, "Who Turned the Mechanical Ideal into Mechanical Reality?" *Technology and Culture* 29 (1988): 744–788.

8. Cyril Stanley Smith, *A History of Metallography* (Chicago: University of Chicago Press, 1960), sec. 1.

9. The conceptualization needed in making a one-off object is examined in Charles M. Keller and Janet Keller, *Thinking and Acting with Iron*, Cognitive Science Technical Report CS-91-08, Learning Series (Urbana–Champaign: Beckman Institute for Advanced Science and Technology, University of Illinois, 1991).

10. The shifts in the components of skill needed by artisans as the manufacture of firearms changed from craft to factory production are described in Gordon, "Mechanical Ideal into Mechanical Reality."

11. Ibid.

12. Robert B. Gordon, "Strength and Structure of Wrought Iron," *Archeomaterials* 2 (1988): 109–137.

13. Robert B. Gordon, "English Iron for American Arms: Laboratory Evidence on the Source of Iron Used at the Springfield Armory in 1860," *Journal of the Historical Metallurgy Society* 17 (1983): 91–98. On James Burton, see Edward C. Ezell, *The AK47 Story* (Harrisburg, Pa.: Stackpole, 1986).

14. Robert B. Gordon and M. S. Raber, "An Early American Integrated Steel Works," *IA, Journal of the Society for Industrial Archeology* 10 (1984): 17–34.

15. See, for example, Alfred Chandler, *The Visible Hand: The Managerial Revolution in American Business* (Cambridge, Mass.: Harvard University Press, 1977).

16. James Conrad, "The Making of a Hero: Samuel Slater and the Arkwright Frames," *Rhode Island History* 45 (1986): 3–13; Gary Kulik, "The Beginnings of the Industrial Revolution in America: Pawtucket, Rhode Island, 1672–1829" (Ph.D. diss., Brown University, 1980), chap. 2; Paul Rivard, *Samuel Slater: Father of American Manufacturers* (Pawtucket, R.I.: Slater Mill Historic Site, 1974); David J. Jeremy, *Transatlantic Industrial Revolution: The Diffusion of Textile Technologies Between Brit-*

ain and America, 1790–1830s (Cambridge, Mass.: MIT Press, 1981), pp. 79–89; Gary Kulik, Roger Parks, and Theodore Z. Penn, eds., *The New England Mill Village, 1790–1860* (Cambridge, Mass.: MIT Press, 1982), pp. 55, 65–67, 93–97; Robert Macieski, "Samuel Slater and the Cotton Bicentennial," *Slater Mill Historic Site Newsletter* 20 (Winter 1990): 1–3; Steven Kasierski, "Giving Out the Psalm" (honors thesis, Stanford University, 1988). We are grateful to James Conrad for letting us read a draft of a new article showing that Slater was also technologically progressive in his later promotion and adoption of power looms.

17. The independence of applied science and technology is developed in A. Hunter Dupree, "The Role of Technology in Society and the Need for Historical Research," *Technology and Culture* 10 (1969): 528–534; Edwin T. Layton, Jr., "Technology as Knowledge," *Technology and Culture* 15 (1974): 31–41; and an outstanding case study: Walter P. Vincenti, "Technological Knowledge Without Science: The Invention of Flush Riveting in American Airplanes, ca. 1930–ca. 1950," *Technology and Culture* 26 (1984): 540–576.

18. The calculation of the costs of developing the different power sites within a drainage basin is explained in Robert B. Gordon, "Cost and Use of Water Power During Industrialization in New England and Great Britain: A Geological Interpretation," *Economic History Review* 36 (1983): 240–259.

19. M. King Hubbert, "Energy Resources," in Committee on Resources and Man of the National Academy of Sciences, *Resources and Man* (San Francisco: Freeman, 1969), pp. 207–209.

20. H. R. Schubert, *History of the British Iron and Steel Industry from c. 450 B.C. to A.D. 1775* (London: Routledge and Kegan Paul, 1957), pp. 222, 430.

21. Y. K. Rao, *Stoichiometry and Thermodynamics of Metallurgical Processes* (Cambridge: Cambridge University Press, 1985), table 4-3.

22. The fuel reserves of North America are reviewed in Hubbert, "Energy Resources." A comprehensive survey of the availability of natural resources is found in D. J. McLaren and B. J. Skinner, eds., *Resources and World Development* (New York: Wiley, 1987).

23. One of the first studies of early attempts at cost accounting is Judith McGaw, "Accounting for Innovation: Technological Change and Business Practice in the Berkshire County Paper Industry," *Technology and Culture* 26 (1985): 703–725. See also Daniel Nelson, *Managers and Workers: Origins of the New Factory System in the United States, 1880–1920* (Madison: University of Wisconsin Press, 1975), p. 50.

24. Rosenberg, *Perspective on Technology,* pp. 213–219.

25. Schubert, *British Iron and Steel Industry,* pp. 218–222. There has been a great deal of debate among historians as to the actual amount of the depletion of English forest resources by the iron industry, and it now appears that the deforestation was not so great as once believed (Oliver Rackham, *Trees and Woodland in the British Landscape* [London: Dent, 1976], p. 91).

26. A brief history of the environmental movement in the United States and a list of background books is in the *Wilson Quarterly* 11 (1987): 51–83.

27. For discussion of American attitudes toward wilderness and of the conflicting philosophies of Muir and Pinchot, see Roderick Nash, *Wilderness and the American Mind* (New Haven, Conn.: Yale University Press, 1967). For the role of government and of the science establishment in conservation issues, see A. Hunter Dupree, *Science and the Federal Government* (Cambridge, Mass.: Harvard University Press, 1957), pp. 232–255.

28. Paley Commission [U.S. President's Materials Policy Commission], *Resources for Freedom* (Washington, D.C.: Government Printing Office, 1952); H. D. Meadows and others, *The Limits of Growth: A Report for the Club of Rome's Project on the Predicament of Mankind* (New York: New American Library, 1970).

29. Robert B. Gordon and others, *Toward a New Iron Age? Quantitative Modeling of Resource Exhaustion* (Cambridge, Mass.: Harvard University Press, 1987).

30. Kenneth Thompson, "Forests and Climatic Change in America: Some Early Views," *Climatic Change* 3 (1980): 47–64.

31. English locomotives burned coke until 1852, when fireboxes suitable for coal were finally designed (J. B. Snell, *Mechanical Engineering: Railways* [London: Longman, 1971]). "Report of the Trial of an Indictment Preferred Against Messrs. Benjamin Gott & Sons, for an Alleged Public Nuisance in Neglecting to Consume the Smoke of their Steam Engine Furnaces at Leeds," in *History at Source: Men and Machines, 1717–1896* (London: Evans, 1972). Testimony at the trial showed that smoke entering neighboring dwellings had caused significant damage. For public health problems caused by industry, see Anthony S. Wohl, *Endangered Lives: Public Health in Victorian Britain* (London: Dent, 1983).

32. Barrie Trinder, *The Making of the Industrial Landscape* (London: Dent, 1982), pp. 126, 174.

33. Carl Gersuny, *Work Hazards and Industrial Conflict* (Hanover, N.H.: University Press of New England, 1981), p. 20; Keith Dix, *Work Relations in the Coal Industry: The Hand-Loading Era, 1880–1930* (Morgantown: West Virginia University Press, 1977).

34. Alice Hamilton, *Exploring the Dangerous Trades* (Boston: Little, Brown, 1943), pp. 131–133.

35. Earl J. Malone, Jr., diary, 25 January 1911, in the possession of Patrick M. Malone.

36. Larry D. Lankton, "The Machine Under the Garden: Rock Drills Arrive at the Lake Superior Copper Mines, 1868–1883," *Technology and Culture* 24 (1983): 1–37.

II

INDUSTRIAL LANDSCAPES

3

Wood and Water

The early Spanish adventurers came to America primarily to mine precious metals. Some colonists in eastern North America also had hopes of finding gold and silver, but more turned to the abundant timber and water resources of the New World and undertook lumbering and ironmaking to produce goods for export to the mother country. Through the next 200 years, most American industrial entrepreneurs used energy from wood and from flowing water.[1] Water was a renewable resource, while wood was so abundant that new sources were easily found when a local supply was depleted. The years in which wood had a dominant place in American technology have been described by historian Brooke Hindle as "America's Wooden Age";[2] on much of the continent, metal was used only where wood would not serve, as in nails, gun barrels, and cooking pots. Iron was the only metal made in significant quantities in North America during the Wooden Age.

Settlers along the American coast reached the roadless interior by ascending the numerous rivers and, until well into the nineteenth century, preferred to move heavy or bulky cargoes by boat or raft. They used the flow and drop of water in streams as their principal source of mechanical power for industry, and only after 1870 did Americans generate more power with steam engines than with waterwheels.[3] Visitors to Old Sturbridge Village, a living-history museum in Massachusetts that re-creates community life in the early years of the nineteenth century, find wooden buildings, tools made of wood and iron, the smell of wood smoke, and machinery powered by waterwheels.

Along the east coast, wood, water in lakes and streams, and iron ore were abundant but had to be used near where they were found until entrepreneurs with access to capital and technological expertise built canals, railways, and, later, electrical power-transmission systems. A craftsman who started a shop with human-powered machinery in town and subsequently wanted to use water power often had to move to a rural site. As more people did this, they spread manufacturing over the landscape of the Northeast. In addition, not all sites could provide the same amount of water power. The amount of power that could be generated at a given place was fixed by the flow and fall of water available. Before manufacturers had alternative sources of cheap energy, this limited the amount of industrial development in a community. Entrepreneurs were unable to concentrate industry based on wood or water resources in large industrial towns except at a few places, such as Lowell, Massachusetts, where the substantial water power and the configuration of the land made it possible to build power canals for numerous mills.

Natural Resources

Wood

The great tracts of forest found by colonists on the east coast of North America and the tall white pines suitable for masts of the ships of the Royal Navy have a prominent place in American literature and history. By 1600, the forests of England already had a long history of hard use, and people were turning to mineral coal as an alternative fuel.[4] Because of the strong demand for timber in England, one of the quickest ways for colonists to start an export trade from America was by cutting trees and splitting or sawing them into boards with handsaws; the first cargo the Pilgrims at Plymouth sent back to England was a load of clapboards.[5]

Not only were eastern forests abundant, but they were made up of diverse species and were near numerous streams that could supply both the power to saw the logs and a means of moving the timber to the coast. Americans made full use of these characteristics. The forests of North America had reached the climax stage of development well before the arrival of Europeans. Since the retreat of the ice of the last glaciation (about 12,000 years ago), change in the climate had been slow enough for the forest to approach the optimum distribution of species, which would change further only through the slow process of biological evolution. This climax forest had a great diversity of species, each adapted to a specific habitat. Its complexity was further enhanced by windfalls caused by hurricanes and fires started by lightning or Indians. Because the distribution of species could be different between a

FIGURE 3.1. Particular kinds of wood are suitable for specialized uses. An artisan has been fitting teeth made of hard maple into a large bevel gear used in the wheel pit of a water-powered mill. With wooden rather than metal teeth, the gears in the mill power train run more quietly and are easier to repair. Through experience, American artisans learned which of the many species of wood available to them were best suited for specific tasks. With this specialized knowledge, they were able to make optimum use of wood in the machinery they built for American factories in the nineteenth century. (Photographed in Holyoke, Massachusetts, 1981)

hillside and its adjacent valley, many kinds of wood were often available within walking distance of one another.

Diversity of tree species can contribute to the sophistication of artisans' work because the properties of specific kinds of wood make each particularly suitable for particular uses. Characteristics that differ among tree species include resistance to rot; the ease with which the wood can be cut or bent; its appearance, hardness, rate of burning, and suitability for making charcoal; and the chemical composition of its ashes.[6] In America, shipwrights favored white oak for ship timbers, found that black oak was a better choice for planking hulls because of its resistance to marine worms, and chose white pine for masts. Carpenters used chestnut to sheathe buildings because it resisted weathering. Mechanics used maple to make teeth for gears (Fig. 3.1) and various hardwoods to make the spools used in textile mills.

Woodsmen could bring felled trees out of the forest on horse-drawn sleds in winter, but they found that the most convenient means of moving timber to distant users was to float it down rivers. Hence, the many rapidly flowing rivers and the abundance of sites suitable for water-powered sawmills enhanced the value of the North American forests. In the nineteenth century, axmen cut timber in the winter and drew it through the woods with horse teams to ice-covered ponds. They floated it downstream to sawmills in organized timber drives or in rafts during the spring runoff.[7] It was only in the 1870s that lumbermen began to substitute railways for timber drives and place steam-powered sawmills in the woods.

Wooden artifacts are archaeological evidence of the different ways Americans used forest resources. The type of wood in an artifact can be identified from its grain structure.[8] The size of trees cut is shown by the size of boards found in early buildings and the structural parts of wooden ships, such as the *Charles Morgan,* preserved at the Mystic Seaport Museum. Successive layers of pollen preserved in the sediment on the bottoms of lakes and ponds are a record of the past composition of forests. Some idea of our early forest resources can be had from observing the wilderness areas of the national parks, but park managers have found it difficult to decide how to react to natural disturbances, such as fires ignited by lightning strikes, that were a part of forest ecology in the past.

Water

Climatological maps show the great range of hydrological variables across North America.[9] Rainfall is greatest in the Northwest, but has a strong seasonal variation; in the Southwest, average annual evaporation exceeds rainfall for extended periods, and many streams flow only during the intense, but infrequent, rains. In the Northeast, the annual variation in rainfall is smallest, and the steady flow, frequent waterfalls or rapids, and small amount of sediment in river water made it easier for Americans to start industries that used water power. These characteristics of rivers are similar to those in regions where industrialization began in northern Europe.[10]

There has been a continuing debate about how much river flow has changed in North America during historic time. Disappearance of streams and diminution of water available at mill sites was reported in many eighteenth- and nineteenth-century accounts, and usually ascribed to changes in climate due to deforestation; these accounts were thereafter repeated uncritically by others. They should be read critically because some streams have been diverted underground in urban areas, while the apparent shortages of water at mills were often due to earlier, uninformed, and overly optimistic estimates of the stream flow that was available. Hydrologists have been gauging the flow of American rivers for more than a century. Even where no gauge data exist, it has been possible to reconstruct the history of river flow with indirect evidence, such as the relation of discharge to tree-ring spacing.[11] In historic time, climatic change has had much less effect on stream flow than have changes in land use. Hydrologists have found that cutting the trees in a watershed reduces the water loss by evapotranspiration and, so, increases the average discharge of a river. Among experimental drainage basins covered with pine, oak, wheat, and grass, the runoff is least for pine cover and greatest for wheat. In one trial, researchers found that clear-cutting an oak forest in North Carolina increased runoff by about 30 percent; others have observed increases as great as 300 percent.[12] The increased runoff is accompanied by greater susceptibility to flooding and soil erosion during heavy rains and diminished flow during droughts because of the smaller infiltration capacity of the deforested land. Where steady flow is important, as when we use water to generate power, the disadvantages linked with these variations can outweigh any advantage gained from the increased total flow. Americans observed and reported some aspects of drainage-basin hydrology in the early nineteenth century,[13] but had no theoretical framework for their observations until about fifty years ago. The slow development of the science of hydrology was one cause of poor management of water resources in the industrialized areas of North America.[14]

State legislatures often commissioned surveys of water-power resources from 1865 onward in their efforts to attract industry,[15] but the first comprehensive inventory of the water-power resources of the United States was not made until the Tenth Census (1880).[16] We can use the archaeological technique of engineering analysis (Chapter 1) to find the *power potential* (how much power could have been generated if all the flow and fall of water of a river had been used) and the *power density* (the power potential per unit area of a watershed). These characteristics differ greatly among the rivers of the Northeast (Table 3.1).

How much of the power potential of a river system entrepreneurs develop at a given time depends on the cost of using it. Most of the cost of water

TABLE 3.1 Water-Power Characteristics of Drainage Basins

Principal River	Total Power Potential	Power Density
Housatonic	343 megawatts	69 kilowatts/square kilometer
Merrimack	851	59
Blackstone	26	23
Charles	8	11
Taunton	6	6

Source: Robert B. Gordon, "Cost and Use of Water Power During Industrialization in New England and Great Britain: A Geological Interpretation," *Economic History Review* 36 (1983): 245.

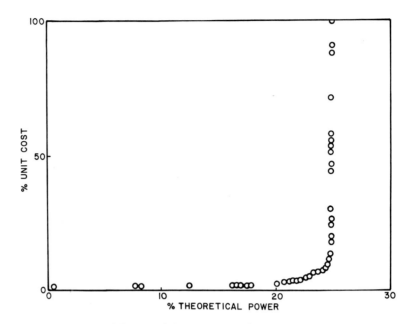

FIGURE 3.2. Most of the cost of obtaining power from a river is in the construction of the physical plant and is lower per unit of power obtained at sites where the topography makes construction easy. The cost of obtaining power at each of the thirty-nine cheapest privileges on the Housatonic River is placed in rank order in this graph, showing the unit cost as a percentage of that at the thirty-ninth site and the percentage of the potential power of the river realized by development of each site. Once the most favorable water privileges are developed, the cost of obtaining more power from the river increases very rapidly. Hence only about one-quarter of the power potential of the river is economically useful.

power is the initial investment in engineering works and machinery, and this depends on the topographical and flow characteristics of each water privilege. When we compute the relative cost of power at the water privileges within a drainage basin, we find a cost function like the one in Figure 3.2. This example shows that after about 25 percent of the power that is theoretically available in the Housatonic basin is developed (corresponding to all the easily developed privileges), the marginal cost of obtaining more power increases very rapidly. The remaining power potential of the drainage basin is physically available but is not economically useful. After the low-cost power potential is used up, persons wanting water power either locate elsewhere or use alternative sources of energy. The industrial significance of the drainage basins listed in Table 3.1 changes when we compare the amount of economically useful power in them. In the Blackstone drainage basin, 53 percent of the power potential is economically useful, while in the Merrimack basin only 15 percent is. The economically useful power density in the Blackstone is 12 kW/km² but only 9 kW/km² in the Merrimack. The Blackstone had the most intense industrial development of any river in New England, prompting the observation in the 1880 census that "it would be hard, in fact, to find another stream in the country so completely utilized." Of the 438-foot drop between Worcester and Providence, 400 feet were used in manufacturing.[17]

Iron

Ore rich enough for smelting could be found near most of the settlements on the east coast of North America either as bog ore, which was regenerated by the flow of groundwater, or as rock ores, iron minerals formed in past geological times.

Bog ore is formed on the bottom of shallow wetlands by precipitation of iron from upwelling water that reaches a source of oxygen. Its formation may be aided by bacteria. The unconsolidated crusts of iron oxide are called "loam ore" and are relatively low grade. With time, the loam ore consolidates into "seed ore," which contains about 45 percent iron, and, eventually, "massive ore," which contains up to 53 percent iron. Layers of bog ore harvested from the bottoms of wetlands can be replaced by the natural accretion of more iron in as short a time as sixteen years. The extensive deposits along the east coast from Massachusetts through Virginia were the principal iron ores used until well into the eighteenth century.[18] Iron-workers in boats harvested bog ore with long-handled tongs, like oyster tongs, or they diverted water from an area of wetlands by means of temporary dams to expose the ore.[19] When David Harvey undertook experimental iron smelting at Colonial Williamsburg in 1985 (Chapter 1), he was able to dig up the ore that he needed along the banks of the nearby James River.[20] Bog ore was highly variable in composition and often had a high phosphorus content, so, while it was easy to smelt, the resulting iron was sometimes of poor quality.[21]

In the early decades of the republic, ironmasters were abandoning bog ore in favor of rock ores. They preferred the ores found in eastern Pennsylvania, but also established works near the limonite deposits of western Connecticut and Massachusetts as well as the magnetite ores in northern New Jersey and the Adirondack region of New York State. The rock ores they used cropped out at the surface and could be dug in open pits by persons with little special knowledge of mining. William Keating, in a pamphlet written in 1821, complained that Americans were slow to adopt the more advanced mining techniques then common in Europe.[22] Actually, they probably had little need for these methods and found it easier and more economical to move on to a new mine than to improve an old one. The remains of small mines and test pits are common in the woods and fields of eastern North America, but investigation of early mining methods has not yet attracted much attention from archaeologists or historians.

Earliest Industries

Many English immigrants to North America in the seventeenth century were sponsored by proprietors who expected the colonists to produce goods for the home market from American natural resources. The industrial products they favored included timber, metals, glass, and chemicals.

Less than two years after the initial settlement at Jamestown, members of the Virginia Colony began small-scale industrial enterprises that were to produce glass, pitch, tar, soap ashes, and lumber products for export. Records mention the arrival in 1608 of a group of skilled men: "Eight Dutchmen [probably Germans] and Poles." Some of these non-English artisans erected a glasshouse and, using local sand (with lime and potash), quickly produced trial samples of glass that the colony shipped back to England. That first glasshouse was abandoned after only a few months, but a second one was in sporadic operation from 1621 to 1624. Archaeologists discovered four wood-fired glassmaking furnaces used in 1608 and 1609 and glass fragments that reveal, for the first time, the nature of the original glass exports. Based on the 1948 excavations by J. C. Harrington and on artifactual analysis, the National Park Service reconstructed the main working furnace, as well as the annealing and fritting furnaces and a furnace or kiln for firing pots. Demonstrators use these working furnaces of stone cobbles and clay to show glassmaking to the public. The preserved and interpreted ruins of the first furnaces are nearby, allowing easy comparison.[23]

Sawmills

The forest was one of the easiest natural resources to use in North America. Colonists could cut timber in nearby woods for themselves and to make products for export. They felled trees, hauled them out of the forest with draft animals, and exported them as baulks or sawn timber. Felling was done with axes, and the needs of woodsmen stimulated the domestic manufacture of edge tools, at first by individual smiths and, in the early nineteenth century, in factories that became major American industries. Because hauling logs and sawing them into planks by hand with pit saws was heavy physical labor that also required considerable skill,[24] colonists quickly adopted water flow in rivers for sawing and transporting timber. As settlers advanced into forested lands, they usually built a sawmill first and then put up houses and barns. Water-powered, up-and-down sawmills were in use by at least 1634 and soon became common throughout the forested parts of eastern North America; by 1830, the people of Sturbridge, Massachusetts, had sixteen.[25]

FIGURE 3.3. This sawmill built by staff members at Old Sturbridge Village stands just below the millpond dam. When constructing this substantial wooden building, they left siding off part of it so they could move large logs onto the saw table. They placed the waterwheel under the sawing floor. (Photographed at Old Sturbridge Village, 1990)

The archaeological remains of sawmill operations are modest and not easy to find in the woods. Even some of the large mills were washed away by floods and their remains scattered far downstream. The earliest sawmills recorded by industrial archaeologists date from the early nineteenth century, but the basic sawmill mechanism and the context in which it was used had not changed much from the seventeenth century.

Ten years ago, the staff at Old Sturbridge Village reconstructed their sawmill from the plans of the Nichols-Colby Mill in Bow, New Hampshire, made just before its destruction in a 1938 hurricane.[26] Local farmers had built a sawmill at the Sturbridge site sometime before 1795; it was rebuilt after a fire in 1802 and continued to operate for many decades. Sawmills could be housed in rudely made, temporary buildings, but Sturbridge researchers designed a substantial building because sawing had become a year-round enterprise by the early nineteenth century (Fig. 3.3). The mill mechanism consists of a pair of waterwheels on a horizontal shaft fitted with cranks at each end to drive the saw frame up and down through connecting rods called "pitmans," after the sawyers they replaced. (Before 1800, a flutter wheel, which had a lower efficiency than the Wing reaction wheels in the Sturbridge mill, would have been used.[27]) The saw blade is stretched within a wooden saw frame whose up-and-down motion is guided by wooden "fender posts" fitted with iron bearing plates. A horizontal carriage holds the log and feeds it into the saw. An up-and-down sawmill in its simplest form is an example of mechanization that imitates the method of working with hand tools.

One way to appreciate how much physical labor was avoided by using a sawmill is to compare the power developed by a pair of pit sawyers with the power available at the Sturbridge mill. Working a pit saw is similar to operating a pump, a task at which a man can work at the rate of about 0.060

FIGURE 3.4. This section of the U.S. Geological Survey topographic map for Sturbridge shows how the sawmill (S) and gristmill (G) at Old Sturbridge Village draw power from the Quinebaug River. In the early nineteenth century, David Wright, Jr., built the power system by making a cut through the hill at C, building a dam between G and S, and digging the tailraces from G and S back to the Quinebaug. In creating this small industrial complex, he substantially altered the landscape.

horsepower for a ten-hour day.[28] The joint effort of the two men operating a pit saw would be about 0.12 horsepower. The power available at the Sturbridge sawmill, calculated from the flow and fall of water, is some 12 horsepower, 100 times greater than that of the sawyers.[29] But to use this power, the mill proprietor had to make a substantial investment in preparing the site. David Wright, Jr., obtained water power for the sawmill at Sturbridge by cutting an opening between a swamp and an adjoining pond, building a dam across the outlet to the swamp, and digging a tailrace to return the water to the Quinebaug River (Fig. 3.4).[30] The dam provided the fall needed to turn the mill wheel, and the water stored in the pond allowed Wright to operate the mill during periods of low river flow. The hills and swamps at this mill site were used by Wright to develop a water-power system that was capable of operating several mills. He made a substantial change in the landscape to realize the potential power of the stream. A site such as this could easily become the nucleus of a community.

The economic context in which a sawmill operated could be quite small. A sawyer and a helper ran the mill (one person could do it if necessary); it could be used when needed and then left unattended with only occasional maintenance and repair. The sawyer did not have to collect a large stock of logs before starting work or to organize a work force to provide a continual supply of logs. Planks, timbers, or boards could be cut as needed or accumulated against future demand. The operation of the mill could fit easily into the scope of a family enterprise, but it was not independent of the outside commercial and industrial communities. Although the sawmill was built mainly of wood,[31] iron parts such as the crank pins and saw frame guides were essential components. These could be made by a skilled smith. However, the large, steel saw blade was not an item that a blacksmith could make. Even when a domestic saw industry was started in the United States, sawmakers continued to depend on steel plates made in Sheffield, England.[32] A basic commercial and trade network had to be in place before sawmills could be used extensively in America.

Ironworks

In the seventeenth century, Americans used cast and wrought iron freely. Cast iron, an alloy of iron, carbon, and silicon, has a melting temperature low enough that it can be melted in a simple furnace and poured into molds to make articles such as pots and fire backs. It is a brittle material that breaks in a rough, finely faceted fracture (Fig. 3.5). Wrought iron (also called "bar iron" or "malleable iron") is a mechanical mixture of nearly pure iron and particles of slag. Depending on its purity and the distribution of slag particles, wrought iron is a more or less ductile material that can be bent when cold and forged when hot. When broken, it has a characteristic fibrous texture (Fig. 3.6). Steel has a carbon content intermediate between cast iron and wrought iron, and can be hardened by heat treatment. Cast iron is made in a blast furnace from ore, flux (a mineral such as limestone containing calcium that aids formation of a liquid slag), and fuel that in America before about 1840 was always charcoal. Ironmasters had two alternative ways of making wrought iron with charcoal fuel. They could reduce iron ore directly to metal in a small hearth called a bloomery or convert cast iron (usually in the form of pigs cast at a blast furnace) to wrought iron by removing the carbon and silicon in it with a charcoal-fired finery hearth. (After 1800, they might substitute a puddling furnace that used either wood or mineral coal for the finery.) The product of either a bloomery or a finery was solid rather than liquid iron that had to be hammered while hot to expel excess slag. The term *forge* could signify a place where artisans carried out bloom smelting, fining, or shaping of previously made iron.

Making iron for sale in England was one of the enterprises favored by the financial backers of English colonies in America. The first attempt, made in 1621 at Falling Creek, Virginia, ended in the Indian uprising of March 1622. Archaeological evidence suggests that Falling Creek was intended to be an integrated ironworks with a blast furnace to make pig iron and castings and a finery to convert pig into bar iron.[33]

The next attempt at iron production for the export market was made in Massachusetts. Economic difficulties in 1640 led the General Court of that colony to promote domestic industries.[34] John Winthrop, Jr., went to England in 1641 to raise capital and recruit experienced workers for an ironworks. Winthrop and his associates abandoned their first blast furnace, at Braintree, after a few years, when they found it too costly to bring ore to it. They made a second attempt at Saugus and in about 1647 completed works capable of making pig, bar, plate, and nail rods. While they succeeded in making iron, they did not make profits, and after 1652 the works were operated only occasionally. In 1676, the plant was abandoned. Nearly a hundred years elapsed before anyone attempted an industrial enterprise of comparable technical complexity in America. Archaeologists uncovered remains of the Saugus works in the 1950s, and a reconstruction was undertaken that has since become the Saugus Ironworks National Historic Site.[35] The excavations provided only part of the information needed for the reconstruction (no traces of the slitting mill building were found, for example), and, where archaeological information was lacking, the builders followed plans of comparable European works.[36]

The natural resources needed by the Saugus entrepreneurs were fuel, ore, flux, and water. The only economical way of transporting bulk commodities in seventeenth-century America was by water, so they needed access to

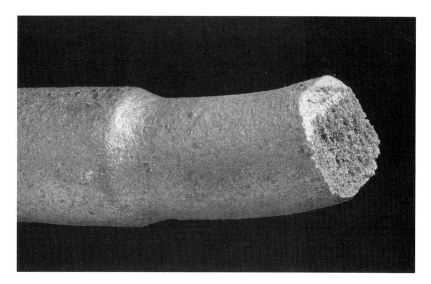

FIGURE 3.5. Cast iron, an alloy of carbon and silicon with iron, is easy to cast into complex shapes, but it is a brittle material. To demonstrate this, we clamped one end of this bar of cast iron in a vise and struck the other end with a heavy hammer. The bar bent slightly and then fractured. The fracture has the characteristic rough texture of a break in a brittle material; the dark color is due to the graphite flakes that are a component of the structure of this cast iron. (Photograph by William Sacco)

FIGURE 3.6. Wrought iron is nearly pure iron containing fibers of slag. When free of phosphorus and well hammered to disperse the slag into fine fibers, it can be a very ductile material. When we bent this bar of wrought iron back on itself, the iron ruptured but did not break apart. The fibrous fracture is due to the elongated bands of slag in the iron. (Photograph by William Sacco)

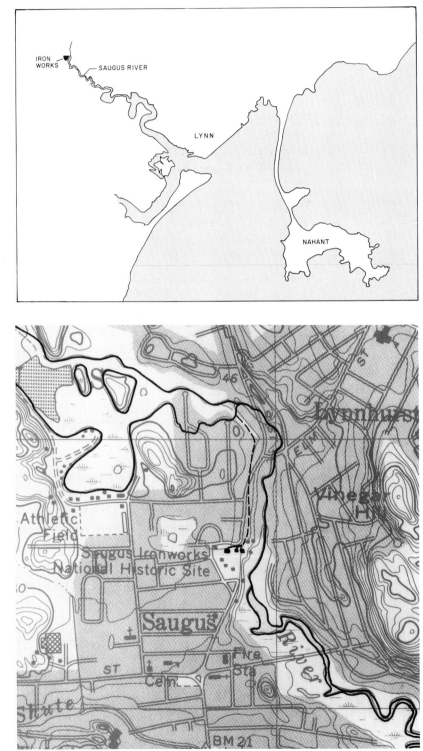

a

b

a navigable waterway. Their siting of the Saugus works, in a well-wooded area on a navigable river with many wetlands, served these needs well (Fig. 3.7). They mined bog ore from the wetlands, made charcoal in the neighboring woods, and got water power by damming the Saugus River and constructing a race to bring the water to the works.

Today it seems surprising that the Saugus proprietors chose a site with no convenient source of lime for flux, but in the seventeenth century there was no generally accepted practice in fluxing a blast furnace. The Nahant gabbro, a rock containing about 10 percent calcium, could be reached from the mouth of the Saugus River by crossing the outer reaches of Lynn Harbor. With this as flux, the ironmaster at Saugus succeeded in making a blast-furnace slag containing about 12 percent lime, lower than desirable but adequate for successful smelting.[37]

The works at Saugus included the blast furnace (Fig. 3.8), which was placed against the hillside so that its top could be reached by a level charging bridge; the forge (Fig. 3.9), which housed two finery hearths (for converting pigs to wrought iron), a chaffery hearth (for reheating the iron), and the forge hammer; and the slitting mill. Water power was essential to the operation of the entire plant. The blast-furnace bellows had to be pumped continuously (except when the blast was shut off for charging and tapping the iron) and would have required about 1 horsepower. Smaller bellows were used for the finery and chaffery hearths, but the forge hammer would have used about 5 horsepower.[38] Winthrop took advantage of the topography of the site by placing the buildings on the scarp of the glacial outwash plane that stands 20 feet above the level of the Saugus River (Fig. 3.7b). A race dug across the plane delivered water to all the wheels through a system of flumes. Overshot, undershot, and pitchback wheels were used in the reconstruction for purposes of illustration; there is no way of knowing from the archaeological evidence what types of wheels were used originally (except for the overshot wheel at the blast furnace).

Unlike sawmill operators, the Saugus proprietors worked in large economic and social contexts. Workers had to burn charcoal, mine ore and flux, haul these supplies to the site, and keep a sufficient stock on hand to ensure

FIGURE 3.7. (a) The Saugus proprietors took advantage of the site of the ironworks on the Saugus River to produce water power and to transport their raw materials and finished products. They brought flux for the blast furnace by boat from a quarry in Nahant across Lynn Harbor. (b) Part of the U.S. Geological Survey topographic map for Saugus showing the location of the Saugus Ironworks National Historic Site and the course of the Saugus River. Artisans at Saugus got water to power the machinery from the wetlands and ponds above the ironworks by cutting a raceway, the probable location of which is shown by the dashed line. (Today, water is pumped up from the river to demonstrate the operation of the waterwheels.)

FIGURE 3.8. The blast furnace at the Saugus Ironworks National Historic Site. The filling crew brought ore, fuel, and flux to the top of the furnace over the charging bridge. The founder and molders worked in the casting house in front of the furnace; the bellows and waterwheel are out of sight to the right. This furnace is a reconstruction that shows what the original furnace may have looked like.

FIGURE 3.9. Reconstruction of the finery forge and, behind, the rolling and slitting mill at the Saugus Ironworks National Historic Site. The undershot wheel at the forge drives one set of bellows, while the pitchback wheel behind it drives the hammer; both wheels discharge into the tailrace that can be seen in the foreground. The placement of the works well above river level shows that the full power potential of the site was not needed. The locations of the hearths within the finery forge are shown by the stacks.

continuous operation of the blast furnace in the event of an interruption of supply. During a smelting campaign, the crew tapped the furnace every twelve hours or so and poured the iron into castings (such as pots or fire dogs) or into pigs that would subsequently be taken to the finery forge for conversion to wrought iron. This wrought iron could be either sold as hammered bar or taken to the mill to be rolled into plate or slit into nail rods. The managers of the works thus had to assemble three kinds of raw materials, provide workers skilled in five or more specialties, and distribute their output among at least five classes of products that were to be sold on both domestic and foreign markets. They had to judge the product mix for the foreign market to be sold six months in the future on the basis of price information that was already six months old. Quite apart from difficulties with the quality of their products (Chapter 6), it is easy to see why the complexities of management overwhelmed the entrepreneurs at Saugus.

An idea of the technological difficulties of the production process, but not the context, can be gotten by visiting the site. Since the neighborhood has

FIGURE 3.10. The waterfront at the Saugus Ironworks National Historic Site. The ridge in the foreground is a pile of slag from the blast furnace. The rise of sea level since 1660 has caused so much silt to accumulate that much of the former river channel has become wetlands. This has left the site of the ironworks pier well back from the present channel.

been suburban for many years, one can sense neither the character of the surrounding seventeenth-century landscape nor the community in which the ironworkers lived.

The Saugus works was not large enough and did not operate long enough to cause permanent alteration to its site other than the accumulation of the slag pile that extended as a ridge toward the river (Fig. 3.10). By 1945, this was the only visible feature left. However, significant changes have taken place in the Saugus River, which had been a navigable waterway. The works are located just at the upland end of the Saugus estuary. Accompanying the rise in sea level at the rate of about 3 millimeters a year that has been going on along the Atlantic coast for the past several thousand years is an upward growth of estuarine marshes; marsh now extends well beyond what used to be the wharf serving the Saugus works (Fig. 3.10).[39]

The greatest significance of the Saugus ironmaking venture was that its decline released artisans and managers who had acquired industrial skills for employment elsewhere in the colonies. They established modest industrial enterprises that were better matched to the colonial economy.

Second Generation of Industries

As the demand for raw materials and manufactures grew in the colonies, Americans produced more products for the home market. Their managerial tasks were simplified, but the demands on artisans' skills remained high. A sawmill or gristmill could serve either the local or the export market. An integrated ironworks, such as Saugus, was too complex an organization to function successfully within the limits of seventeenth-century communication and transportation systems, but its component units—blast furnace, finery, and slitting mill—could be operated as independent producers of iron products for local needs.

Gristmills

Americans built both gristmills and sawmills (sometimes combined in one building) as they settled along the frontier. A gristmiller had backward linkages to the farm community and to the suppliers of millstones, the wood and iron components of the mill mechanism, and millwrighting services; he might have forward linkages to grain markets and international trade. The miller needed technical and commercial skills to make and market products of good quality. Grain was a high-value product that could be transported more easily than timber. Since the value of grain was enhanced by high-quality milling, farmers would prefer to take grain to a well-equipped mill run by a competent miller.

Except for a few wind- and animal-powered mills, Americans built water-powered gristmills with a dam and millpond. The simplest way to build a mill was to attach the stone directly to the top of a vertical shaft rising from a horizontal waterwheel, but the quality and quantity of the flour that could be made with this equipment were limited. Millers preferred to drive the millstones with a gear train from the horizontal axle of a vertical waterwheel.

Any gristmill was a potential nucleus for a community. The mill at Philipsburg Manor, now a museum in North Tarrytown, New York, is within 100 yards of the manor house and was the commercial center of this eighteenth-century estate that exported flour to overseas markets. Since milling involved either waiting while one's grain was ground or returning to the mill, farmers found it convenient to visit and transact other business while attending to their milling. The nature of the miller's work could also contribute to the nucleation and growth of a town. The miller was a technical specialist who handled many people's grain, exacting payment from each. Millers with business talent could accumulate capital and acquire information about the financial affairs of their customers that might be turned to commercial advantage.

There were many opportunities in a gristmill for the miller to refine and improve the equipment. With better-dressed stones and better machinery, he could compete with other millers on quality and cost. A miller could further mechanize his operations by installing the power-driven bolters and hoists designed by Oliver Evans in 1786.[40] A miller could enhance his prestige by putting up a well-made and sturdy building; this would also make it easier to keep the stones and machinery in proper alignment. The miller's activities could assume commercial and social functions extending beyond the preparation of grain. Because of their substantial construction, a relatively large number of gristmills from the wood-and-water era have survived; many have been restored to operating condition or adaptively reused.[41]

To achieve economic growth, the miller had to deal with a difficult problem in natural-resource management. A small water privilege could be developed with little capital but would offer no scope for growth other than what could be achieved with more efficient water motors. A large water privilege could be used only with a large initial investment that might be difficult to find or expensive to service. A shrewd choice of water privilege gave a miller a better chance of prospering. Since people often built communities around gristmills, the distribution of sizes of water-power privileges was one geographical factor influencing the pattern of community development in agricultural regions. Although the machinery was different, some of the characteristics of gristmills were found in mills that provided other services to agricultural communities, such as fulling cloth and processing oilseed, snuff, and tanbark.[42]

Ironworks

After the failures of the integrated ironworks at Falling Creek and Saugus (along with a similar Winthrop works in East Haven, Connecticut), which produced primarily for export, American colonists reverted to small-scale iron production for local markets. The Massachusetts General Court canceled the monopoly held by the Company of Undertakers of Ironworks in 1657, thereby allowing individuals to erect bloomery forges. One was operating in Concord by 1660. It was only one of many small successors of the Saugus venture that were better suited to the needs of communities and to the limitations on management that existed in the colonies.[43] Settlers on the frontier often built a bloomery along with their first sawmill and gristmill, as at Rocky Mount, Virginia.[44] Traces of seventeenth-century bloom smelting are being uncovered in tidewater Virginia,[45] but the existing archaeological evidence of this stage of American metallurgy is sparse. The proprietors of bloomery forges made wrought iron but could not supply cast-iron products, such as pots. Only a few colonists were operating blast furnaces in the late seventeenth century, and cast goods, mostly obtained from England, were dear.[46]

Americans began to expand their ironmaking in the 1720s, in part because political differences with iron suppliers such as Sweden made American ironworks a more attractive investment for British capitalists. Population growth was enlarging the American market.[47] Some proprietors reestablished ironworks that produced for the English market, such as the Principio works (situated at the head of Chesapeake Bay), the Baltimore Company (which produced pig iron with furnaces built in Maryland after 1731), and Governor Spotswood's works in Virginia (staffed with German immigrants in 1719).[48] We have no archaeological studies of these enterprises as yet. Production for the local market began in Pennsylvania with the erection of a bloomery forge near what is now Pottstown and a blast furnace at Colebrookdale, Berks County, in 1720.[49] Additional bloomeries, fineries, and furnaces were soon built in the area west and north of Philadelphia. These works were often undertaken by recent British immigrants, who brought with them the necessary skills, and staffed by a combination of local artisans and workers recruited in Britain, but were financed with local capital derived from trade. They owed little to the heritage of the Saugus enterprise and were organized differently. Many of the blast furnaces were on plantations—partially self-sufficient communities with large landholdings that supplied fuel, ore, and flux for the furnace and agricultural products for its crew.[50] The proprietors of bloomery and finery forges often preferred to locate their works at a water privilege of convenient size rather than on a plantation, but there was no fixed pattern.

Since woodland and water-power sites were abundant along the eastern seaboard, the principal geographical factors that proprietors considered in selecting locations for their ironworks were the proximity of markets, the availability of ore, and the existence of transportation routes. Some Philadelphia capitalists invested in iron plantations along the coast that used bog ore. The new ironworks in Maryland, Virginia, and northern New Jersey were in the piedmont, or eastern margin, of the mountains and used rock ores.[51] New Englanders sometimes located blast furnaces in established towns. The Livingstons, an eastern New York landed family, incorporated ironworks into the economic system of their manor by hiring their tenants to supply fuel and by marketing the iron through the manor's existing commercial network.[52]

Abandoned blast-furnace stacks dominate the publically displayed remains of ironmaking in the colonies and the early republic because they survive much better than most industrial artifacts; many have been studied under the sponsorship of local authorities or interest groups, and some have become the foci of parks and historical sites. The bloomeries and fineries were an equally large component of the industry, but are poorly represented in the historical literature and are almost absent from the archaeological record because so few sites have been excavated.

BLOOMERY FORGES

At a bloomery, one person, the bloomer, converted ore directly to wrought iron with charcoal fuel in a small hearth. In addition to one or more hearths, a bloomery forge had an air pump, a helve hammer, and, sometimes, ore-crushing machinery, all driven by waterwheels. A person with the necessary skills could set up a bloomery forge almost anywhere in eastern North America, but in northern New Jersey and the eastern Adirondack region of New York—where high-grade ore, water power, and abundant charcoal were available—forge proprietors pushed bloomery technology to its highest level of sophistication. The sites of some New Jersey bloomeries have been located by archaeologists; many more have been found in New York, where there has been less disturbance of the sites.[53]

In 1828, Allen Penfield and Timothy Taft started to make wrought iron near Crown Point, New York, with a forge having two hearths located on a water privilege on Putnam Creek. They used ore brought by wagon or sled from mines a few miles away and charcoal made in the adjacent woods. Their iron was hauled to Lake Champlain to be shipped to local users or to distant markets by way of the Champlain Canal. Successive owners enlarged the forge to four hearths and, in the 1840s, added the new technology of preheating the air blast. They rebuilt the forge again in 1879 but, as the demand for bloomery iron diminished, finally closed it in 1883. The village of Ironville was home to the sixty persons who worked at the forge and ore separator, and at the local sawmill and gristmill (Fig. 3.11). After the forge was closed, many residents left Ironville, while those who stayed turned primarily to agriculture; today, Ironville survives because of the amenities available in its setting. The site, now in the care of the Penfield Foundation, still gives a visitor a sense of the isolation and self-sufficiency of an industrial community that, while producing for a national market, depended entirely on the wood–water–iron natural-resource base. Up to 1,000 persons worked at some Adirondack bloomery forges, such as the one at Clintonville, but the associated communities were similar to Ironville.

Bloomery forges have often been described as technologically primitive, backwoods enterprises.[54] Some were, but despite the geographical isolation of Ironville, the proprietors of the forge had close connections with the national scientific and business communities. The original entrepreneurs, Penfield and Taft, made iron for Joseph Henry to use in his experiments on

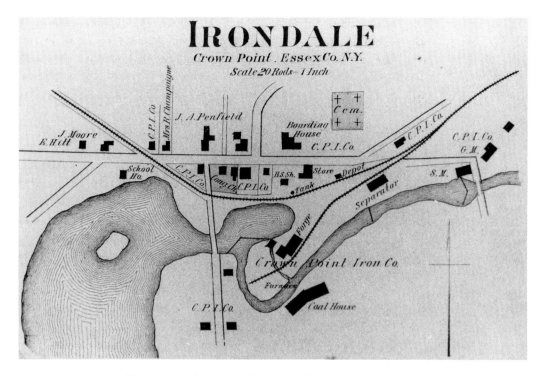

FIGURE 3.11. Artisans made iron at a bloomery forge in Ironville (also known as Irondale), New York, from 1828 to 1883. They obtained water power for the blowing engines and helve hammers from Putnam's Creek, and charcoal from pits and kilns in the surrounding woods. They hauled ore by wagon or sled and, later, by narrow-gauge railway from mines a few miles to the west. This industrial community also had an ore separator, a sawmill (S.M.), and a gristmill (G.M.), all powered by water. Some sixty artisans dressed ore and smelted iron with charcoal. The town had a school, church, store, and boardinghouse. Many workers lived nearby in their own houses; the manager lived in the center of town, and today his house is the Penfield Museum. A visit to the site makes it easy to see how industrial life in Ironville remained closely tied to the surrounding landscape and the rhythm of the seasons. (From *New Topographical Atlas of Essex County, New York* [Philadelphia: Grey, 1876])

electromagnetism, and, with Henry's aid, they developed a magnetic separator in 1831 for the beneficiation of their ore. Subsequent rebuilding of the forge carried the bloomery process to its highest technical development. The Penfield forge was a skillful adaptation of metallurgical technology to the characteristics of the wood–water–iron resource base and existing markets. It remained economically viable for seventy-five years.[55]

FINERY FORGES

A blast furnace might make 400 to 900 tons of pig iron a year and could supply several finery forges, which converted only 100 to 200 tons of pig to bar iron annually.[56] A finery forge usually had two to four fining hearths, each small enough to be worked by one person, and a helve hammer driven by a substantial waterwheel. Proprietors of finery forges selected water privileges capable of supplying the relatively large amount of power needed for the hammer, and, since these facilities were usually well removed from the blast-furnace sites, they depended on a network of wagon roads to bring in their raw materials and get their products to customers.

After the initial failure at Saugus, American ironmasters did not make much use of the finery process again until the early eighteenth century. Valley Forge, the finery that gave its name to the Continental Army's campground, was built on Valley Creek in 1742. John Potts, owner of a blast furnace and two other forges farther up the Schuylkill River, acquired it in 1757. Surviving ledgers show that Potts made about 2 tons of bar iron a week from pig received from Warwick furnace (18 miles distant). He shipped the bar iron to Philadelphia for sale. In 1773, David Potts (John's son) and William Dewees bought the forge, expanded the landholdings to more than

FIGURE 3.12. The builders of the forge at Valley Forge, Pennsylvania, drew water from Valley Creek, which descended between Mount Joy and Mount Sorrow to the Schuylkill River, to power their works. The creek was a convenient size for this ironworks; the Schuylkill was too expensive to use for power, but it served as a transportation link to Philadelphia. (From Henry D. Rogers, *The Geology of Pennsylvania* [Philadelphia: Lippincott, 1858], vol. 2, map follows p. 674)

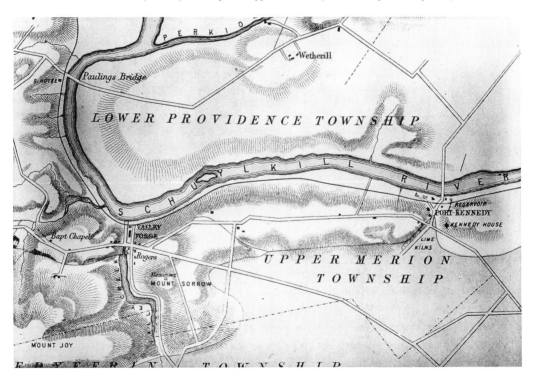

1,000 acres, and, apparently, built a second forge just upstream of the first. Both forges were damaged during the Revolution. After the war, the owners raised the dam at the lower forge as part of a rebuilding scheme, thereby flooding the upper forge. All metallurgical activity at the site ended before 1824.[57] The site of the upper forge was gradually covered by silt from the millpond and so was preserved. It was excavated by the Valley Forge Park Commission in 1929, but subsequently re-covered with soil so that the remains cannot be viewed today.[58]

The finers at Valley Forge worked in a stone building about 35 feet square with hearths in the northeast and southeast corners, one probably the finery and the other, the chafery. Races along the east and south sides brought water to undershot wheels that drove the forge hammer and the bellows for the hearths. The excavators located part of the wheel for the forge hammer and the anvil base. The size and general plan of the forge were similar to the plan of Chingley Forge on the boundary between Kent and Sussex near Lamberthurst, England, as it existed in the late seventeenth century,[59] suggesting that finery technology transferred to America needed little alteration for local conditions. The upper Valley Forge was smaller than most of those operating in Pennsylvania in 1783 (most had two hammers),[60] but the technology used there is probably representative.

The original builders of Valley Forge chose a site on Valley Creek that was small enough to dam easily but large enough to provide the power needed for the forge hammer (the largest consumer of power at an ironworks) (Fig. 3.12). Developing the Schuylkill for water power would have been too costly, but the river did provide a useful transportation route. The archaeologists found a partially fined pig marked "Andover" within the forge building. Thus some time after 1770 (when Andover furnace went into blast), pig was brought from Andover, New Jersey, a trip of 20 miles down the Musconetcong Valley, 65 miles down the Delaware River, and 23 miles up the Schuylkill River to Valley Forge. Road and river transportation were important parts of the context of these dispersed units of production.

BLAST FURNACES

Pennsylvanians built more blast furnaces than any other colonists in the eighteenth century, and many of their furnace stacks survive, several in parks.[61] At the Hopewell Village National Historic Site, the National Park Service has preserved an iron plantation at which pig iron and castings were made from 1771 to 1883 (Fig. 3.13).[62] Mark Bird, son of a Pennsylvania ironmaster, assembled the estate, but it passed through several changes of ownership before new proprietors were able to establish a profitable operation in the early nineteenth century. The Hopewell entrepreneurs made domestic ware and castings for agricultural equipment, but they were best

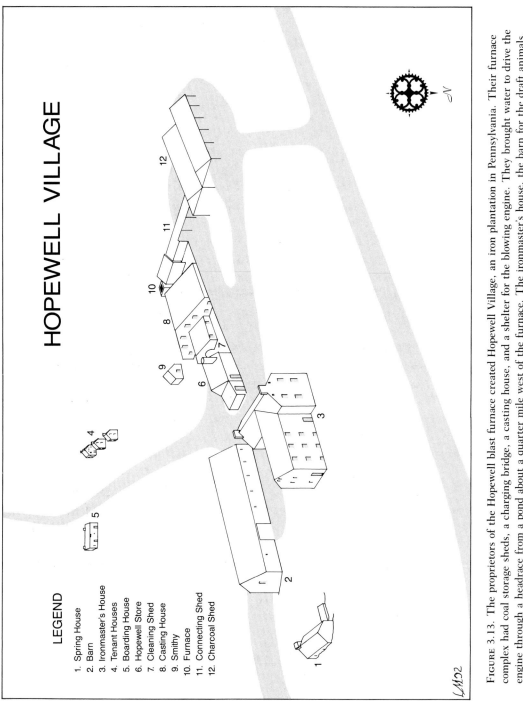

HOPEWELL VILLAGE

LEGEND

1. Spring House
2. Barn
3. Ironmaster's House
4. Tenant Houses
5. Boarding House
6. Hopewell Store
7. Cleaning Shed
8. Casting House
9. Smithy
10. Furnace
11. Connecting Shed
12. Charcoal Shed

FIGURE 3.13. The proprietors of the Hopewell blast furnace created Hopewell Village, an iron plantation in Pennsylvania. Their furnace complex had coal storage sheds, a charging bridge, a casting house, and a shelter for the blowing engine. They brought water to drive the engine through a headrace from a pond about a quarter mile west of the furnace. The ironmaster's house, the barn for the draft animals, and the combined office and store were also near the furnace. Dwellings for workers and a boardinghouse were located farther away and were surrounded by fields. Hopewell was a largely self-sufficient agricultural and industrial complex. (Drawing by Lyn Malone, based on a drawing by L. Kenneth Townsend for the National Park Service)

known for their stoves, which usually had the Hopewell name cast in, making them easy to identify. In 1830, near the peak of Hopewell's prosperity, about 170 persons were making more than 1,000 tons of iron a year, 700 tons of which were used for cast products. The proprietors attempted to avoid the high cost of charcoal by experimenting with anthracite fuel. They were unsuccessful and, after the market for stoves declined, continued to produce cold-blast, charcoal pig iron for those customers who still valued this product enough to pay a premium price for it. By 1848, other ironmasters were making equally good pig iron with anthracite fuel at a labor cost of $2.50 a ton; the Hopewell product, which then had a labor cost of $15.44 a ton, could not compete for long.[63] The furnace was blown out for the last time in 1883, and, after a long period of disuse, the federal government acquired the site in 1935.

Hopewell is located on the upper reaches of French Creek and has only a small water-power potential (as can be seen easily on a visit to the site), insufficient to operate a forge of any size. (The nearby ponds have been constructed recently.) The Park Service has been able to preserve the rural setting of Hopewell but is allowing the surrounding woods, which would have been cut every twenty years for charcoal, to grow. Aside from this and the absence of smoke from charcoaling, the landscape is probably much as it was when the furnace was operating.[64] Unlike ironworks in mountainous regions, Hopewell had land suitable for farming. Agriculture was practiced both on the plantation and nearby. Local farmers could sell produce and animals to the plantation and could work at woodcutting and other chores during the off-season. Consequently, life at Hopewell was closely linked to the local economy.

Teamsters hauled ore to Hopewell from mines 3 to 5 miles away and carried iron about 5 miles to the Schuylkill River for transport to Philadelphia. To gain the advantages of nearby ore and a large acreage of woodland, the Hopewell proprietors had to accept the disadvantages of limited power potential and dependence on overland transportation. Some of the numerous draft animals they kept to haul raw materials and products were quartered and fed in the barn that is adjacent to the casting shed. Many workers lived in company-owned houses on the plantation, but no uniform housing style or ordered layout developed at Hopewell.

Another iron plantation that survived to become a museum is at Batsto, New Jersey, where a blast furnace was erected between 1765 and 1768 by investors from Philadelphia. Their large landholdings included inland wetlands that provided water power, bog ore, and a convenient means of transporting the ore to the furnace. (A reconstructed ore boat is on display.) The Batsto proprietors cast kitchen ware; forge hammers; parts for sawmills, gristmills, and sugar mills; and stoves. They rebuilt the furnace in 1829 and blew it out for the last time in 1848. It failed, not from exhaustion of resources, but because the cast-iron products they made could be manufactured more cheaply at furnaces in Pennsylvania that used mineral coal for fuel.[65]

Batsto was a more nearly self-sufficient and somewhat more diversified community than Hopewell in that it contained a gristmill, sawmill, and glassworks as well as the blast furnace. The proprietors built standardized worker houses arranged in two uniform rows on one side of town. The ironmaster's house was located on the other side of town and closer to the furnace.

Iron-industry investors in western New England and, later, in southern Ohio set up works on a pattern different from that in the Middle Atlantic states. They did not build iron plantations, and they sometimes placed their furnaces within existing communities. Sharon, Connecticut, was already a center for agricultural trade and manufacturing when local entrepreneurs built three blast furnaces within the town (Fig. 3.14). After ironmaking was no longer profitable, workers were able to turn easily to other industrial and agricultural pursuits in these diversified communities.[66] Sharon was in the Salisbury district. Although ironmasters in that area specialized in making cast-iron lye pots, they sent most of the output of their furnaces to finery forges for conversion to bar iron until about 1850. Some of the forge proprietors had rolling and slitting mills by 1780. They produced rolled iron for gun barrels, standardized parts for machinery, and heavy forgings for mills and factories, including Eli Whitney's armory. The district forgemasters acquired a reputation for the superior quality of their bar iron and were able to sell to distant customers that demanded iron of the highest quality, such as the Harpers Ferry Armory in Virginia. After about 1840, most blast-furnace proprietors converted to hot blast. They also shifted production to specialized castings, particularly chilled-iron railroad wheels. They continued to trade on their ancient reputation for high-quality iron until the last furnace was blown out in 1923. The Salisbury ironmasters were important in the industrial development of the United States because they supplied iron for machinery as well as the metal stock used by Eli Whitney, Simeon North, and other manufacturers in the Connecticut Valley who were developing the manufacture of metal goods with interchangeable parts in the early decades of the American republic. Probably the only site of a New England ironworks built after Saugus to remain largely intact is in Roxbury, Connecticut, where the roasting ovens and a furnace stack survive as standing structures on grounds that include mines, railway routes, ore storage, and slag dumps.[67]

Ironmasters built charcoal-fired blast furnaces along the industrial frontier that moved westward across Pennsylvania, Ohio, Kentucky, Tennessee,

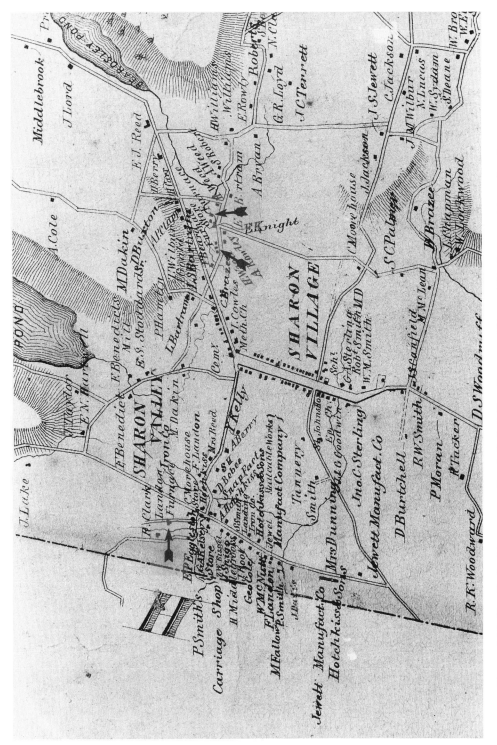

FIGURE 3.14. New England ironmasters often built their blast furnaces within established communities rather than on iron plantations, as in Pennsylvania, or on proprietary estates, as in eastern New York. There were three furnaces (arrows) within the village of Sharon, Connecticut. (From Clark's *Map of Litchfield County* [Philadelphia, 1859]. Courtesy of Sterling Memorial Library, Yale University. Photograph by William Sacco)

and Missouri to Michigan. Fayette Historic Townsite and State Park preserves the community that housed workers at two blast furnaces built in
1867 at the edge of the forest on the shore of Lake Michigan. These furnaces
smelted ore from the Marquette range. As colliers cut the surrounding
forest to make charcoal, the proprietors sold the newly cleared land to
farmers rather than reforesting it. Over twenty-four years, the cost of hauling wood from the ever more distant forest increased to the point at which it
was no longer profitable to operate the furnaces. The smelting plant at
Fayette was more sophisticated than that at Hopewell, but the community
was similar to the iron plantations that had been established in the East a
hundred years earlier.

ENVIRONMENTAL EFFECTS

Writers of ironmaking history have said much about the exhaustion of forest
resources, asserting that some ironworks closed because they had exhausted
their wood supplies. What "exhausted" actually meant was that the proprietors did not have enough woodland, had failed to provide for a sustained
yield from their woodland, or were unwilling to pay to bring wood from a
greater distance. In their reminiscences, some ironworkers inflated the
acreages they cut to sustain iron production, and others further inflated
these figures in successive retellings.[68] An acre of woodland in sustained
production on a twenty-year rotation in the Middle Atlantic region yielded
between 500 and 1,200 bushels of charcoal. The largest annual consumption of charcoal among the New Jersey ironworks listed in the census of
1850 was 200,000 bushels a year; so between 167 and 385 acres would have
been cut each year, and between 3,300 and 7,700 acres would have sufficed
for sustained operation.[69] To give an example, a square of woodland between
2.3 and 3.5 miles on a side would have been divided into twenty squares in
successive stages of regrowth. Of course, not all proprietors operated their
ironworks on a sustained-yield basis (most of those in Michigan did not), and
there were many other sources of demand for wood, but charcoal was always
available when customers were willing to pay a sufficiently high price for
iron made with it.[70] Small logs made the best charcoal, so woodland was cut
before the trees got very big. It never returned to mature forest as long as
charcoaling continued.

Air pollution from coaling was a nuisance, but it is easy to see that the
long-term environmental effects of charcoal ironmaking are minimal. Where
blast furnaces, forges, and foundries have been abandoned, the land returns
to forest, and all that remains is evidence of a furnace stack, some stone
foundations, and overgrown slag piles. At some sites, even these features are
difficult to find.

Mechanization with Water Power

Until the last decade of the eighteenth century, Americans spun and wove fibers into cloth in their homes or in shops, while individual craftsmen—such as carpenters, turners, cabinetmakers, and blacksmiths—working with their own tools, turned the timber and iron made by the primary-materials industries into finished goods. Tools and products rather than work sites are the primary artifacts that survive from this activity.[71] In 1793, Samuel Slater and his business partners began to manufacture textiles in the first American factory. Early accounts of American industry often focus on textile mills because of the novelty of the factory system and because the mills were the largest and most visible of the new industrial establishments. The more numerous, smaller industries where most people worked were often overlooked.[72]

The first managers of the Springfield Armory attempted large-scale production of muskets by assembling a group of gunsmiths to work together, but using traditional methods.[73] They did not achieve much of an increase in productivity. Eli Whitney found that because he could not produce cotton gins by craft methods fast enough to satisfy the demand for gins in the cotton-growing regions of the South, he was unable to keep others from copying his invention and depriving him of the rewards that he should have earned from his patent.[74] Experiences such as these helped Whitney and others to realize that productivity could be increased by using factories for three purposes that could not easily be achieved in craft shops: division of labor, manufacture of uniform (interchangeable) products, and mechanization. Simeon North illustrated the reduction of costs that could be attained with division of labor by his observation that "by confining a workman to one particular limb of the pistol until he has made two thousand," at least a quarter of the labor cost was saved and the quality of the product was improved.[75]

When entrepreneurs mechanized work by applying power-driven machinery to tasks such as forging iron, they found they could lift the limits on production rates set by the physical endurance of artisans and allow them to concentrate their efforts on those aspects of the work that required skill rather than strength. To achieve this end, they had to locate factories where sufficient water power could be obtained with affordable equipment. As with gristmills, this requirement posed a site-selection problem. If an entrepreneur chose a water privilege that was too small, there would be insufficient power available for subsequent growth of the enterprise; but if an attempt was made to establish a factory at too large a privilege, the burden of debt resulting from the capital expenditure might ruin the enterprise.[76] A region that had a range of sizes of water privileges, as much of New England did, had a natural advantage for the initiation of manufacturing.

Components of industry necessary to utilize water-power resources for manufacturing included artisans who were willing and able to learn new methods of working, an agricultural surplus, producers of the primary materials used, a transportation system capable of delivering raw materials and distributing products at acceptable cost, sufficient capital to make the initial investments, and a minimum of restrictive trade and labor practices. A conjunction of all these factors in the late eighteenth century helped entrepreneurs start the new American manufacturing technology.

The distribution of water-power resources and the characteristics of direct-drive power placed some constraints on industries that used these resources. A factory could obtain power only up to a limit fixed by the flow and fall of water at a given site. Factory designers had to concentrate production in a compact area because of the inefficiency of mechanical-power-transmission systems. They also had to cluster factory buildings near the watercourse, where they were susceptible to damage from floods.

We sometimes find it difficult to appreciate just how little power and capital were needed to launch a manufacturing enterprise in the 1790s. Simeon North, the fourth son of a farmer, was thirty years old when, in 1795, he purchased a sawmill on Spruce Brook near the family farm and built a factory there for making scythes. A few years later, he obtained a contract to make 500 horse pistols for the federal government. Additional contracts followed, and by 1809 about forty men were at work at the Spruce Brook factory in Berlin, Connecticut. Archaeologists recently located the site of this factory; they found traces of building foundations and unfinished pistol parts. Spruce Brook, a very small stream, has a power potential of only about 1.5 horsepower at the factory site. With forty artisans working, the horsepower per person would have been only 0.04, somewhat less than a "man power." By 1809, the growth of the business had overtaxed the power potential of the site.[77]

When more power was needed at a factory, the proprietors could move to a site with a larger power potential, adopt steam power, or try to utilize the water power available at their original site more fully. The stream was so small at North's Spruce Brook factory that there was no possible way he could obtain more water power. But North and his workers had accomplished enough at Spruce Brook by 1813 to enable him to raise the money to build a new factory at a water privilege that could supply 95 horsepower. This amounted to an average of 1.9 horsepower for each of the fifty men employed in 1816. It allowed North to make use of newly invented machine tools in the operation of his armory and become one of the principal innovators in mechanized manufacturing.[78]

The different devices by which proprietors of a factory could obtain more power to meet the needs of a growing business at one site are illustrated by the experiences of the Collins Company. This celebrated maker of axes and machetes was responsible for many innovations in mechanized manufacturing. In 1826, the brothers David C. and Samuel W. Collins, along with William Wells, chose a site, then occupied by a gristmill, on the Farmington River in what is now Collinsville, Connecticut, to manufacture axes with power-driven machinery. In 1832, E. K. Root joined the company and over a period of years built production machinery that, as it mechanized axe-making, created ever-increasing demands for power. Water shortages developed, and in the summer of 1845, low water limited the Collins factory to half-time operation.

Samuel Collins, by then president of the enterprise, was unusual among nineteenth-century entrepreneurs in being willing and able to make the fullest possible use of the water-power resources available at the site of his works. He adopted three measures: he raised the dam to provide a larger pond, replaced the waterwheels with more efficient turbines, and built a large storage reservoir at Otis, 25 miles upstream from Collinsville, to provide additional water in periods of low flow. By 1870, the works had twelve turbines and one breast wheel with average efficiency of 67 percent and capable of producing 1,000 horsepower. Over the next thirty years, the company replaced all this machinery with improved turbines. There were further replacements in the twentieth century and then adoption of electric-power distribution. Through these various devices, the Collins Company, which had an international reputation and sold on a worldwide market, was able to operate on water power generated by the Farmington River until the works were finally closed in 1967.

In addition to willingness to invest in new equipment, proprietors of factories had to manage closely and carefully the water resources of the drainage basin to achieve self-sufficiency. Because it took more than a day for water from the Otis reservoir to reach Collinsville, release of water had to be planned well in advance of need. Not many entrepreneurs had the managerial skills needed to make this kind of careful, husbanding use of a natural resource; many found it more convenient to shift to steam power, which was simpler to manage and thereby offered opportunities for "managerial deskilling."[79]

SITE LAYOUT

There were two basic ways of distributing power in a direct-drive water-powered factory. Power from a waterwheel could be transmitted through shafts, gears, and belts to individual machines, or water could be brought to individual wheels placed where needed within the works. Factory designers usually used mechanical transmission to bring power to individual machines within a factory building, but because long lengths of shafting were inefficient and difficult to maintain, they were used sparingly to transmit power between buildings.

Multiple wheels were often installed for independent operation in large factory buildings, in factory complexes, and at industrial operations with a number of shops. The water-power system at the Tredegar Iron Works in Richmond, Virginia, was unusual in the extent of the dispersion of prime movers on the site. According to a list at the Valentine Museum, which is developing a museum complex at the Tredegar site, the ironworks had seventeen turbines in 1920. It was not, however, the only metalworking plant built with a highly decentralized pattern. In 1865, the Collins axe works had water-powered manufacturing in nine buildings, four of which had two separate turbines (Fig. 3.15).

The factory pond made an open space adjacent to many water-powered factories. Since the upper margins of the pond had no power potential, they generally remained nonindustrial. Nathan Starr's sword factory near Middletown, Connecticut, is located at the downstream end of a factory pond that is surrounded by fields and dwellings. The setting has changed little since 1813, even though the factory was rebuilt and enlarged. The lower, brownstone portion of the building is the remaining part of the sword factory, which operated until 1864 with power from waterwheels in the basement that discharged through the tailrace arches visible in Figure 3.16. In 1865, new owners built a brick textile mill on the foundation of the sword factory and installed a turbine at the side of the building. If we walk from the factory past the housing for workers adjacent to the open space created by the millpond, we move from an industrial to a rural setting in a space of only a few hundred yards.[80]

The largest millpond in Rhode Island was at Valley Falls on the Blackstone River. The first two dams, built there around 1813 and in 1828, were timber framed. Although a lawsuit by a manufacturing company upstream forced the owner of the 1828 dam to reduce its height by about 1.4 feet, his lowered dam still created an extensive millpond that is now part of the Valley Falls Marsh, a pleasant recreational area. The major framing members of both dams are intact, submerged beneath the surface of the pond. The expanding Valley Falls Company erected the present stone dam in 1853. When engineers dewatered the 1853 dam in 1940 as part of an inspection and repair project, they found and photographically recorded the other dams. We would not understand the structure of the wooden dams if the pond had not sheltered and preserved them. The physical evidence also clarifies their relative positions. No surviving map of the area shows the first dam. Archae-

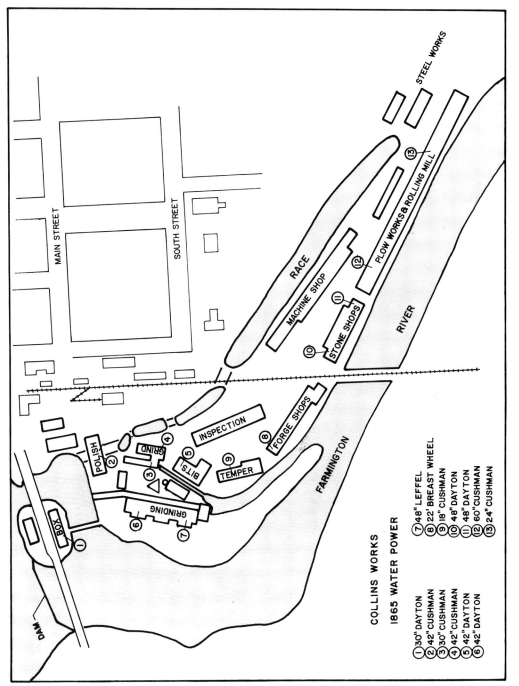

COLLINS WORKS
1865 WATER POWER

① 30" DAYTON
② 42" CUSHMAN
③ 30" CUSHMAN
④ 42" CUSHMAN
⑤ 42" DAYTON
⑥ 42" DAYTON

⑦ 48" LEFFEL
⑧ 22' BREAST WHEEL
⑨ 18" CUSHMAN
⑩ 48" DAYTON
⑪ 48" DAYTON
⑫ 60" CUSHMAN
⑬ 24" CUSHMAN

FIGURE 3.15. The power system at the Collins axe works in 1865. Twelve turbines and a waterwheel provided power at the different buildings. Water flowed from the millpond to the buildings through a series of races that created open space in the industrial complex. (From R. B. Gordon, "Material Evidence of the Development of Metal Working Technology at the Collins Axe Factory," *IA, Journal of the Society for Industrial Archeology* 9 [1983]: 23)

FIGURE 3.16. Nathan Starr's sword factory, erected in 1813, was one of a series of works built along the Coginchaug River near Middletown, Connecticut, at this time. The factory was built at the end of the dam that created the power pond partially visible in the background. Waterwheels inside the building powered the original factory. One of the tailrace arches can be seen. In 1865, new owners built a brick textile mill on the brownstone ashlar foundation of the sword factory and replaced the interior waterwheels with the external turbine visible in the photograph. The concrete blocks used to construct a parking lot at the edge of the millpond are a late-twentieth-century addition.

ologists have demonstrated significant inaccuracies or omissions in every known cartographic representation of Valley Falls before 1915.[81]

The designers of a complex that contained a number of manufacturing buildings could use canals or raceways to supply water to each by clustering the buildings along the open waterways. At the Collins axe works, which was spread out along the Farmington River, water was distributed to the thirteen wheels by a network of open raceways and underground channels and then returned to the river by tailraces. Mechanical transmission was confined to relatively short distances within each building of the plant. The races make open areas that run through the plant complex between the industrial buildings.

In order to place power-producing machinery at a lower elevation than the dam, entrepreneurs had to put factory buildings in the river valley, leaving the surrounding high land open for residential, civic, and commercial uses and free of industrial intrusion. At Collinsville, housing for workers and other residents of the town occupies the high ground overlooking the works. In the great flood of 1955, the factory buildings were heavily damaged, but the town was unscathed.

We think of communities with water-powered factories as typical of New England, but they were also common elsewhere in the East. Because Harpers Ferry, West Virginia, is at the junction of the Potomac and Shenandoah rivers, eighteenth-century traders with the Ohio Company found it a convenient place to transship goods. George Washington, who had a continuing interest in the commercial development of the Potomac Valley, recognized the large water-power potential at Harpers Ferry and induced the federal government to establish a manufacturing armory there in 1795. Starting in 1824, local entrepreneurs built gristmills, sawmills, and cotton mills on Virginius Island, where the Potomac Company had a canal to bypass the rapids in the Shenandoah. New England John Hall made his breech-loading rifles here under the sponsorship of the federal government. By 1859, the Ordnance Department had built the armory into an industrial complex, with the twenty-eight buildings of the musket factory along the Potomac River supplied with water by a power canal from a dam upstream. The rifle works, rebuilt on the site of Hall's factory, drew water from the Shenandoah canal. After the Civil War, several large floods on the Shenandoah damaged the mills of Virginius Island, and only a pulp mill survived into the twentieth century. Archaeologists with the Harpers Ferry National Historical Park are excavating the water-power system on Virginius Island (Fig. 3.17). They find that interpreting the remains is complicated by the succession of mills and the many changes made to canals and raceways in the nineteenth century. Visitors to the park can explore what is left of this southern industrial complex.[82]

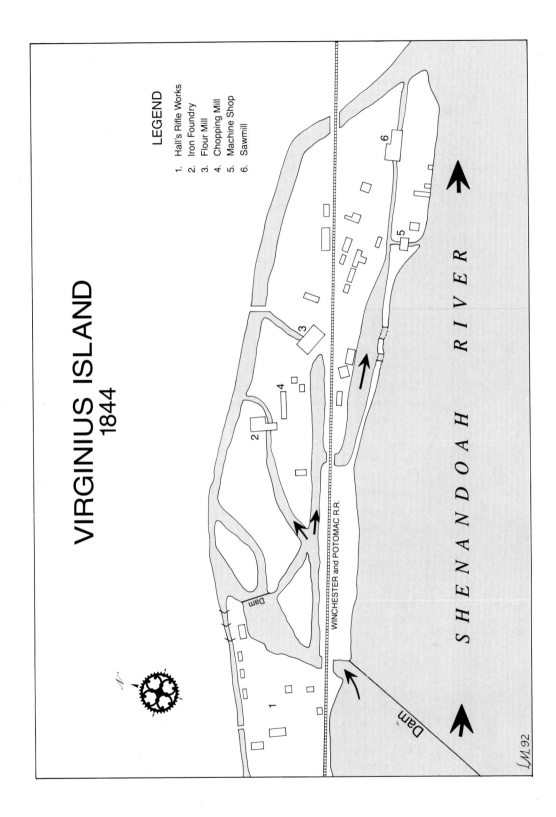

VIRGINIUS ISLAND
1844

LEGEND

1. Hall's Rifle Works
2. Iron Foundry
3. Flour Mill
4. Chopping Mill
5. Machine Shop
6. Sawmill

WINCHESTER and POTOMAC R.R.

SHENANDOAH RIVER

Dam

Dam

LM 92

COMMUNITY STRUCTURE

There often was no preexisting community at a water privilege, and the surrounding land was owned by the factory proprietors. They could then build a town to their own plan. Eli Whitney built one of the first factory villages, Whitneyville, adjacent to his armory in Hamden, Connecticut. Factory villages are usually easy to identify on topographic maps. In Wauregan, Connecticut, a cotton-mill community built between 1853 and 1867, the mill with its power canal is in the valley, and housing for the 700 to 800 persons who worked in the mill is on the adjacent hillside. Most of the houses were duplexes of standard design, but there were also boarding-houses for unmarried workers and a company store in town.[83] At Ashton, Rhode Island, the mill is across railroad tracks from the company village, with its ordered rows of multiple-occupancy, standardized dwellings (Fig. 3.18). Here, as at Wauregan, the mill stands between the community and the river. In these towns, the river was a working resource.

Proprietors of factory villages sometimes imposed their social values, in addition to their architectural ideas, on residents. Samuel Collins, believing that drinking alcoholic beverages was wicked, kept saloons out of Collinsville. The Shakers at Canterbury Village in New Hampshire built another variant on this theme as they arranged their community around a set of water-power sites. Since they lacked a substantial river with a steady flow, they created a series of millponds and dug ditches to channel water from natural ponds and swamps 2 miles away. In order to create a community under their sole control and large enough to be economically viable, the Shakers went to great effort to make the best possible use of a limited amount of water power.[84]

At some locations where the water-power potential was sufficient to support numerous factories, investors organized partnerships or corporations to

FIGURE 3.17. The water-powered industries located on Virginius Island, Harpers Ferry, West Virginia, in 1844. Harpers Ferry is at the confluence of the Potomac and Shenandoah Rivers. By 1834, Harpers Ferry could be reached from the coast on either the Chesapeake and Ohio Canal or the Baltimore and Ohio Railroad. The main part of the Harpers Ferry Armory, built by the federal government, was on the Potomac side of town, and the Hall Rifle Works were on the Shenandoah side. Private entrepreneurs were operating oil, flour, and sawmills by 1824 on Virginius Island and later added cotton and paper mills. The rifle works drew water from the Shenandoah Canal (first opened in 1803), running north of the site, while the private users depended on a dam across the Shenandoah River and a complex system of raceways. Floods damaged the mills and factories on Virginius Island repeatedly during the nineteenth century. Confederate troops destroyed many of the mills and factories when they retreated from Harpers Ferry. The buildings are gone, but remains of the water-power system survive on Virginius Island. This map is based on examination of the remains and old maps of the island. (Map by Lyn Malone)

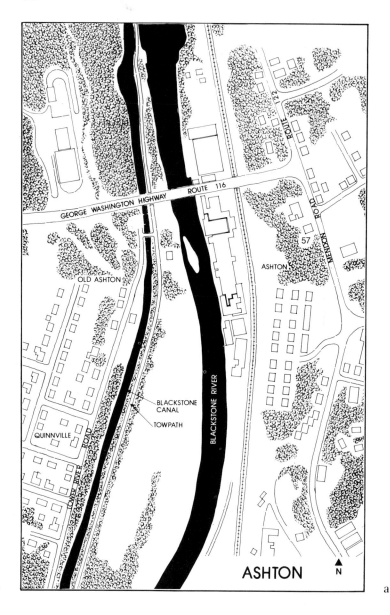

build dams and canal systems that could deliver water to factory sites. They planned to sell the sites, along with permanent water-power leases, to manufacturing enterprises. In 1791, Alexander Hamilton and friends made an attempt at this kind of enterprise in Paterson, New Jersey, but they had limited success for many years because of inadequate capital and managerial expertise.[85] Casper Wever tried this scheme on the Potomac at Weverton, Maryland, in 1834, with even less success. The water-power proprietors of Lowell, Massachusetts, began works to harness the power of the Merrimack

b

FIGURE 3.18. (a) Ashton, Rhode Island, showing the mill built along the east side of the Blackstone River and rows of workers' houses on the hillside separated from the river by the mill and the tracks of the Providence and Worcester Railroad. (Courtesy of the Rhode Island Department of Environmental Management) (b) Looking south from the Route 116 bridge, the mill, railway, and residential community are visible.

River in 1822, and by 1850, two other large manufacturing cities—Manchester, New Hampshire, and Lawrence, Massachusetts—were also in place on the Merrimack. The three together had a capacity of 28,000 horsepower in 1880.[86]

The Lowell proprietors used a complex, two-level system of multiple power canals to convert an area of farms and small rural mills into an urban manufacturing center. The ideal way to power a series of factories was with a single canal running parallel to a river that had a large drop in elevation. The land between the canal and the river became an extended island on which factories could be placed in a line. Water from the canal (still at approximately the same level as the upper river) entered the factories on the island, dropped through their power-producing wheels or turbines, and exited back into the river below. A simple system of this type was not feasible in early Lowell because of the high, rocky ground rising from the river's edge below Pawtucket Falls,[87] but it was adopted at Lawrence in 1846 (Fig. 3.19). The investors in Manchester borrowed the two-level concept from Lowell, with tailraces from the upper mills supplying water for the lower-level canal.

FIGURE 3.19. An 1876 bird's-eye view of Lawrence, Massachusetts, showing the placement of factories between the north power canal and the Merrimack River. The dam is at the left edge of the view. (Courtesy of the Museum of American Textile History)

However, unlike in Lowell, there were only two canals at Manchester, and both were parallel to the river.

Textile production dominated the economies of Lowell, Lawrence, and Manchester. Each city had scores of textile mills as well as great machine shops. The powerful manufacturing corporations that controlled the development of these cities ensured that the urban plans met the needs of the factories. The first priority was the efficient placement of power canals and mills. Next came the orderly rows of corporate housing for the workers, usually built close to the mills. An impressive main street lined with commercial establishments was essential, and a park or two added to the community's progressive image. The last concern was private housing; most residential neighborhoods lacked the precise planning that was characteristic of the corporate districts, and they were located where they would not interfere with industrial activity.[88]

After Henry David Thoreau traveled on the Merrimack River in 1839, he wrote that it "falls over a succession of natural dams, where it has been offering its *privileges* in vain for ages, until at last the Yankee race came to *improve* them." There was "a city on each successive plateau, a busy colony of human beaver around every fall."[89] Lowell, Lawrence, and Manchester were the biggest and best known, but they accounted for just over one-third of the 77,000 horsepower used in the entire Merrimack River basin. Sizable tributaries such as the Nashua and Suncook rivers also supported concentrations of industry, and even modest brooks in the wooded hills had their share of mills. Walking the small streams of New Hampshire today, one finds numerous stone foundations of former sawmills and gristmills, furniture and bobbin shops. There were approximately 900 water-powered mills in the basin in 1880, but those on the small tributaries averaged only about 30 horsepower.[90] The typical American mill was a modest affair that needed relatively little power (Fig. 3.20).

As might be expected, the large water-power developments on New England's major rivers attracted much more attention in the nineteenth century than the ubiquitous rural watermills. But it was the labor system and the attractive corporate architecture of the three great Merrimack River cities that brought them international fame. Lowell was more renowned for its boardinghouses and thousands of female operatives than for its achievements in textile production, civil engineering, and hydraulic science. With many of its manufacturing and water-power structures intact but few of its boardinghouses left, Lowell became the first urban, industrial national historical park in 1978. Holyoke generated more power from the Connecticut River than Lowell did from the Merrimack and has joined it as the site of a Massachusetts state heritage park. Papermaking became the dominant industry in Holyoke, where the canal system provided water to process the paper and power the mills.

FIGURE 3.20. The stone headrace of the Hallville Mill in Rhode Island, a small "negro-cloth" factory that burned after the Civil War. Cheap cloth for slave clothing was no longer in demand, and many mills of this type were destroyed by suspicious fires. The impressive elevated race ran for more than 200 feet from a dam and millpond.

There were only a few large-scale, direct-drive water-power developments outside the Northeast. Those in Augusta, Georgia, and Minneapolis, Minnesota, were among the most significant. The city of Augusta built and operated a three-level canal system fed by the Savannah River to supply power primarily for textile manufacturing and flour milling. It supplied power for a variety of industrial operations, including textile manufacturing, gunpowder and munitions production (the enormous Confederate States Powder Works was on the upper canal), flour milling, foundry work, and the pumping of Augusta's municipal water.[91] Minnesota investors used St. Anthony's Falls on the upper Mississippi at Minneapolis first for sawmills and then for flour mills that, by 1880, were producing more than 2 million barrels a year. Despite persistent problems caused by erosion of the sandstone and limestone formations at the falls, Minneapolis became the center of flour milling for the north-central states.[92]

Steam power played an important role in the continuing industrial expansion of these and other cities that depended heavily on water power; their present-day urban structure represents the superimposition of two industrial styles. In Lowell, for instance, only ten textile corporations and the

Lowell Machine Shop leased power from the Proprietors of Locks and Canals. A few mills situated by the Concord River got water power from the small Wamesit Canal, but in many of the city's manufacturing buildings, steam engines were the only prime movers. Even for those manufacturers with access to water power, steam was an attractive option for processes that required heat or that produced scrap wood that could be burned under boilers. Using steam was often the only way to increase the scale of existing operations. By 1880, installed steam power had surpassed net horsepower from water leases, not only in Lowell as a whole but also among the corporations on the canal system. There were then 119 engines in Lowell, providing a total of 16,157 horsepower.[93]

COMMUNICATION AND TRANSPORTATION

Before the construction of canals or railroads, the operators of water-powered industries that were dispersed over the countryside depended on coastal shipping, riverboats, and wagons to deliver raw materials and carry away finished products. When manufacturers wanted to ship heavy products, such as iron forgings, they hauled them by wagon to the nearest navigable waterway, where they could be carried by boat easily, if slowly, to any destination on a river or the coast. People moved between industrial sites quite freely,[94] but the difficulty of transporting goods was a significant drag on the economy at this time; for example, it limited specialization in the manufacture of large or bulky products. Heavy machines, such as forge hammers, were built as close as possible to where they were to be used because it was costly to ship them long distances.

INNOVATION

Both the material evidence and the historical record show that there was an extraordinary burgeoning of innovation in American manufacturing technology in the decades after 1790. Entrepreneurs were aided by some of the geographical, social, cultural, and economic factors that had been important in the industrialization of Europe. One was an abundance of sites where machinery could be set up to apply power to manufacturing with small initial investment, as at Simeon North's Spruce Brook plant in Berlin, Connecticut. Innovators were able to try out their ideas promptly, often without having to convince wealthy individuals to supply venture capital. The distances between these water-power sites were often large enough to encourage innovators to work out independent solutions to manufacturing problems and to try out their ideas at their own establishments. Yet these artisans were still close enough that they could frequently compare and exchange ideas with their peers. This was both a stimulus to the improvement of technology and part of the process of reaching a consensus on best practice.

Additionally, the varied nature of the products made at these sites created opportunities for "technological convergence," the transfer of new developments in one line of work to another.[95]

All these factors contributed to the development of machinery for milling metals at the factories of Simeon North, Nathan Starr, and others located along the Coginchaug River just outside Middletown, Connecticut. Each was a mile or two from its neighbors and had abundant water power to operate machine tools. Artisans often shifted jobs between these factories, transferring their skills and experiences as they moved.[96]

ENVIRONMENTAL EFFECTS

Entrepreneurs who developed a water privilege changed the surrounding environment by building dams and millponds. Building a dam on a navigable stream might aid navigation (if fitted with lift locks) by creating slack water, but without a fishladder or some opening, the passage of anadromous fish would be blocked. This contributed to the decline of the shad, alewife, and salmon fisheries.[97] Land behind the dam was flooded. During periods of low flow, factory managers might use all the available water to refill their millponds, causing the stream below it to go dry for a few hours. During these periods, sewage dumped in the stream would not be diluted by flowing water. Disputes over minimum releases of water were common wherever there were several users along one stream. Counterbalancing these adverse effects were the open space created by the millpond and the benefits of not using steam power. These benefits included the absence of smoke and sulfurous emissions to the atmosphere, of hot water discharges to streams, and of the solid wastes from burning fuel, as well as independence from distant suppliers of fuel. Many of these factors are debated today in arguments over proposals for new hydroelectric installations.

Archaeological evidence reveals an important, long-term environmental consequence of the use of water power. When millponds are drained or their bottoms are sampled by taking cores, they are often found to be filled with silt; some have accumulated so much silt that they have become inland wetlands. The new owner of an abandoned textile mill in Sandy Hook, Connecticut, drained the power pond by opening a gate at the bottom of the dam and found that it was almost filled with sediment. The flow of water out of the gate cut a deep channel into this deposit, and when we looked closely at its edges, we found successive layers of leaves covered by sand and silt (Fig. 3.21). Each layer of leaves marked the bottom of the pond in the fall; sand was deposited in the spring runoff, and the silt during the low flow in the summer months; floods deposited thick deposits of sand. By counting layers, we found that the sediment in the pond had accumulated between 1936 and 1978; by then, it had destroyed the storage capacity of the pond.

FIGURE 3.21. A drained millpond on the Pootatuck River near Sandy Hook, Connecticut. Sediment carried down the river over a period of fifty years had nearly filled the pond, which had become an inland wetland with no storage capacity. When drained, the river cut a deep channel (seen in the photograph) through the accumulated sediment. Each horizontal band in the bank is a layer of leaves deposited in the pond in the fall. The material between the layers is sand and silt. The space between each layer of leaves shows the amount of sediment that accumulated in a year.

Silt accumulations behind mill dams in industrial districts may contain high concentrations of pollutants. In 1974, the removal of the power dam on the Hudson River at Fort Edward, New York, released silt contaminated with PCBs and polluted a long reach of the river.

DECLINE AND DISUSE

In the second decade of the nineteenth century, some factory managers were already beginning to install steam engines, either as their principal source of power or as a supplement to waterwheels. Once investors built canals and railroads that could transport coal from mining regions at reasonable cost, steam power became an increasingly attractive alternative to water power at many sites. Improvements in the efficiency of boilers and engines reduced the costs of steam-powered manufacturing, and safer boiler designs calmed fears of explosions. Better governors allowed close speed regulation under varying loads. Steam power removed the constraint on growth at a given site set by the water-power potential; it was not subject to curtailment due to drought or flood; and it did not require such skilled management in either

FIGURE 3.22. The Horatio Ames Iron Works at Falls Village, Connecticut, in 1853. Ames's artisans made heavy forgings, such as cranks and axles for locomotives, and, during the Civil War, heavy wrought-iron, rifled cannon. Ames was so confident of the quality of his cannon that he offered to sit on one when it was fired. (From L. Fagan, *Map of Canaan* [Philadelphia, 1853]. Courtesy of Sterling Memorial Library, Yale University)

FIGURE 3.23. The site of the Horatio Ames Iron Works as it appeared in 1981. All above-ground traces of heavy industry have vanished. The low concrete dam diverts water to a hydroelectric plant located below the falls.

the development of the water resource or the scheduling of work to allow for periods of low stream flow. By about 1870, as much industrial power was obtained from steam as from water in the United States. Thereafter, the relative importance of water power declined rapidly. There were plenty of unused water privileges, but claims for the convenience and reliability of steam were very persuasive.

Steam from coal released industry from the geographical immobility of direct-drive water-power systems and allowed entrepreneurs to concentrate manufacturing in cities. Rural water-powered factories and their renewable power sources gradually fell into disuse. Today it is often hard to find the remaining traces of these industries. Artisans made heavy cannon and machinery at the Ames Iron Works on the Housatonic River in Falls Village, Connecticut, during the Civil War (Fig. 3.22); today, virtually every trace of this major industry, which drew power from the river, has vanished (Fig. 3.23). The sites of other water-powered industries are being reused with the transformation of the dam, pond, and raceway that formerly served the needs of manufacturing into recreational facilities. But some of the largest water-powered factories, such as the Mastodon Mill at Cohoes, New York, have so far proved to be too costly to reuse.

Hydroelectric Power

While factory managers were abandoning direct drive of their machinery by water power, new methods of generating and transmitting electric power were making some previously undeveloped water privileges economically attractive. Turbines could drive dynamos or alternators, and the energy they produced could turn motors. In 1895, at Silverton, Colorado, water was brought 9,750 feet in a flume to turn two Pelton wheels coupled to 150-kilowatt alternators that supplied power for milling ore. It was also possible to generate the power at one point and use it at a distant industrial plant. Edward Terry had already demonstrated that it was practical to transmit hydroelectric power to a distant customer in 1889. He generated electricity with two 600-kilowatt alternators at a dam on the Farmington River, raised it by transformers to 10 kilovolts, transmitted it 11 miles, reduced it to lower voltage, and distributed it to the streetlights of Hartford, Connecticut, with a loss of less than 10 percent. The transmission was over six copper wires with a combined cross section of about $1/4$ square inch. These would have been a hardly visible feature on the landscape had it not been necessary to elevate them on wooden poles. A similar effort was successful at a Taftville, Connecticut, cotton mill in 1894, when electric current arrived by overhead wires from water-powered generators 4.5 miles away in Baltic.[98]

Entrepreneurs found the largest water-power sites in North America difficult to use when the only way to distribute power from them was in canals, like those at Lowell. At Niagara, a canal from above the falls was completed in 1861, and by 1885 it was supplying 7.5 megawatts (0.3 percent of the power now generated on the United States side) to mills and factories perched along the edge of the gorge below the falls. The discharge from their tailraces dotted the cliffs with many small, man-made plumes of water (Fig. 3.24). To preserve the appearance of the falls and gain a twelvefold increase in the power developed, in 1889 a consortium of engineers proposed building

FIGURE 3.24. Entrepreneurs first used hydropower at Niagara by diverting water above the falls into a canal that carried it to mills and factories on the cliffs below the falls. Much of the potential power was wasted because the factory operators did not use the full drop. They released the spent water at the cliff edge in the white plumes seen in the photograph. To get rid of this intrusion on the natural appearance of the Niagara gorge, engineers cut a single, deep tailrace well back from the cliffs. Factories could then discharge spent water into this tunnel, and since it was released at the base of the cliff, it was not visually intrusive. This photograph shows the cliffs of the Niagara gorge before the benefits of the tailrace tunnel were realized. (Courtesy of the Smithsonian Institution)

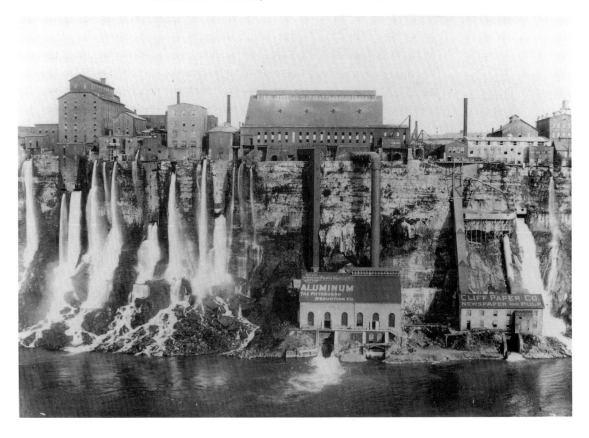

a central powerhouse located upstream with a tailrace tunnel discharging at the base of the falls. At first, the members of the consortium thought that the only way to distribute the power generated would be by compressed-air mains, which would have been less than 40 percent efficient. Instead, they found two large customers for electric power willing to build works adjacent to the powerhouse. Both were makers of new products; the Pittsburgh Reduction Company (known after 1907 as the Aluminum Company of America) used electrolytic cells to make aluminum, and the Carborundum Company made abrasives in electric furnaces. The confidence and optimism Americans felt about engineering at that time were reflected in the care taken with the appearance of the powerhouse and its adjoining stone structures; nearby, the power company also built a model industrial village, Echota, designed by Stanford White. The designers made sure that their diversion of water did not lower the falls more than 2 inches.[99] Subsequent industrial development in nearby communities and the commercialization of the village of Niagara Falls largely wiped out these early efforts to preserve natural features in the industrial use of the power resources of Niagara. Today a superhighway sweeps across the site of the powerhouse (1895) of the Niagara Falls Power Company, and since 1961, 2,400 megawatts have been generated with Niagara water at the Robert Moses power complex, which visually dominates the central part of the gorge.

Across the Niagara River on the Canadian side, more survives from the early years of hydroelectric generation. Three turn-of-the-century plants are in place near the falls, and two of them are still generating. The plant operating above Horseshoe Fall was built by the American-owned Canadian Niagara Power Company between 1901 and 1924. The powerhouse with the most spectacular location faces both of the falls from a position deep in the gorge. Reaching this plant by elevator and tunnel, one finds sixteen turbines, complete with the graceful scroll cases originally installed by the Buffalo-based Ontario Power Company when the plant was built (1902–1905). Canada's Ontario Hydro now keeps twelve of these units working and operates the Adam Beck Plant No. 1 (1917–1930) and No. 2 (1950–1958) downstream. Using a section of the Welland River and an 8.5-mile canal to deliver water with 295 feet of head, the Canadians made Adam Beck No. 1 the world's greatest hydroelectric development at its completion. It could produce 400 megawatts. The continuing drop in the river below Niagara Falls has made the Adam Beck and Robert Moses plant locations much more effective than any site near the cataracts.[100]

Traces of the plants built below American Fall at the base of the cliff have almost disappeared. From the Canadian side, it is difficult to tell where penstocks once ran down the cliff to the powerhouse (1895–1896) of the Niagara Falls Hydraulic and Manufacturing Company. You can pick out a pile of rubble and fallen rock at the site of the Schoellkopf Power Plant, which was built in three stages from 1903 to 1924. The Canadian Niagara Power Company kept the plant in operation until 1956, despite escalating problems with leaks through the cliff, which was subject to natural fractures and had been perforated since the 1860s by numerous cuts, tunnels, and tailraces. Seepage into the plant had worsened by June 7, 1956, when a large crack suddenly opened in the back wall. Workers scrambled to escape as a torrent of water rushed into the generator room and the cliff above collapsed onto the plant, crushing most of it in minutes. Luckily, only one man lost his life.[101]

A better impression of the hydropower systems envisioned by turn-of-the-century engineers can be had at the Soo hydro in Sault Sainte Marie, Michigan. The quarter-mile-long, carefully designed, dressed-stone power-house facing the Saint Marys River retains its original appearance. The developers of the Soo hydro anticipated creating an industrial city in an undeveloped site, as had been done at Lowell, but a Union Carbide plant that manufactured calcium carbide was the only industrial customer attracted to this remote location. When the carbide works closed in 1963, the technique of long-distance energy transmission was used to sell power to distant customers.[102] In this way, investments made in the development of a renewable power source nearly a century ago continue to be useful today.

Notes

1. Nathan Rosenberg, *Perspectives on Technology* (Cambridge: Cambridge University Press, 1976), pp. 43–44.

2. Brooke Hindle, ed., *America's Wooden Age: Aspects of Its Early Technology* (Tarrytown, N.Y.: Sleepy Hollow Restorations, 1975). On the continued importance of forests, see Michael Williams, "Industrial Impacts on the Forests of the United States, 1860–1920," *Journal of Forest History* 31 (1987): 108–121.

3. Louis C. Hunter, *A History of Industrial Power in the United States, 1780–1930,* vol. 1, *Waterpower* (Charlottesville: University Press of Virginia, 1979), chap. 10.

4. Many of the long-held beliefs about the deforestation of Britain, the depredations of the ironmasters in the woodlands, and the shortage of timber for shipbuilding are not substantiated by hard evidence. These matters are discussed in Oliver Rackham, *Trees and Woodland in the British Landscape* (London: Dent, 1976), pp. 91–95, 99–102.

5. For descriptions of the forests of colonial New England and their use by European immigrants, see William Cronon, *Changes in the Land* (New York: Hill and Wang, 1983), chaps. 1, 6, and Charles F. Carroll, *The Timber Economy of Puritan New England* (Providence, R.I.: Brown University Press, 1973). For a general review, see Michael Williams, *Americans and Their Forests* (New York: Cambridge University Press, 1989). There were also two hogsheads of furs in the first cargo from Plymouth.

6. There is a full account of the physical properties of different kinds of wood and the suitability of particular woods for different uses in R. Bruce Hoadley, *Understanding Wood* (Newtown, Conn.: Taunton Press, 1980). Potash extracted from wood ashes was used in the manufacture of soap and glass and was one of the principal commodities that could be sold for cash in the Wooden Age (Cronon, *Changes in the Land*, p. 117; Robert P. Multhauf, "Potash," in *Material Culture of the Wooden Age*, ed. Brooke Hindle [Tarrytown, N.Y.: Sleepy Hollow Press, 1981], pp. 227–240; Harry Miller, "Potash from Wood Ashes: Frontier Technology in Canada and the United States," *Technology and Culture* 21 [1980]: 187–208).

7. Timber drives are described in Harold K. Hochschild, *Lumberjacks and Rivermen in the Central Adirondacks, 1850–1950* (Blue Mountain Lake, N.Y.: Adirondack Museum, 1962). On the geography of forest use, see Michael Williams, "The Clearing of the Forests," in *The Making of the American Landscape*, ed. Michael P. Conzen (Boston: Unwin Hyman, 1990), pp. 146–168. Timber harvesting is shown in the lumbering building at the Adirondack Museum and at the Pennsylvania Lumber Museum, Coudersport.

8. The characteristic structures of the grain of different species of wood are shown in Hoadley, *Understanding Wood*.

9. See, for example, *The National Atlas of the United States of America* (Washington, D.C.: U.S. Geological Survey, 1970).

10. The geological similarity arises because the two continents were once one.

11. Jamie Eves, "'Shrunk to a Comparative Rivulet': Deforestation, Stream Flow and Rural Milling in 19th-Century Maine," *Technology and Culture* 33 (1992): 38–65; P. D. Jones and K. R. Briffa, "Riverflow Reconstruction from Tree Rings in Southern Britain," *Journal of Climatology* 4 (1984): 461–472.

12. L. W. Swift and others, "Simulation of Evapotranspiration and Drainage from Mature and Clear-cut Deciduous Forests and Young Pine Plantations," *Water Resources Research* 11 (1975): 667–673; P. J. Sellers and J. G. Lockwood, "A Numerical Simulation of the Effects of Changing Vegetation Type on Surface Hydroclimatology," *Climatic Change* 3 (1981): 121–136; J. H. Patric and R. G. Reinhart, "Hydrologic Effects of Deforesting in Two Mountain Watersheds of West Virginia," *Water Resources Research* 7 (1971): 1182–1188.

13. Cronon, *Changes in the Land*, pp. 122–126.

14. Robert B. Gordon, "Hydrological Science and the Development of Water Power for Manufacturing," *Technology and Culture* 26 (1985): 204–235.

15. An example of this type of survey is Walter Wells, *The Water Power of Maine* (Augusta, 1869). Compilers who relied on the reports of selectmen and other local officials were often told that the water power in a given town was "all that anyone could possibly want" or "as much as Niagara"; reliable reporting of the seasonal variation in stream flow was especially difficult before flow gauges were established. Later, the U.S. Geological Survey reported on Maine in Henry A. Pressey, *Water Powers of the State of Maine*, Water Supply Paper No. 69 (Washington, D.C.: Government Printing Office, 1902).

16. U.S. Bureau of the Census, Tenth Census, *Reports on the Water-Power of the United States*, vols. 16 and 17 (Washington, D.C., Census Office, 1885, 1887). A summary of the results of this survey is given in Hunter, *Waterpower*, chap. 3.

17. Bureau of the Census, *Reports on the Water-Power of the United States*, vol. 16, p. 15. The computations are explained in Robert B. Gordon, "Cost and Use of Water Power During Industrialization in New England and Great Britain: A Geological Interpretation," *Economic History Review* 36 (1983): 240–259.

18. J. P. Lesley, *The Iron Manufacturer's Guide* (New York: Wiley, 1859), pp. 731–742; Paul T. Gundrum, "The Charcoal Iron Industry in Eighteenth-Century America: An Expression of Regional Economic Variation" (Master's thesis, University of Wisconsin, Madison, 1974), pp. 46–48.

19. Gundrum, "Charcoal Iron Industry in Eighteenth-Century America," p. 52.

20. David Harvey, "Reconstructing the American Bloomery Process," *Historic Trades Annual* 1 (1988): 19–37.

21. Robert B. Gordon, "Strength and Structure of Wrought Iron," *Archeomaterials* 2 (1988): 109–137.

22. William Keating is quoted to this effect in Darwin H. Stapleton, *The Transfer of Early Technologies to America* (Philadelphia: American Philosophical Society, 1987), p. 19.

23. J. C. Harrington, *Glassmaking at Jamestown* (Richmond, Va.: Dietz Press, ca. 1952).

24. For an illustrated account of the technology of pit sawing and the sawyer's skills, see Roy Underhill, *The Woodwright's Companion* (Chapel Hill: University of North Carolina Press, 1983), chap. 14.

25. The evidence for New England is summarized in Theodore Z. Penn and Roger Parks, "The Nichols-Colby Sawmill in Bow, New Hampshire," *IA, Journal of the Society for Industrial Archeology* 1 (1975): 1–12. See also Richard M. Candee, "Merchant and Millwright: The Water Powered Sawmills of the Piscataqua," *Old Time New England* 60 (1970): 131–149; Harry B. Weiss and Grace M. Weiss, *The Early Sawmills of New Jersey* (Trenton: New Jersey Agricultural Society, 1968); and John Englund, "Sawmills of Worcester County" (File report, Old Sturbridge Village, 1982). For other areas, see Hunter, *Waterpower*, pp. 6–8, 15–21.

26. The careful documentation of this mill was an early project of the Historic American Buildings Survey (HABS).

27. The shaft of the flutter wheel in Grant's Mill, Cumberland, Rhode Island, was still in place when this site was recorded by one of the authors. It had been recycled as the wooden shaft of an iron impulse wheel (Gary Kulik and Julia C. Bonham, *Rhode Island: An Inventory of Historic and Engineering Sites* [Washington, D.C.: Government Printing Office, 1978]).

28. The power that a person can develop in various kinds of tasks is tabulated in William Kent, *The Mechanical Engineer's Pocket Book* (New York: Wiley, 1903), p. 433.

29. The power is calculated from the relation $P = QHe/11.8$, where P is the power in kW; Q, the mean flow in ft^3/s; H, the head in feet; and e, the efficiency. The mean flow at the mill site is estimated from the stream gauge on the Quinebaug River just below Sturbridge to be about 140 ft^3/s (*Surface Water Supply of the United States, 1966–70*, part 1, *North Atlantic Slope Basins*, vol. 1, *Basins from Maine to Connecticut*, U.S. Geological Survey Water Supply Paper No. 2101 [Washington, D.C.: Government Printing Office, 1975]); the fall is 7 feet; and for a Wing reaction wheel, $e = 35$ percent (Hunter, *Waterpower*, p. 304). There are three mills on the site, so the power at the sawmill has been taken as one-third of that available.

30. John Worrell and Ted Penn, "Of Ice and Men," *Old Sturbridge Visitor* 23 (1983): 6–7; Englund, "Sawmills of Worcester County."

31. An archaeological study of a mill built after 1822 and destroyed by a flood before 1831 found that most of the surviving parts of the mill mechanism were made of wood (John S. Wilson, "Upper Factory Brook Sawmill," *IA, Journal of the Society for Industrial Archeology* 3 [1977]: 43–52).

32. Geoffrey Tweedale, *Sheffield Steel and America: A Century of Commercial and Technological Interdependence, 1830–1930* (Cambridge: Cambridge University Press, 1987), p. 25.

33. James A. Mulholland, A *History of Metals in Colonial America* (University: University of Alabama Press, 1981), p. 24.

34. Ibid., p. 30.

35. A full history of the Saugus enterprise is in E. N. Hartley, *Ironworks on the Saugus* (Norman: University of Oklahoma Press, 1957). See also Mulholland, *History of Metals in Colonial America,* pp. 30–36.

36. Comparison of artifacts recovered in the excavation at Saugus with those recovered in subsequent excavations in England suggests that proprietors in Massachusetts closely followed the design of English ironworks. The waterwheel and wheel pit uncovered at the blast furnace site, for example, are nearly identical to the wheel and wheel pit excavated by David Crossley at Chingley furnace, which was operated between about 1560 and 1580 (see Crossley, *The Bewl Valley Ironworks* [London: Royal Archaeological Institute, 1975], plate 14, and the photograph of the excavation of the wheel pit at Saugus in Hartley, *Ironworks on the Saugus*).

37. The chemistry of the Saugus blast-furnace slag is discussed in Hobart M. Kraner, "Ceramics in the Saugus Blast Furnace Circa 1650," *Ceramic Bulletin* 37 (1960): 354–358, and M. M. Hallet, "A Note on Slag from the First American Blast Furnace," *Bulletin of the Historical Metallurgy Group* 7 (1973): 6.

38. The estimates of power required are based on Ronald F. Tylecote and J. Cherry, "The 17th Century Bloomery at Muncaster Head," *Transactions of the Cumberland and Westmorland Antiquarian and Archaeological Society* 70 (1970): 69–109.

39. For an account of sea-level changes in New England and the resulting changes in the coastal topography, see Robert B. Gordon, "History of Sea Level Changes Along the Connecticut Shore," in *Connecticut Archaeology: Past, Present, and Future,* Occasional Papers in Anthropology, ed. R. E. Dewar, K. L. Feder, and D. A. Poirier (Storrs: Department of Anthropology, University of Connecticut, 1983), pp. 61–78. Tide gauge records and geochemical evidence indicate that the rate of submergence has been the same in historic time along all of the coast of southern New England.

40. Eugene S. Ferguson, *Oliver Evans: Inventive Genius of the American Industrial Revolution* (Greenville, Del.: Hagley Museum, 1980).

41. Examples of gristmill buildings are illustrated in Martha Zimiles and Murray Zimiles, *Early American Mills* (New York: Potter, 1973).

42. The mill complex serving the Moravian community at Bethlehem, Pennsylvania, which included oilseed, hemp, tanbark, groat, and snuff mills as well as a water-powered municipal water supply in use from 1745 onward, was unusually well recorded in documents and drawings that were sent back to the sponsors of the community in Germany (Carter Litchfield and others, *The Bethlehem Oil Mill, 1745–1934* [Kemblesville, Pa.: Olearius Editions, 1984]).

43. Mulholland, *History of Metals in Colonial America,* pp. 57–59.

44. John S. Salmon, *The Washington Ironworks of Franklin County, Virginia, 1773–1850* (Richmond: Virginia State Library, 1986).

45. Harvey, "Reconstructing the American Bloomery Process."

46. The great scarcity of manufactured goods in the Middle Atlantic colonies is described in James P. Horn, "'The Bare Necessities': Standards of Living in England and the Chesapeake, 1650–1700," *Historical Archaeology* 22 (1988): 74–91.

47. Mulholland, *History of Metals in Colonial America,* pp. 62–63, chap. 6.

48. Ibid., pp. 63–66; James M. Swank, *History of the Manufacture of Iron in All Ages,* 2d ed. (Philadelphia: American Iron and Steel Association, 1892), chaps. 22, 23.

49. Swank, *History of the Manufacture of Iron,* pp. 166–167; Deborah Ducoff-Barone, "Marketing and Manufacturing: A Study of Domestic Cast Iron Articles Produced at Colebrookdale Furnace, Berks County, Pennsylvania, 1735–1751," *Pennsylvania History* 50 (1983): 20–37.

50. Mulholland, *History of Metals in Colonial America,* pp. 69–71.

51. For Virginia, see Salmon, *Washington Ironworks of Franklin County, Virginia;* for Maryland, Michael D. Thompson, *The Iron Industry of Western Maryland* (Morgantown, W.Va., 1976); for New Jersey, James M. Ransom, *Vanishing Ironworks of the Ramapos* (New Brunswick, N.J.: Rutgers University Press, 1966).

52. Sally A. Botiggi, "An Iron Experiment: The Livingston Ironworks and the Colonial Iron Industry, 1743–1790," in *The Livingston Legacy: Three Centuries of American History,* ed. Richard C. Wiles and Andrea K. Zimmerman (Annandale-on-Hudson, N.Y.: Bard College, 1987), pp. 283–298.

53. For an archaeological report on a New Jersey bloomery forge site, see George P. Sellmer, "Windham Forge Revisited," *New Jersey Highlander* 20 (1984): 3–33. The Adirondack sites are described in R. F. Allen and others, "An Archaeological Survey of Bloomery Forges in the Adirondacks," *IA, Journal of the Society for Industrial Archeology* 16 (1990): 3–20.

54. The idea that the bloomery is primitive technology may have originated with Swank, who so describes bloomeries in *History of the Manufacture of Iron,* chap. 30.

55. For the history of Ironville, see Richard S. Allen, *Separation and Inspiration,* Historical Publication No. 1 (Ironville, N.Y.: Penfield Foundation, 1967), and Elmer E. Barker, *The Story of Crown Point Iron,* Historical Publication No. 3 (Ironville, N.Y.: Penfield Foundation, 1969). A technical description of the American bloomery process is given in Robert B. Gordon and D. Killick, "The Metallurgy of the American Bloomery Process," *Archeomaterials* 6 (1992): 141–167.

56. In 1783, 8 blast furnaces made 5,100 tons of iron, and 17 finery forges converted 4,300 tons (84 percent) of this output to 3,180 tons of bar iron, according to Samuel G. Hemmerlin, *Report About the Mines in the United States of America,* trans. Amandus Johnson (1783; Philadelphia: John Morton Library, 1931), pp. 72–74.

57. Swank, *History of the Manufacture of Iron,* pp. 174–175.

58. Helen Schenck and Reed Knox, "Valley Forge: The Making of Iron in the Eighteenth Century," *Archaeology* 39 (1986): 27–33.

59. For the Chingley Forge excavation report, see Crossley, *Bewl Valley Ironworks.*

60. Hemmerlin, *Report About the Mines,* pp. 72–73.

61. M. B. Sharp and W. H. Thomas, *A Guide to the Old Stone Blast Furnaces in Western Pennsylvania* (Pittsburgh: Historical Society of Western Pennsylvania, 1966). There is a list of sites with significant remains of pre-twentieth-century blast furnaces in *Hopewell Furnace: A Guide to Hopewell Village National Historic Site,* National Park Handbook No. 34 (Washington, D.C.: Department of the Interior, 1983). In Pennsylvania, Hopewell Village, Cornwall Iron Furnace, and Curtin Furnace have interpretive programs for visitors.

62. A full description of Hopewell is given in Joseph E. Walker, *Hopewell Village* (Philadelphia: University of Pennsylvania Press, 1966).

63. The reasons for the continued demand for iron made in charcoal-fired furnaces are discussed in Robert B. Gordon, "Materials for Manufacturing: The Response of the Connecticut Iron Industry to Limited Resources and Technological Change," *Technology and Culture* 24 (1983): 602–634. Data on labor costs are for 1851 to 1853 (Walker, *Hopewell Village*, p. 62).

64. National Park Service policy has been to allow woodlands to grow at industrial sites such as Hopewell. As the woods are allowed to grow, the site looks less and less like it did when the ironworks was in operation.

65. Jack E. Boucher, *Of Batsto and Bog Iron* (Batsto, N.J.: Batsto Citizens Committee, 1980). On the glassworks, see Budd Wilson, "The Batsto Window Light Factory Excavation," *Bulletin of the Archeological Society of New Jersey*, no. 27 (1971): 11–18; no. 29 (1972): 28–31.

66. For New England, see Gordon, "Materials for Manufacturing," and Robert B. Gordon and M. S. Raber, "An Early American Integrated Steel Works," *IA, Journal of the Society for Industrial Archeology* 10 (1984): 17–34. We do not have an archaeological study of the Ohio charcoal iron industry, but there is a description in Frank H. Rowe, *The History of Iron and Steel in Scioto County* (Columbus: Ohio State Archaeological and Historical Society, 1938).

67. Gordon and Raber, "Early American Integrated Steel Works." This site is now in the care of the Roxbury Land Trust.

68. Statements such as "1,000 acres per year per charcoal furnace, previously predicted as fact, might be on the low side" have been traced by David C. Mudge to recollections of retired ironworkers who offered guesses about the amount of wood they cut ("Charcoal & Iron: Some Interpretations of the Use of Charcoal by the Early Iron Industry in New Jersey" [Paper presented at the Society for Industrial Archeology Iron Workshop, Greenwood Lake, New York, 10 November 1984).

69. These estimates are based on ibid. See also Williams, "Industrial Impacts on the Forests of the United States."

70. Gordon, "Materials for Manufacturing."

71. Carolyn Cooper and Patrick Malone, "The Mechanical Woodworker in Early Nineteenth-Century New England as a Spin-off from Textile Industrialization" (Paper presented at the Old Sturbridge Village Colloquium, 17 March 1990).

72. The McLane report of 1833, for example, enumerates only textile mills in the industrial census of Rhode Island (Louis McLane, *Documents Relative to the Manufactures in the United States* [New York: Burt Franklin, 1969]).

73. Michael S. Raber and others, "Conservative Innovators and Military Small Arms: An Industrial History of the Springfield Armory, 1794–1968" (Report for the National Park Service, 1989), chap. 1.

74. Jeanette Mirskey and Allan Nevins, *The World of Eli Whitney* (New York: Macmillan, 1952), p. 175.

75. S.D.N. North and R. H. North, *Simeon North: First Official Pistol Maker of the U.S.* (Concord, N.H.: Rumford Press, 1913), p. 64.

76. The Harpers Ferry Armory drew water power from the Potomac, a river with an average flow much larger than was needed. Repairs and replacement of the dam were a major expense that probably would have put the armory out of business had it been a private concern.

77. Robert B. Gordon, "Simeon North, John Hall, and Mechanized Manufacturing," *Technology and Culture* 30 (1989): 179–188.

78. Merritt Roe Smith, "John H. Hall, Simeon North, and the Milling Machine:

The Nature of Innovation Among Antebellum Arms Makers," *Technology and Culture* 14 (1973): 573–591.

79. Gordon, "Hydrological Science." A reconstruction of the water-power system at the Collins works in 1865 can be found in Robert B. Gordon, "Material Evidence of the Development of Metal Working Technology at the Collins Axe Factory," *IA, Journal of the Society for Industrial Archeology* 9 (1983): 19–28.

80. Matthew Roth, *Connecticut: An Inventory of Historic Engineering and Industrial Sites* (Washington, D.C.: Society for Industrial Archeology, 1981), p. 133.

81. Patrick M. Malone, Michael S. Raber, and Beth Parkhurst, "Historical and Archaeological Assessment: Valley Falls Heritage Park" (Report for the Town of Cumberland, Rhode Island, 1991).

82. David T. Gilbert, *Where Industry Failed: Water-Powered Mills at Harpers Ferry, West Virginia* (Charleston, W.Va.: Pictorial Histories, 1984).

83. Roth, *Connecticut,* p. 259. Additional examples, such as the village of Ashton, Rhode Island, are found in *Working Water: A Guide to the Historic Landscape of the Blackstone River Valley* (Providence: Rhode Island Department of Environmental Management, 1987). A number of these communities have survived with their textures largely intact.

84. An archaeological study of this site is in David R. Starbuck, "The Shaker Mills in Canterbury, New Hampshire," *IA, Journal of the Society for Industrial Archeology* 12 (1986): 11–37. Collinsville and Canterbury survive as examples of planned communities.

85. Hunter, *Waterpower,* p. 209. Chapters 5 and 6 cover water power in large industrial cities. For Paterson, see Russell Fries, "European vs. American Engineering: Pierre Charles L'Enfant and the Water Power System of Paterson, N.J.," *Northeast Historical Archaeology* 4 (1975): 68–96.

86. George F. Swain, "Report on the Water-Power of the Streams of Eastern New England," in Bureau of the Census, *Reports on the Water-Power of the United States,* vol. 16, pp. 75, 85, 129. We followed the census suggestions and used 73 percent efficiency to convert gross to net horsepower.

87. Patrick M. Malone, *Canals and Industry* (Lowell, Mass.: Lowell Museum, 1983).

88. John Coolidge, *Mill and Mansion* (New York: Russell & Russell, 1967), pp. 22–27.

89. Henry David Thoreau, *The Concord and the Merrimack* (New York: Bramhall House, 1954), p. 77. For a discussion of efforts to control the natural flow of the Merrimack and to use lakes as storage reservoirs, see Theodore Steinberg, *Nature Incorporated: Industrialization and the Waters of New England* (New York: Cambridge University Press, 1991).

90. Swain, "Report on the Water-Power," pp. 222–250.

91. Ibid., pp. 126–129; James L. Greenleaf, "Report on the Mississippi River and Some of Its Tributaries," in Bureau of the Census, *Reports on the Waterpower of the United States,* vol. 17, pp. 163–177; Hunter, *Waterpower,* pp. 222–250.

92. *Saint Anthony Falls Rediscovered* (Minneapolis: Minneapolis Riverfront Development Coordination Board, 1980), pp. 10–11.

93. Data compiled from *Statistics of Lowell Manufactures* (Lowell, Mass., 1835–); Malone, *Canals and Industry,* pp. 20–22.

94. See, for example, Anthony Wallace, *Rockdale* (New York: Knopf, 1978), pp. 217–218.

95. Rosenberg, *Perspectives in Technology,* p. 16.

96. The development of metal-milling technology is discussed in Smith, "John H. Hall, Simeon North, and the Milling Machine"; Edwin A. Battison, "Eli Whitney and the Milling Machine," *Smithsonian Journal of History* 1 (1966): 9–34; and Battison, "A New Look at the 'Whitney' Milling Machine," *Technology and Culture* 14 (1973): 592–598.

97. The construction of the Housatonic Dam was held up from 1838 to 1867 by concern for the shad fishery (James Leffel, *Construction of Mill Dams* [Springfield, Ohio: Leffel, 1881], chap. 9). See also Gary Kulik, "Dams, Fish, and Farmers: The Defense of Public Rights in Eighteenth-Century Rhode Island," in *The New England Working Class and the New Labor History,* ed. H. G. Gutman and Donald H. Bell (Urbana: University of Illinois Press, 1987), pp. 187–213, and Steinberg, *Nature Incorporated,* pp. 172–176, 193–204.

98. William H. Corbin, *Edward Clinton Terry, Ph. B.* (Hartford, Conn.: Louise E. Terry, 1943).

99. Francis L. Stanton, "The Use of Niagara Power," *Cassier's Magazine* 8 (1895): 173–192.

100. Mark Fram, ed., *Niagara: A Selective Guide to Industrial Archaeology in the Niagara Peninsula* (Toronto: Ontario Society for Industrial Archaeology, 1984), pp. 64–80; *Power from Niagara* (Ontario Hydro Booklet); exhibits in the Hydro Hall of Memory, now closed, at the Adam Beck location. The second plant above the falls on the Canadian side was built by Toronto Power Company from 1903 to 1906 and operated up to 1974. The handsome Beaux-Arts building would be a perfect location for a new museum of hydroelectric power.

101. *Niagara Falls Gazette,* 6 June 1976; "The Niagara Falls Power Company" (Niagara Falls Power Company, ca. 1924); Daniel Mead, *Water Power Engineering* (New York: McGraw-Hill, 1920), pp. 605–607.

102. Terry S. Reynolds, "The Soo Hydro: A Case Study of the Influence of Managerial and Topographical Constraints on Engineering Design," *IA, Journal of the Society for Industrial Archeology* 8 (1982): 37–56; Reynolds, *Sault Ste. Marie: A Project Report* (Washington, D.C.: Government Printing Office, 1982).

4

Coal, Canals, Railways, and Industrial Cities

During the decades after the 1820s, Americans reshaped the industrial landscape by gradually substituting coal for the wood and flowing water they were using as energy sources and iron for wood in structures and machinery. The amount of power they could obtain from wood or water at a given place was limited, but coal resources were so large that more was always available. Coal could be transported to distant consumers by the newly built canals and railways. With it, the resource constraints that had led entrepreneurs to favor small, dispersed mills and factories were less important.

Production of coal was concentrated in Pennsylvania in the first part of the nineteenth century. At first, the largest markets were in the East, and as long as the Appalachians were a barrier to shipment of bituminous coal from the West, the anthracite coalfields of eastern Pennsylvania remained the principal source of industrial fuel. Ironmasters using anthracite to smelt ore mined in eastern Pennsylvania dominated American ironmaking until the last quarter of the nineteenth century. Industrialists west of the Appalachians experimented with bituminous coal and with coal converted to coke. They built furnaces around Pittsburgh and Cincinnati (where rivers provided good access to coking coal), and then through Ohio, Indiana, and, eventually, Illinois. But it was in eastern Pennsylvania that artisans and entrepreneurs established many of the economic and social practices followed by American heavy industry well into the twentieth century.

Industries based on wood and water starkly contrasted with those based on coal and iron. Death and injury from mine accidents, social strife in mining communities, and environmental degradation from mine wastes were new costs of wealth created by the digging of anthracite. Because coal could

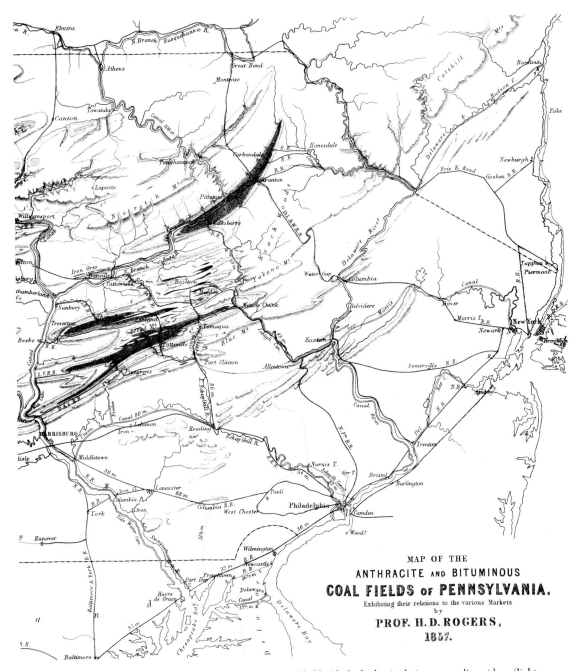

FIGURE 4.1. The anthracite coalfields (dark shading), their surrounding ridges (light shading), and the canal and railway routes used to deliver coal to distant consumers. In 1857, canals and railways shared the coal traffic. (From Henry D. Rogers, *The Geology of Pennsylvania* [Philadelphia: Lippincott, 1858], vol. 2, map follows p. 1018)

118

be hauled long distances and still be sold at a lower cost per unit of energy than locally cut wood, it could be shipped profitably to distant customers. They used it to make primary materials, such as iron, glass, and brick, and to convert these materials into finished, high-value-added goods. The social and environmental costs of getting the coal were left behind at the mines.

Mineral Fuel

Anthracite Coal

The anthracite coal in northeastern Pennsylvania was formed from plant remains buried under deep layers of sediment more than 100 million years ago. Subsequent erosion cut away the mountains and most of the coal, but some survived in basins protected by surrounding ridges of sandstone (Fig. 4.1). The water gaps cut into these ridges by a few large rivers, such as the Susquehanna and the Schuylkill, were the most economical routes to carry out the coal and were utilized by canal and, later, railroad builders.

The mountain-forming processes that created the coal basins also folded and faulted the coal veins in complex patterns that can be seen now in strip mines (Fig. 4.2). Where folded veins intersected the surface, early adventurers could extract coal without expensive equipment or previous knowledge of mining techniques. One such individual, Thomas Bedwell, learned what he knew about mining from an encyclopedia article.[1] Underground mining was more difficult, and it was often hard to know where and how deep to dig because there were few means of inferring the underground course of coal veins. Guesses could be made, but in places like the one shown in Figure 4.2, they were often wrong.[2]

Pennsylvanians began mining small amounts of anthracite for the use of local blacksmiths in the late eighteenth century, and shortly thereafter the Lehigh Coal Mine Company brought coal to Philadelphia to sell. At first, there was only a small market for it outside the forging and smithing trades because anthracite could not be burned without specially designed grates. As inventors developed these, more people used anthracite for heating buildings (from about 1815) and firing steamboat boilers (from about 1830). Ironmasters adapted both the blast and puddling furnaces to anthracite fuel by 1840. Thereafter, Americans used increasing amounts of anthracite until they shifted to petroleum and natural gas in the twentieth century.

Because the rivers passing through the water gaps in the coal basins were not deep enough for safe navigation, moving coal from the mines to urban markets was a chancy business at first. Beginning in 1822, the Lehigh Coal and Navigation Company first improved the river navigation on the Lehigh and then built a canal to move coal to the Delaware. Other entrepreneurs used the Schuylkill to bring coal to Philadelphia after 1825[3] (thereby touching off the first coal rush) and opened routes to New York and Albany through the Delaware and Hudson Canal in 1829, and to Baltimore via the North Branch Canal along the Susquehanna in 1831.[4] Railway owners subsequently captured much of the coal traffic, beginning with the Philadelphia and Reading in 1844 and the Lehigh Valley in 1855 (see Fig. 4.1).[5]

The first adventurers in the coalfields dug anthracite from easily worked, small quarries. At the Summit Hill Mine, where the Lehigh Coal and Navigation Company got its start, a fold of the Mammoth coal vein was close to the surface, and large-scale quarrying was easy. Where the coal veins had a

FIGURE 4.2. When modern miners dug this open-pit anthracite mine near Tamaqua, Pennsylvania, they cut through old, underground workings. The folded and faulted anthracite veins that had been mined from below in the nineteenth century can be seen on the far wall of the pit. The horizontal lines across the wall are benches spaced 40 feet apart. Miners drove motorized vehicles on them as they excavated the pit. The coal veins are dark and are partially obscured by loose rock and soil. The tops of the folds and several faults that offset the veins are visible. This pit is no longer in use and is gradually filling with water.

FIGURE 4.3. At the Baltimore Company mines in Wilkes Barre, Pennsylvania, miners dug coal by excavating rooms while leaving pillars of coal to support the roof. When this method of working was carried farther underground, the rooms were called breasts, and each breast became the workplace of one miner with one or more helpers. (From Henry D. Rogers, *The Geology of Pennsylvania* [Philadelphia: Lippincott, 1858], vol. 2, frontispiece)

gentle slope, miners followed them underground, leaving about half the coal in place to support the roof (Fig. 4.3). By 1830, most of the coal that could be easily quarried had been taken, and miners began driving drifts (horizontal tunnels) into veins exposed in the sides of ravines. Five years later, they were mining below the water table with the aid of steam-powered pumps.[6] Underground mining was initiated by inexperienced individuals who knew little about mine operation and by British immigrants who were confronting unfamiliar geological conditions. The mining practices and customs they established remained firmly in place for more than a hundred years and were the cause of many of the social and environmental costs of anthracite mining.

Because of the steep inclination of most anthracite veins, miners had to make a place for themselves to stand while they dug the coal. The rock above the coal veins was weak and liable to fall into the miner's work space unless the roof was supported by timber props. Mine operators had to provide for the continuous circulation of air throughout the mine, for the removal of water, and for the efficient transport of coal to the surface. In the system adopted in eastern Pennsylvania, miners dug coal out of the veins in rooms (called "breasts") separated by pillars of coal that, together with timber props, supported the mine roof. The breasts opened out from gangways, horizontal tunnels that provided access to the workings and routes for circulating air and hauling out the coal. Miners worked upward within a breast so that the loosened coal would fall to the gangways and also provide a place for them to stand (Fig. 4.4). In a large mine, the gangways and breasts made a complex, underground labyrinth. Americans had had little previous experience that would guide them in the design and operation of safe and efficient coal mines. They made serious mistakes, as at Avondale Mine; a fire in the

FIGURE 4.4. Diagram showing the method of mining coal from a steeply dipping vein by means of a gangway and breast. The miner and his helper reached the working face from the gangway by climbing up the manway. They blasted coal out of the vein overhead and kept enough loose coal in the breast to provide a footing that allowed them to reach the coal above them. (From H. M. Chance, *Mining Methods and Appliances Used in the Anthracite Coal Fields* [Harrisburg: Second Geological Survey, 1883], plate 21)

FIGURE 4.5. The breaker and shaft of the Kohinoor Colliery in Shenandoah, Pennsylvania, in the late nineteenth century. The head frame of the mine shaft is at the right. Coal lifted from the mine moved by gravity through the breaker, where it was crushed and passed through screens to select different sizes. Breaker boys picked slate and other rock out of it by hand. The breaker operator dumped the resulting waste into culm piles nearby. The sized coal was hauled away in railcars. Steam engines provided power for the mine hoist and the breaker. The building at the right of the head frame was the engine house. Because mine operators used large quantities of wood for mine timber, only a few trees remain on the hillside behind the mine. (Photograph by William Rau. Courtesy of Hugh Moore Historical Park and Museums)

shaft on September 6, 1869, trapped the miners below because the mine design provided for no alternative way out of the underground workings.[7]

Coal brought to the surface was prepared for the market by breaking it into lumps and picking out the slate that came up with it. Fine particles of coal and rock also had to be removed, since they blocked the flow of air through a coal fire, causing it to burn poorly. After 1844, coal was mechanically crushed in breakers and the slate in it picked out by youths (breaker boys) and disabled, older miners.[8] The breaker building and the waste heaps around it became the dominant surface features at an anthracite mine (Fig. 4.5).

ENVIRONMENTAL EFFECTS OF MINING ANTHRACITE UNDERGROUND

Coal mining changed the landscape in ways unlike anything previously seen in North America. Only about one-third of the coal in a vein was recovered in the breast-and-pillar system of mining; the rest was left underground or broken into particles too fine to sell.[9] Mine operators dumped culm, fine coal mixed with rock waste, in piles near the breaker; culm piles soon became prominent features of the landscape near underground anthracite mines. Only now, decades after mining ended, are stunted plants beginning to cover the culm piles.

Continuous pumping from a mine could lower the adjacent water table and cause neighboring wells to go dry. When the water table was depressed by pumping and the mine operation subsequently stopped, the resulting rise in groundwater could flood the basements of houses built near the mine. To prevent this, pumping would have to continue at worked-out mines for the indefinite future. The quality of water in streams and ponds in the mining districts was often degraded by water from the mines. Anthracite contains on average about 0.6 percent sulfur,[10] and underground mine workings often channeled groundwater over strata that contained sulfur. Water from mines was actually dilute sulfuric acid that destroyed life in the streams it entered. Rainwater flowing through culm piles also turned into dilute acid. Culm washed from the piles by rain often choked nearby streams.

Even when miners intended to leave adequate support for a mine roof, they were often uncertain about how much coal they had to leave in the pillars to maintain adequate support for the roof. Mine operators often began to rob the pillars after they had extracted from the breasts as much coal as they could safely take. Miners cut out the pillars in the distant parts of the mine and worked back toward the entrance as the roof gradually collapsed. This practice caused subsidence of the land above the mine (Fig. 4.6). Many nineteenth-century holders of coal lands marked out towns and sold building lots for houses while retaining the mineral rights to the land. They wrote deeds that released themselves from responsibility for any damages that might result when the coal was mined. Subsidence often occurred while mining was in progress, but it also might happen many years later, when the restrictive clauses in property deeds had been forgotten by house owners.[11]

In the past, culm piles were often set on fire by hot ashes thrown out from the mine engine houses. Today, underground mine workings above the water

RESULT OF A MINE CAVE

FIGURE 4.6. Mine subsidence in the anthracite region is shown in this postcard image from Pennsylvania. Subsidence resulted from the collapse of underground workings, which was often caused by robbing coal from the pillars that supported the mine roof. When entrepreneurs in the coal-mining regions sold building lots, they usually reserved the right to mine coal underneath the lots regardless of resulting damage. Subsidence might occur long after mine operations had ceased.

table are susceptible to fire because of the large amount of coal that was left in them. It is often impossible to seal all the openings of older mines—in many cases there are no records of where these openings are, particularly where bootleg mines were opened to take coal without paying royalties—so that extinguishing a fire by cutting off the air supply may be impossible. Residents started a fire in old mine workings under the village of Centralia, Pennsylvania, in 1962 when they burned trash in an abandoned strip mine that opened onto underground workings; the fire was still spreading in 1990.[12] Where the Centralia fire approached the surface, the ground became hot, vegetation was destroyed, and smoke and fumes were released (Fig. 4.7), calling to mind Ele Bowen's description of the Schuylkill coal basin in 1848: "jealous art has despoiled it . . . stripped the mountains of their gaudy foliage, and levelled the venerable and sturdy forest trees to the earth—with here and there one remaining, stripped of bark and branches—as if intended for monuments to their perished fellows."[13] Seepage of carbon monoxide into buildings in Centralia made many dwellings unsafe to occupy.

FIGURE 4.7. When this photograph was taken in 1988, an underground mine fire was burning just below the surface in this area immediately south of Centralia, Pennsylvania. Carbon monoxide and sulfur dioxide released at openings in the ground together with the heat from the fire have killed the trees.

Since federal and state mine officials saw no prospect of extinguishing the fire, they decided to relocate all those residents of Centralia who were willing to move, and then raze their homes.

MINING COMMUNITIES

The anthracite fields of eastern Pennsylvania were largely wilderness when the first adventurers in the coal trade arrived.[14] The Lehigh Coal Mine Company acquired 8,665 acres of "unlocated" land in the 1790s.[15] Then,

FIGURE 4.8. St. Nicholas, Pennsylvania, a mine patch in the shadow of a coal breaker built in the early 1930s, survives little changed today because it is surrounded by highway embankments and rail yards on two sides.

Philadelphians who had made money in commerce, such as the Carey and Wetherill families, began to buy large blocks; Stephen Girard purchased 30,000 acres at auction from the First Bank of the United States in 1830.[16] Most of the coal land of the Schuylkill district was bought up during the coal rush of 1829 with the intention of monopolistic control of the coal trade.[17]

Mines were first opened at outcrops of coal veins, which were numerous, dispersed, and often small. The miners lived in "patches" that grew or withered as the fortunes of their associated mines waxed or waned. Proprietors of the coal tracts sold lots for homes set out in a rectangular grid pattern, the plan of many coal-district towns today. Visitors can experience some aspects of a nineteenth-century anthracite miner's patch at the Eckley State Historic Site in Pennsylvania. Here houses are arranged in regular rows along two parallel streets, with the residences of the manager and mine supervisors at one end. The open space around each dwelling provided land for large gardens. St. Nicholas is the remnant of a one-street mining patch located between a breaker and adjacent rail yards (Fig. 4.8). The tough and gritty character of this community has resisted the twentieth-century intrusion of highway embankments that have all but walled in the dwellings and the church that remain under the shadow of the breaker.

The mine communities were isolated from the neighboring agricultural areas by the high ridges surrounding the coal basins. The owners of the routes through the water gaps in these ridges controlled the only economical means of moving coal out and manufactured goods in. By 1901, railroads, the successors to the canal companies, controlled all but 4 percent of the area of the anthracite coal lands.[18] Because there was little iron ore associated with the coal, few ironworks were established within the anthracite districts. The only other industries attracted to the mining patches and villages were the silk mills that employed the female relatives of coal miners. It was only in the larger towns and cities that entrepreneurs were able to create a more diversified industrial base.

Anthracite miners and their families bore the costs of death, injury, and debilitation as coal was extracted. Environmental damage was also evident in the nineteenth century, but was then considered an unavoidable consequence rather than a cost that should be included in the price of coal. These human and environmental costs (Fig. 4.9) were for the most part ignored outside the mining communities because of their geographical isolation, which kept the patches out of the direct purview of industrial and political

FIGURE 4.9. Coal hauled to industrial centers by rail contributed to the creation of wealth in manufacturing and provided cheap fuel for heating homes and workplaces; the environmental and social costs remained largely in the mining districts. This picture shows how difficult it is to present the context of coal mining in museums. (Courtesy of Hugh Moore Historical Park and Museums)

officials; the extensive holdings of land by a few absentee landlords, who left the management of their property in the hands of agents; the political power of the anthracite and railroad interests; and the transport of coal by canal and railway to distant users, who were spared the indirect costs of mining.

SILK MILLS IN EASTERN PENNSYLVANIA

The commanding physical presence in most mining communities was the coal breaker, where the sons in mining families labored as breaker boys. Traveling through the region today, we see decaying breakers, but there are also brick or wood factory buildings in many of the towns, even in relatively small and isolated mining patches where their presence seems strangely out of place, evidence of an industry that has received less attention from historians than anthracite mining.

During the widely publicized 1903 hearings of a presidential commission on labor unrest in northeastern Pennsylvania, Clarence Darrow asked: "Is there any man so blind that he does not know why the anthracite region is dotted with silk mills? Why are they not on the prairies of the West? Why are they not somewhere else?"[19] The silk mills were there, the famous lawyer and social reformer went on to explain, "because the miners were there," with large families and inadequate incomes. The boys went into the breakers, and the girls went into the mills to supplement the wages of the coal miners. The silk industry was an opportunistic transplant from less hospitable communities with higher labor costs, and it took root quickly in the landscape of anthracite mining.

In 1870, Paterson, New Jersey, was the largest producer of silk in the United States. Skilled workers, many of whom had come from Europe to work in Paterson's mills, made up a large part of the labor force. As mechanization of silk making reduced the need for operatives' skills, the manufacturers tried to cut costs and expand the industry. It was difficult to reduce wages and speed up machine operations in a city with Paterson's reputation for labor militancy, but northeastern Pennsylvania offered much cheaper labor and minimal regulation. Communities such as Hazelton, Pennsylvania, campaigned aggressively to attract silk mills. The silk industry was well established in the anthracite region by the 1880s and growing rapidly. After Paterson's bitter silk strike of 1913, Pennsylvania quickly became the number-one state in silk production.[20]

Many families needed the income that working daughters could provide, and there were few opportunities for girls or young women in mining towns. Pennsylvania, home of the breaker boys, had some of the weakest child-labor and child-education laws in the nation; enforcement of these regulations was notoriously lax. Even very young girls worked in the mills, many of which ran both day and night shifts.[21] An article in *McClure's* in 1903 commented on the makeup of the work force and the location of the typical mill:

> Sometimes in a mining town, sometimes in a remote part of the coal fields, one comes across a large substantial building of wood or brick. When the six o'clock whistle blows, its front door is opened, and out streams a procession of girls. Some of them are apparently seventeen or eighteen years old, the majority are from thirteen to sixteen, but quite a number would seem to be considerably less than thirteen. Such a building is one of the knitting mills or silk factories that during the last ten years have come into Anthracite.[22]

The local availability of inexpensive fuel for steam boilers was another inducement for silk mills to locate in the anthracite region. Machinery tended by the daughters of mining families was driven with energy from some of the anthracite extracted by their fathers and brothers. Steam power, which was largely responsible for the heavy concentration of late-nineteenth-century manufacturing in urban areas, in this case helped to promote the diffusion of factory production into rural areas of northeastern Pennsylvania.

Just as silk manufacturers had moved from New Jersey to Pennsylvania seeking cheaper and more docile labor, so did they desert the anthracite region as its silk workers began to demand better treatment. Pennsylvania's child-labor laws had finally become more effective by the 1940s. The decline in anthracite production after World War I eventually forced large numbers of miners and their families to move away from the anthracite towns, reducing the pool of young women who were willing to work in local mills. In the 1920s, silk mills began to close in Pennsylvania, while new ones opened in the South. In addition to the competition from southern silk mills, there was a sharp drop in the national demand for silk because of the introduction of rayon. Synthetic fabrics were made in Pennsylvania, but it was usually more profitable for manufacturers to set up new rayon mills in the South and to hire inexperienced workers from depressed agricultural areas. Today only a few silk or rayon mills are operating in Pennsylvania or, for that matter, in the southern states. The cheap labor is now overseas.[23]

Bituminous Coal

Miners began shipping fuel from the small field of bituminous, or soft, coal on the James River just west of Richmond, Virginia, to ports on the east coast during the eighteenth century. Although the interruption of this supply during the War of 1812 helped create a market for Pennsylvania anthracite, by 1818 Virginians were lifting coal from seams 350 feet deep and pumping water from their mines with a Bolton & Watt steam engine.[24]

American entrepreneurs opened the large bituminous coalfields west of the Appalachian mountains in the late eighteenth century. They were moving soft coal down the Monongahela River on flatboats in 1789 and on to Cincinnati by way of the Ohio by 1793. Travelers commented on the pall of coal smoke that hung over Pittsburgh as early as 1808. Little soft coal was carried east until later in the century, but much was moved north and west with the completion of the canals from Pittsburgh to Erie (1834) and Akron (1838).[25]

Unlike the anthracite coal veins, the soft coal seams were nearly horizontal and did not ordinarily crop out at the surface. However, the edges of bituminous seams were often exposed in the deep valleys cut by rivers into the Appalachian plateau. Miners dug this coal by the room-and-pillar system (analogous to the breasts used in anthracite mining) and loaded it directly on boats destined for Pittsburgh, Cincinnati, or other downriver towns. When they could not reach the coal from a stream bank, they sank shafts and hoisted the coal to the surface, where it was screened and loaded from tipples into railway cars.[26] Miners encountered problems with safe operation and inadequate supervision of underground bituminous mines similar to those faced in the anthracite regions, but while anthracite mining remained largely hand work, the horizontal nature of veins of soft coal made mining operations easier to mechanize. Mechanical mining appliances eased some of the manual labor of undercutting and loading coal but created new hazards, such as increased concentrations of dust. Because of the adversarial climate that developed between miners and managers in the early years of their industry, it was difficult for the two factions to cooperate to find methods of organizing mine work that would improve both safety and productivity.[27]

In western Pennsylvania, Maryland, and West Virginia, where coal was often mined from seams exposed on the walls of narrow valleys, a mining community, mine machinery, and a railway were likely to be crowded together in the valley bottom. Towns such as Thurmond, West Virginia, often had a sinuous plan following natural valley contours instead of the rectangular grid layout common in the anthracite districts. Where valleys were particularly narrow, there was little space to pile mine waste.[28] Other environmental problems at bituminous coal mines were similar to those encountered with anthracite. The severe environmental impact of strip-mining on the Appalachian plateau has been well publicized, but, as in the anthracite districts, continued effects of the release of acid water into streams from abandoned underground mines has attracted less attention. Water seeps into most coal mines, and the flow can be considerable where mining and coal removal have collapsed overlying strata and disrupted aquifers. The National Coal Association admits that "it is unlikely that acid mine drainage will ever be totally avoided."[29]

Users of bituminous coal often wanted it in purified form (coke), while anthracite was always burned as raw coal. Coke ovens were a feature of the landscape not seen in the East but common in areas such as Fayette County, Pennsylvania, from 1850 onward. Until the twentieth century, most coke in the United States was made in beehive ovens—domed, circular firebrick structures about 12 feet in diameter with a vent at the top. They were arranged in long banks, usually near the mine that supplied the coal. Each oven was charged with 5 to 7 tons of coal that was ignited and allowed to burn with a small airflow until its volatile constituents were driven off. Smoke and fumes were vented directly into the atmosphere and became a major nuisance in places such as Birmingham, Alabama, where the coke works were within the city. The landscape of coke making can be seen at the site of the Elkin Coal & Coke Company near Masontown, West Virginia, now on the National Register of Historic Places. The remains of 140 beehive ovens built of stone and brick stretch in long lines over 36 acres.[30] Only a few ovens, hidden in dense vines, have survived in the most famous coke district of all, Connellsville, Pennsylvania. A historic marker by the roadside directs the reader's attention to a large group of coke ovens and explains their historic significance, but nothing is there—only a cleared area, the tracks of bulldozers, and surveying markers for a commercial development.

Transportation

Coal at the mine was of little value unless customers had easy access to it, through either proximity or efficient transportation. Few industries migrated to the coalfields. Instead, coalfield entrepreneurs invested in new transportation systems that could deliver coal to consumers at prices low enough to be competitive with those of other sources of energy. First, they built a network of canals; later, their railroads carried most of the coal trade. Many bituminous coal mines in western Pennsylvania and West Virginia were on waterways such as the Monongahela River, along which coal could be moved to nearby industrial users or to the Ohio River. These river valleys were also convenient routes for railways. Coal mining, ironmaking, and the railways were economically linked because the rail network that hauled the coal was made of iron smelted and refined with coal fuel.

Bulk Transportation

Before they built canals and railways, Americans found it difficult and costly to move bulk commodities except in boats along the coast and navigable rivers. The limitations of overland haulage are shown by the load that a single horse could draw in different modes of transportation (Table 4.1).

TABLE 4.1 Load Drawn by a Single Horse

Method	Ton
Average packhorse load	0.1
Wagon on a dirt road	0.6
Wagon on a macadam road*	2
Wagon on iron rails	8
Barge on river	30
Barge on canal	50

*A macadam road was made of well-compacted broken stone, small on top and larger below. For a discussion of the development and technology of the macadam system of constructing roads, see W. J. Reader, *Macadam: The McAdam Family and the Turnpike Roads, 1798–1861* (London: Heinemann, 1980).

Source: L.T.C. Rolt, *Navigable Waterways* (London: Longman, 1969), p. 1.

Interest in canal building grew in the early nineteenth century as Americans created the political, intellectual, and financial organizations needed to undertake large civil works. Canals cost more to build and operate than did roads but had a much greater carrying capacity because, while the speeds of canal boats and road vehicles were about the same, much heavier loads could be drawn along a canal. Canals were risky investments in North America, and if traffic did not reach the level expected, their owners could be quickly ruined. Americans had a substantial canal network in place by 1830, and more routes were under construction. Beginning with the Baltimore and Ohio Railroad in 1829, the proprietors of railways began to compete for passenger and, later, freight traffic. Railroad operators had the decisive advantage of all-weather operation. Canals in the northern states, where most industrial activity was concentrated, were closed by ice for about a third of every year, suffered diminished carrying capacity during periods of dry weather, and were often damaged by floods. Railway operations were little influenced by cold or drought and were less vulnerable to high water than canals. They could make inexpensive spur connections right into mill yards, and the introduction and general adoption of standard gauge enabled interconnections to be made without reloading. Canal boat and lock sizes were never standardized.

Transportation by canal and railway made it economical for industrialists to use natural resources from distant places. As entrepreneurs located factories well away from their sources of raw materials, the environmental costs of primary production, such as deforestation and the accumulation of mine wastes, were left behind for others to deal with. As they concentrated factories in cities served by canals and railways, they began to deindustrialize the countryside.

To keep a canal filled with water at the correct elevation, its builders had to maintain accurate levels over long distances, a skill less important in road building. Attempts by enthusiastic but inexperienced Americans to design canals and, later, railways often led to difficulties. Experienced civil engineers were needed; some were recruited from Europe, some learned on the job, and others came from West Point (founded in 1802) or private schools such as Rensselaer Polytechnic Institute (founded in 1824).[31] While engineers in the early years of the republic were gaining experience with construction technology, they also had to keep up with new sciences, such as hydrology, that were just being developed. Engineers designing civil works broadened the intellectual life of Americans through their interest in the application of natural science and architecture to practical ends.

Canals

Americans made two principal kinds of inland waterways in the nineteenth century. They "improved" rivers in various ways to make them navigable for boats, barges, or rafts, and they built canals. River "navigations" were particularly successful on the main rivers and major tributaries of the Ohio and Mississippi systems. In general, canals were entirely new watercourses, although a few like the Blackstone Canal used stretches of navigable river for parts of their route. Canals were popular in the industrialized East, where most linked interior areas to tidewater, and in the Midwest, where they usually connected the Ohio River valley with the Great Lakes. One canal, the Pennsylvania Main Line, brought boats across the Appalachians by carrying them part of the way on the Allegheny Portage Railroad. Another, the famous Erie Canal, stretched from the Hudson River to Lake Erie.

Canal builders aimed to make an almost level channel having minimal current and wide and deep enough for canal boats to pass freely. In the nineteenth century, mules or horses walking on an adjacent towpath hauled the canal boats (Fig. 4.10). Boats were shifted from one level to another with locks or incline planes, a process that will be described in the next section. A nearly level ditch filled with water ran between the locks or planes. Canal builders could avoid locks and planes, which were expensive, by following the natural contours of the land, but in hilly terrain it was necessary to build a sinuous path through the valleys, resulting in longer canals. Lengthy sections of many canals paralleled rivers that meandered through the landscape. The original Erie Canal used 363 miles of ditch to traverse 290 route miles.[32] If enough capital was available, canal builders could avoid some changes in elevation by piercing hills with tunnels and crossing valleys with aqueducts.

FIGURE 4.10. The Delaware Canal at Narrowsville, Pennsylvania, about 1915. Mules on the towpath are pulling empty coal barges belonging to the Lehigh Coal and Navigation Company on the return trip from Philadelphia. The wharf of a small community beside the canal and a covered bridge crossing the canal are visible in the background. Beyond the towpath is the Delaware River. (Courtesy of the Pennsylvania State Archives)

Canal engineers often found that providing enough water to keep the canal ditch filled and operate the locks was their most vexatious problem. Some early canals were so badly made that when completed, they could not be filled because water seeped out faster than it could be supplied by flow down the canal channel.[33] Even a well-made canal lost 5 to 10 inches of water a day through evaporation and seepage. This had to be made up by a flow of water along the channel from feeder inlets. All canals needed a reliable supply of water at their highest points. In the early years, American designers often failed to slope the canal ditch enough to provide an adequate flow of water. Inaccurate (usually overly optimistic) estimates of the amount of water available from streams and reservoirs as well as poor design or construction of canal banks caused difficulties in operating many canals (Fig. 4.11).[34]

FIGURE 4.11. The North Branch Canal near Beach Haven, Pennsylvania, about 1880. The canal boats grounded when this section of the canal was drained for emergency repairs to the bank. The Susquehanna River is to the right of the towpath; to the left, houses and trees of a small town are adjacent to the canal. (Courtesy of Hugh Moore Historical Park and Museums)

LOCKS, PLANES, AND AQUEDUCTS

To move a boat from one level to another, a lock tender used the weight of water to change the level in a lock chamber that was fitted with gates at either end. (This operation is described briefly in Fig. 4.12.) Incline planes were used on some canals, such as the Morris Canal in New Jersey, as an alternative to locks. Boats were floated onto cradles fitted with wheels running on rails and drawn along the incline by cables. By operating the cradles in tandem, the weight of the ascending boat was balanced by that of a descending one. Waterwheels or turbines running on water drawn from the canal itself often powered the incline.

Because the length and width of the lock chambers or plane carriages limited the size of boat that could pass through a canal, designers faced a difficult decision in balancing the higher initial cost and increased water consumption of larger locks against the revenue to be gained in the future from larger boats. It was difficult to design a canal that was well adapted to both the economy in which it was to operate and the landscape it was to traverse. Owners of many successful canals often found that they had to enlarge their locks (and often their channel as well) to achieve a profitable volume of traffic. Poor designs ruined many canal investors.

Crossing a river on an aqueduct in a horse-drawn canal boat would have been a novel sensation for travelers in the early nineteenth century. Major aqueducts attracted popular attention and were often selected as symbols of engineering achievement to illustrate canal-company documents. The Chesapeake and Ohio Canal, promoted as a Grand National Project, used carefully constructed stone aqueducts (Fig. 4.13), but most proprietors were more concerned with economical operation than with grandeur and settled for more utilitarian designs, such as a timber trough supported on masonry piers. A unique covered timber-bridge aqueduct is in service for tour boats on the Whitewater Canal in Metamora, Indiana, and a rebuilt timber trough supported by original masonry piers can be seen on the Enfield Canal in Windsor Locks, Connecticut.

The aqueduct over the Delaware River at Lackawaxen, Pennsylvania,

FIGURE 4.12. Lock No. 9 on the Muskingum River Improvement in Philo, Ohio. To allow a boat to enter the lock from upstream, the lock tender opens valves to admit water to the chamber until the elevation of the water in the chamber matches that of the slack water behind the dam. The upstream gate is then opened to admit the boat. After closing the gate, the tender opens valves to lower the water level to that of the downstream section of the canal, and then opens the second gate to allow the boat to exit. He reverses the procedure to raise a boat from the downstream to the upstream level. In this case, he opens valves to flood the lock, and the rising water inside it lifts the boat.

FIGURE 4.13. The Monocacy Aqueduct on the Chesapeake and Ohio Canal in Maryland near the point where the Monocacy River enters the Potomac River. This 438-foot-long aqueduct was built between 1829 and 1833. The designers intended to use a locally available red sandstone for the structure, but when it proved to be of indifferent quality, they substituted white granite for some of the sandstone. The aqueduct was dewatered when operation of the canal ended in 1924. The six piers are set on bedrock, and the arches have 54-foot spans. The canal prism is 18.5 feet wide at the bottom and 19.5 feet at the top; the water depth was 6 feet. Part of the top of the aqueduct was swept away in a flood in 1971, but the National Park Service stabilized the structure and it now carries a bicycle path over the Monocacy River. (Courtesy of the Smithsonian Institution)

now a National Historic Landmark, illustrates engineering sophistication in an unadorned design. Before 1849, boats moving anthracite along the Delaware and Hudson Canal had to be pulled across the Delaware River in a slack-water pool created by a low dam. Because floods and collisions with timber rafts being floated down the Delaware impeded the coal traffic, the canal company engaged John Roebling to design a suspension aqueduct similar to one he had recently completed near Pittsburgh. The company chose Roebling's design because it required only three piers in the river instead of the five that would have been needed for a conventional pier-and-trough aqueduct. The flexibility of suspension road bridges often caused difficulties and, with a few exceptions, made them impractical for railways, but this design worked well for the aqueduct because the load on the cables was not increased by the passage of boats and the stiffness of the wooden trough prevented flexing. When the canal was closed in 1898, a new owner used the dewatered aqueduct as a toll bridge. The passage of vehicles imposed live loads on the structure that it had not been designed for, and this problem was exacerbated by removal of the aqueduct trunk in 1930. The cables became worn from sliding over the saddles on the tops of the piers, and when the National Park Service acquired the aqueduct in 1980, repairs were needed. The restorers kept the appearance of the original aqueduct (Fig. 4.14) but, since it is still a highway bridge, modified the structure by building a large, dead load into the roadway to simulate the weight of the water that would have been in the trough. By making the dead weight large compared with the weight of the crossing vehicles, the designers reduced

FIGURE 4.14. A view of the Delaware Aqueduct, Lackawaxen, Pennsylvania, from the southwest. This photograph, taken in 1989, shows the National Park Service's reconstruction of John Roebling's aqueduct as a bridge for vehicles. (For a view of the original aqueduct in service, see H. J. Magaziner, "The Rebirth of an Engineering Landmark," *APT Bulletin* 18 [1986]: 52.) (Photograph by Jet Lowe. Courtesy of the Historic American Engineering Record, HAER No. PA-1)

flexing enough that the original Roebling cables could still be used. The reconstruction is a sensitive balance in providing a vehicular bridge at Lackawaxen and preserving and interpreting an important cultural resource.[35]

LANDSCAPE AND COMMUNITIES

Travelers on canals proceeded at the walking speed of a horse or mule and, when self-propelled boats appeared, still had to move slowly to avoid damaging the canal banks with waves. Since a boat was never far from the towpath, canal travelers were not separated from the adjacent countryside by either speed or distance; the landscape with its farms, industries, and communities passed slowly and in full view. Compared with the pace of travel familiar to us, canal passages appear to have been tranquil, although this is partly because a canal that no longer carries commercial traffic does not have the congestion and confusion that formerly existed at heavily used locks and planes.

A new canal was not always welcomed by its neighbors. To many, it was a long barrier that could not be crossed conveniently, much like a limited-access highway today. The bridge needed at every canal crossing was an additional expense for the canal proprietors. A bridge high enough to allow canal boats to pass underneath often had steep approach grades that were difficult to negotiate with a loaded farm wagon. There were no grades at drawbridges, but they were an inconvenience to both land and canal traffic when used frequently. Groundwater levels and runoff patterns were likely to be changed by diversion of water into a canal and by its release through seepage along the canal route, perhaps creating wetlands where none existed before. Water pouring from breached canal banks could flood neighboring fields or homes. Canal construction carried the promise of benefits to landowners who could anticipate a rise in values near terminal basins and of loss to others whose water privileges were diminished or whose property was transected. As the first extended intrusion of a built environment in North America, canal construction created conflicts that existing social institutions were ill prepared to deal with. Many felt themselves injured by canal building and sometimes expressed their hostility by suing canal owners or by piercing canal banks, dumping loads of stone into the canal by night, or committing other acts of vandalism.[36]

Opportunities for trade arose as boats waited to pass locks or planes. Store- and tavern keepers often set up nearby—there are many examples along the Chesapeake and Ohio Canal, such as the tavern at Great Falls National Park, Maryland—and some of these clusters of businesses grew into communities. They prospered by providing services to canal travelers or through industries along the canal that could send and receive goods directly by boats and, sometimes, draw water from the canal for power. In these communities, there was often a line of factories and warehouses bordering the canal, with commercial districts and then residences spreading outward from the central artery. Danville, Pennsylvania, was a small market town when the North Branch Canal along the Susquehanna River reached it in 1831. Warehouses were built along the canal, creating a new commercial center; these were followed by ironworks that used the canal to receive coal and to ship out finished products. Curiously, the Montour Iron Works, for a time the largest maker of iron rail in the United States, dispatched all its rails on the canal until 1853; the canal facilitated the expansion of its archrival just as in the 1950s some railways earned profits for a few years by hauling construction materials for the interstate-highway system. Danville industries soon stretched in a line along the canal (Fig. 4.15). Today only traces of the canal remain and many of the industries are gone, but the layout of the town based on the canal still dominates the geography of Danville.

WATER POWER

On the Morris Canal, wheels driven by water from the canal powered the wire cables that hauled boats between levels at some inclined planes.[37] One of the Morris Canal turbines that replaced overshot waterwheels for this job has been restored in its original wheel pit at plane nine west, near Phillipsburg, New Jersey.[38] Proprietors of transportation canals often found that they could sell water for power. They might draw water out of a canal above a lock and run it to a mill or factory that would then discharge it back into the canal below the lock.

More often, the canal served as a raceway taking water from a river to a mill, which then returned it to the river. A canal that relied on locks to change levels might remain at an upper elevation, while a nearby river dropped significantly through rapids or falls. A mill could be placed anywhere the difference in water level between the canal and the river was great enough to operate a waterwheel. The mill would draw water from the man-made waterway, drop it through a waterwheel, and return it to the river through a tailrace. Good examples of this arrangement survive along the Enfield Canal in Windsor Locks, Connecticut, and in Richmond, Virginia, where the Confederacy's famous Tredegar Iron Works drew power from the James River and Kanawha Canal.[39] Canal historians, fascinated by the romance of canal boats and the mechanical ingenuity of locks, have often ignored the value of transportation canals as sources of power for manufacturing.

The biggest problem for canals with dual functions was ensuring that there was enough water to supply the demands of manufacturing operations. A lesser problem was excessive current created by supplying those de-

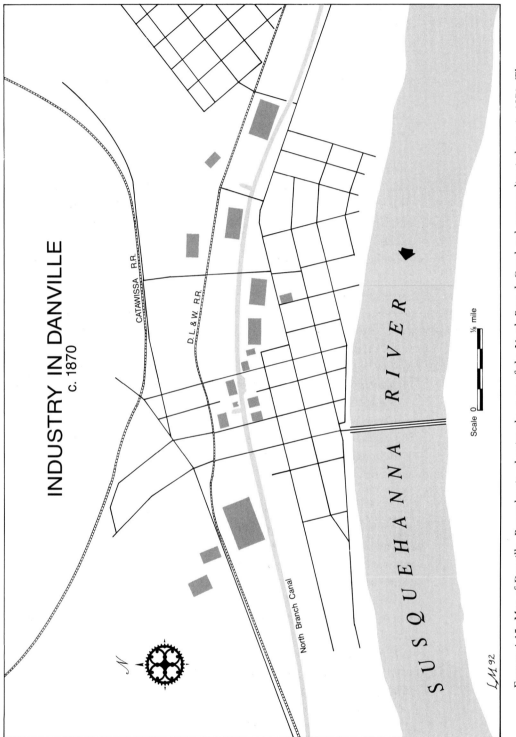

INDUSTRY IN DANVILLE
c. 1870

CATAWISSA R.R.

D. L. & W. R.R.

North Branch Canal

S U S Q U E H A N N A R I V E R

Scale 0   ⅛ mile

LM 92

FIGURE 4.15. Map of Danville, Pennsylvania, showing the route of the North Branch Canal and surrounding industry in 1870. The first railroad reached the town in 1853, twenty-two years after the completion of the canal. (Map by Lyn Malone)

mands.[40] Visitors to the National Park Service's waterborne interpretive programs on the Lowell Canal System, which is still producing electrical power as well as attracting tourism, get a sense of the effects of current in a canal. As long as mills on a canal did not demand too much water, the current in the canal would remain low enough for mule-drawn boat traffic. A well-designed canal with a cross-sectional area of sufficient size could be both a feeder for water-powered mills and a man-made channel for transportation.

ABANDONMENT

When they could no longer haul goods profitably on their canals, some proprietors sold water to adjacent factories or transferred ownership to manufacturers. Others abandoned their canals. The ditches might then dry out or, less frequently, remain watered as long, stagnant ponds. Aqueducts carrying canals across streams were subject to flood damage and to deterioration when not maintained, while abandoned lock chambers were often robbed for building materials.[41] The Chesapeake and Ohio Canal is an exception to the usual fate of abandoned waterways. It follows the Potomac River between Washington, D.C., and Cumberland, Maryland, and the towpath for its entire 184-mile length has been made into a national historic park. A few sections of the canal remain watered.

Disused canal ditches and basins in urban areas were frequently filled to create additional land for industrial or commercial use, causing a corresponding diminution of open space. The idea that a watercourse through a city added open space with an attractive texture arose after many canal routes had been destroyed; where they have survived, canal districts are often desirable places for redevelopment, as in Georgetown in Washington, D.C.

Navigations

An inland navigation is a modification of an existing river, stream, or lake made to facilitate boat or barge traffic. The projectors of a navigation might deepen shallows or clear obstructions from the natural channel of a river, or they might build locks and short canals around rapids. George Washington and his fellow proprietors of the Potomac Company used both of these techniques in their attempt to open the river to trade from the West and make the nation's capital a commercial center. Government agencies, such as the U.S. Army Corps of Engineers, had the resources to make slack-water navigation systems by building dams to create successive pools along the length of major rivers.[42]

The history of the Ohio–Mississippi waterway, one of the largest navigations in the United States, is particularly important because its development set the pattern of river management in the West that continues today. By 1820, the United States had acquired all of the Mississippi River, and in 1824 Congress made the first of many appropriations for navigational improvements. Continuing problems with property damage due to flooding and with obstructions to navigation prompted Congress to commission studies of the Mississippi. The authors of two of these reports opened a long-continuing debate over national policy for the management of the western rivers. In 1849, Charles Ellet, Jr., had on his own initiative prepared a plan for maintaining a 5-foot depth for navigation throughout the Ohio River by release of water from reservoirs on tributary streams rather than by dikes and levees. The next year, Congress commissioned two independent surveys of the Mississippi, one by Ellet and the other by A. A. Humphreys of the Army Corps of Engineers. Ellet's plan called for levees south of the mouth of the Red River, a floodway (alternative channel for flood waters) along the Atchafalaya River, and a system of holding reservoirs upstream. Humphreys's plan, developed between 1857 and 1861 in collaboration with H. L. Abbot, proposed construction of levees along the length of the Mississippi below Cairo, Illinois.

In a general way, Ellet proposed using the forces of nature to maintain an open channel for navigation while limiting the magnitude of floods by reservoirs and natural spillways; Humphreys proposed confining the river between levees and creating an artificial channel. The Corps of Engineers, with Humphreys at its head, vigorously promoted the levees-only policy in the face of contrary views originating outside the official establishment. Humphreys published a rebuttal of Ellet's plans in the *Report on the Physics and Hydraulics of the Mississippi River,* in which he claimed the discovery of new scientific laws for the transport of sediment by rivers. These laws have not stood the test of time, but the invocation of the authority of science by Humphreys helped convince Congress of the desirability of the Corps of Engineers' plans. The federal government adopted Humphreys's levees-only design for the lower Mississippi as well as the Corps' navigation plan for the Ohio based on a lock-and-dam system. Ellet had also opposed the construction of locks and dams on the Ohio; he thought that they would slow river traffic and would make flood conditions worse by obstructing the river channel. Among others who challenged Humphreys and the Corps of Engineers was James B. Eads (the builder of the famous St. Louis bridge). In 1879, Eads proved that he could keep the mouth of the Mississippi open to navigation by directing the natural erosive power of the river with jetties, a plan that Humphreys had denounced as unworkable. Nevertheless, the power of bureaucracy prevailed in subsequent policy concerning the Mississippi and Ohio rivers.

Once the commitment to levees was made, irreversible changes in the landscape were inevitable. Sediment formerly deposited over the Mississippi River floodplain by frequent flooding was carried to the Gulf of Mexico. It no longer compensated for the naturally occurring subsidence that lowered the land. In addition, the capacity of swamps and bayous to store floodwater was lost as they were cut off from the river by the levees; more water came down the Mississippi in rainy seasons than had before the construction of the levees. Consequently, the levees had to be rebuilt repeatedly and ever higher. This policy created projects for the Corps of Engineers and its contractors, but it also established both the potential for catastrophic destruction if the levees were breached and continuing problems with local drainage. In places like New Orleans, the river's surface is higher than the city's streets.[43]

Mark Twain, who earned a pilot's license on Mississippi steamboats before the Civil War, had little faith in the ability of engineers to control the Mississippi:

> One who knows the Mississippi will promptly aver—not aloud but to himself—that ten thousand Mississippi River Commissions, with the mines of the world at their back, cannot tame that lawless stream, cannot curb it, or confine it, cannot say to it, "Go here," or "Go there," and make it obey; cannot save a shore which it has sentenced; cannot bar its path with an obstruction which it will not tear down, dance over, and laugh at. But a discreet man will not put these things into spoken words; for the West Point engineers have not their superiors anywhere; they know all that can be known of their abstruse science; and so, since they conceive that they can fetter and handcuff that river and boss him, it is but wisdom for the unscientific man to keep still, lie low, and wait till they do it.[44]

A view of the Mississippi River in southeastern Missouri during the flood of 1973 shows that Twain's view was closer to the mark than Humphreys's (Fig. 4.16).

Between 1878 and 1929, the Army Corps of Engineers converted the entire Ohio River to a navigation with the construction of fifty dams that had movable gates or weirs. The gates of a dam (and thus its pool) were raised during periods of low flow, when an adjacent lock provided for the passage of vessels. The government's engineers also improved navigation on the Mississippi above Alton, Illinois, with locks and dams. A long-term project to replace the older locks and dams on the Ohio River with nineteen larger locks and higher dams has been under way since the 1950s. At Louisville, Kentucky, site of the greatest drop in the river, three generations of locks remain in place. The creation of slack-water pools along the Ohio has not altered the river landscape as drastically as the levees have on the lower Mississippi.[45]

FIGURE 4.16. The Mississippi River flooding part of southeastern Missouri in 1973. The protective levee running through this aerial photograph has failed to hold back the exceptionally high water.

Railways

A railway, like a canal, carries heavy vehicles along a dedicated route. A canal uses a cushion of water to reduce resistance to the motion of the vehicle; a railway uses the low friction of a metal wheel rolling on a metal rail. The wheel-and-rail combination does not reduce friction as much as the water cushion does (Table 4.1), but it is not stopped by frost or drought, and trains can run at much higher speed than a canal boat. Railway speed is limited not by the formation of waves, as in a canal, but by the much lower resistance of air passing the cars. English railway builders used iron rails placed on stone blocks. Americans found this design too expensive, but their attempts to build track with wood covered with iron straps quickly proved to be misguided, and they turned to iron rail.[46] Railway, coal, and iron enterprises soon became intimately intertwined.

It is easiest to move traffic over a railway when the route has low grades and gentle curves. Railway designers had to balance the heavy cost of building tunnels, bridges, cuts, and fills against the benefits these improvements would make in the subsequent operation of the line. Choices made by nineteenth-century designers still determine the usefulness of many American railways. Where a route was constructed with sharp curves and heavy grades to minimize the initial investment and the surrounding land subsequently became urban, route improvements needed to make high-speed railway operation possible are often too costly to undertake.

LANDSCAPE

A line of railway is a linear barrier, but, unlike a canal, it can be crossed at grade (with precautions about oncoming traffic).[47] A heavily used highway creates nearly continuous noise, while passage of a train is a discrete event that returns the countryside to its undisturbed condition. Features close to the tracks are often difficult to see from a train at speed, but the distant vista reveals an unfolding view of the countryside that is difficult to experience any other way. At station stops, the traveler may sample the neighboring community. Railway travel displays the texture of the land and its people to those who care to look.[48]

The environmental impact of a railway line is generally less than that of a highway or canal. Unlike a canal, railway track has little effect on local groundwater and drainage, and there is no risk of damage or injury from burst banks or failure of dams at supply reservoirs (the cause of the famous 1889 Johnstown flood). Since the railway is not paved and the roadbed is permeable to water, it does not reduce the infiltration of rain, as a highway does. A railway track can carry ten times as much passenger traffic as a highway lane[49] because railway vehicles are coupled together and no space need be provided between them to allow for individual variations in speed, the factor that limits highway-traffic density. Of the alternative overland transportation systems, a railway intrudes the least on the landscape (Fig. 4.17).

The major engineering and architectural works built for railways included cuts, fills, bridges, tunnels, and stations. Where a hill or a mountain was to be pierced, either a cut or a tunnel might be used. Because of the high cost of excavation before dynamite and powered digging machines were available, railway designers used small cuts and numerous tunnels. (Many of these small tunnels were later opened out into cuts to reduce maintenance.) The large railway tunnels, such as the Hoosac Tunnel in northwestern Massachusetts and the Summit Tunnel in California's Sierras, were major engineering undertakings, but they have little visual effect on the landscape because the volume of spoil removed from them is small enough that it does not create significant disposal problems.[50] Granite shards from cutting the Summit Tunnel made excellent road ballast, and the Central Pacific also sold larger pieces of granite waste to construction companies.[51] Cuts and fills are much more intrusive because they alter the natural shapes

FIGURE 4.17. The construction of Interstate 70 near Glenwood Springs, Colorado, as seen from the Denver and Rio Grande Western Railway. Because the valley of the Colorado River is narrow, the highway is being built out over the river. The railroad tracks are barely visible on the left and have made a relatively minor intrusion in the valley.

of hillsides or create barriers across valleys. However, bridges and viaducts are often the most noticeable railway features on the nonurban landscape.

Railway companies that were promising investments or that became prosperous could attract the capital needed to build large, handsome viaducts and bridges. The Starrucca Viaduct built for the New York and Erie Railroad in 1848 was one of the largest (Fig. 4.18). It crosses the valley of Starrucca Creek in northern Pennsylvania on seventeen masonry arches, making a span 1,040 feet long and 100 feet above the creek. Because it is built of local sandstone, it has a visual connection with the adjacent landscape; because the arch is a structure that occurs in nature, it appears more an extension of the landscape than an intrusion on it.[52] Jaspar Cropsey's painting *Starrucca Viaduct* suggests this.[53] The arched viaduct of the Great Northern Railway over the Mississippi River at Minneapolis (now abandoned for rail service) has much the same effect in an urban setting.

Although a few nineteenth-century railroads, such as the Baltimore and Ohio and the Erie, were willing to expend the time and money to construct substantial masonry bridges and viaducts, the engineers on most lines built in a hurry, using wood trusses or trestles for most of their early spans. This

FIGURE 4.18. The Starrucca Viaduct near Lanesboro, Pennsylvania, was built over Starrucca Creek for the New York and Erie Railroad in 1848. Today it carries freight trains for Conrail. In the intervals between trains, rural tranquility returns to the yards of the houses adjacent to the viaduct.

FIGURE 4.19. Building railroads through rugged terrain called for construction techniques different from those originated by British railway builders. The narrow-gauge Durango and Silverton Railway has been cut into the edge of a cliff in southwestern Colorado. The train is being pulled by two locomotives.

150

was a striking departure from the conservative practices of British railroads, where great stone viaducts were common features. Philip Nicklin, a traveler on the Columbia Rail Road in 1835, commented on its light construction: "In this part of Pennsylvania, until the construction of the rail road, all the houses, mills, barns, bridges and roads were made of stone. Solidity was the peculiar characteristic of the state. The fashion has changed, and there is now an iron road and wooden bridges."[54] Nicklin went on to complain about another characteristic feature of American railroads: their sharp curves in rugged terrain. Speaking again of the Columbia Rail Road, he said that its "curves are too numerous, and their radii generally too short." It was usually quicker and less expensive to follow curving contours than to cut or tunnel through them. Designers of American locomotives and rolling stock adapted their equipment to handle the demanding curves of their customers' lines. A ride today on the narrow-gauge Durango and Silverton Railway through the San Juan Mountains of southern Colorado shows just how challenging the American landscape could be (Fig. 4.19).

Because of the physical demands of heavier loads and the need to reduce maintenance expenditures, railway engineers often preferred wood and metal or all-metal bridges after 1850. By the turn of the century, they were replacing both wrought and cast iron with steel in bridge construction. The 2,053-foot-long Kinzua Viaduct, now part of a Pennsylvania state park, demonstrates the structural capabilities of steel (Fig. 4.20). It was erected in 1900 as a replacement for an obsolete wrought-iron viaduct. This steel trestle over the valley of Kinzua Creek has a light, open appearance, but it is rigid and strong. A few railroad owners chose to project a different image with monumental concrete viaducts. The Tunkhannock Viaduct, completed by the Delaware, Lackawanna, and Western Railroad in 1915, is 2,375 feet long and contains 167,000 cubic yards of concrete. It is more than twice as long and high as the stone Starrucca Viaduct, but its size is not the only reason that it appears as a dominant insertion on the natural landscape. The Tunkhannock Viaduct's concrete construction gives it a bright, white surface and an aura of overwhelming solidity.[55]

COMMUNITIES

The changes on the open landscape caused by railways were much smaller than the indirect effects of railroads on cities and towns. A railway is operated efficiently only if stopping places along it are widely spaced. The advent of a railway encouraged the growth of towns separated by the distance of a convenient train trip. Trains did not stop between stations, and the railway had little effect on land use. Once a railway was built, people tended to move their industrial and commercial activities into urban centers. Trains

FIGURE 4.20. Deep valleys cut into the Allegheny plateau by rivers such as Kinzua Creek were barriers to railway construction. The Kinzua Viaduct near Mount Jewett, Pennsylvania, is 2,053 feet long and 301 feet above the creek. This steel structure built in 1900 replaced an earlier wrought-iron viaduct. It is no longer used for railway traffic and is part of the Kinzua Bridge State Park.

delivered coal to run steam engines in factories, allowing entrepreneurs to move away from water-power sites that were spread across the countryside and into cities, where they could hire workers and specialist services more easily. These trends were reversed when Americans shifted most of their freight and passenger traffic to highways and motor vehicles. Because independently operated cars and trucks could be stopped conveniently anywhere along a road, merchants and entrepreneurs built strip developments on highways; long stretches of roads, unlike railways, became surrounded by a built environment. The proliferation of limited-access highways in the past fifty years has brought a return to the settlement patterns associated with railways. Interchanges on the interstate-highway system are now settings for the tightly clustered commercial development that once surrounded train stations.

Residents of towns that benefited from railways saw in the train station a symbol of civic pride. As railways and their associated towns prospered, railway managers hired distinguished architects to design imposing stations.[56] These buildings housed telegraph and express offices and became focal points of communities. When railways withdrew passenger train service and the downtown areas of communities deteriorated, the train stations decayed. But because they are often substantial structures, reuse of stations no longer served by trains can be a part of the revitalization of downtown neighborhoods. The city of Wheeling, West Virginia, has converted the former Baltimore and Ohio station (Fig. 4.21) into a community college.

Major railway yards covered large areas with track layouts and could be a source of open (but not accessible) space within cities (Fig. 4.22). The environment of the yards was likely to be both noisy and dirty; the replacement of steam by diesel-electric traction eliminated much of the dirt and some of the noise. Where rail yards were clustered along waterfronts, they prevented the erection of buildings that would cut off the view of the shore from the central city. With the abandonment of many railways, these yards have become prime land for development.

FIGURE 4.21. The trains no longer run to Wheeling, West Virginia, where both the Baltimore and Ohio Railroad and the National Road reached the Ohio River. The tracks are gone, and the Wheeling station is now a community college.

Figure 4.22. The rail yards at the entrance to Union Station in Washington, D.C., in the early twentieth century. These yards created a large but generally inaccessible open space in the center of the city. The building on the left stands today, but has been converted to offices. (Courtesy of the Smithsonian Institution)

Mills and Factories

Before the advent of electrical-power transmission, industries that obtained their power from flowing water had to be located at water privileges. The power potential set a limit on the growth that was possible at each site, and the spacing of the sites was a barrier to the concentration of factories or mills. Since most of the water privileges in northeastern North America were small and well separated, entrepreneurs built industries in a dispersed pattern that required them to do much hauling of raw materials and finished goods with transportation systems that were slow and subject to interruption by adverse weather. Community services and housing for workers often had to be provided by the proprietors because their enterprises were not located in established cities or towns. While this offered opportunities for social experimentation and paternalistic control that were welcomed by some entrepreneurs, it also entailed added managerial responsibilities that later generations of managers often did not want. The widespread adoption of power from steam engines fueled by coal from 1830 onward allowed entrepreneurs to concentrate industries in urban settings.

The substitution of coal for wood fuel is an example of the replacement of one resource by another that had been made less costly through innovation and investment—in this case, in mining, combustion methods, and transportation systems.[57] One technological barrier that had to be overcome before anthracite could be substituted for wood was its inability to burn in fireplaces, stoves, or the fireboxes of locomotives and steamboats designed for wood fuel. Americans established the value of anthracite as a fuel by experimenting with it until they learned the necessary firing skills. By the 1830s, they had mastered the use of steam power in factories, and the proprietors of many American engineering works were capable of building boilers and stationary steam engines suitable for driving factory machinery.[58]

Ironworks

The large reduction in costs achieved after 1840 by ironmasters who substituted mineral coal for charcoal made it easier for Americans to build railways and use iron in place of wood in ships, buildings, and bridges. But after 1867, designers increasingly chose steel over iron in structures and machines, and, by the early twentieth century, steelmaking rather than ironmaking was the paradigm of American heavy industry. In Britain and in Europe, the transformation of ironmaking from wood to mineral fuel was accomplished with coke made from bituminous coal. Americans had few supplies of bituminous coal large enough to be useful in ironmaking on the east side of the Appalachians. They made the transformation to mineral fuel primarily with anthracite and concentrated the iron industry in eastern Pennsylvania. In 1847, Pennsylvanians made more iron than was made in all the United States just seven years earlier, and it was not until 1875 that iron production from coke-fired furnaces in western Pennsylvania exceeded that from the anthracite-fired furnaces in the eastern part of the state.[59] When ironmasters began to use anthracite, their customers wanted wrought iron as much as cast iron. Wrought iron could be made from pig with mineral coal instead of charcoal if the fuel was kept away from the metal in the furnace to avoid contamination of the iron by sulfur in the coal. British ironmasters had solved this problem by 1800 with the puddling process, carried out in a reverberatory furnace fired with bituminous coal that produced a long flame. They considered anthracite unsuitable fuel for a puddling furnace,[60] but well before 1841 Americans whose names are unknown to us had puddling furnaces running with anthracite.[61] They redesigned the firebox and added a forced-draft blower to the British furnace design.[62]

Pennsylvanians began experiments with anthracite blast-furnace fuel in 1821,[63] but, since anthracite will not reach a temperature hot enough to melt iron without preheated air, they had no success with their cold-blast furnaces. Within three years of Scottish ironmaster James Neilson's 1828 British patent for a preheating stove, Frederick Geissenhainer was conducting experiments in the United States on smelting iron with anthracite and hot blast. As with puddling, he and other practicing artisans gradually solved the technical problems, and by 1840 anthracite smelting was successfully under way at seven blast furnaces in Pennsylvania; six more were blown in in Pennsylvania and New Jersey the following year.[64]

GEOGRAPHY

With railroads to transport ore and fuel, and steam power to drive blowing engines, ironmasters could locate furnaces where none had existed before. Pennsylvania entrepreneurs put them in communities of all sizes, from the small Alburtis, to the medium-size Danville, and large Scranton. Alburtis was a railway junction amid farms in Lehigh County that happened to be midway between ore and coal mines. In 1869, the Lock Ridge Iron Company erected two blast furnaces, two- and four-family houses for workers, and, for the ironmaster, the largest house in this previously agricultural community. However, employment at the ironworks never exceeded about ninety persons, and Alburtis remained a small community. The physical and social fabric of the town survived the closing of the works in 1921, but the machinery and equipment were gradually removed, ending with the processing of the slag banks to make aggregate for construction of a section of the Pennsylvania Turnpike. Lehigh County officials converted the site of the works and the remaining buildings into a park and museum.[65]

There were iron-ore deposits just outside Danville that were little used until the North Branch Canal from the northern coalfield reached town in 1831. Pennsylvania capitalists put up four anthracite-fired blast furnaces in Danville between 1840 and 1842. In 1845, they completed a large puddling and rolling mill, the Montour Iron Works (Fig. 4.23), and rolled some of the first "T" rails made in the United States. The Montour works was using 100,000 tons of anthracite annually to make 20,000 tons of rail by 1856. Subsequent enlargements and improvements brought the capacity of the works to 45,000 tons of wrought-iron rail a year with 1,400 persons employed.[66] It was the largest rail mill in the United States. The contrast between the old and new ironworks is illustrated by the Hopewell iron plantation 70 miles to the southeast; while Montour was turning out rails,

FIGURE 4.23. The Montour Iron Works in Danville, Pennsylvania, photographed during a spring flood of the Susquehanna River. The large building in the center contained the puddling furnaces and rolling mills. To the left are the machine and carpenter shops where mill equipment was repaired. The blast furnaces are just out of view to the left. The commercial and civic center of the town is visible behind the mill. (Courtesy of the Montour County Historical Society)

Hopewell was still making pig iron with charcoal and ore hauled in by draft animals supplied with fodder grown on the plantation.

William Henry of Oxford, New Jersey, and several members of the Scranton family started the Lackawanna Coal and Iron Company in the town that later became Scranton during the great expansion of the anthracite iron industry that began in 1840; it was one of the few ironworks established within a coal basin. The first blast furnace produced little iron until the proprietors hired J. E. Davis away from Danville to be their ironmaster in 1842. They then built five puddling furnaces, two trains of rolls, and twenty nail machines in 1844. The nail-making enterprise was not successful, and after 1847 they concentrated on making iron and, later, steel rail.[67] The Lackawanna works were located along Roaring Brook, which provided the mechanical power for blowing engines and mill machinery, and the city of Scranton grew around this industrial nucleus. In 1902, the Lackawanna Company moved all its operation to a new site near Buffalo, New York, that was better placed to receive the lake ores and coke that were by then the dominant raw materials used in steelmaking. Then the Scranton site was abandoned. The city, however, remained a rail, manufacturing, and commercial center after the departure of ironmaking.[68]

The ironworks fueled with anthracite were located where raw materials could be brought together by canal and, later, by rail. A map of their sites shows them dispersed over an area centered in eastern Pennsylvania but, unlike their charcoal-fired predecessors, in towns instead of on plantations. Only a few were integrated by incorporating blast furnaces, puddling furnaces, and rolling mills in one plant. The proprietors of many blast furnaces chose to produce only pig iron for sale to others, and many puddling works used only iron purchased on the open market. No one community grew to dominate the industry, nor did the iron industry dominate the region. Later, as customers chose steel over wrought iron and ironmasters replaced coal with coke, they shifted the center of the industry to western Pennsylvania. Back east, entrepreneurs found that ironworkers in towns such as Danville could turn their skills from primary metal production to manufacturing. But in the anthracite patches, where for generations the men had been miners, this transition proved nearly impossible. When oil fuel displaced coal and the silk mills moved south, residents in these communities found it hard to turn to other industries.

The factors that made anthracite iron cheap—low-cost fuel and transportation—also led to its demise as entrepreneurs developed the less expensive coal and ore resources west of the Appalachians. Iron and, later, manufactured goods made in the West could be shipped east at low cost on the new trans-Appalachian rail routes while the market west of the Appalachians was also growing. The increase in the scale of operations at the western ironworks was larger again than the difference between the anthracite and charcoal works in the East.

SURVIVALS

The archaeological record of anthracite ironmaking before 1850 is very uneven. Because of the large size of a blast-furnace plant, the smelting branch of the nineteenth-century iron industry attracted most of the attention of contemporary writers and photographers; the archaeological record is similarly biased because an abandoned blast-furnace stack often stands long after its surrounding plant and equipment are gone. Some of these stacks, particularly those that happen to be in attractive, rural settings, have been incorporated into parks. There are no above-ground remains of the Montour Iron Works in Danville, Pennsylvania, and there are no surviving sites from the anthracite iron industry as extensive as those from the industry based on charcoal. Fully half of the industry is forgotten because no wrought-iron works has yet been studied by industrial archaeologists and no puddling

FIGURE 4.24. Scranton Iron Furnaces Park, in Pennsylvania, the site of the Lackawanna Coal and Iron Company until 1902, when it moved to a site on Lake Erie. Only the masonry of four blast furnaces remains; the metal roof where the furnace stacks would have been is a recent addition.

furnace is on public display in the United States. After the Lackawanna works closed, industrial remains were gradually removed from the site, leaving only the four stone blast-furnace stacks. These have been made a part of Scranton Iron Furnaces Park, a grassy open space between the furnaces and the creek where puddling furnaces and rolling mills were once densely packed (Fig. 4.24). It is a challenge to an observer's powers of imagination to visualize the Lackawanna works from these physical remains (Fig. 4.25).

Coke and Steelworks

Ironmasters found that most bituminous coal worked best as blast-furnace fuel when converted to coke. Americans began to experiment with coke and anthracite at about the same time. The Lonaconing blast furnace, near Frostburg, Maryland, was operating with coke made from Cumberland coal by 1839, and a year later four coke-fired furnaces were producing iron at Pittsburgh. About 1850, western entrepreneurs found that a superior grade of coke could be made from the coal mined in Fayette County, Pennsylvania. With coke-fired blast furnaces, they were able to make iron at a much lower cost than was possible with the older, charcoal-fired furnaces.[69] Where the Allegheny plateau was incised by rivers (Fig. 4.20), the iron-ore and coal

FIGURE 4.25. A view of the furnaces shown in Figure 4.24 in the late nineteenth century, showing how much of the industrial texture of the site has disappeared. The stone stacks were surmounted by hot-blast stoves and charging ramps. The casting shed was in front of the furnaces. A footbridge allowed workers to cross the stream that originally provided the power to flow the furnaces. (For a view of the interior of the casting shed in 1892, see Ralph Greenhill, *Engineer's Witness* [Boston: Godine, 1985], fig. 51.) (Courtesy of Robert Vogel)

seams of the plateau were exposed on the valley walls. Ironmasters built new works on the long, narrow strips of flatland between the rivers and the scarps of the plateau. One of these new ironmaking enterprises was in Johnstown, Pennsylvania.

Johnstown was a small settlement on the Pennsylvania Main Line transportation system at the junction of the canal from Pittsburgh along the Conemaugh River and the Allegheny Portage Railroad when men from the East found high-grade ore in Prospect Hill, just outside the town. They built a charcoal-fired blast furnace to smelt iron for the Pittsburgh market. The Cambria Iron Company, organized in 1852 to make rail, built four coke-fired blast furnaces and a set of puddling furnaces. The company also erected a foundry, machine shop, smithy, pattern shop, and, on the edge of town, houses to accommodate its expanded work force. Cambria was already in financial difficulties when the first rails were rolled in 1854. Wood, Morrell and Company leased the works, and sustained production got under way a year later.

Cambria at this period is best known for its colorful superintendent, John Fritz, and the spectacular but unsuccessful trials of the Kelly converter. John Fritz arrived at Cambria in 1854 and had a three-high rail mill operating in 1857; the mill building burned and was rebuilt, and production resumed in January 1858. William Kelly was invited to demonstrate his pneumatic converter for making steel from pig iron at Cambria by D. J. Morrell, the general manager, in 1856. In the first trial, the liquid iron in the converter was blown out of the vessel by the air blast, and subsequent experiments by Kelly at Cambria seem to have been unsuccessful. Later, A. L. Holley designed a Bessemer plant for the company,[70] and when steel production began in 1871, Cambria, with its buildings spread along the Conemaugh and Little Conemaugh rivers, was the largest iron- and steelworks in the United States.[71] The owners further enlarged the works and introduced new products, such as barbed wire. In 1895, they built the first by-product ovens for blast-furnace coke in the United States.[72]

One structure survives from the original ironworks, the smithy built in 1854 (Fig. 4.26), a polygonal brick building that originally housed forge fires but now contains gas furnaces for heating metal and air hammers for forging repair parts for the rolling mills. Most of the fabric of the integrated steelworks into which the Cambria Iron Company evolved is now derelict (Fig. 4.27); only an electric-furnace melt shop and the blooming mill are still in use.[73]

The Johnstown site of the Cambria works was chosen because of the ore and coal in the Conemaugh Valley. By the time Bessemer steel production began, the local ore supplies were inadequate and the works depended on rail transport of raw materials from distant sources. The narrow valley made

FIGURE 4.26. The smithy of the Cambria Iron Company, built in 1854 and now surrounded by more recent buildings of the Bethelehem Steel Company works at Johnstown, Pennsylvania. The foreground is the area in which William Kelly carried out an abortive demonstration of his pneumatic converter in 1856. At one time, Cambria was the largest steelworks in the United States.

FIGURE 4.27. Remains of the last blast-furnace installation at the Bethlehem Steel works in Johnstown, Pennsylvania, in 1988. The furnace is gone, but several hot-blast stoves can be seen in the background. The blowing engines were in the building to the right of the stoves.

162

FIGURE 4.28. Steelworks on the south shore of Lake Michigan at Gary, Indiana, were so large by 1940 that they dominated the landscape totally. Ore was delivered by ship from ports on the Great Lakes in the United States and Canada. This picture shows the turning basin for ore ships. In the background are twelve blast furnaces and, beyond, the open-hearth shops. (Photograph by F. G. Korth. Courtesy of the Smithsonian Institution)

it difficult for engineers to design an efficient plant layout and left the works susceptible to flooding. The next generation of steelmaking entrepreneurs preferred to build on navigable water. The owners of the Lackawanna works moved from Scranton to Buffalo to gain access to the Great Lakes; others chose the Cleveland area or the south shore of Lake Michigan. All these sites could be supplied with ore ports on Lake Superior[74] and, later, from Quebec, by ship (Fig. 4.28). The scale of the lakeside steel plants, which can still be viewed east of Chicago, is so large as to dominate the landscape to the visible horizon.

ENVIRONMENTAL EFFECTS

Ironworks of the nineteenth century were noisy, dirty, and smoky while in operation. But, unlike coal mines, they left few lasting effects on the environment. Blast furnace and puddling slags may be unsightly, but they are not chemically active and have been used successfully as building materials. The absence of long-term environmental effects may be seen in Danville at the site of the Montour Iron Works. Danville High School and its grassy playing fields now occupy the site of the puddling and rolling mill that once employed more than 1,000 men; townhouses are being built on the dumps of slag from the adjoining blast furnaces.

The twentieth-century steelworks were so large that their smoke emissions could dominate the atmosphere of an entire city, as at Pittsburgh, and, under unfavorable atmospheric conditions, become a health hazard. Closure of these works creates vast tracts of derelict buildings. Unlike ironworkers, steelworkers used chemicals, such as pickling solutions for cleaning, and produced toxic wastes in by-product coke ovens. When a steelworks site is cleared, residual chemicals may render the vacant land unusable.

SURVIVALS

The preservation of an integrated steelworks as an industrial monument would be a costly undertaking because of its size and the high maintenance costs; just the regular painting of all the exposed metal structures would be a burdensome task. Civic authorities in former steel towns usually want their communities to project a prosperous image and have little use for reminders of the past. No Bessemer steelmaking works has been preserved. It is unlikely that future generations will be able to see an open-hearth shop. However, a blast-furnace plant in Birmingham, Alabama, is now a public park and museum. The Sloss Furnaces, described in a 1978 article as the "central element of the city's skyline,"[75] began iron production in 1881, were rebuilt in 1927 and 1928, and closed in 1970. Since the furnaces produced pig iron for foundries, the site illustrates blast-furnace technology, but not the steelmaking component of an integrated works.

Factories in Cities

Zachariah Allen, like many New Englanders, found virtue in the region's lack of coal resources:

> It may be intended as a blessing that an all-wise Providence has denied to the barren hills of New England the mines of coal, which would allow the inhabitants to congregate in manufacturing cities, by enabling them to have recourse to artificial power, instead of the natural water power so profusely furnished

by the innumerable streams, that in their course to the ocean descend over beds furrowed in the rocks of an iron bound country. Whilst a cold climate and an ungrateful soil render the inhabitants from necessity industrious, thus distributed in small communities around waterfalls, their industry is not likely to be the means of rendering them licentious; and of impairing the purity of those moral principles, without which neither nations nor individuals can become truly great or happy.[76]

However, cities had many advantages over rural villages as settings for manufacturing enterprises once canals and railways linked them to markets, sources of fuel, and raw materials. Cities had existing physical and cultural infrastructures that reduced or eliminated the need for direct company expenditures on housing, stores, parks, churches, meeting halls, recreational facilities, domestic water supply, and waste disposal. Newly arrived immigrants came to them seeking employment opportunities.

The countryside offered many more water-power sites than did the cities, but improvements in steam engineering in the nineteenth century made it increasingly cost efficient to locate factories where coal could be delivered by rail or ship. Mass-production of textiles in Providence, Rhode Island, where there was almost no water power, got under way in 1827, when Samuel Slater built a steam-powered mill on the waterfront near what later became a district of factories making jewelry, iron products, and rubber goods. Anthracite from the Pennsylvania coalfields came by sea to the port of Providence, with its appropriately named Scranton and Wilkes-Barre piers. The famous Corliss steam engine, patented in 1849, provided substantial fuel savings over earlier engines. This improved efficiency convinced many American manufacturers to build steam-powered mills. The Corliss Steam Engine Works, located on the main rail line and appropriately powered by steam (Fig. 4.29), was part of a long tradition of engine building and engine use in Providence. Until tall commercial buildings were erected in the late nineteenth and early twentieth centuries, smokestacks and factory towers competed with church steeples as the most prominent features of America's urban skyline.

Steam also helped to transform many industrial communities whose utilization of water power was already approaching its limit, thus allowing expansion of their manufacturing base and continued urban development. The Wilkinson Mill in Pawtucket, Rhode Island, had a steam engine to help drive the machinery in the new cotton factory and machine shop built in 1810. Edward Wilkinson, who worked there, called it a "steam mill," but other sources and physical evidence indicate primary reliance on water power. The dimensions of the first waterwheel and the fall at the site are known from documents and archaeological research (Chapter 1);[77] these

FIGURE 4.29. The Corliss Steam Engine Works in Providence, Rhode Island. This picture dates from the time when smoke emissions were considered a sign of prosperity. (From *Rhode Island Industries Catalogued and Illustrated* [Providence: Chamber of Commerce, 1904])

data show that the installed water power was insufficient for the mill. Oziel Wilkinson had built a substantial manufacturing plant despite the shortage of water power at his crowded urban site, and even the wider wheel installed in 1826 produced less than 15 horsepower. Excavations in the wheel pit have also uncovered fill containing coal, cinder, and ash. Thus, like many water-powered mills in the years to come, this early factory depended on steam as a source of supplementary power as well as of heat in the work spaces.

The largest industrial complex in Pawtucket today is the vast site of the former Conant Thread–J. P. Coats mills, located far above the Blackstone River and for many years completely dependent on steam engines for power. By 1880, installed steam power had surpassed water power even in Lowell, and because of it, Fall River, on the Massachusetts coast, became the most productive of all the great textile cities. The falls that gave Fall River its name are now buried beneath buildings and highways, while the surviving smokestacks of textile mills seem insignificant when measured against those of the immense coal-fired generating station just across the bay.

Smokestacks, now strongly associated with air pollution, grime, and acid rain, were regarded by many nineteenth-century civic boosters as positive features of the urban industrial landscape. Smoke rising into the sky indicated industrial productivity, and clusters of tall factory chimneys were viewed by many as signs of economic strength. Charles Cowley counted chimneys and smoke among the beautiful features of Lowell in 1868:

> The whole valley of the Merrimack is noted for its picturesqueness; but from the mountains to the main, there is no lovelier scene than that which meets the eye . . . when we look down upon Lowell, and survey the varied landscape unrolled like a beautiful map before us. The spacious natural amphitheatre surrounded by hills, —the sky-blue rivers, —the long lines of mills, —the labyrinth of brick and masonry, —the obeliscal chimneys curtaining the heavens with smoke, —the spires of churches, belfries of factories, and gables of houses, . . . —all combine to form a scene that must be pleasing to every eye that has been quickened to the beauties of art and nature.[78]

Charles Dickens, who had seen the English "Black Country" and the enormous stacks of Lancashire mills, said of Pittsburgh in 1842 that "it certainly has a great quantity of smoke hanging over it." Attitudes about air pollution gradually changed in America as blankets of coal smoke from various sources began to have an adverse affect on the quality of life in many cities. Public health was suffering, and grime was damaging the built environment. In 1882, Mark Twain remarked that "in St. Louis, as in London and Pittsburgh, you can't persuade a thing to look new; the coal-smoke turns it into an antiquity the moment you take your hand off it." The encrusted dirt on some urban buildings has its own microscopic stratigraphy that records the history of local air quality. Providence had an inspector of smoke (with little regulatory power) as early as 1904, but the city did not begin measuring soot fall until 1930. The Smoke Prevention Association of America was formed in Chicago in 1907. Despite growing public concern, little was accomplished to abate smoke emissions until after World War II.[79]

Whatever the associations produced by billowing factory smoke, the prominence of smokestacks and their visibility to an audience traveling by rail made them ideal platforms for signs advertising companies or products. The practice of painting signs on chimneys (and on factory walls) persists today, although this promotional activity is now directed primarily at people in automobiles. John Stilgoe, in *Metropolitan Corridor,* describes the physical form and peculiar aesthetics of "the industrial zones surrounding commercial downtowns" and the experience of railway passengers who regularly traveled through these factory districts.[80] Steam-powered factories were clustered along rail lines (and along seaport or river frontage) in urban areas. People traveling by rail between cities or from outlying suburbs to city centers passed through the industrial landscape and observed its striking features at close range. The rail sidings, coal bunkers, smokestacks, and loading docks of factories swept by in a blur seen through the window of a moving train.

Electrical Power from Coal

Transmitting power by shafts, belts, and gears over any significant distance is difficult and inefficient.[81] Designers of factories with mechanical-power systems had to make them compact; they also had to locate them at water privileges or where bulk shipments of coal could be received. With electrical transmission, engineers could concentrate the equipment for generating power from coal in large central stations, where they could attain economies of scale in fuel use and monitor the release of effluents more closely than at dispersed generating units. In the early twentieth century, utility companies built substantial, coal-fired power stations for industrial cities (Fig. 4.30). In them, steam raised in coal-fired boilers drove engines (piston engines at first, but, later, turbines) coupled to alternators. To achieve high efficiency, the steam exhausted from the engines had to be condensed with circulating cold water. The best sites for steam plants were along rivers or estuaries because fuel could be delivered cheaply and there was plenty of water available to dissipate the waste heat from the condensers. With the construction and operation of these central stations, highly visible new features were added to the industrial landscape: stock piles of coal; powerhouses with tall stacks. The invisible effluents from the stacks, particularly sulfur dioxide,

FIGURE 4.30. This formerly coal-fired power plant in Providence, Rhode Island, is surmounted by clusters of smokestacks and surrounded by coal-handling conveyors. This equipment was left in place when the plant was converted to oil fuel.

could cause changes in the landscape miles away from their source. Ash and clinkers, the solid wastes from burning coal, had to be removed to landfills. With the ash buried and the stack gases dispersed high in the atmosphere, a coal-fired power plant conveyed a sense of clean, controlled power, an impression that was heightened by the uncluttered layout and polished metalwork of the interior. Actually, the environmental costs of generating energy were being sent elsewhere or buried. The spatial separation of costs and benefits in the generation of energy, which began as Americans replaced wood fuel with coal, is the cause of many regional disputes today.

Energy from a central station is carried to users on copper or aluminum wires. Engineers minimize the energy loss in transmission by using high voltage to reduce the current that must flow for a given amount of power transmitted. High-voltage lines have to be insulated from the ground, and the cheapest way to do this was to place them high in the air, suspended from poles by ceramic or glass insulators. Power companies soon began to fill the sides of city streets with webs of wires strung on poles and to trace the countryside with towers carrying cables hung on insulators in swaths of cleared land.

As Americans adopted mineral fuel, constructed the transportation systems to deliver it, and concentrated industries using power from coal in cities, they profoundly changed the industrial landscape. At the same time, they adopted new ideas about the use of natural resources and the social setting of work; the consequences of these changes were to remain unresolved through the twentieth century.

Notes

1. H. Benjamin Powell, *Philadelphia's First Fuel Crisis: Jacob Cist and the Developing Market for Pennsylvania Anthracite* (University Park: Pennsylvania State University Press, 1978), p. 10.

2. A tunnel was dug 200 feet below the ridge of the Summit Mine of the Lehigh Coal and Navigation Company to reach the coal vein being worked from above. The tunnel was undertaken on the assumption that the vein dipped to the south; it did not, and the tunnel was abandoned after having been driven 790 feet (Ele Bowen, *The Coal Regions of Pennsylvania* [Pottsville, Pa.: Carvalho, 1848], p. 24).

3. Frederick M. Binder, *Coal Age Empire: Pennsylvania Coal and Its Utilization to 1860* (Harrisburg: Pennsylvania Historical and Museum Commission, 1974), p. 136.

4. Ibid., pp. 146–147.

5. W. Julian Parton, *The Death of a Great Company: Reflections on the Decline and Fall of the Lehigh Coal and Navigation Company* (Easton, Pa.: Center for Canal

History and Technology, 1986); Bowen, *Coal Regions of Pennsylvania*, table opposite p. 56; Binder, *Coal Age Empire*, pp. 136–144.

6. Bowen, *Coal Regions of Pennsylvania*, pp. 23, 26. Open-pit mining was impractical until mechanized earth-moving equipment became available in the twentieth century because of the large volume of rock covering the coal veins. Anthony Wallace, *St. Clair: A Nineteenth-Century Coal Town's Experience with a Disaster-Prone Industry* (New York: Knopf, 1987), p. 80.

7. Ellis W. Roberts, *The Breaker Whistle Blows* (Scranton, Pa.: Anthracite Museum Press, 1984), chap. 2. The principal source for the summary up to 1848 is Bowen, *Coal Regions of Pennsylvania*, pp. 17–22.

8. Bowen, *Coal Regions of Pennsylvania*, p. 38.

9. About 45 percent of the coal in a vein was left in pillars to support the roof, and 7 percent was lost through adhering to shale. In blasting the coal out of the veins, about 8 percent of it was broken into sizes smaller than three-eighths of an inch, the finest that could be burned successfully (Franklin Platt, *Causes, Kinds, and Amount of Waste in Mining Anthracite* [Harrisburg, Pa.: Second Geological Survey, 1881], p. 23). At the breaker, 16 percent was broken into particles too small to use. Hence, in mining a vein, only about one-third of the coal present underground was sent to market when mining was completed (H. M. Chance, *Mining Methods and Appliances Used in the Anthracite Coal Fields* [Harrisburg, Pa.: Second Geological Survey, 1883], p. 475).

10. Y. K. Rao, *Stoichiometry and Thermodynamics of Metallurgical Processes* (Cambridge: Cambridge University Press, 1985), p. 97.

11. Peter Roberts, *The Anthracite Coal Industry* (New York: Macmillan, 1901), chap. 10.

12. David DeKok, *Unseen Danger: A Tragedy of People, Government, and the Centralia Mine Fire* (Philadelphia: University of Pennsylvania Press, 1986); Renee Jacobs, *Slow Burn: A Photodocument of Centralia, Pennsylvania* (Philadelphia: University of Pennsylvania Press, 1986); Kelly Kissel, "Centralia Celebrates 125th," *Reading Times*, 5 July 1991.

13. Bowen, *Coal Regions of Pennsylvania*, p. 26.

14. Ibid.

15. Powell, *Philadelphia's First Fuel Crisis*, p. 9; Bowen, *Coal Regions of Pennsylvania*, p. 19.

16. Wallace, *St. Clair*, pp. 54–63; Nicholas B. Wainwright, "The Age of Nicholas Biddle, 1825–1841," in *Philadelphia: A 300-Year History*, ed. Russell F. Weigley (New York: Norton, 1982), p. 273; more examples are quoted in Powell, *Philadelphia's First Fuel Crisis*, p. 16.

17. Bowen, *Coal Regions of Pennsylvania*, pp. 29–30.

18. Roberts, *Anthracite Coal Industry*, p. 66. The efforts of the railroads to control the coal trades and thereby drive up prices in the 1880s is discussed in I. Lowthian Bell, *Principles of the Manufacture of Iron and Steel* (London: Routledge, 1884), p. 555.

19. Quoted in Arthur Weinberg, ed., *Attorney for the Damned* (New York: Simon and Schuster, 1957), pp. 347–348.

20. Bonnie Stepenoff, "Child Labor in the Silk Mills of Northeastern Pennsylvania" (Paper presented at the Third Textile History Conference, Museum of American Textile History, North Andover, Massachusetts, 22 September 1990). The authors are grateful to Stepenoff for sharing the results of her research on this subject.

21. *Some of Pennsylvania's Child Workers* (Pittsburgh: Pennsylvania Child Labor Association, 1913), p. 3. See also Stepenoff, "Child Labor in the Silk Mills."

22. Francis H. Nichols, "Children of the Coal Shadow," *McClure's*, February 1903, p. 440.

23. Stepenoff, "Child Labor in the Silk Mills."

24. Howard N. Eavenson, *The First Century and a Quarter of American Coal Industry* (Pittsburgh: Eavenson, 1942).

25. Ibid., pp. 161–185.

26. Ibid., pp. 201–204; Stan Cohen, *King Coal: A Pictorial Heritage of West Virginia Coal Mining* (Charleston, W.Va.: Pictorial Histories, 1984).

27. Keith Dix, *Work Relations in the Coal Industry: The Hand-Loading Era, 1880–1930* (Morgantown: West Virginia University Press, 1977).

28. For a discussion of waste dumps and of town layouts, see Richard Francaviglia, *Hard Places: Reading the Landscape of America's Historic Mining Districts* (Iowa City: University of Iowa Press, 1991), pp. 23–33. The collapse of a dam made of mine waste was responsible for the devastating flood at Buffalo Creek, West Virginia, whose social impact was studied by Kai T. Erikson, *Everything in Its Path: Destruction of Community in the Buffalo Creek Flood* (New York: Simon and Schuster, 1976).

29. *Coal and Your Environment* (Washington, D.C.: National Coal Association, n.d.), p. 27. This is not an unbiased report, but it recognizes a serious problem with abandoned mines.

30. Cohen, *King Coal*, p. 50.

31. Daniel H. Calhoun, *The American Civil Engineer: Origins and Conflict* (Cambridge, Mass.: MIT Press, 1960); Darwin H. Stapleton, *The Transfer of Early Industrial Technologies to America* (Philadelphia: American Philosophical Society, 1987), chap. 2. For an example of learning on the job, see Neal Fitzsimmons, ed., *The Reminiscences of John B. Jervis* (Syracuse, N.Y.: Syracuse University Press, 1971).

32. W. B. Langbein, *Hydrology and Environmental Aspects of Erie Canal (1817–99)*, U.S. Geological Survey Water Supply Paper No. 2038 (Washington, D.C.: Government Printing Office, 1976), p. 59.

33. An example is described in Albright G. Zimmerman, "The First Years of the Delaware Division Canal," *Canal History and Technology Proceedings* 8 (1989): 176.

34. Langbein, *Hydrology and Environmental Aspects of Erie Canal*, p. 30; Robert B. Gordon, "Hydrological Science and the Development of Water Power for Manufacturing," *Technology and Culture* 29 (1985): 204–235.

35. Robert M. Vogel, *Roebling's Delaware and Hudson Canal Aqueducts*, Smithsonian Studies in History and Technology No. 10 (Washington, D.C.: Smithsonian Institution Press, 1971); Harlan D. Unrau, *Historic Structure Report (Historic Data Section): The Delaware Aqueduct* (Denver: National Park Service Center, 1983); Henry J. Magaziner, "The Rebirth of an Engineering Landmrk," *APT Bulletin* 18 (1986): 52–64.

36. Charles R. Harte, "Connecticut's Canals," *Proceedings of the Connecticut Society of Civil Engineers* 54 (1938): 137, 140. The banks of the Farmington Canal were cut by property owners who had not been compensated for the taking of their land. In Rhode Island, mill owners sued the proprietors of the Blackstone Canal over water losses (Richard Greenwood, "A History of the Blackstone Canal, 1823–1849" [Report for the Rhode Island Historical Preservation Commission, 1984], pp. 84–88).

37. William M. Ferraro, "Biography of a Morris Canal Village: Bowerstown, Washington Township, Warren County, New Jersey, 1820–1940," *Canal History and Technology Proceedings* 8 (1989): 3–74.

38. James Lee, *The Morris Canal: A Photographic History* (Easton, Pa.: Delaware Press, ca. 1979, 1988), pp. 28–32.

39. Michael S. Raber and Patrick M. Malone, "Historical Documentation, River Canal Feasibility Study and Master Plan, Windsor Locks Canal Heritage State Park" (Report for the Connecticut Department of Environmental Protection, 1991); Charles B. Dew, *Ironmaker to the Confederacy: Joseph R. Anderson and the Tredegar Iron Works* (New Haven, Conn.: Yale University Press, 1966), p. 20; W. E. Trout III, *A Guide to the Works of the James River & Kanawha Company from the City of Richmond to the Ohio River* (n.p.: Virginia Canals and Navigation Society, 1988), p. 5. A good case study of the Blackstone Canal in Rhode Island and Massachusetts is in Richard Greenwood, "Natural Run and Artificial Falls: Waterpower and the Blackstone Canal," *Rhode Island History* 49 (1991): 51–62.

40. Patrick M. Malone, *Canals and Industry* (Lowell, Mass.: Lowell Museum, 1983), p. 9. High currents hindered boat traffic, caused erosion of banks, and, as this study shows, were even detrimental to generation of water power. By 1867, the demand for water power at the east end of the James River and Kanawha Canal had increased the current so much that boatmen were forced to use double their normal team of horses to navigate the Richmond level (Michael Raber, P. M. Malone, and R. B. Gordon, "Historical and Archaeological Assessment of the Tredegar Iron Works Site, Richmond, Virginia" [Report for the Valentine Museum and the Ethyl Corporation, 1992]).

41. Of the thirty-two aqueducts on the improved Erie Canal, only four have original masonry that is largely intact. Wooden components, such as trunks, have almost entirely disappeared (Michael S. Raber and others, "Preliminary Cultural Resources Assessment, New York State Barge Canal Study" [Report for the New York District, U.S. Army Corps of Engineers, 1983]). Recent excavations have revealed details of some of the earliest canal locks built in the United States (Richard J. Dent, "On the Archaeology of Early Canals: Research on the Patowmack Canal in Great Falls, Virginia," *Historical Archaeology* 20 [1986]: 50–62).

42. The different types of navigations are described in Patrick M. Malone, Michael S. Raber, and Charles Parrott, "Muskingum River and Dam Study, Ohio Department of Natural Resources: Historical Significance" (Report for Woolpert Consultants, 1991).

43. For a detailed account of the "official" history, see D. O. Elliott, *The Improvement of the Lower Mississippi River for Flood Control and Navigation* (Vicksburg, Miss.: U.S. Waterways Experiment Station, 1932), vol. 1, chaps. 1, 11; for an account of Humphreys's disputes with Eads and others, Martin Reuss, "Andrew A. Humphreys and the Development of Hydraulic Engineering: Politics and Technology in the Army Corps of Engineers, 1850–1950," *Technology and Culture* 26 (1985): 1–33; and, for a summary of Ellet's work and the development of the Ohio navigation, Donald Sayenga, "The Ohio Mississippi Waterway," *Canal History and Technology Proceedings* 7 (1988): 73–123. There are detailed histories of western river projects. See, for example, Roald Tweet, *A History of the Rock Island District, U.S. Army Corps of Engineers, 1866–1983* (Rock Island, Ill.: U.S. Army Engineer District, 1984), and Leland R. Johnson, *The Falls City: A History of the Louisville District, Corps of Engineers, U.S. Army* (Louisville, Ky.: U.S. Army Corps of Engineers, 1975).

44. Mark Twain, *Life on the Mississippi* (New York: Bantam, 1963), pp. 138–139.

45. Edward Wegmann, *The Design and Construction of Dams* (New York: Wiley, 1922); *The Ohio River Handbook and Picture Album* (Cincinnati: Young and Klein, 1969).

46. John H. White, Jr., "Tracks and Timber," *IA, Journal of the Society for Industrial Archeology* 2 (1976): 35–46.

47. Grade crossings in the landscape and the problems they posed for horse-drawn vehicles are described in John R. Stilgoe, *Metropolitan Corridor: Railroads and the American Scene* (New Haven, Conn.: Yale University Press, 1983), chap. 6.

48. For a different interpretation, see Wolfgang Schivelbusch, *The Railway Journey*, trans. Anslem Hollo (New York: Urizen Books, 1977), chap. 4.

49. John A. Jakle, "Landscapes Redesigned for the Automobile," in *The Making of the American Landscape*, ed. Michael P. Conzen (Boston: Unwin Hyman, 1990), p. 300.

50. The Hoosac Tunnel is a 4.75-mile-long railway tunnel connecting North Adams and Florida, Massachusetts. It was built over twenty-one years and completed in 1876. Nitroglycerine was first used for blasting rock, and compressed air was first used for rock drilling at the Hoosac. The high cost of construction became a major political scandal in Massachusetts (J. L. Harrison, *The Great Bore* [North Adams, Mass.: Advance Job Print Works, 1891]; George M. Mowbray, *Tri-Nitro Glycerine as Applied in the Hoosac Tunnel, Submarine Building, Etc.* [North Adams, Mass.: J. T. Robinson, 1872]; R. Pumpelly, J. E. Wolf, and T. N. Dale, *Geology of the Green Mountains in Massachusetts*, U.S. Geological Survey Monograph No. 23 [Washington, D.C.: Government Printing Office, 1894]).

51. John H. Williams, *A Great and Shining Path* (New York: Times Books, 1989), p. 116.

52. The structural and aesthetic qualities of the Starrucca Viaduct are discussed in Carl W. Condit, *American Building* (Chicago: University of Chicago Press, 1968), p. 74.

53. Susan Danly and Leo Marx, eds., *The Railroad in American Art* (Cambridge, Mass.: MIT Press, 1988), pp. 11–13.

54. Peregrine Prolix [Philip Nicklin], *Journey Through Pennsylvania—1835, by Canal, Rail and Stage Coach* (York, Pa.: American Canal and Transportation Center, 1978), pp. 18–19.

55. The structural and aesthetic qualities of the Tunkhannock Viaduct are discussed in Condit, *American Building*, p. 252. See also David Plowden, *Bridges: The Spans of North America* (New York: Viking Press, 1974), pp. 29, 71, 317–318.

56. Carroll L. V. Meeks, *The Railroad Station: An Architectural History* (New Haven, Conn.: Yale University Press, 1956).

57. Resource substitution is discussed in Robert B. Gordon and others, *Toward a New Iron Age? Quantitative Modeling of Resource Exhaustion* (Cambridge, Mass.: Harvard University Press, 1987), chap. 3.

58. Carroll W. Pursell, Jr., *Early Stationary Steam Engines in America* (Washington, D.C.: Smithsonian Institution Press, 1969); Louis C. Hunter, *A History of Industrial Power in the United States*, vol. 2, *Steam Power* (Charlottesville: University Press of Virginia, 1985).

59. Craig L. Bartholomew and Lance E. Metz, *The Anthracite Iron Industry of the Lehigh Valley* (Easton, Pa.: Center for Canal History and Technology, 1988), pp. 50–53.

60. Thomas Turner, *The Metallurgy of Iron* (London: Griffin, 1900), p. 306.

61. Walter R. Johnson, *Notes on the Use of Anthracite in the Manufacture of Iron* (Boston: Little, Brown, 1841), p. 11.

62. Frederick Overman, in H. S. Osborn, *The Metallurgy of Iron and Steel* (Philadelphia: Baird, 1869), p. 669.

63. Bowen, *Coal Regions of Pennsylvania*, p. 31.

64. Johnson, *Notes on the Use of Anthracite*, table 1.

65. Bartholomew and Metz, *Anthracite Iron Industry*, chap. 3.

66. Edwin T. Freedley, ed., *A Treatise on the Principal Trades and Manufactures of the United States* (Philadelphia: Young, 1856), pp. 263–264; J. H. Battle, ed., *History of Columbia and Montour Counties* (Chicago: Warner, 1887), p. 98.

67. W. David Lewis, "Early History of the Lackawanna Iron and Coal Company," *Pennsylvania Magazine of History and Biography* 96 (1972): 424–468.

68. In 1983, the Lackawanna works were, in turn, abandoned (John Strohmeyer, *Crisis in Bethlehem: Big Steel's Struggle to Survive* [Bethesda, Md.: Adler and Adler, 1986], chap. 17).

69. Binder, *Coal Age Empire*, p. 77. The remains of the coal, coke, and iron industry in Fayette County are described in Sarah P. Heald, ed., *Fayette County, Pennsylvania: An Inventory of Historic Engineering Sites* (Washington, D.C.: National Park Service, 1990).

70. Jeanne McHugh, *Alexander Holley and the Makers of Steel* (Baltimore: Johns Hopkins University Press, 1980), pp. 124–126, 227–228, 234–239.

71. Sharon Brown, "The Cambria Iron Company of Johnstown, Pennsylvania," *Canal History and Technology Proceedings* 7 (1988): 19–46.

72. William T. Lankford and others, eds., *The Making, Shaping and Treating of Steel*, 10th ed. (Pittsburgh: United States Steel, 1985), p. 156.

73. The abandonment of steelmaking in the valleys of western Pennsylvania is described in John P. Hoerr, *And the Wolf Finally Came: The Decline of the American Steel Industry* (Pittsburgh: University of Pittsburgh Press, 1988).

74. The early history of the Great Lakes iron mines is described in Harlan Hatcher, *A Century of Iron and Men* (Indianapolis: Bobbs-Merrill, 1950).

75. Gary Kulik, "Birmingham: Old Iron Furnaces Still Central Element of Industrial City's Skyline," *American Preservation* 1 (1978): 20–23.

76. Zachariah Allen, *The Practical Tourist* (Providence, R.I., 1835), vol. 1, p. 155. For more information on Allen and industrialization, see Richard E. Greenwood, "Zachariah Allen and the Architecture of Industrial Paternalism," *Rhode Island History* 46 (1988): 117–135.

77. Gary Kulik and Patrick M. Malone, *The Wilkinson Mill*, Landmark Dedication Program (Pawtucket, R.I.: American Society of Mechanical Engineers, 1977), pp. 3–6.

78. Charles Cowley, *Illustrated History of Lowell* (Boston: Lee and Shepard, 1868), pp. 84–85.

79. Charles Dickens, *American Notes for General Circulation*, quoted in Walter C. Kidney, *The Three Rivers* (Pittsburgh: Pittsburgh History and Landmarks Foundation, 1982), p. 24; Twain, *Life on the Mississippi*, p. 113; Scott Nixon, "A History of Metal Inputs to Narragansett Bay" (Report for the Narragansett Bay Project [preliminary draft], 1990), pp. 40–44.

80. Stilgoe, *Metropolitan Corridor,* pp. 77–103.

81. For a thorough discussion of both mechanical and electrical transmission of power, see Louis C. Hunter and Lynwood Bryant, *A History of Industrial Power in the United States, 1780–1930,* vol. 3, *The Transmission of Power* (Cambridge, Mass.: MIT Press, 1991).

5

Scarce Metals and Petroleum

Lured by the potential for substantial wealth, Americans have focused a disproportionate share of their industrial effort on extracting and processing resources that are both scarce and in high demand. Gold and silver were always valuable and eagerly sought, but in the nineteenth century, the demand for other nonferrous metals and for petroleum rose to unprecedented levels. Obtaining these scarce, nonrenewable resources brought new patterns of industrial land use and new environmental consequences. The continuing effects on our land, water, and air are serious concerns in American society today.

Mining and Metallurgy

The hope of finding gold and silver, the metals of wealth and display, drew numerous adventurers to North America in the seventeenth century. In the East, those hoping to repeat the Spanish experience in South America and Mexico were disappointed. Although colonial prospectors did discover small deposits of nonferrous-metal ores on the east coast and in the Appalachians, most of the metals were not in the precious category. There was a demand for utilitarian metals as well: English colonists depended on lead for pipes, window cames, and shot; they cooked with copper kettles, drank the products of copper stills, and set their tables with pewter (a tin alloy) tableware. Nevertheless, Americans generally found it cheaper and easier to use imported nonferrous metals until the mineral resources of the center of the continent were exploited in the nineteenth century. Iron was the only metal extensively mined in the English colonies.[1]

One of the few relicts of pre-Revolutionary nonferrous metallurgy is the Simsbury Copper Mine in East Granby, Connecticut. This mining enterprise obtained its charter in 1706. The state now preserves the site, not as an industrial monument but because the mine served for a time as the state prison. Visitors can enter the underground workings. Physical evidence of the first gold discovery in the United States, in 1799, exists at the Reed Gold Mine, a state historic site near Georgiaville, North Carolina. Most of the milling survivals are from later development at the mining site in 1854 and 1896. North Carolina led the nation in gold production until the California gold rush of 1849.[2]

In the early decades of the nineteenth century, the production of nonferrous metals increased at about the same rate as the growth of the American industrial economy. Then the relative demand soared as entrepreneurs introduced such new products and services as the metallic cartridge (made of brass, an alloy of copper and zinc), daguerreotype photography (done on silver-coated copper plates), galvanized (zinc-coated) iron, and electric power (transmitted on copper wires). In the Mississippi Valley, Americans found abundant, new supplies of nonferrous metals, particularly lead ore deposits. Lead was considered so vital to national defense that until 1846 lead-bearing lands were held by the federal government and administered by the Ordnance Department for lease to miners. The names of towns such as Galena, Illinois, and Leadington, Missouri, are reminders of the former importance of this industry. In Wisconsin, settlers paid Indians to do much of the early mining. By the 1820s, Cornish immigrants had begun to take over this work, introducing some of the extraction and milling technology of their homeland. At first, miners took ore from shallow mines worked by hand-turned windlasses. The resemblance of their pits to the work of hordes of badgers is said to have given Wisconsin the nickname "Badger State." After they exhausted the lead deposits, many of the Wisconsin miners used their earnings to set up as farmers, and their region made a transition, unusual in mining districts, to a new economic base.[3] The remains of the twentieth-century lead industry in the Mississippi Valley are more prominent. Two abandoned mines in Missouri may be visited today: the Federal Lead Company mine and mill at Flat River (Fig. 5.1), now a Missouri Mines Historic Site, and the partially flooded mine at Bonne Terre, which is the scene of both walking tours and guided scuba dives.

At Herculaneum, Missouri, the bases of nineteenth-century shot towers scar a steep limestone bluff along the Mississippi River. Lead workers built their first tower in 1809. They used the natural drop of almost 150 feet and the force of gravity to advantage. Droplets of molten lead assumed a spherical shape as they fell inside the masonry towers, cooling on the way down and landing in water-filled tubs as solid shot. Water-borne transport at the lower level was ideal for shipping the heavy product, sorted by size, for use in ammunition.[4] Ammunition entrepreneurs in the East competed by building the Phoenix shot tower in Baltimore in 1828. At 234 feet, this brick tower was once called the world's tallest building. It was reconstructed after a fire in 1878 and continues to dwarf multistory structures near it.[5]

From mid-century onward, prospectors discovered rich deposits of precious metals in the western states and territories. In exploiting these resources, miners helped push the frontier across the continent. The mines they opened were often in remote places and difficult terrain. The costs of

FIGURE 5.1. The head frame of the Federal Lead Company mine in Flat River, Missouri, is at the left in this photograph, and the mill for preparing the ore is at the right. The waste, or "chat," from the milling operations has been piled up behind the mine buildings. The size of the waste pile can be appreciated from the scale of the rail cars on the track beside it. (Courtesy of the Smithsonian Institution)

bringing supplies and equipment in and taking the product out were high. Consequently, the first miners sought to take the most valuable ore as quickly as possible and then move on to richer workings. By the end of the century, these adventurers were being replaced by professional engineers operating large-scale metallurgical works owned by eastern capitalists. However, the professionals inherited frontier attitudes about the environment that led to some of the greatest industrial intrusions ever made on the American landscape.

Industrial Archaeology of Mining

The average amounts of copper, lead, zinc, silver, mercury, and gold in the earth's crust are so low that they can be mined economically only where geological processes have concentrated them into ore. These ores often have been found in wilderness or frontier areas, but almost every region of the United States has experienced some type of extraction or refining process for scarce metals. The physical, documentary, and oral evidence of this industry is particularly well suited for the interdisciplinary approach of the industrial archaeologist.

At Ely, Vermont, a walled trench, now only partially covered with stone lintels, runs up a mountainside. A few hardy birch trees grow within this mid-nineteenth-century flue of a copper smelter that once stood in the valley, and bats use the open entrance to the mine. The mining community at Ely is gone, but many other abandoned metallurgical sites have changed little. The New Jersey Zinc Company built its works at a greenfield site in Palmerton, Pennsylvania, in 1897 to smelt ore from New Jersey with coal from Pennsylvania. Photographs taken in 1899 show a rural setting with wooded hills adjacent to the smelter.[6] The company expanded the industrial plant as well as the housing for workers and their families. For three-quarters of a century the community prospered, but costs of mining, transportation, smelting, and fuel were gradually rising. Emissions of smelter fumes and defoliation of neighboring woods, practices that had long been tolerated, were no longer acceptable. Today the closed smelter reflects the new economic reality of a community that once depended on a single company and a single metal (Fig. 5.2).

Sometimes, as in the Mississippi Valley, rich mines were in country that was also good farmland. Miners could take up farming when working ore deposits was not profitable. But in northern Michigan and the arid and mountainous West, there were few alternative uses for the land; if mining declined, communities were depopulated or abandoned.[7] A mining camp could become a boomtown almost overnight, and then sink into oblivion just

FIGURE 5.2. The former New Jersey Zinc Company smelter in Palmerton, Pennsylvania, sits in the narrow valley of the Lehigh River. When the smelter was in operation, the high ridges around it restricted the dispersion of smoke and fume. Rising costs and environmental regulations forced the Palmerton smelter to close, solving the air-pollution problem and leaving behind this industrial ruin and the barren hillsides.

as quickly if metal prices fell or the ore became exhausted. The remains of mining activities are abundant where equipment and buildings were left in place to decay. A remarkable amount of historic machinery escaped later scrap drives and salvage efforts. Some depressed towns, such as Cripple Creek, Colorado, have attempted to take advantage of mining detritus to revive their faltering economies with mine tours or museum displays.

Horizontal Stratigraphy

To an archaeologist, the word *stratigraphy* describes the layering of artifactual evidence; in the simplest case, deposits of recent materials lie above the artifacts from earlier periods. Mining sites are more likely to be stratified horizontally,[8] with newer features added where space was available, not in locations already used for structures, shafts, or heavy machinery. To some extent, this behavior was promoted by a frontier environment, where there was usually sufficient space to spread out, and a frontier culture, which was not offended by littering or dereliction. Few mine operators expected to occupy a site for decades. They were not concerned with appearances or long-term effects. It made sense to leave old equipment in place if it was still functional, could be a source of parts or building materials, or was too difficult to move. Demolition took effort and could cause temporary halts in production. If done at all, it was for reasons of minimal concern at most mining sites, such as liability, property taxes, or scarcity of land. Mine operators had no qualms about destroying things or completely rebuilding a plant when it was to their economic advantage, but it could be wise to put up the new hoist house beside the operating one, to sink a large access shaft while saving the small one for ventilation, to add a new set of boilers by simply extending the boiler house, to try out a ball mill while keeping the stamps in place, just in case they might be needed.

The major technological changes in nineteenth-century mining and met-allurgical practices are well documented and offer good evidence for the relative dating of equipment and the interpretation of process sequences with material evidence at mining sites. Only remnants of obsolete systems can be expected to remain at sites where there were multiple changes or that went through cycles of abandonment and reuse. Some destruction occurs in almost any program of industrial replacement, and mining operations (even those with horizontal stratigraphy) were no exception.[9] Extensive salvaging of metal for its scrap value and collection of artifacts in the twentieth century have further reduced, but not eliminated, the material record of defunct enterprises.

Isolation and Difficult Terrain

On balance, the difficulty of getting to and carrying things from isolated mining sites has helped to preserve the artifacts of extraction technology and life in mining communities. Although vandals may be more inclined to damage historic features if they feel safe from observation, they have to make a significant effort to reach remote mines in the mountains or deserts. For students of mining history, it is helpful to discover by personal observation the relative inaccessibility of so much of this industrial landscape. The challenges presented to miners by steep mountains must have been terribly intimidating in the nineteenth century, when bad weather could cut off every link to the outside world for weeks at a time. Trips today into rugged mining areas by foot path, by mountain road, or by narrow-gauge railroad (Fig. 4.19) are a revelation, even for those who have studied topographic and historic maps and surveys of mining operations.

During the Klondike gold rush, which began in 1897, a prospective miner's greatest problem was getting himself and several thousand pounds of supplies and equipment over the coastal mountain range so that he could

FIGURE 5.3. A narrow-gauge Baldwin steam locomotive, built around 1900, used by the White Pass and Yukon Railroad. It was scrapped in the 1940s and placed as riprap in the bank of the Skagway River at Skagway, Alaska. It and another locomotive hulk have since been hauled out. The railway still uses a 2-8-2 Baldwin locomotive for special passenger trains.

travel down the Yukon River to the goldfields. Hikers today in Klondike Gold Rush National Historical Park can follow the arduous Chilkoot Trail, which leads from Dyea, Alaska, up the Golden Stairs of the mountain pass to British Columbia, and see en route the remains of aerial tramways that charged fees to carry cargo for miners with enough money to afford such luxury. Passengers taking the historic White Pass and Yukon Railroad, an alternative route through the mountains from Skagway, can assess the terrible cruelty of the earlier and aptly named Dead Horse Trail, visible at various points below the rail line as a ledge or defile in the sharp rocks. The narrow-gauge railroad (Fig. 5.3), an engineering marvel that connected with steamboats on the Yukon River (Fig. 5.4) in 1899, made the Chilkoot obsolete; the railroad acquired the tramways along the trail and demolished them.[10]

At White Pass, another aerial tramway, now in ruins, that carried gold and silver ore down from John Conrad's mine on Montana Mountain cost $90,000 to construct in 1905. It rose 3,500 feet and was 18,000 feet long. In 1907, Conrad built a much shorter tramway from his Venus Mine to a new concentration mill at the side of a lake (Fig. 5.5). Buckets of ore came down

FIGURE 5.4. The graveyard of steamboats downstream of Dawson, Yukon Territory, on the west bank of the Yukon River.

on cables, supported by towers, and went directly into the top of the mill, where the rock was dumped into a crusher.[11]

Tramways had already proved their worth in Colorado in mountain ranges such as the San Juans.[12] Mines had to be where the ore was located, even if that was far up a mountainside. It was best to locate mills, which needed water for wet processes and often for power, near streams below. Tramcars on rails could not handle a steep descent between mine and mill, and an ore chute was ineffective or impossible to build in many types of terrain.[13] An aerial tramway was a daring but common solution, as one can see in numerous Colorado examples: near Telluride, at sites along the route of the Durango and Silverton Railroad, and at the Paris Mine outside Alma.[14]

Buildings perched near mine entrances at these mountainous sites provided temporary storage for ore and lodging for miners. Some miners who worked at almost inaccessible places had no choice but to stay there for extended periods. Despite rules against riding in ore buckets, men did go up and down in them occasionally, particularly if a tramway was operating when snow blocked the path from a mine.[15] However, snow was not the explanation for one fatal trip at a Silverton mine in 1930. According to a report by the Colorado Bureau of Mines, after a vacation Edward Shimin was returning to his job as a blacksmith at the Iowa-Tiger Mine, accompanied by a woman, whom he was taking to the mine with him. Both appeared to be under the influence of liquor. In violation of the company's order in such cases and over the strong objections of the tram operator, he placed the woman in one bucket and he took the bucket immediately following some 200 or 300 feet. . . . It is quite evident that in some unaccountable manner the woman loosened the clasp holding the bucket . . . allowing it to descend . . . with terrific force until it collided with the bucket in which Shimin was riding. The collision knocked Shimin from the bucket and threw the woman's bucket from the tram, causing them both to fall a considerable distance to the ground, killing Shimin instantly and very seriously injuring the woman.[16]

Mountains and western deserts were not the only geographic features that created isolation. Water could also cut off mines and miners from easy access to the nearest vestige of civilization. Nowhere was this more obvious than at Silver Islet, originally an 80- by 65-foot rock outcropping a mile from the Ontario shore in Lake Superior. Only a very costly coffer dam and a system of breakwaters made it possible to expand the surface area and develop a profitable and technically innovative mining complex in the 1870s.

FIGURE 5.5. The lower tramway terminal and concentration mill of the Venus Mine on Tagish Lake near Carcross, Yukon Territory. It was completed by 1909 and is now abandoned. (There is a photograph of the tramway in operation in D. D. Cairns, *Report on a Portion of Conrad and Whitehorse Mining Districts, Yukon* [Ottawa: Dawson, 1908].)

Miners stayed on the tiny island in company boardinghouses during cold months and storms. The company provided separate housing for Cornishmen, Norwegians, and "others."[17] The lake made it even more difficult to reach Isle Royale, a much bigger island that had many copper mines and small communities of year-round inhabitants. Isle Royale was located so many miles from land that traveling to it was like a sea voyage, when the lake was not frozen and impassable.

Diffusion, Variation, and Innovation

Much of the technology used at North American mines, ore mills, and smelters was based on foreign practices. Early European mining practices were well documented, and methods of ore crushing had continued to evolve in the New World colonies of the Spanish. Chinese miners in northern California introduced Chinese pumps, bucket bailers on an endless chain driven by an undershot waterwheel. These were based on traditional irrigation devices used in southeastern China, but the concept was also known in Europe.[18] The Cornish had developed skills of hard-rock mining that had made them the most respected miners in the world. The immigration of thousands of experienced miners, engine operators, and mill men from the copper and tin regions of Cornwall in the nineteenth century provided a ready source of practical information and experience. When faced with complex ores that were difficult to reduce, Americans frequently sought advice from experts in Swansea, Wales, or at the Frieberg School of Mines in Saxony.[19] After mid-century, mining journals and an outpouring of technical books aided the diffusion of information between nations and regions.

Yet, for all the borrowing, there was even more adaptation and innovation. The Cornish stamp mill for pulverizing ore was altered in California, and changed again to fit particular needs in Michigan's copper country. European smelting processes (Chapter 6) had to be radically modified to be effective on many American ores. A mine captain named William Frue on Silver Islet came up with an improved form of concentration table (see the discussion on mills later in this chapter), the "Frue Vanner," which Dianne Newell calls "the ultimate development of the (mechanical) type of concentration process and a fine example of local invention." In Ontario, "the borrowing of technology always entailed some degree of experimentation, adaptive change, and perhaps improvement of existing techniques. At the very least, the equipment would have to be modified and its components arranged to suit the particular minerals being developed in each setting."[20]

Much of the modification and experimentation with extraction or processing equipment took place in small blacksmith and machine shops, often part of the surface complex at a mining site. The twentieth-century repair facilities at Bear Creek in the Yukon and the Quincy Mine in Michigan were

FIGURE 5.6. In this historic photograph, foundry workers pose beside a recently cast mine-hoist sheave wheel at the Knight Foundry in Sutter Creek, California. The wooden jib of the foundry crane is at the right. The mold for the wheel was made in the sand floor. After the casting cooled, it was broken free of the sand and lifted out with the crane. (Courtesy of David Weitzman and Knight Foundry)

exceptionally well equipped,[21] but even small mines might have a blacksmith shop and an engine lathe. Although isolation could force mining companies to acquire their own capability for repairing broken machinery and building things on site, convenience and independence were also important factors.

Shops such as the Knight Foundry (1873 onward) in Sutter Creek, California, did custom casting for mine operators and sometimes produced items of their own design for sale (Fig. 5.6). Today, the foundry allows

visitors to watch the weekly pour of molten metal. The Knight tangential
waterwheel, patented in 1875, before the better-known Pelton wheel, was
made from parts cast and machined at the foundry. One of these Knight
wheels is displayed at the Empire Mine State Historic Park in Grass Valley,
California. [22]

Mines

Men have mined in North America with pans and crude sluice boxes, with
hammers and drill rods, pneumatic drills, black powder, dynamite, hydraulic nozzles, dredges, and giant shovels. The physical evidence is everywhere,
on the surface and far below ground. Shallow Native American copper mines
in Michigan, which are difficult, if not impossible, to distinguish from
nineteenth-century test pits, [23] lie close to shafts driven thousands of feet
through rock with powered tools and explosives.

Access to many deep mines was through shafts, some of which went down
vertically to the workings, while others followed an inclined, or angled,
path. Head frames, engine foundations, and occasionally a fully equipped
hoist house can be found above or near some mine openings, but most shafts
are now isolated features, nothing more than holes or depressions in the
ground. It was often possible, particularly in mountainous terrain, to tunnel
in with a horizontal entrance, or adit. Mines might have multiple levels,
each with interconnected passages; they might need a series of shafts or adits
to the surface and a number of shorter, interior shafts to connect the levels.
It was not unusual to have special shafts dedicated to ventilation or pumping, and tunnels for no purpose other than draining water. There was no
standard solution to the technical problems of extracting and transporting
ore from a deep mine while maintaining an environment in which men could
work. [24]

Open-pit mining was possible when ore was located near the surface, but
without self-propelled earth-moving equipment, it was usually impractical.
The scale of these operations changed dramatically in the twentieth century
as heavy equipment (shovels, draglines, loaders, bulldozers, trucks) and
more powerful explosives became available. Open-pit mining of low-grade
ore has created enormous holes in the ground that may become permanent
parts of the landscape. Their great volume makes it costly to fill and regrade
them after mining operations cease. A relatively recent example is the
Berkeley pit at Butte, Montana, which was mined from 1955 to 1982 and is
now gradually filling with water (Fig. 5.7).

BELOW-GROUND LANDSCAPE
Relatively few Americans have been in an underground mine, and many look
on the prospect of entering one with a mixture of fear and loathing. Mines

are, after all, one of the most dangerous working environments; the terrible toll taken by accidents and occupational lung disease is well documented. The vision of dark, dripping passageways, with creaking supports holding up tons of rock, haunts the imagination. Most of us have no qualms about riding through railroad, subway, or highway tunnels. We will gladly get in a crowded elevator and travel into the subterranean levels of a parking garage. Somehow a mine is different; it makes almost everyone feel uncomfortable. For many, it arouses the primordial fear of being trapped underground, of being buried alive.

A well-interpreted visit to a mine can relieve some of the irrational horrors of an underground industrial experience without glossing over the historic and continuing dangers. It is a broadening experience to be far below the surface in a place where men once worked, even when many compromises are necessary to make that experience safe for the visitor. The Pioneer Tunnel and the Lackawanna Coal Mine, formerly active anthracite opera-

FIGURE 5.7. The Berkeley pit in Butte, Montana, was opened in 1955; by 1982, its operation was no longer economical. The stepped benches of this enormous open-pit copper mine indicate levels of excavation and routes for removal of material by truck. The tall steel head frame of a deep mine, which is surrounded by waste piles, is just beyond the top of the pit.

FIGURE 5.8. An underwater scene in the former Bonne Terre Lead Mine. Scuba divers on a guided tour of this flooded lead mine in Bonne Terre, Missouri, pause to examine the frame of an ore elevator. Ore cars, tracks, drills, and other artifacts were left behind in the open rooms and tunnels of this mine's extensive underground workings. (Photograph by Richard Frehsee. Courtesy of West End Diving)

tions in northeastern Pennsylvania, give visitors a realistic impression of work underground.

The Molly Kathleen Mine in Cripple Creek, Colorado, packs visitors (with authentic crowding) into a mine "cage" and, after a hurtling descent down a vertical shaft, delivers them safely to a drift at the 1,000-foot level. Mining began here in 1892, but for almost fifty years, the Molly Kathleen has served as both tourist attraction and underground-mining museum. The

interpreted tour of the gritty workings below is worth the somewhat claus-
trophobic trip. Riding back up in the cage, equipped with safety brakes, one
can only imagine the same trip in one of the open buckets that were used to
transport men (as well as ore, waste rock, and water) at many nineteenth-
century mines.[25] Unfortunately, improved technology and government inspection could only promote mine safety; it could not remove all risks. Many
accidents happened in the shafts of working mines even with up-to-date
signaling and hoisting equipment. Not far from the Molly Kathleen in 1902,
a miner was torn to pieces in the Elkton Mine when the drill rods he was
holding caught against the timbering of a shaft while his cage was in
motion.[26]

Some experiences on public mining tours are truly memorable. In addition to the cage at the Molly Kathleen, there is the tram ride through total
darkness to the proverbial light at the end of the Pioneer Tunnel in Ashland,
Pennsylvania, and the underwater tour for certified divers through the enormous, flooded rooms of the Bonne Terre Lead Mine in Missouri (Fig. 5.8).
The walking entry to the Chollar Mine on the Comstock Lode in Virginia
City, Nevada, is not as dramatic as any of these, but the view of square-set
timbering within is a thrill for any reader of Mark Twain's *Roughing It*:

> Virginia was a busy city of streets and houses above ground. Under it was
> another busy city, down in the bowels of the earth, where a great population of
> men thronged in and out among an intricate maze of tunnels and drifts,
> flitting hither and thither under a winking sparkle of lights, and over their
> heads towered a vast web of interlocking timbers that held the walls of the
> gutted Comstock apart. . . . One . . . cannot well imagine what that forest of
> timbers cost, from the time they were felled in the pineries beyond Washoe
> Lake, hauled up and around Mount Davidson at atrocious rates of freightage,
> then squared, let down into the keep maw of the mine and built up there.
> Twenty ample fortunes would not timber one of the greatest of those silver
> mines.[27]

SQUARE-SET TIMBERING, STOPING, AND GLORY HOLES

Fears of roof collapse are somewhat eased in the Chollar Mine by the solidity
of the great timbers that support it—a modest example of the three-
dimensional grid system developed at the nearby Ophir Mine in 1860 by the
young German mining engineer Philipp Deidesheimer.[28] The underground
rock of the Comstock was often badly fractured and notoriously weak. Fear
of collapse prompted many miners to fill unnecessary spaces between timbers with waste rock as soon as they could. It is difficult to imagine pressures that could crush the square-set timbering devised by Deidesheimer,
but nothing built by man in a mine is completely secure; one of the first
photographs taken with magnesium light is of a "Crash of timbers in cave-in,

FIGURE 5.9. Shot holes ready for firing in a rock face of the instructional mine operated by the Michigan Technological University in Houghton. The holes are drilled in the rock and filled with explosive. Timed electrical impulses sent through the wires detonate the explosives in the correct sequence to break the rock to the desired size.

Gould & Curry Mine, Virginia City Nevada." It is one of Timothy H. O'Sullivan's famous series of photographs taken of mines and miners at the Comstock Lode in 1868.[29]

The common practice of stoping increased the danger of collapse. In many hard-rock mines, operators found it efficient to open up large underground spaces called stopes. There was often no better way to extract large ore bodies, but roofs could cave in if there was inadequate support from stone pillars, timber posts, or square-set framing. The great expense of wood led some operators to skimp on their timbering. Also, water seeped into the workings, causing wooden members to rot and framing to weaken. If a stope near the surface collapsed, the resulting glory hole was sure to attract attention. The Chollar Mine had two cave-ins in the late 1860s, both attributed to rotting timbers: in the first incident, a Virginia City store disappeared into the hole; in the second, a mine superintendent's house hung on the edge.[30] Glory holes have become prominent landscape features in heavily mined areas of the West, and others will continue to appear as water weakens the timbering of closed mines.

Miners used a combination of drilling and blasting to open up stopes, to drive horizontal drifts and crosscuts, and to sink shafts in hard rock. The technique is demonstrated in a copper mine that has become an underground classroom of the Michigan Technological University. The university took over part of the abandoned Quincy Mine at Hancock, Michigan, entering through an adit on a hillside below most of the company's surface structures. Demonstrations introduce students to mining technology in an authentic setting. The noise and dust of power drilling are disturbing but not unexpected. However, nothing in the literature of mining prepares a neophyte for standing in front of a solid wall of stone pierced with a carefully designed pattern of drilled holes, charged with explosives, and wired for ignition (Fig. 5.9). The instructor explains how the timed, sequential blasts will first remove rock from the center, then shatter the surrounding mass to a depth of 9 feet, and finally heave the fractured pieces onto the floor of the tunnel. After leading everyone to a safe location in the mine (distance and corners provide protection from blast effects), he sets off the series of programmed explosions. The deep, muted sounds of those blasts and the strong waves of air pressure that race through the mine leave no doubt that a pile of shattered rock now lies where the group had been standing.

Copper Mining

MICHIGAN

Outcrops of native copper in northern Michigan were the principal source of the copper artifacts that were extensively traded across North America by Indians before contact with Europeans. Adventurers from the eastern states started mining these deposits after 1845, and the opening of the Sault Sainte Marie Canal in 1855 allowed copper from Michigan not only to replace imports, but also to make the United States a net exporter of copper. Michigan remained the principal North American source of copper until miners and capitalists began to extract great quantities of copper ore in Montana, Utah, and Arizona later in the nineteenth century. Few of the Michigan copper companies that struggled through the Great Depression could survive the elimination of price supports that existed during World War II. The last of the native-copper mines closed in 1969. Because Michigan mines were underground and unusually deep, the remains that are easiest to see are the surface structures and the openings to shafts, adits, and ventilation passages. The rockhouse at the No. 2 shaft at the Quincy Mine is about a mile north of Hancock, Michigan, on the Keweenah Peninsula (Fig. 5.10). Miners drew ore in skips up the inclined shaft, which had reached a depth of 9,000 feet when the mine was closed in 1931, and dumped it into the crushing plant in the rockhouse.

The No. 2 hoist house at Quincy still contains the 1921 Nordberg steam hoist that drew skips from the mine at a speed of 36 miles an hour (Fig. 5.11). One has to see this great, cross-compound, condensing engine—the

FIGURE 5.10. The rockhouse at the No. 2 shaft at the Quincy Mine in Hancock, Michigan. This 150-foot-tall structure was built in 1908 over the deepest of the Quincy Mine shafts. It contained machinery for crushing, classifying, and separating the ore brought up the shaft. The hoist cable passed over the steel tower in the foreground to an engine, or hoist, house some 600 feet away.

world's largest steam hoist—to appreciate its size. The winding drum is 30 feet in diameter. The operator's elevated platform, reached by a spiral stairway, has dials to indicate the position of skips in the mine and a set of levers to control the immense, 2,500-horsepower hoisting apparatus. Standing on that platform, it is easy to imagine the heady sense of power that an operator must have felt with his hands on the levers; but even with the automatic safety devices on the hoist, he would also have felt a sobering burden of responsibility as he moved men and materials through the subterranean levels of the mine.[31]

The crushed ore was hauled about 10 miles by rail to a stamp mill on the shores of Torch Lake, where water was plentiful. In the hundred years after 1868, some 200 million tons of tailings were dumped into the lake (Fig. 5.12). At first, the separation procedures at the mill were not very good, and much metal went into the lake with the tailings. In the twentieth century, the mining company dredged these tailings, reprocessed them, and dumped the remains back into the lake along with the chemicals from the flotation plant used to recover the copper. Although they decomposed relatively rap-

FIGURE 5.11. The Nordberg steam hoist at the No. 2 hoist house at the Quincy Mine. It took a year to install and put this gigantic piece of machinery in operation. Wire rope ran from the drum, shown here, to the top of the No. 2 shaft rockhouse and then down into the Quincy Mine. (Courtesy of Larry Lankton and The Quincy Mine Hoist Association)

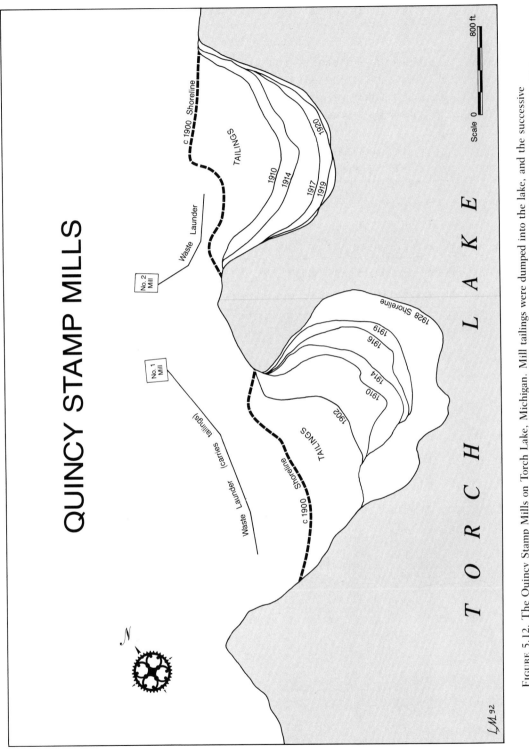

FIGURE 5.12. The Quincy Stamp Mills on Torch Lake, Michigan. Mill tailings were dumped into the lake, and the successive positions of the shoreline as more tailings were dumped are shown by the dated lines. (Map by Lyn Malone, based on a map by Eric Hansen for the Historic American Engineering Record)

idly, the flotation chemicals may have caused tumors that appeared in fish there. We still do not know the long-term effects of the metals in the tailings, but the Environmental Protection Agency has designated this a Superfund site and is continuing to investigate.[32] When it was operating, the Quincy Mining Company's smelter on Portage Lake was undoubtably a contributor to local air pollution, but its emissions were far less noxious than those from western plants that reduced sulfide ores.

JEROME, ARIZONA

High in the mountains of Arizona is a once-prosperous community that has suffered both direct and indirect damage from almost eight decades of intensive mining activity. The town of Jerome clings precariously to the steep side of Cleopatra Hill and is built on a geologic fault. From the formation of a copper-mining camp in 1876 to the closing of the Phelps Dodge mining operations in 1953, Jerome depended on rich deposits of ore that lay beneath or near its streets. It was a classic boomtown, with a population that peaked at 15,000 in 1929.[33]

Fires above and below ground plagued Jerome. Like many congested mining towns, it suffered several disastrous urban conflagrations in the late nineteenth century. A longer-term problem appeared in 1894 when sulfide ores in the United Verde Mine ignited and continued to burn for years. After several ineffective efforts to extinguish the fire, the mining company tried to seal off the burning areas with concrete bulkheads and kept mining at lower levels. In 1905, water leaking into the sealed spaces caused steam pressure to build up behind the bulkheads. The resulting explosion released steam and hot, poisonous gases into working areas of the mine and left six men dead.[34]

The persistent underground fires in the United Verde Mine made it difficult to reach most of the ore body. Surface mining with steam shovels was one way to get at the copper, but the large United Verde smelter stood right over much of it. In 1912, construction began on an even bigger smelter far below in the valley. The "big pit" in Jerome today is the site of the original smelter, which the company demolished soon after opening its Clarkdale plant in 1915. A 6.7-mile railroad connected the company town of Clarkdale to the end of United Verde's ore-haulage tunnel. Ore from the stripping operations was dumped down special shafts in the pit area and then moved more than 1 mile on rails through the tunnel.[35]

Long before the company shifted its smelting to the Verde Valley, nothing green (*verde,* in Spanish) was left on the mountain slopes around Jerome. All the trees had been cut to supply the demand for building materials, mine timbers, railroad ties, and fuel. The sulfurous fumes from Jerome's reduction of copper ores had killed the rest of the vegetation, and rapid runoff of rainwater and snowmelt from the denuded terrain was causing periodic floods and landslides. The foundations of buildings were being undermined by erosion and soil movement.

Beneath Jerome, mining had created a labyrinth of shafts, horizontal passageways, and large open stopes that could cave in with little or no warning. The natural fault in the hill was dangerous enough without the additional problems of altered hydrology, subsidence in old workings, and continuing disturbance by the mining companies. Blasting had always been an integral part of hard-rock mining in Jerome, but surface operations at the "big pit" in the 1920s required unprecedented amounts of explosives. [36]

Huge charges placed in tunnels at the sides of the pit shook the whole area and probably contributed to a subsequent movement of the fault. [37] By 1928, spreading cracks were obvious in many of the masonry structures on Main Street. Part of Jerome's business district gradually slid down the hillside, and numerous buildings collapsed in the fault area. A rugged concrete jail now sits intact more than 200 feet from its original location. It has become something of a tourist attraction. Another of Jerome's historic sites is known as the powderbox church, because most of the wood in its stuccoed walls came from recycled dynamite boxes. [38]

Use of Water in Mining

HYDRAULIC MINING AND DREDGING

Water has always played an important role in the recovery of precious metals, particularly gold. It has assisted in the prospecting for gold by panning, the separation of placer deposits (flakes or lumps of free gold) from sand or gravel deposits, and the concentration of ores. Placer gold, because of its high specific gravity, tends to settle at the bottom of a pan or sluice, while lighter materials are washed away. Water has also been the major source of mechanical and electrical power for mining, milling, and refining operations in many regions, even some of the most arid. Miners built elaborate ditch and flume systems to convey water for long distances over rugged terrain. Even a small flow of water could have tremendous energy if it was delivered from a high elevation in a tubular flume, or penstock. The pressurized flume was often a coopered structure, built of wood staves with wrought-iron constraining bands, like an extended barrel.

Hydraulicking in California. By the mid-1850s, gold miners in California's Sierra Nevada had begun to use high-velocity jets of water to cut away earth and gravel deposits, not only along the banks of streams but also on hillsides above. Pivoting iron nozzles (monitors), which were directed like artillery pieces at the natural landscape, released the energy of water under great

FIGURE 5.13. Scars left by hydraulicking for gold at the "Malakoff Diggins," now a state historic park at North Bloomfield, California. (Photograph by David Weitzman)

pressure. In this environmentally destructive process, known as hydraulicking, miners could excavate a vast quantity of possibly gold-bearing material, washing it down in a filthy torrent to sluices that trapped most of the heavy particles of gold. Owners who invested in these expensive industrial operations made little or no effort to prevent the runoff of wastes into creeks and rivers. Damage to farms in California's downstream valleys by heavy siltation and flooding caused outrage in the 1860s, followed by litigation and state regulation that ended most of the large-scale hydraulicking in the Sierras by 1884.[39]

Scars at the sites of this deliberate, mechanized erosion persist more than a century later (Fig. 5.13). California has made the extensive "Malakoff Diggins" at North Bloomfield into a state historic park with a visitors' center. It is a good place to learn about the problems caused by hydraulic mining. Serrated cliffs of earth and gravel rising from the water's edge at the park's pond are not natural features; they appear prominently in historic photographs that show multiple jets of water cutting away at their faces. Nowhere else did hydraulic mining take place on such a scale. The main pit is 7,000 feet long and up to 3,000 feet wide.[40]

Mining in the Klondike. The need for water to mine hillside claims in the Klondike region of Canada's Yukon Territory allowed a few heavily capitalized firms to gain control of the local goldfields in the early twentieth century. In 1907 to 1909, the Yukon Gold Company built a 70-mile-long "ditch" to deliver water for hydraulicking. Although open channels, flumes, and redwood pipes would suffice at upper elevations, pressures were very high where the conduit had to dip down into the Klondike River valley before rising on the other side. There the company's engineers installed an "inverted siphon" of steel, 15,000 feet long and 42 inches in diameter. Water at the lowest point was under 1,100 feet of head, exerting more than 450 pounds per square inch pressure and requiring special lap-welded joints between sections of the siphon.[41]

Some hydraulic mining continues in the Yukon, but the settling ponds and recycling systems used by the best operators keep the Klondike River relatively clean as it rushes through an upended landscape of historic tailings. Permafrost in the subarctic still creates difficult problems; the cutting action of the antique nozzles becomes ineffective as the water blasts reach a

FIGURE 5.14. Hydraulic mining for gold in the Klondike. Water from a monitor (nozzle) is directed at a gravel deposit in a permafrost layer. Another monitor, temporarily idle, is in the foreground. This modern operation uses antique monitors.

thick stratum of hillside permafrost that is as hard as concrete (Fig. 5.14).

Earlier in this century, mining companies in the Yukon had to thaw thick layers of frozen soil before they could reach much of the gold-bearing gravel. They tried wood fires and steam points (pipes driven deep into the ground) before discovering that cold-water points could do the job. By the late 1930s, they had learned to strip surface "muck" with powerful pumps and hydraulic monitors and then to use points in the stripped areas more than a year before they began their gold-recovery operations. After the permafrost thawed, it was possible to excavate and process gravel in the valleys with enormous, electrically powered, chain-bucket dredges assembled in the goldfields. In 1938, the Yukon Consolidated Gold Company stripped off 2,818,000 cubic yards of "overburden," thawed 4,141,000 cubic yards of ground, and dredged 8,551,000 cubic yards. Two-thirds of the ground processed by the company's dredges had already been worked at least once by other miners.[42]

The dredges floated in man-made ponds that moved with the process of excavation and backfilling. Canadian No. 2, constructed in 1910, sits rotting in its last pond. It was one of thirty-five such dredges that operated in the Klondike goldfields, digging up more than 100 miles along the creeks. Yukon Consolidated Gold Company Dredge No. 4, a wooden-hulled bucket dredge, is now preserved by Environment Canada (Fig. 5.15). Built in 1912 and 1913, the survivor of a sinking, a dismantling, and a rebuilding, it last ran in 1959. This 3,000-ton behemoth had seventy-two buckets, each with a capacity of 16 cubic feet and the capability to scrape off even some of the bedrock.[43] The incredible noise levels of this machine can only be imagined, but shock-absorbing suspension systems for interior incandescent lights give an indication of the vibrations that its operators endured. Because grease or oil might hinder the separation of gold from rock and gravel in the dredge's revolving screen and its sluices, much of the moving machinery could not be lubricated.[44]

The long tailing piles that cover the dredged areas of the Yukon have curved striations that make them look like earthworms, as they are sometimes called (Fig. 5.16). These are marks of deposition by the radial swings of a dredge's rear stacker, which dropped wastes from a conveyor belt. The distance between striations measures the incremental movement of the entire rig as it was winched forward in its pond by cables attached to the shore. The concavity of the arcs reveals the direction of the dredging process.[45] These surficial markings of a large-scale industrial operation can be read much as one reads the cutting marks of a machine tool.

WATER AS A LIABILITY IN MINING

Miners and engineers faced a tremendous challenge in keeping water out of workings, a fact that is evident in the number of abandoned mines that are flooded. If there was no reasonable way to construct a drain, water had to be

FIGURE 5.15. Yukon Consolidated Gold Company Dredge No. 4. This wooden-hulled dredge floated in its own pond and excavated gravel with a chain of seventy-two heavy buckets. The supporting apparatus for these buckets extends forward (to the right in this photograph). At the rear, a long conveyor called the "stacker" dropped the tailings that had passed through the processing machinery inside. Technicians from Environment Canada have refloated the dredge since this photograph was taken in 1990, and the site is now operated as a museum.

lifted out of a mine with a hoist or pump. At mines on the Comstock Lode in Nevada, the situation was complicated because the offending water was sometimes unbearably hot due to geothermal action. There, and at many other western sites, operators relied heavily on imported Cornish pumping technology, adapted for American conditions. The steam engines they favored had a flywheel, which was a departure from normal Cornish practice. A Cornish pumping engine with a 40-foot flywheel is preserved today at Iron Mountain, Michigan. Designed by the great American steam engineer Edwin Reynolds, it could raise 4 million gallons from a depth of 1,500 feet in twenty-four hours.[46] A water-powered pump of the Cornish type is on display at the North Star Mining Museum and Pelton Wheel Exhibit in Grass Valley, California.

Drainage tunnels, although sometimes difficult to cut, were less trouble to maintain than mechanical pumps and did not require fuel to operate. Whether drained by gravity or pumped, water from mines could cause severe

FIGURE 5.16. An aerial view of the Klondike River valley showing the tailings from past dredging and recent scars from hydraulic or strip-mining in the distance.

environmental damage. The acid and metal content of mine water was not fully understood. Even if it had been, most mine operators were not concerned about the long-term consequences of sending polluted water into nearby streams. The 3-mile-long Sutro Tunnel, built to carry water away from an entire group of Comstock mines, is the best-known drainage project in the history of American mining, but there were many smaller projects. Unfortunately for gullible investors in Adolf Sutro's enterprise, his tunnel was very costly to construct and was not completed until 1878, when most of the mines it was to serve were already going into decline. It automatically drained water long after the boom was over. The tunnel was also supposed to improve ventilation, reveal substantial ore bodies, and serve as a route for hauling ore from the mines. It did none of these, but it was opened again for mineral exploration in the 1970s.[47]

Mills

Because even rich nonferrous ores contained a low percentage of metal, they had to be concentrated by milling before they were smelted. Miners in the Lake Superior area sometimes found substantial pieces of relatively pure metal, or mass copper, which did not require milling. However, surrounding rock often had to be broken or crushed to release these mass-copper deposits.[48] Because of the difficulty of transporting heavy ore, mining companies set up the process of concentrating their ores as close to the mine as possible, and concentration mills are conspicuous landscape features at many metal mines.[49]

The Kennecott Mining Company's copper concentration mill in Alaska, subject of a recording project by the Historic American Engineering Record,[50] is one of the most spectacular of American mining buildings, with its fourteen timber-framed stories stepping in multigabled profusion down a steep hill. The height of the building is evidence of the way in which gravity helped to move ore through successive stages of concentration at this and other mills. Gravity also played a role in the operation of mechanical equipment, such as the shaking or vibrating tables that separated heavier concentrates from lighter gangue.[51] Large quantities of tailings, the waste from milling, often remain on a site long after buildings have disappeared.

The Kennecott copper mill has equipment that demonstrates the frequent adoption of new milling methods, local adaptation of older methods, and horizontal stratigraphy. When one type of machinery or process was replaced by another, the older form was often left in place or simply moved aside. Original design drawings of the Kennecott mill do not match the as-built forms or machinery placement found at the site; the building was expanded or altered many times. It must have been a cluttered and confusing place during its operating years. Researchers who interviewed former Kennecott workers found that they "only knew the operation of their particular machines or stations (such as a jig or crusher), and could not provide accurate information about the complete process through the mill. Thus, . . . documentation through oral interview proved less effective than observation of in place machinery."[52]

Smelters and Refineries

Gold and some copper were found as native metals, but miners got most of their copper, lead, silver, and zinc from ores that also contained sulfide, oxide, or carbonate minerals. Frequently, they found several metals together, as in the lead–silver ores of the Rocky Mountains. Sulfide minerals, such as chalcopyrite (copper–iron sulfide) were common and were usually converted to oxides by roasting before reduction to metal. At first, smeltermen practiced heap roasting—placing the ore on open wood fires—a process that used much labor and fuel and released the sulfur into the atmosphere as fumes. For every ton of copper they produced by smelting sulfide ores, they released approximately a ton of sulfur in the form of sulfur dioxide. Visitors can see some of the effects of heap roasting at Ducktown, Tennessee, where the Ducktown Basin Museum has displays on the local copper industry. Reverberatory and shaft roasters cut labor costs and improved fuel efficiency but did little to control emissions. Even after some plants began to recover their sulfurous fumes to make marketable sulfuric acid, smelter emissions remained a problem. Concentrations of sulfur dioxide as low as 0.01 parts per million are injurious to plants and many aquatic animals. Western smeltermen constructed very tall stacks so the sulfurous fumes would be emitted high enough in the atmosphere to be diluted and blown away from the source, but this only partially alleviated the effects of air pollution in the immediate area and spread the damage many miles downwind.

Some of the most notorious smelter emissions were in Butte, Montana, where public outrage over the rising death rate from respiratory disease in the early 1890s led to the passage of an ordinance against the heap roasting of copper ores. Thick smoke, with poisonous levels of sulfur and arsenic, had given the city an unhealthy, ugly environment. The situation in Butte improved somewhat as local smeltermen gradually adopted more effective processes, but the main cause of better atmospheric conditions at Butte was the shift of large-scale smelting operations to the nearby town of Anaconda. Gertrude Atherton, a novelist, described the effects on Butte:

> They [smelters] ate up the vegetation, and the melting snows and heavy June rains washed the weakened earth from the bones of the valley and the mountain, leaving both as stark as they must have been when the earth ceased to rock and began to cool. Since the smelters have gone to Anaconda, patches of green, of a sad and timid tenderness, like the smile of a child too long neglected, have appeared between the sickly grey boulders of the foothills, and, in Butte, lawns as large as a tablecloth have been cultivated.[53]

In Anaconda, farmers and ranchers decided to sue the smelter operators, despite their protestations that taller stacks and dust chambers had solved the worst smoke problems.[54] In 1919, the lingering controversy prompted the company to erect the ultimate smokestack. The 585-foot behemoth is the only surviving structure of the great Anaconda Copper Mining Company smelter and refinery. This giant artifact and the off-limits perimeter defined by the Environmental Protection Agency remain as symbols of earlier attitudes toward the environmental costs of the wealth derived from the copper mines. A visitor has to see the Anaconda stack, the tallest freestanding masonry structure in the world, from various distances to comprehend its scale.

By the early 1980s, Anaconda was shipping ore to Japan for smelting. Preservationists managed to save the stack when the company razed the vast complex. The old works nearby had been demolished in the early twentieth century.[55] Little is left of the nineteenth-century western smelters, particularly those that were in or near the Rocky Mountains. The concentrations of smelting facilities that developed in Denver and Pueblo, Colorado, were at considerable distance from the mines (locations made possible by rail service and promoted by cheaper coal and labor), but most were close to the ore sources, as in Butte, Montana; Blackhawk and Leadville, Colorado; and Jerome, Arizona.[56]

The sulfide ores of copper contained arsenic and other heavy metals that had to be removed in smelting and refining. Some were recovered, but a great deal ended up in waste dumps or spillage, forming toxic deposits that remained after operations ceased and smelters were razed. Problems with heavy metals have been linked to former nonferrous-metal mining sites throughout the Rocky Mountains. The sites of silver and lead smelters are among the worst. At Leadville, Colorado, acidic runoff from abandoned mines, mill tailings, and smelter wastes carries an estimated ton of toxic metals into the Arkansas River drainage system every day. Rainwater and groundwater react with sulfides to form acids that can dissolve heavy metals.[57]

Many of the new uses for nonferrous metals depended on high standards of purity. Traces of arsenic or antimony in copper greatly reduce its electrical conductivity, for example. The managers of the large copper companies often placed electrolytic refining plants and the factories for subsequent drawing of copper into wire, or alloying to make brass, in the East. There were major copper refineries in Perth Amboy, New Jersey, and Baltimore, Maryland; wire works in Hastings, New York; and brass mills in Waterbury, Connecticut, among other places.[58] Railways took the primary metal from the mining districts to industrial cities where most of the value of the finished products was added; the severe environmental costs of mining and smelting were left behind.

Archaeology of Technological Failure

Archaeology is particularly valuable for examining the demise of industrial operations, a common historical experience that is seldom documented in any detail. Mining enterprises had a high rate of failure, and in many cases were intended to produce profits for only a short time. Although metal mining has richer documentation than most American industries, large companies received the most attention and left more records than small operations. The history of ordinary mines, mills, and smelters is much harder to determine from written sources alone. When they shut down, no archive was likely to preserve their complete business correspondence and account books. The material evidence of their operations is sometimes quite extensive and revealing, however.[59] It was difficult to salvage equipment from the more isolated mining sites, and few owners worried about the waste dumps or tailing piles they left behind. Miners abandoned above-ground structures that no longer had value. They left their underground workings to bats or perhaps to water that pumps had once kept at bay.

Causes of mining failures included undercapitalization, poor management, changes in metal prices, environmental restrictions, labor problems, excessive transportation or fuel costs, exhaustion of ore, inaccurate geological assessments, and technological mistakes. The extraction and processing of ores has always been a risky business. A significant part of that risk was in the choice of industrial equipment and in the technological experimentation that was often necessary to deal with variable conditions and unusual ores. The material evidence that remains at the sites of abandoned mining operations can sometimes yield information obtainable no other way. It can help to unravel twisted paths of trial and error, exposing dead ends and roadblocks. With integrated programs of documentary research and archaeological investigation at mining sites, we can begin to understand the difficulties and see why so many of them closed.[60]

Norwich Mine

Archaeologists working at the site of the Norwich Mining Company in Michigan found physical evidence of much more extensive and longer-lasting copper-mining operations than was suggested by an initial documentary survey. That evidence then provided directions for further archival investigation. Seven copper-mining companies had worked the site over a period of seventy years. None was successful; the copper lodes were neither rich enough nor of sufficient size to bring a reasonable return on investment. Rising copper prices and hopes generated by improved technology (such as diamond drilling for core samples in 1916) spurred additional attempts, but to no avail. Archaeologists found and identified more than forty shafts and adits, three stamp-mill foundations, three dams, and the ruins of numerous buildings, roads, and trams.[61]

Isle Royale

Investigation of copper mines at Isle Royale National Park in Lake Superior is a long-term, cooperative effort of the National Park Service and university scholars. One of the sites examined in recent years is the Isle Royale and Ohio Mine, which commenced operations in 1847. Study of the physical remains of this mine's smelter, the first to operate in the region, revealed its design and operating principles. Brief references to it in documentary records did not explain its form or the reasons for its abandonment. Operating much like a blast furnace, the smelter did not work as well as the owners hoped. It is still "clogged with the slaggy remains of its final charge." The mine closed for good in 1849, soon after the failure of this risky, experimental technology. The Siskowit Mine Company, 2 miles away, which also had sent stamp-mill concentrates to the smelter, continued in operation until 1855, but its managers had to depend on distant processing facilities in Detroit, Cleveland, or cities on the east coast.[62]

Charles H. Spencer Mining Operations

Efforts by Charles H. Spencer to recover gold by dredging and hydraulic mining at Lee's Ferry, Arizona, between 1910 and 1913 were not successful. They are, however, highly instructive for historians of technology. A historical and archaeological study conducted by the Submerged Cultural Resources Unit of the National Park Service[63] has revised the accepted explanations for Spencer's failure at this site and shown the potential for technical analysis of both artifacts and geology at abandoned mining sites.

Spencer went to Lee's Ferry after trying to develop profitable gold-mining operations at two other sites in the region. This time he tested a newly patented pipe dredge beside the Colorado River, but hit ledge at a shallow depth. Steam boilers fired with driftwood supplied power for the futile dredging operation and for his next effort, hydraulic mining using water supplied by pumps. His miners were soon breaking up shale with the jets from monitors and sluicing it down to an amalgamator (the foundations of which are still in place), where the gold in the broken shale was supposed to combine with mercury brought to the isolated site. The resulting amalgam would then be heated in retorts to extract the gold and free the mercury for reuse.[64]

Spencer planned to use driftwood fuel for his stationary boilers (one survives) only until he could mine coal deposits that he knew were in the region. In 1911, his backers ordered a stern-wheel steamboat for transporting coal 28 miles down the Colorado River. San Francisco shipbuilders prefabricated the *Charles H. Spencer* and shipped its components to the river for assembly. The vessel made numerous trips in 1912, but now rests partly submerged and partly buried near Spencer's gold-mining area.

The failure of Spencer's mining venture in 1912 has been blamed on a number of factors, including the supposed ineffectiveness of his steamboat. It is clear from many witnesses that he had a serious problem with his amalgamator, and just as clear that no one at the time understood why the mercury was not catching enough of the gold. Neither Spencer's on-site laboratory nor the mining experts to whom he sent samples could determine what was clogging his mercury. Many years later, with improvements in metallurgical analysis, it was determined that rhenium was the element in the shale that had caused the clogging. In the 1960s, Spencer, then a senior citizen, actually went back to another of his claims to mine this valuable metal, but success eluded him once again.

The *Charles H. Spencer,* maligned in local lore and in the 1929 testimony of a disgruntled former crewman, became a convenient excuse to help explain technical and managerial failures. The vessel was accused of being too underpowered for upstream travel and so wasteful of fuel that it burned up almost its entire cargo of coal in a single round trip. However, studies conducted since the early 1960s have challenged that interpretation. One plan and numerous photographs of the vessel have been discovered. Interviews were conducted with men who had been on it or seen it running. Field recording of the wreck from the surface and underwater confirmed the *Spencer's* dimensions and engine configuration, added detailed information on its impressive construction, and demonstrated that the boiler actually installed was different from the one shown on the plan. The power available was more than sufficient to handle normal currents in the river, an engineering conclusion supported by historical documentation that the boat completed upstream trips in reasonable time. Extrapolating from reliable data on coal consumption by similarly equipped vessels, Park Service specialists proved that the sternwheeler did not use an excessive amount of coal and that it could deliver all the fuel needed for mining operations at Lee's Ferry.

Rhenium, not the inadequacy of a steamboat, was the principal cause of the miserable return from mining at Lee's Ferry. The *Spencer* was simply a scapegoat. Although the identification of rhenium took place before the Park Service's investigation, that type of technical determination is part of industrial archaeology today. It is possible, using modern analytical and diagnostic techniques, to find causes of industrial failure that were unrecorded, covered up, or not known by participants. The answers may lie in broken parts, chemical residues, slag heaps, or the shale particles around the foundations of an amalgamator.[65]

Petroleum Production

Petroleum and natural gas, unlike coal, can be extracted without anyone having to go down to their source in the fuel-rich strata underground. Since only the oil and gas are brought to the surface and the reservoir rock remains below, little debris accumulates at the wellheads. If something goes wrong with a well, drillers attempt to fix it by lowering tools or, in extreme cases, explosives. Well proprietors do not have to fund the complicated life-support systems needed by underground miners. Oil-field and refinery workers face the hazards of handling flammable liquids and gases rather than the dangers of working in coal mines. Still, the transportation of petroleum and gas presents risks to people and to the environment that are not present with coal.

Successive oil rushes in North America have had all the rawness associated with the early stages of an extractive industry. Drill rigs make a spectacular scene, but once drilling is completed, only pumps, pipes, and sometimes storage tanks remain at a typical producing site. When wells are pumped out, they can be capped, and the pumping equipment removed. The effects on the landscape vary: usually the surface marks of oil extraction are not permanent, but sometimes the very level of the ground has dropped significantly because the pumping of fluids has weakened supporting strata.

Derricks, Pumps, and Boomtowns

Temporary by intention, wooden derricks were erected in dense clusters over recently discovered pools of subterranean petroleum. It is fortunate that photographers recorded their profusion before they were dismantled or destroyed in one of the many oil-field fires. The Drake Well Museum in Titusville, Pennsylvania, has an accurate replica of a covered drilling rig used at the first American oil well in 1859 (Fig. 5.17). Also in the "stovepipe" building with the rig is a re-created horizontal steam engine that powers a simulated pump. Pennsylvania oilmen were instrumental in the development of a standard form of derrick by the 1870s. Usually 65 to 85 feet tall, these wooden supports for drilling equipment appeared in oil fields throughout the world.[66]

Derricks, also called rigs, were built quickly. They remained within the American tradition of wood construction into the 1920s, when steel frames

FIGURE 5.17. The replica of the derrick and engine house at Drake Well in Titusville, Pennsylvania. The first wooden structure at this site burned soon after the well began to produce oil in 1859. This replica is based on the replacement, which was recorded by photographers.

were adopted. They were rough, impermanent, yet sturdy and resilient structures. As we will show in Chapter 7, special skills were required to build them.[67] Californians developed their own variation of the cable drilling rigs used in Pennsylvania. Both used a percussion principle that was based on earlier brine-drilling methods. In Ontario, where wells were shallow, drillers switched from cables to lengths of readily available hardwood that were screwed together as the work progressed.

There was a great deal of local invention in regions that had oil resources. Some of the cleverest mechanical devices were developed to operate pumps on groups of small wells. Jerker rods or cables driven from a central engine house actuated multiple pumps (Fig. 5.18). Ontario oil workers are still operating some wooden-rod jerkers.[68] At the Drake Well Museum, metal rods fan out over a large area, moving back and forth in regular rhythm. The system demonstrates how it was possible to turn corners and even change elevation to pass over roads when necessary.

SPINDLETOP *Camille*

In Beaumont, Texas, Gladys City Boomtown uses reproductions, including two wooden derricks, to suggest the boomtown environment at the nearby Spindletop strike in 1901. Its tall replica of the Lucas Gusher derrick, which began the mass extraction of oil for the automobile age of the twen-

FIGURE 5.18. An endless wire system for pumping oil wells near Petroleum, West Virginia, in the 1890s. The powerhouse is at the left, and one of the pumps is just right of center. The wire cable is in place running over sheave wheels. (Photograph by William Barrett. Courtesy of the Historic American Engineering Record)

tieth century, is powerfully evocative (Fig. 5.19). A photograph taken just after the strike shows oil spraying more than 100 feet into the air above the original structure. However, only an image like Figure 5.20 can give any sense of the dense concentration of derricks at the height of some oil booms. The cable drilling technology that worked so well in many areas was not effective in the geological formations at Spindletop, but a heavy rotary drilling rig mounted on a standard derrick brought in the first well.[69] After two oil booms and a recent period of sulfur mining, the pronounced rise of the Spindletop salt dome has sunk physically into the coastal lowlands. There are a few pumps left in the area, their rusting heads rising like dinosaurs from the brush. When the price of oil rises enough, perhaps they will begin to bob up and down again.

FIGURE 5.19. Replicas of the Lucas Gusher derrick and Gladys City buildings at the Spindletop oil field in Beaumont, Texas. No previous oil well had produced anything like the estimated 80,000 to 100,000 barrels a day from Anthony Lucas's well in 1901. (Photographed at Gladys City Boomtown, a museum operated by Lamar University)

PITHOLE

The town of Pithole, now a Pennsylvania state historic site, demonstrates even more dramatically the transience of industrial success. This 1865 boomtown, located in the heart of the first oil rush a few miles south of Titusville, was built in a few months. It was already dying in 1867 and was largely abandoned five years later. One almost expects to see an inscription by Ozymandus etched into the stone of a crumbling foundation wall buried by vines. A brochure provided by the Pennsylvania Historic and Museum

FIGURE 5.20. Oil wells clustered together in the Burkeburnett field in northern Texas, around 1919. The oil boom at this rich site produced a dense concentration of wooden derricks (Pennsylvania rigs), engine houses, maintenance sheds, boiler houses, offices, oil-storage tanks, and railway buildings. (Courtesy of Robert Vogel)

Commission directs visitors on a walking tour through the grid of former city streets, now little more than paths in the fields and thickets. Figures 5.21 and 5.22 show Holmden Street, the main thoroughfare of a city that once had fifty-seven hotels. Near the brook where most of the wells were located, a trench marking the path of the world's first crude-oil pipeline (salvaged after Pithole's decline) is still visible.[70]

Refineries

Raw petroleum was not of much use until a refiner separated it into its constituent hydrocarbons by distillation. Oilmen collected the output of many wells to feed the stills of a refinery (Fig. 5.23). The first oil-refining center in the United States, at Corry, Pennsylvania, was, like many of its

FIGURE 5.21. Holmden Street in Pithole, Pennsylvania, in 1866. Dozens of hotels and other commercial establishments lined the main street of Pithole in its very brief heyday. The petroleum boom of 1865 drew thousands to this once rural spot and created an instant urban landscape. (Courtesy of the Drake Well Museum)

FIGURE 5.22. Holmden Street at the site of Pithole as it looks today. There are few surface indications of the oil boomtown that was once here. Buildings lined both sides of this formerly busy street. (Photographed at Pithole City, Plummer, Pennsylvania, where there is a visitors' center and self-guided walking tour)

FIGURE 5.23. Batch stills at a refinery in Oil City, Pennsylvania. Refiners heated petroleum in the iron tank of the still with an oil or a coal fire in chambers in the brick base. The fire doors can be seen at the base of each still. The vaporized constituents of the petroleum condensed in the vertical, domed pipes above the tanks. The stacks discharged the smoke from the heating fires. Oil derricks are visible in the background, and metal tank cars sit on the railroad in front of the refinery. (Courtesy of Robert Vogel)

successors, devastated by fire. Today, there is little trace of these early refineries. However, the subsequent increase in the scale of oil extraction, transportation, and refining as well as the movement of industrial operations to more sensitive terrain has greatly increased the environmental consequences of petroleum production. The huge refineries, petrochemical plants, and transshipment facilities that light up the night on the bays and rivers of the Gulf Coast are part of the price we pay for our personal automobility, our electricity, our plastics, and our synthetic fabrics.

Because of railway tank cars, ocean and Great Lakes tankers, inland river barges, and pipelines, the presence of refineries has not been limited to the major oil-pumping states (Texas, Louisiana, California, Oklahoma, Wyoming, Kansas, Arkansas, Illinois, Ohio, Indiana, Pennsylvania, West Virginia), as a trip on the New Jersey Turnpike will quickly confirm. In general, American plants that continue to refine petroleum have been modernized and altered so radically that the structural and mechanical evidence of early processes has largely disappeared. Obsolescence has come quickly, and the chemical effects of oil have helped to ensure that most refining equipment does not last for decades.[71] Exceptions to this pattern do exist, however, in some of the smaller refineries.

Representatives from Standard Oil claimed in 1919 that their refinery at East Providence, Rhode Island, would be "the most important oil terminal on the Atlantic coast." Intended to receive large stocks of petroleum from ships after ocean voyages, the Rhode Island refinery soon took a back seat to larger Texas facilities near the oil fields. The corporation scaled down its plans for expansion at this site in the 1920s, but the facility remained an active producer until 1975. The refinery's main product was heavy petroleum distillates, with a concentration on asphalt after 1950. It also made some gasoline to satisfy the heavy demands of automobile owners. Despite the development of more effective catalytic cracking in 1937, the thermal-cracking process was used at this refinery until after World War II. Much of the early thermal equipment was converted for asphalt applications, and one furnace survived relatively unchanged into the 1980s, reused as an asphalt heater. The riveted storage tanks from the first decade of the plant's history are now being demolished, but a concrete arch bridge built by the corporation in 1919 continues to carry a public road over a deep cut made for the company railroad that ran between the refinery and its dock.[72]

Environmental Effects

We have allowed significant damage to North American environments because of our hunger for metals and our thirst for petroleum. In mountainous terrain and arid regions, scars of mining may not heal for thousands of years—if ever. Runoff from long-abandoned mines still poisons streams in the Rockies, and subsidence changes the surface contours of both mining lands and petroleum fields. Despite stringent regulatory efforts, emissions from petroleum processing and combustion are major contributors to smog conditions and other types of atmospheric pollution. Oil spills damage coastal habitats, killing wildlife and forcing massive cleanups. Many who work in or live near petroleum refineries or petrochemical plants have learned to tolerate the dangers of accidental leakage, fire, and explosion; but almost everyone is threatened by the transit of combustible or poisonous materials on highways and railroads.

Today there is relatively little mining of nonferrous metals in the United States. Yet our consumption of these materials has not diminished. We import most of them, in effect exporting the environmental costs of mining, milling, and smelting to nations that have not adopted (and often cannot afford) the environmental controls that are now in place in North America. We actually extract and concentrate copper ore from a few open-pit mines in western states, ship it overseas for smelting and final processing, and bring back the resulting metal or metal products.

Notes

1. James A. Mulholland, *A History of Metals in Colonial America* (University: University of Alabama Press, 1981). For coverage of Spanish silver mining and milling technology in North America, see Otis E. Young, Jr., *Western Mining* (Norman: University of Oklahoma Press, 1970), chap. 3. Mining in western North America depended heavily on Spanish milling technology until the late nineteenth century.

2. Matthew Roth, *Connecticut: An Inventory of Historic Engineering and Industrial Sites* (Washington, D.C.: Society for Industrial Archeology, 1981), p. 36; Brent Glass, *North Carolina: An Inventory of Historic Engineering and Industrial Sites* (Washington, D.C.: Historic American Engineering Record, 1976), pp. vii, 3. In the Appalachian region of Georgia and North Carolina, there was extensive placer mining with an American form of pan (a modification of a Spanish technique) (Young, *Western Mining*, p. 109).

3. Arthur C. Todd, *The Cornish Miner in America* (Truro: Barton, 1967), chap. 2. A bibliography of mining each of the nonferrous metals in the United States before 1850 is in M. H. Hazen and R. M. Hazen, *Wealth Inexhaustible* (New York: Van Nostrand Reinhold, 1985). There is coverage extending past 1850 in Peter Molloy, *History of Metal Mining and Metallurgy: An Annotated Bibliography* (New York: Garland, 1986). For Canada, see Dianne Newell, *Technology on the Frontier: Mining in Old Ontario* (Vancouver: University of British Columbia Press, 1986).

4. David Gracy II, "Moses Austin and the Development of the Missouri Lead Industry," *Gateway Heritage* 1 (1981): 47.

5. Robert Vogel, ed., *Some Industrial Archeology of the Monumental City & Environs* (Washington, D.C.: Society for Industrial Archeology, 1975), pp. 4–5.

6. *The First Hundred Years of the New Jersey Zinc Company* (New York: New Jersey Zinc Company, 1948).

7. The interpretation of the remains of nonferrous-metal mining is discussed in Donald L. Hardesty, *The Archaeology of Mining and Miners: A View from the Silver State,* Special Publication Series No. 6 (n.p.: Society for Historical Archaeology, 1988). After years of decline, a few western mining communities—such as Aspen, Telluride, Breckinridge, and Crested Butte in Colorado, and Park City in Utah—have rebounded as ski resorts.

8. Donald Hardesty, "The Archaeological Significance of Mining Districts," in *Proceedings of the Workshop on Historic Mining Resources,* ed. Jeff Beuchler (Vermillion, S.D.: State Historical Preservation Center, 1987), pp. 77–90.

9. Robert L. S. Spude, "Mining Technology and Historic Preservation with Special Reference to the Black Hills," in *Workshop on Historic Mining Resources,* ed. Beuchler, pp. 45–58; Hardesty, "Archaeological Significance of Mining Districts," pp. 77–90.

10. Archie Satterfield, *Chilkoot Pass* (Anchorage: Alaska Northwest, 1983); Frank Norris, "The Tramway Story" (Paper presented to the Society for Industrial Archeology—Yukon Study Tour, 1990); Roy Minter, *The White Pass: Gateway to the Klondike* (Toronto: McClelland and Stewart, 1987). Bridges, snow sheds, snow fences, a mountain tunnel, and a preserved steam-powered rotary snowplow are physical evidence of the White Pass and Yukon Railroad's problems due to terrain and climate.

11. Rob Ingram, "Conrad and the Venus Mine," in *Site Guide for the SIA Study Tour of the Yukon and Alaska,* ed. Ken Elder (Ottawa: Society for Industrial Archaeology, 1990), p. 15.

12. See the descriptions in Thomas A. Rickard, *Journeys of Observation Part II: Across the San Juan Mountains* (San Francisco: Dewey, 1907), chaps. 5, 11. Rickard was a well-known mining engineer as well as a prolific editor and author.

13. Otis E. Young, Jr., *Black Powder and Hand Steel* (Norman: University of Oklahoma Press, 1975), pp. 110–111.

14. Peter Molloy, then director of the Western Museum of Mining and Industry, took us up Buckskin Gulch to go through the Paris Mill and to see the tramway remains associated with it. An unexpected fall snowstorm nearly stranded us at the mill and provided a lesson in how weather can quickly isolate mining sites.

15. Young, *Black Powder and Hand Steel,* pp. 110–111.

16. *State of Colorado Bureau of Mines Annual Report for the Year 1930* (Denver: State of Colorado Bureau of Mines, 1931), pp. 34–35.

17. Newell, *Technology on the Frontier,* pp. 74–77.

18. Chinese pumping technology is discussed in Jeffrey LaLande, "Sojourners in Search of Gold: Hydraulic Mining Techniques of the Chinese on the Oregon Frontier," *IA, Journal of the Society for Industrial Archeology* 11 (1985): 39–41, and Young, *Western Mining,* pp. 114, 271n. LaLande finds no significant physical evidence of distinctively Chinese technology in the pressurized hydraulic-mining practices of the sojourners in the Applegate Valley. Miners there apparently adopted the same types of nozzles and water-delivery systems used by non-Chinese miners.

19. On technological diffusion, see John Rowe, *The Hard Rock Men: Cornish Immigrants and the North American Mining Frontier* (New York: Barnes & Noble,

1974); James E. Fell, *Ores to Metals: The Rocky Mountain Smelting Industry* (Lincoln: University of Nebraska Press, 1979), pp. 23–24, 27–28, 42; and sections by Rodman Paul and Clark Spence in *The Reader's Encyclopedia of the American West,* ed. Howard R. Lamar (New York: Crowell, 1977), pp. 733–740.

20. Newell, *Technology on the Frontier,* pp. 80–81, 143. Newell, a veteran industrial archaeologist, says that the subject of Ontario mining first attracted her attention when, as a child, she saw "the evidence of early mining ventures etched into the local landscape."

21. See Environment Canada archaeologist John Light's discussion of the Bear Creek Compound in *Site Guide for Yukon and Alaska,* ed. Elder, p. 60, and Larry D. Lankton and Charles K. Hyde, *Old Reliable: An Illustrated History of the Quincy Mining Company* (Hancock, Mich.: Quincy Mine Hoist Association, 1982), pp. 74–76. Both of these studies show extensive surface support structures for mining operations. The maps of the Quincy property over time, prepared as part of a Historic American Engineering Record survey project, are very helpful.

22. We are grateful to David Weitzman for suggesting a visit to the Knight Foundry and for sharing the results of his observations and photographic recording. We are also indebted to Carl Borgh, the present owner-manager, for granting us an interview at the foundry–machine shop in 1989. For information on the Knight wheel and other California variations on the tangential (impulse) design, see Louis C. Hunter, *A History of Industrial Power in the United States, 1780–1930,* vol. 1, *Waterpower* (Charlottesville: University Press of Virginia, 1979), pp. 404–413. An exceptionally large Pelton wheel, 30 feet in diameter, which was built by A. D. Foote in 1895, is on display at the North Star Mining Museum and Pelton Wheel Exhibit in Grass Valley.

23. Patrick Martin, quoted in discussion, in *Workshop on Historic Mining Resources,* ed. Beuchler, p. 104.

24. There are good descriptions of historic gold- and silver-mining technology in Hardesty, *Archaeology of Mining and Miners,* and Young, *Western Mining.*

25. Young, *Black Powder and Hand Steel,* chap. 5.

26. Mark Wyman, *Hard Rock Epic: Western Miners and the Industrial Revolution, 1860–1910* (Berkeley: University of California Press, 1979), pp. 84–117. The Western Museum of Mining and Industry in Colorado Springs has the fatal cage from the Elkton Mine. The drill rods also left their marks on the metal. For proof of continuing dangers, see the Annual Reports of the State of Colorado Bureau of Mines in the 1920s and 1930s. These reports describe fatal accidents that occurred each year, but too often they excuse mine operators of liability and blame worker carelessness.

27. Mark Twain, *Roughing It* (New York: Penguin, 1983), pp. 380–381.

28. Grant H. Smith, *The History of the Comstock Lode, 1850–1920,* University of Nevada Bulletin, vol. 37, no. 3 (Reno: Nevada Bureau of Mines and Geology, 1943), pp. 22–24; Rodman Paul, *Mining Frontiers of the Far West, 1848–1880* (Albuquerque: University of New Mexico Press, 1963), p. 64.

29. Alan Trachtenberg, *Reading American Photographs* (New York: Hill and Wang, 1989), pp. 144–154.

30. Smith, *History of the Comstock Lode,* pp. 89–90.

31. Lankton and Hyde, *Old Reliable,* pp. 117, 120–129; Charles K. Hyde, *The Upper Peninsula of Michigan: An Inventory of Historic Engineering and Industrial Sites* (Washington, D.C.: Historic American Engineering Record, 1978), p. 27.

32. "Michigan Department of Natural Resources Remedial Action Plan" (Michi-

gan Department of Natural Resources, Lansing, 27 October 1987), pp. 1, 42–47; "Final Remedial Investigation Report, Operable Unit 1, Torch Lake," vol. 1 (Environmental Protection Agency, Chicago, November 1990); "Superfund Fact Sheet: Torch Lake Superfund Site" (Environmental Protection Agency, Chicago, August 1989).

33. James W. Brewer, *Jerome* (Tucson: Southwest Parks and Monuments Association, 1987), pp. 2–11. The Jerome Historic District was designated a National Historic Landmark in 1967. Arizona now has a state historic park in this "billion dollar copper camp."

34. Herbert V. Young, *They Came to Jerome* (Jerome, Ariz.: Jerome Historical Society, 1972), pp. 36–37; *Jerome Tourguide* (Jerome, Ariz.: Jerome Community, 1987), p. 3; Brewer, *Jerome,* p. 6.

35. Brewer, *Jerome,* pp. 6–7; Young, *They Came to Jerome,* p. 47.

36. Young, *They Came to Jerome,* pp. 49–50.

37. C. E. Mills, "Ground Movement and Subsidence at the United Verde Mine," *Transactions of the American Institute of Mining and Metallurgical Engineers* 109 (1934): 153–172.

38. Young, *They Came to Jerome,* pp. 48–50; *Jerome Tourguide,* pp. 16–17, 21. Young, a former executive of United Verde Copper Company, claims that 260,000 pounds of explosives were used for the largest blast, in 1927.

39. Paul, *Mining Frontiers of the Far West,* pp. 91–92; Young, *Western Mining,* pp. 125–131; Duane Smith, *Mining America: The Industry and the Environment* (Lawrence: University Press of Kansas, 1987), pp. 67–74. For a thorough history of the controversy in California, see Robert L. Kelley, *Gold vs. Grain: The Hydraulic Mining Controversy in California's Sacramento Valley* (Glendale, Calif.: Arthur Clark, 1959).

40. Kelley, *Gold vs. Grain,* frontispiece, photograph on p. 275. For a discussion of the site history and park development, see Howard Sloane and Lucille Sloane, *Pictorial History of American Mining* (New York: Crown, 1970), pp. 126–127, and *Malakoff Diggins State Historic Park* (brochure) (Sacramento: California Department of Parks and Recreation, 1988).

41. Margaret Carter, "Yukon Gold Company," in *Site Guide for Yukon and Alaska,* ed. Elder, p. 61; Lewis Green, *The Gold Hustlers* (Anchorage: Alaska Northwest, 1977), pp. 122–130.

42. W.H.S. McFarland, "Dredging Operations of the Yukon Consolidated," *The Miner,* November 1939, pp. 44–48.

43. Green, *Gold Hustlers,* pp. 103–107, 154–163; Alex Barbour, "YCGC Dredge No. 4" (Extracts from "Status Report," Parks Canada, March 1985), p. 9; Margaret Carter, "Dredging" and "Dredge No. 4," in *Site Guide for Yukon and Alaska,* ed. Elder, pp. 65–66.

44. Conversation with Alex Barbour of Parks Canada. Young explains that the oil and grease that could make gold flakes float on water could also prevent the close contact with mercury that was necessary for amalgamation (*Western Mining,* p. 98).

45. We are grateful to John Gould, veteran Yukon miner, for suggesting the way to read tailing piles.

46. Young, *Black Powder and Hand Steel,* pp. 135–157; William J. Cummings, *Iron Mountain's Cornish Pumping Engine and the Mines It Dewatered* (Iron Mountain, Mich.: Cornish Pumping Engine and Mining Museum, 1984); conversations with Charles K. Hyde.

47. Smith, *History of the Comstock Lode,* pp. 82–83; Paul, *Mining Frontiers of the*

Far West, pp. 82–83; interview with Roy W. Frailey, Houston Oils and Mineral Corporation.

48. Larry D. Lankton, *Cradle to Grave: Life, Work, and Death at the Lake Superior Copper Mines* (New York: Oxford University Press, 1991), p. 31. Cutting up large pieces of mass copper in a mine was also very labor intensive.

49. Mines too small to build their own mills sometimes used custom mills that served a number of mines in a locality (Young, *Western Mining,* pp. 193–194). One of the best primary sources on milling technology is T. A. Rickard, *The Stamp Milling of Gold Ores* (New York: Scientific Publishing, 1901).

50. Robert L. S. Spude and Sandra McDermott Faulkner, *Kennecott, Alaska* (Anchorage: National Park Service, Alaska Region, 1987); Spude, "Mining Technology and Historic Preservation," pp. 52–54; Jet Lowe and others, *Industrial Eye* (Washington, D.C.: Preservation Press, 1986).

51. Peter Molloy has re-created a gold concentration mill at the Western Museum of Mining and Industry in Colorado Springs. It performs crushing, stamping, and gravity (inertial) concentration of free-milling ores. Visitors to Redruth, in Cornwall, England, can tour the concentration mill at Tolgus Tin, where shaking tables of several types, work with a mix of finely ground minerals and water known as slimes. Cornish stamps begin the processing by recrushing tailings from earlier and less efficient tin mills for this sliming operation.

52. Spude, "Mining Technology and Historic Preservation," pp. 52–53.

53. Gertrude Atherton, quoted in Michael P. Malone, *The Battle for Butte: Mining and Politics on the Northern Frontier, 1864–1906* (Seattle: University of Washington Press, 1981), p. 62. Malone covers the public opposition and legal action (pp. 62–63, 203–204).

54. Smith, *Mining America,* pp. 75–80, 94–96, 165.

55. *The Butte-Anaconda Historical Park System MASTER PLAN* (Butte, Mont.: Renewable Technologies, for the Butte Historical Society, 1985), pp. xi, 112, 191.

56. Fell, *Ores to Metals,* pp. 133, 276.

57. See testimony by Governor Richard Lamm and other Colorado environmental authorities in "Poison in the Rockies," broadcast on "Nova," PBS, 1989 and 1990 (transcripts available from PBS).

58. For example, the activities of the Anaconda Copper Company in an extended array of works are described in the company history by Isaac F. Marcosson, *Anaconda* (New York: Dodd, Mead, 1957). For coverage of the Waterbury brass industry, see William G. Lathrop, *The Brass Industry on the United States,* rev. ed. (Mount Carmel, Conn.: Lathrop, 1926), and Cecelia Bucki and others, *Metal, Minds, and Machines: Waterbury at Work* (Waterbury, Conn.: Mattatuck Historical Society, 1980).

59. Patrick Martin, "An Archaeological Perspective on Nineteenth Century Copper Mining Communities in Upper Michigan, USA," in *Toward a Social History of Mining,* ed. Klaus Tenfelde (Munich: Beck, 1992), pp. 200–203.

60. Hardesty, *Archaeology of Mining and Miners,* pp. 13, 18, 102; Hardesty, "Archaeological Significance of Mining Districts," pp. 77–90; Patrick Martin, "The Perspective of the Historical Archaeologist," in *Workshop on Historic Mining Resources,* ed. Beuchler, pp. 91–107; Spude, "Mining Technology and Historic Preservation," pp. 45–58.

61. Martin, "Perspective of the Historical Archaeologist," pp. 94–95; Patrick Martin, "Cultural Resources Inventory and Evaluation, Norwich Mine Area, On-

tonagon County, Michigan, Ottawa National Forest" (Report, 1985), kindly provided by the author.

62. Martin, "Archaeological Perspective," pp. 204–205; Martin, "Perspective of the Historical Archaeologist," pp. 94, 98, 103–104; Patrick Martin, "Mining on Minong: Copper Mining on Isle Royale," *Michigan History* 74 (1990): 19, 22–25.

63. Toni Carrell, James Bradford, and W. L. Rusho, *Submerged Cultural Resources Site Report: Charles H. Spencer's Mining Operation and Paddle Wheel Steamboat,* Southwest Cultural Resources Center Professional Papers No. 13 (Santa Fe, N.M.: Southwest Cultural Resources Center, 1987). Another contribution to mining history by this unit of the National Park Service is Daniel Lenihan, ed., *Submerged Cultural Resources Study: Isle Royale National Park,* Southwest Cultural Resources Center Professional Papers No. 6 (Santa Fe, N.M.: Southwest Cultural Resources Center, 1987), which covers underwater and coastal components of several mines.

64. For an explanation of amalgamation and discussion of conditions that could make it ineffective, see Young, *Western Mining,* pp. 93–98.

65. Carrell, Bradford, and Rusho, *Spencer's Mining Operation and Paddle Wheel Steamboat,* p. 98.

66. "Let's Visit America's Oil Museums," *Exxon USA* (3d quarter, 1981), pp. 25, 27; *Drake Well* (Titusville: Pennsylvania Historical and Museum Commission, n.d.).

67. Paul Lambert and Kenny Franks, *Voices from the Oil Fields* (Norman: University of Oklahoma Press, 1984), pp. 22, 26–27.

68. David Weitzman, *Traces of the Past: A Field Guide to Industrial Archaeology* (New York: Scribner's, 1980), pp. 178–201; Newell, *Technology on the Frontier,* pp. 34–38, 122–128; Louis C. Hunter and Lynwood Bryant, *A History of Industrial Power in the United States, 1780–1930,* vol. 3, *The Transmission of Power* (Cambridge, Mass.: MIT Press, 1991), pp. 550–555.

69. James J. Clark and Michael Halbouty, *Spindletop* (Houston: Gulf Publishing, 1952), pp. 20–21, 44, 55.

70. See the brochure by the Drake Well Museum, *Walking Tour of Pithole City* (Pithole City: Pennsylvania Historic and Museum Commission, n.d.); *Pithole: A Brief History* (Titusville, Pa.: Titusville Herald, 1962); Ernest C. Miller, *Pennsylvania's Oil Industry* (Gettysburg: Pennsylvania Historical Association, 1974), pp. 38–41; and William C. Darrah, *Pithole: The Vanished City* (Gettysburg, Pa.: Darrah, 1972), p. 77.

71. Stanley Vance, *Industrial Structure and Policy* (Englewood Cliffs, N.J.: Prentice-Hall, 1961), p. 292. See also Harold F. Williamson and others, *The American Petroleum Industry: The Age of Energy, 1899–1959* (Evanston, Ill.: Northwestern University Press, 1963).

72. Patrick Malone, "Standard Oil Refinery," in *Rhode Island: An Inventory of Historic Engineering and Industrial Sites,* ed. Gary Kulik and Julia C. Bonham (Washington, D.C.: Government Printing Office, 1978), p. 81; Matthew Roth and Bruce Clouette, *Historic Highway Bridges of Rhode Island* (Providence: Rhode Island Department of Transportation, 1990), p. 61.

III
INDUSTRIAL
WORKPLACES

6

Countryside, Shops, and Ships

In the early seventeenth century, Americans began setting up shops to manufacture items such as soda ash, gunpowder, glass, charcoal, iron, casks, and wagons on a larger scale than they could manage in their homes. In some establishments, the proprietor was a practicing artisan (usually designated a "craftsman" today), while in others, such as glasshouses and ironworks, a manager coordinated the efforts of a dozen or more people. By the early nineteenth century, many Americans were participating in these industries, either full time or as an adjunct to farming.

When we look at surviving artifacts from the seventeenth and eighteenth centuries, we find evidence that American artisans were steadily increasing the range and depth of their industrial skills. There were few socially constructed barriers to the range of skills that an individual could practice at work, and imaginative artisans could cross the conventional boundaries between trades, enriching the different technologies of each. The diversity of their work experiences contributed to a growing technological sophistication that helped Americans gain industrial maturity in the nineteenth century. Many people, including children, learned about artisans' capabilities as they visited workplaces.

The mechanization of work in America is sometimes associated with the advent of factories, but it was already under way in tasks such as sawing timber, grinding grain, and forging iron by the mid-seventeenth century. Americans gradually adopted machinery to ease the labor of producing goods, and learning about mechanical technology became part of everyday life in agricultural and frontier communities as well as in towns.

Unmechanized Work

Machinery became increasingly important in the work of craftsmen such as silversmiths, gunsmiths, and furniture makers, but work in other industries was never extensively mechanized. Archaeological evidence tells us about work processes in some of these types of enterprises.

Indian Industries

American Indians possessed higher levels of technological skill than many of us realize. The physical evidence of their craftsmanship and well-organized efforts to extract natural resources stand in sharp contrast to the assertions of Indian primitiveness that fill many historical studies.

One component of Indian industry is exemplified by the copper mines in Michigan and steatite (soapstone) quarries in New England that were worked before the arrival of Europeans. The remarkable coincidence of Indian copper mines with nineteenth-century mines on Michigan's Keweenah Peninsula shows how accurately Indians located the rich metal deposits there. The prospectors and mining companies used archaeological evidence of industry left by Indians over a period of some 5,000 years to select sites for their mines. Apparently, the aboriginal miners had abandoned these pits before contact with white explorers in the seventeenth century.[1]

An outcropping of steatite in Rhode Island that was worked by Indians still contains several partially completed bowls that were never broken off for hollowing and final shaping (Fig. 6.1). Numerous scars left by the removal of bowls show that Indians made vessels of several sizes from this soft stone. Ceramic bowls would likely have replaced stone ones in the Early Woodland period, but Indians reopened some of the old steatite quarries to extract raw material for the beautifully carved tobacco pipes of the Late Woodland and Contact periods.

During the seventeenth century, Indians in what is now the eastern United States were adept at using European technology to support their evolving military system. Casting bullets and repairing firearms were soon normal activities in many bands. Material evidence from sites occupied by Indians or from Indian graves shows the technological sophistication that was noted by contemporary colonial observers but forgotten or discounted by most later historians. Archaeologists have found a number of bullet or shot molds carved from stone. William Bradford wrote in the 1640s that Indians had "molds to make shot of all sorts, as musket bullets, pistol bullets, swan and goose shot, and of smaller sorts." When Captain William Turner raided an Indian camp in Massachusetts Bay Colony in May 1675, his men "demol-

FIGURE 6.1. A steatite quarry worked by American Indians. The presence of several partially shaped bowls still attached to the steatite outcrop suggests that more than one artisan worked here when the quarry was last used.

ished the two forges they had to mend their arms; took away all their materials and tools . . . and threw two great pigs of lead of theirs (intended for making of bullets) into the said river."[2]

Hugh Cole witnessed Narragansett craftsmen repairing firearms for the neighboring Wampanoag tribe in 1671. One early grave in Rhode Island has been found to contain the earthly remains of a Narragansett blacksmith who was sent on his way to the afterlife with a full kit of tools, including a hammer and wedges. A Seneca grave in New York contained a cache of 426 flintlock parts. Excavations at the same site uncovered a collection of tools that suggest gunsmithing activities. A drawknife and what appears to be an inletting knife with a curved blade seem to be gunstocking tools. A three-cornered file and a hand vise could have been used to file the sears and tumblers of flintlock mechanisms.[3]

Charcoal Burning

Almost any farmer or woodsman could make charcoal, but making good-quality charcoal with efficient use of wood was not easy. Although Americans began to make charcoal for their homes and workshops in the early seventeenth century, the job soon became one for specialist colliers. At first, colliers simply wanted to make as much charcoal as possible from their wood, but later they also worked to recover by-products, such as methanol. Charcoal remained an important industrial product well into the twentieth century. Colliers might work at isolated sites in the forest (the usual pattern in New England, Pennsylvania, and Maryland), at works fitted with permanent kilns (common in the Adirondacks), or in coaling plants contiguous with ironworks (the practice in northern Michigan). Archaeological studies of the charcoaling grounds for the Hopewell iron plantation in Pennsylvania and the Antietam Ironworks in Maryland show that charcoal was made at

FIGURE 6.2. Charcoal kilns on the shore of Chateaugay Lake, New York, about 1890. Throughout the nineteenth century, colliers made large quantities of charcoal in this region for the local bloomery forges. They have stacked wood ready for conversion in piles behind the kilns. They delivered the finished charcoal to the forges in wagons like the one visible in front of the third kiln from the left; they used boats for deliveries on the larger lakes. The vents that controlled the admission of air are visible on the side of the first kiln. Despite the extensive charcoal production, there were still reserves of timber available near the kilns. (Photograph by S. R. Stoddard. Library of Congress negative number 59233)

pits scattered through the woods.[4] A collier and helper stacked 25 to 50 cords of wood in a circular (oval, if on a hillside) pile (called the pit) 30 to 40 feet in diameter. They covered the pit with old charcoal dust and sod to make a nearly air-tight seal so they could control the rate of combustion of the wood within. This procedure, recorded from the work of a surviving collier some fifty years ago, is the basis for coaling demonstrations that are now performed at Hopewell. To obtain uniform, controlled burning, the collier had to supervise the fire closely, and, since charcoal pits could not be left unattended, colliers lived in nearby huts. At Hopewell, several pits were arranged in a circle around the colliers' huts, but on the steep hillsides in Maryland the pits were placed in lines along narrow plateaus on the hillsides. Once a collier fired a pit, he followed the progress of the conversion to charcoal by the color and smell of the smoke and the feel of the pit as he jumped gently up and down on it (a somewhat risky undertaking, since there was a mass of burning wood beneath the sod cover).

Some charcoal works used kilns for coaling (Fig. 6.2), but the work remained dependent on the collier's skills in interpreting subtle, indirect clues.[5] Typically, a team of four fillers supervised by the collier placed the wood in the kiln according to a specified pattern, leaving a hole in the center of the stack. Then they sealed and fired the kiln; a burn of 80 hours would convert 60 cords of wood to 3,000 bushels of charcoal. As with pit firing, the collier at a kiln needed to observe the smoke. He also tasted the moisture it left on the ground and noted the appearance of an iron test bar thrust into the kiln. Each change in wind speed and direction called for readjustment of the number of vents open on the sides of the kiln. Constant care was needed in order not to lose control of the fire. Every clue available about events inside the kiln had to be heeded to obtain a good yield and to make charcoal free of tar or acids. Even though the workplace might be in the woods, the work was industrial in its intensity and in the range of technical processes that had to be controlled by the collier.[6] Ironworks proprietors considered coaling to be highly skilled work and paid good wages to keep their colliers.

Trying Out Whale Oil

Whaling ships in the age of sail, such as the *Charles W. Morgan*, launched in 1841, retired in 1921, and now on display at the Mystic Seaport Museum in Connecticut, were maritime workplaces with their own on-board blubber-processing capability that was truly industrial in scale. Conservators at the Mystic Seaport Museum have restored the *Morgan*, and museum visitors can examine its equipment for "cutting in" whales and "trying out" their oil-rich blubber.[7]

Whale oil was once in great demand for lighting American homes and factories. By the mid-nineteenth century, residents of many cities and towns could have gas light, while rural customers could buy kerosene ("coal oil" refined from petroleum) in place of whale oil. However, whale oil, sperm oil in particular, remained a valuable lubricant for shafting and machines;[8] it continued to be used for oiling watches because of its resistance to drying.

There are descriptions, drawings, photographs, and even motion pictures of shipboard rendering, including Herman Melville's dramatic depiction in *Moby-Dick* of the tryworks on the *Pequod*. Stuart Frank, director of the Kendall Whaling Museum in Sharon, Massachusetts, surveyed the wide range of information on the subject and concluded that there remained many unanswered questions about the design and operation of tryworks.[9] He and his staff decided to build an interpolated reconstruction. They examined archaeological evidence from excavations of a coastal tryworks in Spitsbergen and studied the restoration efforts on the *Morgan*. To avoid sacrificing whales, they obtained a license to remove blubber samples from carcasses of whales stranded on New England beaches. In two separate experiments conducted on the grounds of the museum, staff members succeeded in rendering oil using procedures suggested by their historic research and readily available modern equipment to simulate historic tryworks.

The museum ran this project in experimental archaeology with close control, recording data and taking samples throughout the process. A chemist assisted with biochemical analyses of the blubber and oil. The public participated, giving a wide audience a chance to take part. The olfactory experience made a lasting impression on everyone in attendance. These experiments provided new data about sperm whales and blackfish, whale products, and the chemical transformation of blubber into oil. They also tested the validity of accounts from the past and provided evidence on critical details missing from the historic record. Just as important, they simulated much of an industrial experience and a working environment, complete with authentic smells, leaving to the imagination only the pitching deck of the whale ship.

Ironworking

BLACKSMITHING

Blacksmiths did all kinds of metalworking tasks in urban and rural communities. Smithing was a well-established trade in Britain and Europe that could be transferred to the New World as its practitioners emigrated. The smith's techniques for shaping hot iron with hammers have been faithfully preserved at several museums, including Colonial Williamsburg, Plimoth Plantation, and Old Sturbridge Village.

A blacksmith worked alone or, perhaps, with a helper, in full view of customers and shop visitors. Smiths could do most of their work with hand-held tools. Most blacksmiths limited mechanization in their shops to simple appliances for shaping items such as wagon tires; only a few invested in power-driven hammers. Before the advent of machines for making products such as nails, many smiths had to undertake work that was highly repetitious. The varied tasks that we associate with smithing were only a part of daily work before the mid-nineteenth century.[10]

A romantic view of the colonial or early American smith is of a skilled, independent craftsman making quality products. The level of skill and the quality of the products actually attained can be assessed more reliably from artifacts. John Light and Henry Unglik's study of artifacts excavated at the site of a blacksmith shop operated between 1796 and 1812 on Fort Saint Joseph Island, Ontario, reveals much about the tools that were available on the American frontier.[11] The shop was a building measuring 19 feet by 16 feet. It had a forge blown by bellows, an anvil, a grindstone, a workbench, and various minor appliances. The archaeologists found more than 8,500 artifacts and concluded from them that two smiths, each with a distinct style, had worked in the shop. Neither smith achieved a high level of skill. The artifacts also showed that in addition to blacksmith's work, tasks usually done by a cooper, gunsmith, or farrier, as well as general repair work on all kinds of metal goods, had been carried out in the shop. Among the artifacts excavated were the remains of twenty axes that had been made either in the smithy or at nearby shops. The smiths had made the axe blades by first folding and welding wrought-iron plate and then welding on a steel bit. The sections of blades examined by Light and Unglik showed that the steel inserted in the cutting edges was badly placed and of inadequate size and that the steel itself had a variable carbon content and abundant slag inclusions. In none of the blades had the bit been properly hardened. These were poor-quality axes that would not have pleased an experienced woodcutter. We will know whether this sample is representative of craft-shop products when additional data become available from fieldwork and studies of tool collections. The data at hand on axes and other kinds of artifacts from this period, such as firearms, indicate that craft-shop products containing iron and steel that were made through the early decades of the nineteenth century were likely to be of variable and uncertain quality.[12] A smith skilled in the shaping of iron might well have only marginal ability in the more abstract tasks of selecting and heat treating steel.

BLOOM SMELTING

Smiths on the frontier may not always have been able to purchase ready-made iron.[13] Could a smith make iron from ore? As has been demonstrated by David Harvey with the experimental bloomery at Colonial Williamsburg

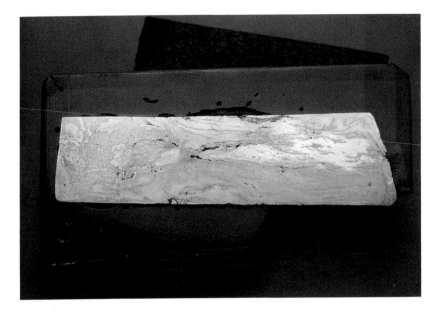

FIGURE 6.3. A section of a bar forged from wrought iron made in David Harvey's bloomery at Colonial Williamsburg. To reveal the distribution of phosphorus in the iron, we treated the polished surface of the section with Stead's reagent, a solution that deposits copper on pure iron, but not on iron that contains phosphorus, which remains bright. The section shows the uneven distribution of phosphorus often found in bloomery iron. The metal in the bright areas of this section is hard and brittle.

(Chapter 1), the equipment and materials needed would have been within the reach of most American smiths. In forming hot metal into finished products, a smith had abundant visual clues about the progress of the work, but in bloom smelting he needed more abstract skills because he could not see the chemical processes going on in the hearth. The difficulties Harvey encountered suggest that a smith would have had to devote much working time to mastering bloom-smelting skills. Harvey's experiments also show some of the difficulties that a seventeenth-century smith would have encountered in trying to make iron with uniform properties. The bog iron ore available along the east coast of North America contained variable amounts of phosphorus, some of which entered bloomery iron, making it "cold short" (brittle at room temperature). Figure 6.3 shows phosphorus-rich bands in bar iron made in Harvey's Williamsburg bloomery. A sample of iron excavated from a late-seventeenth-century context near Jamestown, Virginia, proved to be totally brittle due to a high phosphorus content.[14] It is likely that few blacksmiths mastered the art of bloom smelting and that fewer still would have been able to make high-quality iron. A domestic supply of reliable iron at a reasonable cost would not have been available until bloom smelting by specialists was established in North America. A great deal of

FIGURE 6.4. This artisan is demonstrating the making of a sand mold for a cast-iron stove plate. He has packed sand around a pattern of the plate placed in a wooden box (the flask). He will remove the pattern to leave a cavity in the sand and attach a similar box to this one to complete the mold. With the two halves of the mold fastened together, he will pour liquid metal into the opening left by the pattern. After the metal has solidified, a helper will break away the sand to release the casting. A new mold is made for each casting. (Photographed at the Hopewell Village National Historic Site)

poor iron was probably made, used by smiths, and passed on to customers; the quality of these products must have been a source of continuing difficulty for Americans.

IRON FOUNDING

To make cast-iron products such as pots and cannon, Americans had to learn the industrial skills of pattern making, molding, and casting. These skills are demonstrated today at the Hopewell Village National Historic Site on special occasions, but with aluminum rather than iron. Hopewell was particularly known for its cast-iron stoves. The molders at Hopewell cast stove plates in sand molds made by packing sand around a pattern placed in a container called a flask (Fig. 6.4). The molder lifted the pattern out and closed the flask to make a cavity in the sand in the shape of the stove plate. He poured iron from the blast furnace through the gate (visible at the left side of the plate in Fig. 6.4) to make the casting. After the iron had solidified, boys or other less-skilled workers broke the sand away from the metal to release the casting from the mold. Molders had to make a new mold for each casting poured.

The molder prepared the sand with the correct consistency and moisture content and packed it into the flask in order to reproduce every detail of the pattern. If correctly prepared, the packed sand would be strong enough to hold its shape as the liquid iron was poured into the mold, but porous enough to allow the escape of gases released from the molten metal. The gate had to be placed to allow the iron to fill out the mold properly before it solidified. Dexterity, judgment, and experience were needed to make a mold rapidly and to pour the liquid iron at the right temperature and rate without incorporating dirt or dross into the casting.[15]

Mechanization

Mechanization is the application of machinery driven by hand or by external power to forming, cutting, or joining materials.[16] Americans applied it to manufacturing in four distinct ways. One was to use machinery to carry out tasks virtually impossible to do without machinery, but with full control of the work still in the hands of the artisan. An approximation of a cylindrical surface can be made with a file alone, but, no matter how skillful the artisan, the regularity of a cylinder turned on a lathe cannot be duplicated with hand tools. The second way of using machinery was to reduce the physical labor in doing a task while leaving the manipulation of the work much as when done by hand. A blacksmith who installed a power hammer still manipulated the hot metal with hand-held tongs. A sewing machine left the operator free to concentrate on guiding the work while the machine made the stitches.

The third method was to use "self-acting" machines that did not need continual attention. The operator of a self-acting lathe engaged an external power source to rotate the workpiece and simultaneously advance the cutting tool. By setting automatic stops to disengage the feed when the requisite work was completed, the operator could put the machine in motion and leave it unattended until it was time to insert a new piece of work. A machine builder could carry this kind of mechanization further by fitting guides to direct the cutter along complex shapes, as in the Blanchard gunstock lathe.

In the fourth type of mechanization, a "transfer machine" moved either the work or a set of tools through a sequence of different operations. When the machine was functioning properly, the operator needed only to supply fresh stock and remove the finished product. The Howe pin-making machine, discussed later, and continuous papermaking machines are examples. Since the third and fourth methods of mechanizing work were more likely to be found in factories, most of our examples are discussed in Chapter 9.

Mechanized Work

Soon after arriving in the New World, settlers in eastern North America began to build mechanized sawmills and gristmills. The technology needed for gristmilling was often transplanted from Britain (or, for some Pennsylvanians, from Germany), but since there were virtually no sawmills in England, Americans had to design their mills with only general guidance from the principles of water-powered sawing.[17] Colonists also used extensive mechanization in making iron and iron products, and they developed specialized mills for carding, fulling, and manufacturing oil. In this section, we have also included a nineteenth-century example of basic mechanization, a hand-powered machine that was used on the plantation to spin cotton.

Sawmills

There were sawmills in the American colonies in the early 1630s. To erect one, colonists put up a mill building, a dam, a flume or race to deliver water, a waterwheel, a power-transmission system, a saw frame with its supporting structure, and a saw table with a feed mechanism. The large, heavy saw blade had to be imported from England and carried to the mill site. A substantial, well-fastened structure on a stable foundation was needed to keep the saw frame, its drive mechanism, and the carriage for the logs in alignment while the mill was operating (Fig. 3.3). A carpenter without experience in building structures for industrial use would have difficulty making the saw frame, fender posts, and ratchet-and-pawl mechanism to advance the carriage (Fig. 6.5). Making the metal pitman bearings, the slide tracks for the saw frame, and the mechanism that advanced the table would have been outside the usual range of a blacksmith's work. Since we have abundant evidence of the spread of sawmills in the seventeenth century, we know that American carpenters and smiths acquired these industrial skills early in colonial times.

Although the mechanism of an up-and-down sawmill mimics the work of pit sawyers, the skills needed to operate it were different from those needed in hand sawing.[18] The mill sawyer would keep the dam, millpond, waterwheel, and mill mechanism in order; sharpen, set, and align the saw blade in its frame; and align and secure the timber on the carriage. The sawyer also had to determine the proper rate of feed of the timber into the saw. Working in such a mill offered opportunities to develop mechanical aptitude and a knowledge of basic machinery. The social organization of sawmill work centered around a sawyer who could operate the mill and make small repairs alone, who needed one or more helpers for only the heavy work of moving logs and timbers (Fig. 6.5), and who required only occasional assistance from a specialist for major repairs.

FIGURE 6.5. A demonstration of sawing by museum interpreters at Old Sturbridge Village. The sawyer and his helper are positioning the log on the saw bed with the aid of the wooden mallet. Once the log is clamped securely, they will set the saw in motion, and the mechanical feed will advance the log into the saw. After each board is sawn, the sawyer and helper have to move the log over for the next cut.

Gristmills

The medieval-style gristmill, with its horizontal waterwheel coupled directly to millstones by a vertical shaft, was a simpler mechanism than a sawmill; it is reported to have been used by seventeenth-century Swedish settlers in Delaware.[19] Millers soon found that the low efficiency of the horizontal waterwheel together with the difficulty of controlling its speed and the alignment of the millstones limited the quantity and quality of the grain they could grind with a direct-drive mill. Most began to use mills driven through a gear train from a vertical waterwheel on a horizontal shaft. Some, particularly those living on windswept coasts, built mills with similar gearing but powered by sails. In the power train of the Lefferts tide mill near Huntington, Long Island, New York, the gears were made entirely of wood and were designed to function without a close fit between the parts or careful

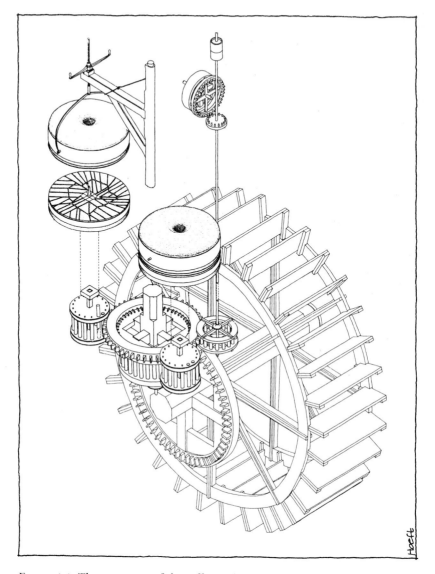

FIGURE 6.6. The power train of the Lefferts tide mill near Huntington, Long Island, New York. The undershot waterwheel, driven by tidal flow, rotated at a slower speed than the miller needed to move the stones adequately. The mill designer used wooden gearing to develop proper speeds for the vertical shafts that drove the two sets of millstones. He included an additional shaft for driving auxiliary equipment, such as bolters. (Drawings by Kathleen Hoeft. Courtesy of the Historic American Engineering Record)

shaping of the teeth (Fig. 6.6). The simplicity of the design helped make the mill mechanism reliable, but the gear teeth wore as they slid over one another so the miller had to replace them frequently. (Sliding motion and the resulting rapid wear can be eliminated if gear teeth are made with the proper shape, but engineers did not achieve this advance until the mid-nineteenth century.) The Lefferts mill used one waterwheel to drive two pairs of stones. When a gristmill had geared drive, the miller could add more shafts to run bolters, grain elevators, or even machinery not directly related to milling. An example of this common elaboration can be seen at the Log Village Grist Mill Museum in East Hartford, New York, where there is a woodworking shop in the attic of the mill.

The skills needed in gristmilling were different from those needed at a sawmill because of the way a millstone works. Grain was milled in two stages with millstones. First, grains entered the furrows on the stone and were sheared by passage of the sharp edges of the furrows on the other stone, much as if the grains were cut by a pair of scissors. The grain fragments then passed between the faces of the stones and were sheared into smaller pieces by sharp edges in the texture of the stone itself. The fineness of the flour was determined by the gap between the millstones, and to grind grain properly, the stones had to have flat, true faces furrowed with sharp grooves and had to be held at an accurately controlled, uniform separation while the upper stone rotated over the fixed lower stone. The miller had many technical choices to make, including the pattern of furrows and the selection of the type of rock used for the stones. The best millstones were made of sandstone (whose sand grains provided the sharp edges for the fine shearing) or porous quartzite. The quality of the flour produced in a mill depended on the design and workmanship of its machinery and on the miller's skill in dressing the millstones. The gristmill was a place where mechanical skills could be learned and refined, and where a miller unusually adept with mill machinery could expect to earn more than competitors.

The sawing process was fully visible in a sawmill, but in a gristmill the grinding took place between the millstones and could not be directly observed. The millstones were normally enclosed in a wooden case that further obscured the view of the grinding process (Fig. 6.7). Visitors could not easily learn the secrets of the miller's craft by direct observation. However, customers could judge the quality of the flour, and a miller's reputation would soon be known to all who cared to inquire. In addition to technical skills, millers needed business experience and access to a network of specialist millwrights for repair work and to a commercial organization that could supply millstones. In the case of the Lefferts mill, these would have had to be brought from a distant source because there were no outcrops of rock

FIGURE 6.7. The interior of a water-powered gristmill. The miller has removed the casing on the left and lifted the upper stone off the lower one for dressing. The assembled stones on the right are enclosed in a wooden casing that collects the grain as it emerges from the edges of the stones. The miller used the two elevator shafts seen in the center of the photograph to lift grain to the floor above. The grain then fell through a chute into a hopper and thence into the opening in the center of the stones to be ground. Elevator belts with some buckets missing have been hung on the outside of the shafts. (Photographed at the Log Village Grist Mill Museum, East Hartford, New York)

suitable for making millstones on Long Island. The operation of a gristmill involved a wide range of social interactions that constantly tested the miller's abilities. A skilled miller could thereby achieve recognition within the larger community, even though he might not have access to a peer group of other millers.

While the grinding process of a gristmill was concealed, the power train could be seen by mill visitors. Watching it would have helped farm and village lads gain familiarity with machinery. Gristmill power-transmission systems were the forerunners of the line shafting later used to distribute mechanical power to individual machines in factories. Millwrights developed the techniques they needed to erect factory power systems as they built and repaired gristmills and sawmills. Milling offered artisans opportunities to learn mechanical skills in long-settled regions and near the frontier. These artisans contributed to the development of industrial maturity in America.

Blast Furnaces

Operating blast furnaces was much more labor intensive than running gristmills or sawmills. Once mechanized equipment was in place, an individual
artisan could saw timber and mill grain; helpers were needed only for heavy
lifting and carrying. A blast furnace not only was too large for one person to
operate, but also was in continuous operation for periods of weeks or
months. It took a disciplined group of about a dozen men to run most
colonial furnaces. Until much larger furnaces were built in the second half
of the nineteenth century, the size of the crew changed little. The founder,
the person in charge, had to organize his work force so that an entire furnace
crew was on hand and at the right places at the right time, day in and day
out. The founder also needed technical skills, for there were few direct
clues about what was going on inside the blast furnace. He judged the
progress of smelting from sounds and smells, the view through the tuyeres,
and the appearance of the slag and iron when tapped. Conditions in the
furnace varied with changes in the composition of the ore, flux, and charcoal, and with the weather (through changes in the temperature and humidity of the air blast). Frequent alterations and adjustments were necessary to
compensate for these conditions. Over time, the founder developed a familiar relationship with the furnace. Founder William Weaver reported to the
owners of his furnace that

> yesterday just before noon the furnace began to hang and did not go down until
> the cast. In the afternoon she did not sink her stock except when blast was
> slacked. Towards evening she got on a black cinder and was very tight. Under
> the circumstances our only way was to blow down, which we commenced after
> cast. She worked very bad all night, but is now improving a little. We will get
> her over this spell in a day or two.[20]

Although this account was written in 1880, it could as well have been from
the founder at Saugus in 1650.

None of the charcoal-fired blast furnaces now preserved in the United
States, including those at the Saugus and Hopewell Village National Historic Sites, are worked, and there is no opportunity to experience the heat,
smell, and sound of this dramatic industrial operation. A general description
of the work can be constructed from surviving documents and physical
remains such as the Roxbury, Connecticut, furnace recently studied by
archaeologists.[21] This furnace made about 9 tons of iron a day in the mid-
nineteenth century. The founder supervised a crew of fifteen that included
three hands to run the blowing engine (steam-driven at Roxbury), two fillers, two coal forkers, one cinderman, two helpers, and five laborers. The
founder and cinderman were on hand whenever they were needed and

always when the furnace was tapped each twelve hours; the rest of the crew was divided into two teams working alternately at the nearly continuous job of charging the furnace. About every half-hour, an engineman shut off the blast. The filler opened the door in the stack at the top of the furnace and, with the aid of a helper, shoveled in 900 pounds of ore, 30 bushels of charcoal, and the necessary limestone they had already brought out on the charging bridge. Then they closed the door, and the engineman put the blast back on. These men, the coal forker, and a laborer then set about preparing the next charge. There does not seem to have been any sharp division of job responsibilities, and there were undoubtedly frequent calls to help out with different tasks and deal with contingencies.

While the charging crew was working on the bridge above, a laborer and helper were preparing the pig bed, a nearly level bed of sand placed directly in front of the furnace within the casting house. They moistened the sand, made rows of parallel furrows having the desired size and shape of the pigs, and connected these furrows with branch channels to a main feeder channel that led up to the tap hole. Sand dams blocked the feeders at intervals. While the furnace was running, slag (also known as "cinder") drained from the hearth into a pit, where it solidified. After the pit was full, the cinderman directed the flow into a second pit, broke up the solid slag in the first pit with a sledge, and dumped the fragments out the back door of the casting shed. When the sand on the pig bed was ready and sufficient iron had accumulated in the furnace crucible, the founder shut off the blast and knocked the clay plug out of the tap hole to release the accumulated liquid iron. Initially, all but the most distant furrows were blocked by sand dams, and a laborer removed these successively to fill rows closer to the furnace. While the pigs were cooling, the laborer and helper made up the other half of the pig bed for the next tapping; then they broke the hot pigs free with sledges, levered them out of the sand, and stacked them.[22]

The work was hot and physically arduous. There was risk of accident. One evening, the founder at Bancroft, Michigan, found that

> the furnace was acting like an animal does after taking a large dose of castor oil and was pretty soft inside, but rather hard at the forebed; and as he was trying to ease her of her burden, she flew at him like a fiend. He succeeded in getting a hole in her and after pulling the bar out, the cinders flew like water from a hose, striking him on the shoulders, back and legs, burning his pantaloons badly. But as he was quick in getting them off, he escaped with little or no injury.[23]

The furnace crew needed teamwork and discipline to keep the furnace running steadily week after week. The work environment at a blast furnace was different from that in a bloomery or finery forge, where the artisans worked largely as individuals. At first, ironmasters had difficulties with drunken, disorderly help, but American workers soon acquired the discipline they needed to operate blast furnaces. A number of factors may explain this behavioral adaptation: the crews were relatively small and interdependent; smooth coordination of effort was essential for technical success and individual safety; the job performance of each person was clearly evident; and there were opportunities for the expression of personal skills and style in much of the work.

One way to evaluate the skills of blast-furnace crews is through analysis of surviving artifacts. So far, only a few of the many artifacts found at Saugus and Hopewell (the two national historic sites devoted to iron smelting with charcoal), at other furnace sites, or in museum collections have been studied. Analyses of pig- and cast-iron artifacts from Saugus and Hopewell are shown in Table 6.1. Iron made at the two sites differs in manganese and phosphorus content because of the different ores used: bog ore at Saugus and magnetite at Hopewell. The absence of uniformity in the iron made at Saugus implies that the founder had difficulty controlling the operation of the furnace. Such differences in composition would have complicated the already difficult task of the finer in converting the product of the blast furnace into wrought iron.

Beginning about 1830, blast-furnace crews had to make their first major adjustments to technological change. American ironmasters adapted the technique of preheating the air blast (developed by Neilson in Scotland in

TABLE 6.1 Analyses of Cast-Iron Artifacts

Iron	Carbon (%)	Silicon	Manganese	Phosphorus	Sulfur
Saugus					
Pig[a]	2.6	0.04	0.02	1.9	0.11
Kettle[b]	3.7	0.77	0.37	1.2	0.09
Crane hook[b]	3.7	0.74	1.15	0.7	0.05
Hopewell					
Stove[c]	4.1	0.70	trace	0.14	0.02
Stove[c]	4.0	1.05	trace	0.15	0.02
English[b,d]	3.6	1.00	0.92	0.5	0.06

[a]Analysis of a pig found at Saugus: K. S. Vecchio and A. R. Marder, "An Analytical Determination of a Saugus Pig," in *Microbeam Analysis, 1984*, ed. A. D. Romig, Jr., and J. I. Goldstein (San Francisco: San Francisco Press, 1984), p. 247.

[b]Ronald F. Tylecote, *A History of Metallurgy* (London: Metals Society, 1976), p. 84.

[c]Analyses of the gate and riser of a stove casting made at Hopewell between 1816 and 1840: Hopewell National Historic site, unpublished data.

[d]Analysis of an iron fireback made in England in 1642, for comparison.

1828 to reduce fuel consumption in coke-fired furnaces) to their charcoal-fired blast furnaces and bloomeries beginning in 1835 with the Oxford furnace in New Jersey.[24] Remains of early hot-blast stoves can be seen on a number of surviving stacks, such as the Nassawango furnace at Snow Hill, Maryland. It was built in 1830, converted to hot blast sometime before 1837, and is now preserved in a park. Making a successful hot-blast stove called for casting thin-walled, curved iron pipes that then had to be fitted together with joints that would stay tight when heated and cooled. Regulating the temperature of the air blast became part of the founder's duties. Next, the adoption of water-cooled tuyeres called for skills in piping liquid water near hot metal. This was followed by the redesign of the furnace top to include conical-shaped valves that the founder could manipulate to charge the furnace without shutting off the blast. Although the charcoal-fired blast furnace might be considered to have been a mature technology by the beginning of the nineteenth century, innovations that increased the sophistication of the smelting process continued to be made into the twentieth century.

Finery Forges

When American ironmasters revived smelting iron in blast furnaces in the early eighteenth century (after the failure of the integrated ironworks at Saugus, discussed in Chapter 3), they often set up separate finery forges to convert pig iron to wrought iron. These forges remained an important component of the iron industry for more than 150 years. The finer worked at a hearth similar to the one at Saugus (Fig. 6.8). He melted the pig in the flame of a charcoal fire immediately in front of the tuyere, where the air blast burned out successively the silicon, the carbon, and some of the phosphorus in the pig iron. The finer (or, in a large forge, a specialist hammerman) took the resulting lump of white-hot, solid iron and liquid slag (called a loup) to the helve hammer and forged it, gently at first and then more vigorously, to expel as much of the slag as possible. The quality of the finer's iron depended on the skill with which he removed impurities by oxidation in the hearth and expelled the slag from the loup under the hammer.[25]

The upper forge at Valley Forge, Pennsylvania (the one that was excavated [Chapter 3]), had one hammer and, probably, one fining and one reheating (chafery) hearth;[26] it could have been operated by a crew of two or three artisans. Since finery-forge proprietors often bought pig iron from different sources, a finer could expect to encounter differences in the composition of the iron, a situation that would complicate his work. Analyses of samples from two pigs found at Valley Forge, one identified as being from the Andover blast furnace in New Jersey, show substantial differences (Table 6.2). As at Saugus, the different contents of silicon and manganese would

FIGURE 6.8. One of the finery hearths at the ironworks at Saugus, Massachusetts. The finer used air pumped by the water-powered bellows to blow the charcoal fire in the shallow finery hearth. He inserted pig iron (one pig is shown in the picture) through the opening in the wall at the side of the hearth and melted its end in front of the tuyere. The air blast oxidized the silicon and carbon in the pig, converting it to nearly pure, solid iron that accumulated under a cover of molten slag in the bottom of the hearth. The finer removed the mass of iron and slag, called the loup, from the hearth with tongs and took it to the adjacent hammer to be forged into bars. (Photographed at the Saugus Ironworks National Historic Site)

have caused these two irons to respond differently in the finery hearth, increasing the difficulty of the finer's task. The analysts also found that four wrought-iron artifacts from the Valley Forge site, while free of excess sulfur and phosphorus, had a highly variable carbon content and a poor distribution of slag particles. They were no better than the artifacts from the Saugus finery described in the following section. If these artifacts are representative, they suggest that the finer and the hammerman at Valley Forge in the 1770s were not better masters of their craft than their predecessors 100 years before at Saugus.

Archaeologists now have data showing the growth of fining skills among nineteenth-century American artisans in the Salisbury district of Connecti-

TABLE 6.2 Analyses of Pig Iron Found at Valley Forge

	Silicon (%)	Manganese	Phosphorus	Sulfur
(No provenance)	0.33	0.099	0.045	0.018
Andover	0.18	2.47	0.027	0.010

Source: Helen R. Schenck and Reed Knox, "Wrought Iron Manufacture at Valley Forge," MASCA Journal 3 (1985): 134.

cut and Massachusetts, where finery forges had been producing "gun iron," the iron plates used to make musket barrels, since the 1790s. By 1830, the iron made there was considered the finest available for this very demanding application, a reputation confirmed by examination of surviving artifacts. Superior iron was also fined in the Juniata region of Pennsylvania. However, there were limits to how well even a highly skilled finer could control the quality of bar iron, and manufacturers found that they could never completely rely on any ironmaker to supply superior-quality metal consistently. Analyses show that one reason for the absence of uniformity in the Salisbury gun iron was the variable phosphorus content of the ore used at the blast furnaces that supplied pig iron to the forges.[27]

Rolling and Slitting

Americans began the mechanized rolling of iron strips for products such as wagon-wheel tires and barrel hoops and the slitting of strips for nail rods at the Saugus works. There, workers reheated iron bars made in the finery forge. They passed the red-hot bars through rolls and, if nail rods were wanted, on through shearing discs mounted next to the rolls. The massive wooden parts of the power train that drove the rolls could have been made by local carpenters who had learned millwrighting skills in building gristmills and sawmills, but the metal parts were probably brought from England, since it is unlikely that there was a lathe capable of turning them in Massachusetts in 1640.

Analysis of artifacts at the site of the slitting mill gives us information about the skills of the Saugus ironworkers. The three samples of bar iron analyzed have more carbon and much more slag than well-made wrought iron should contain. There is further evidence of trouble in a fragment of iron that had become entangled in the mechanism of the slitting mill. The iron was of poor quality, and it had not been heated to a sufficiently high temperature before being placed in the mill. Impressions from the slitting discs in the iron show that they were badly made and improperly aligned.[28] Analysis of more artifacts could show how pervasive this lack of skill was among the ironworkers at Saugus.

Growth of Metallurgical Competence

Although artifacts show that Americans had much to learn about making reliable iron products in the seventeenth and eighteenth centuries, we also have evidence that their skills improved and that they carried their new technological competence throughout the colonies. By 1765, Samuel Forbes of Canaan, Connecticut, had built a reputation that allowed him to sell forge hammers, musket barrels, standardized iron parts for gristmills, and anchors weighing as much as 1,000 pounds through agents in the principal colonial cities. In 1798, Forbes and Adam were able to supply Eli Whitney with a trip-hammer, the iron parts of a water-driven power train for his new armory, and an initial supply of iron and musket barrels.[29] Some iron founders were making very large cast-iron pots to be used for boiling potash. The pots weighed up to 1,000 pounds and were cast in the improved, bottom-down form,[30] which put the best metal where it was most needed, at the bottom.

As the nineteenth century opened, American artisans not only were becoming expert in established technologies, but also began to adapt European innovations to American conditions. Preheating the air for blast furnaces has already been mentioned. The puddling furnace was developed by Henry Cort and others in England in the late eighteenth century for converting pig to wrought iron with mineral coal in place of charcoal. In Britain, only long-flame bituminous coal was considered suitable fuel for puddling furnaces.[31] Since bituminous coal was scarce on the eastern seaboard of the United States, British-style puddling furnaces would have been of little use. However, Americans developed wood-fired puddling furnaces; one was used to increase the production rate of wrought iron at the Tahawus ironworks in New York State in 1846.[32]

These American developments in pyrotechnology have received scant and, sometimes, deprecatory attention from historians.[33] In fact, many practitioners achieved a sophisticated adaptation to local natural resources and economic conditions. One reason for the neglect of these aspects of American technological innovation may be that they are not associated with well-known, individual inventors, but emerged from the growing artisanal competence of many Americans. These developments by anonymous artisans were essential steps in reaching technological maturity.

"Negro Cloth"

The plantation spinner is a good example of mechanization on the site of a primary producer. Slaves used yarn from this machine to make fabric for their hand-sewn clothing, supplementing the supply of so-called negro cloth from northern factories. Curators at the Museum of American Textile History in North Andover, Massachusetts, decided to include a plantation spinner made about 1840 by J. and T. Pearce of Cincinnati in an exhibition on the connections between northern industry and southern slavery.[34] They were already convinced by advertisements and other documentary evidence that it was possible to feed raw cotton (straight from the fields, with seeds attached) into one end of this small machine and wind yarn onto bobbins at the other end; the hand-powered machine combined ginning, carding, drawing, and spinning. There were still many questions about what it was like to run the spinner and about the nature of its product.

Samples of negro cloth that was manufactured in antebellum Rhode Island textile mills were attached to business correspondence now in archival collections, and a slave's vest and trousers made from coarse cotton about 1850 have survived at Shadows-on-the-Teche, in New Iberia, Louisiana.[35] Negro cloth of either cotton or wool is rough to the touch, and some of the woolens would have been about as pleasant to wear as the proverbial hair shirt. The Museum of American Textile History contracted for the production of realistic replicas of negro cloth so that visitors to the exhibit could feel it and make their own judgments about the comfort of an enslaved consumer group.

The missing element was the cotton yarn that slaves made with their own labor on plantation spinners, but Myron Stachiw and Laurence Gross filled that gap by restoring the museum's machine to operating condition and cranking out enough yarn for demonstration and analysis. They soon learned that the yarn made by this machine not only is coarse and uneven, but also is badly flawed by the inclusion of plant fragments. The plantation spinner has no mechanism for the picking process used by textile mills to clean ginned cotton and remove unwanted materials, so it is an incomplete machine. J. and T. Pearce must have known that its spinner made a substandard yarn, unacceptable to even the poorest people of a free society in the North. Wearing scratchy clothing would have been one more trial in the difficult life of a slave.

The Farmer–Artisan

In popular conception, the rural farmer–artisans of the eighteenth and early nineteenth centuries were members of self-sufficient, independent families fed with the products of their farms and the occasional game animal. These families supposedly made and repaired most of their material possessions and needed little help from others. The image is, however, only partly accurate. While there were many men and women in rural areas who had impressive technological versatility, few came close to self-sufficiency. A number of scholars have recently demonstrated the importance of intricate social, kinship, and trade networks in the countryside.[36] People regularly traded goods and services with their neighbors and relatives, often traveling long distances in the process.

The widespread social and economic interaction between rural artisans and their willingness to exchange labor, tools, and technological information promoted the diffusion of skills. It was possible, and often advantageous in this economic system, for an individual to become a jack-of-all-trades. Few artisans in the countryside worked at a specialized craft full-time; most considered themselves farmers by occupation, and in certain seasons they would have been heavily involved in agricultural tasks. But they also manufactured products used in the community and provided skilled services such as sawing timber and repairing tools.

Probate records, account books, and diaries of farmer–artisans provide strong documentary evidence that the legendary jack-of-all-trades was a common figure in the rural population. The archaeological record also supports this conclusion, and it suggests that being a jack-of-all-trades did not rule out becoming a master of at least one.

We can reconstruct aspects of the life of Shadrach Steere, a Rhode Island farmer and wood turner, because his lathe (an unusual foot-treadle design that incorporates both friction and belt drives), some of his turned products, and two of his account books (one dating to 1808) survive. The lathe itself shows technological versatility; it is made primarily of wood with additional parts of iron, leather, and steatite.[37] To use it, Steere needed sharp cutting tools with steel-edged blades set in wooden handles. His accounts show that he was capable of simple blacksmithing as well as woodworking. He made many things himself, used assistants on occasion, and had business dealings with a number of local artisans, several of whom operated sawmills.

Steere sold or traded a wide variety of wood products, including hoe handles, scythe nibs, furniture, lumber, spools, and bobbins. His early experience in the manufacture of hand-spinning wheels and their accessories positioned him well to supply parts for the textile mills that were emerging at water-power sites throughout southern New England. He had his own small shop on a tiny brook at the edge of his farm. Its stone foundation walls are just beyond the suburban housing development that now covers his fields. In this shop, Steere filled the substantial orders for industrial spools and bobbins that appear in his first account book. For reasons that are undocumented, he stopped dealing with mill owners sometime between 1814 and 1836 (a gap in the existing account books), but continued to supplement his farm income with woodworking activities into the 1850s.

While industrialization transformed the American economy, Steere's combination of agriculture and manufacturing provided economic security and a freedom of choice that most urban mechanics lacked. He was not totally dependent on his wood-turning craft, but he apparently enjoyed it and drew economic benefit from it. His skills, practiced whenever personal inclination, financial need, or opportunity dictated, may have kept him from the failure that struck many New England farmers of his period. He did not have to take a job in the urban manufacturing centers, and he chose not to acquire a better water-power site that could support a more mechanized and competitive bobbin business of his own. Perhaps he grew tired of dealing with the new class of industrialists, individuals who may not have understood the complex etiquette of reciprocal obligations and exchanges that governed the rural economy and who had no patience for the alternate bouts of intense labor and idleness that were a part of preindustrial work. Steere was one of a large number of rural craftsmen who chose not to step aboard as the train of industrial change passed by.[38]

The staff at Old Sturbridge Village has re-created the workplace of another, long-lived farmer–artisan from the same historical period as Steere. Hervey Brooks was a Connecticut farmer whose principal manufacturing activity was making pottery. He was apprenticed to a local potter in 1795, at the age of fifteen, and fired his own kiln for the last time almost seventy years later. On occasion, he also made bricks, sawed lumber, did carpentry and blacksmithing, and drove a team. He was an active participant in the complex exchange network of his agrarian community.

The majority of the utilitarian redwares that Brooks produced remained traditional in form and function. He recorded that his final kiln load consisted of "Milkpans, some Pots, Pudding pans & Wash bowls, but mostly of Stove tubs and Flowerpots." Although he adopted some of the improved technology of nineteenth-century ceramic manufacture, he made only a brief attempt at large-scale production, unfortunately just as the demand for redware was beginning to decline. Only in the three years from 1818 to 1820 did he devote most of his time to pottery; from 1828 to 1864, his usual practice was to fire his kiln only one day each year.[39]

Archaeologist John Worrell used documentary and material evidence in combination with physical reconstruction and imitative experiment to gain an understanding of this farmer–potter's craft. Worrell and his assistants began with a study of Brooks's account books and daybooks, and then went on to conduct excavations at the site of Brooks's shop, clay cellar, and kiln. They also studied the surrounding landscape, which once included clay pits and other potteries. Before this project began, relatively little was known about the work processes, spatial organization, and equipment of America's many small, rural potteries. The potters working at Old Sturbridge Village

FIGURE 6.9. Hervey Brooks's restored pottery shop and re-created bottle kiln at Old Sturbridge Village. (Courtesy of Old Sturbridge Village)

served not only as technical experts and experimenters, but also as documentary analysts and occasional excavators. "Insights derived from turning an eye that was skilled in one aspect toward a different medium of research in the company of one trained in that medium proved invaluable."[40] Brooks's account book mentioned "a Stone for a Clay Cellar." The potters, from their experience, thought that Brooks would have needed a cellar to store prepared clay before putting it on his wheel. Excavation soon uncovered a cellar and a large dressed stone that, amazingly, had balls of clay sitting on it.[41] As the archaeologists and historians worked with the potters, incorporating each piece of new evidence into a program of experimental testing, they began to understand the flow of materials, the use of tools and structures, and the skills necessary to make a wide variety of redware items.

Old Sturbridge Village now operates Brooks's restored shop and a recreation of his bottle kiln (Fig. 6.9). The spatial arrangement of equipment and work-in-progress in the shop is based on the findings of this lengthy archaeological research project. Excavated fragments, a few marked pieces that have survived in museum collections, and Brooks's written records indicate the form, the composition, and often the methods of manufacture of many of his wares. Skilled potters at the Village replicate known examples of his work, reenacting the many steps involved in preparing clay, turning, glazing, stacking, and firing. They continue to learn about the work of early craftsmen by actually trying it.

The rapid expansion of American industry in the early nineteenth century drew on the reservoir of skills that artisans in North America had acquired through the previous two centuries. Interpretation of artifactual evidence, in combination with documentary research,[42] clearly demonstrates a substantial growth in the level and distribution of technical ability. With adequate sources of energy and raw materials in place, American entrepreneurs were ready to use these artisanal skills in factory settings.

Notes

1. Larry Lankton and Charles Hyde, *Old Reliable: An Illustrated History of the Quincy Mining Company* (Hancock, Mich.: Quincy Mine Hoist Association, 1982), pp. 1, 3, 10; Roy Drier and Octave du Temple, eds., *Prehistoric Copper Mining in the Lake Superior Region* (Calumet, Mich.: Privately printed, 1961).

2. Patrick M. Malone, *The Skulking Way of War: Technology and Tactics Among the Indians of Southern New England, 1600–1677* (Lanham, Md.: Madison Books, 1991); William Bradford, *Of Plymouth Plantation, 1620–1647*, ed. Samuel E. Morison (New York: Modern Library, 1967), p. 207; Nathaniel Saltonstall, "A New and Further Narrative," in *Narratives of the Indian Wars*, ed. Charles H. Lincoln (New

York: Barnes & Noble, 1959), p. 96; Patrick M. Malone, "Changing Military Technology Among the Indians of Southern New England, 1600–1677," *American Quarterly* 25 (1973): 48–63.

3. "Testimony of Hugh Cole," at Plymouth, March 8, 1670/1671, miscellaneous bound manuscripts, Massachusetts Historical Society, Boston; T. M. Hamilton, "Some Gun Parts from 17th Century Seneca Sites," in *Indian Trade Guns*, ed. T. M. Hamilton, *Missouri Archeologist* [special issue] 22 (1960): 101–107; Paul Robinson, Marc Kelly, and Patricia Rubertone, "Preliminary Biocultural Interpretations from a Seventeenth-Century Narragansett Indian Cemetery in Rhode Island," in *Cultures in Contact: The European Impact on Native Cultural Institutions in Eastern North America, A.D. 1000–1800,* ed. William Fitzhugh (Washington, D.C.: Smithsonian Institution Press, 1985), pp. 120, 122.

4. Jackson Kemper III, *American Charcoal Making* (Hopewell Village, Pa.: Eastern National Park and Monument Association, n.d.); Susan W. Frye and Dennis E. Frye, *Maryland Heights Archaeological and Historical Resources Study,* Occasional Report No. 2, Regional Archaeology Program, National Capital Region (Washington, D.C.: National Park Service, 1989), chap. 3. Previously unpublished illustrations are found in J. Lawrence Pool and Angeline Pool, *America's Valley Forges and Valley Furnaces* (West Cornwall, Conn.: Pool, 1982), pp. 95–96.

5. At ironworks in New York and New England that did not operate on the plantation system, charcoal was often made in kilns located adjacent to the blast furnace with wood purchased from local farmers (Robert B. Gordon and M. S. Raber, "An Early American Integrated Steelworks," *IA, Journal of the Society for Industrial Archeology* 10 [1984]: 17–34).

6. Based on a manuscript description of coaling in the papers of the Peru Steel and Iron Company, Special Collections, Feinberg Library, State University of New York, Plattsburgh. We are indebted to Richard Ward for telling us about this material.

7. Edouard A. Stackpole, *The Charles W. Morgan: The Last Wooden Whaleship* (New York: Meredith Press, 1967).

8. Robert Albion and others, *New England and the Sea* (Mystic, Conn.: Mystic Seaport, 1972), pp. 31, 118; "Statistics on the Distribution of Oil in the Mills," *Proceedings of the New England Cotton Manufacturers Association,* no. 5 (1876): 44–47.

9. Stuart M. Frank, "The Legacy of Stranded Whales," *Whalewatcher: Journal of the American Cetacean Society* 20 (1986): 3–9.

10. The range of smith's work is described in Charles M. Keller and Paul Benson, "Ignatius Streibich, Blacksmith," *Chronicle of the Early American Industries Association* 42 (1989): 47–49.

11. John D. Light and Henry Unglik, *A Frontier Fur Trade Blacksmith Shop, 1796–1812,* rev. ed. (Ottawa: Environment Canada, 1987).

12. Robert B. Gordon, "Strength and Structure of Wrought Iron," *Archeomaterials* 2 (1988): 109–137; Gordon, "Who Turned the Mechanical Ideal into Mechanical Reality?" *Technology and Culture* 29 (1988): 744–778.

13. Smiths preferred to work with wrought iron rather than steel because steel is more difficult to weld with a forge fire and hand hammers. The smithing techniques demonstrated at many museums do not include welding because of the lack of convenient sources of wrought iron. Most modern products described as "wrought iron" are actually made of steel.

14. Gordon, "Strength and Structure of Wrought Iron."

15. An illustrated description of the molder's work is in *Guide to the Hopewell Village National Historic Site,* National Park Handbook No. 124 (Washington, D.C.: Department of the Interior, 1983). The varied problems encountered by moulders are described in L. C. Jewett, "What the Molder Has to Do," *American Machinist* 23 (1900): 323.

16. A useful source of descriptions and illustrations of all kinds of forming and cutting machines is Joshua Rose, *Modern Machine-Shop Practice,* 2 vols. (New York: Scribner's, 1888). A concise history with two chapters on American tools is in L.T.C. Rolt, *Tools for the Job,* rev. ed. (London: HMSO, 1986). An important source on American machine tools remains Joseph W. Roe, *English and American Tool Builders* (New Haven, Conn.: Yale University Press, 1916). Histories of the lathe, milling, grinding, and gear-cutting machines are in Robert S. Woodbury, *Studies in the History of Machine Tools* (Cambridge, Mass.: MIT Press, 1972). The largest collection of machine tools on public display is at the American Precision Museum in Windsor, Vermont.

17. The basic elements of an up-and-down sawmill are shown in Martha T. Gnudi, trans., *The Various and Ingenious Machines of Agostino Ramelli* (1588; New York: Dover, 1976), pl. 136. Considerable mechanical experience would be required to translate this generalized drawing into a practical mechanism.

18. Different kinds of sawing leave distinctive marks, and an example of the use of saw marks to identify machine-sawn boards dating from about 1680 is given in Benno M. Forman, "Mill Sawing in Seventeenth-Century Massachusetts," *Old Time New England* 60 (1970): 110–130.

19. The archaeological evidence on early milling technology in Europe is reviewed in P. A. Rahtz, "Medieval Milling," in *Medieval Industry,* ed. David Crossley, Council for British Archaeology Research Report No. 40 (London: Council for British Archaeology, 1981), pp. 1–15. For the early history of gristmilling in North America, see Charles Howell, "Colonial Watermills in the Wooden Age," in *America's Wooden Age,* ed. Brooke Hindle (Tarrytown, N.Y.: Sleepy Hollow Restorations, 1975).

20. Quoted in Craig L. Bartholomew, "William M. Weaver—Superintendent of the Macungie Furnace," *Canal History and Technology Proceedings* 5 (1986): 151.

21. Gordon and Raber, "Early American Integrated Steelworks."

22. A detailed description of the work of tapping a blast furnace is in Craig L. Bartholomew and Lance E. Metz, *The Anthracite Industry of the Lehigh Valley* (Easton, Pa.: Center for Canal History and Technology, 1988), pp. 74–77.

23. Quoted from *Mining Journal,* 28 February 1874, in Kenneth D. LaFayette, *Flaming Brands* (Marquette, Mich.: LaFayette, 1990), p. 38.

24. Paul S. Leitner, "The Oxford Furnace: Some Surprising Firsts in a Backwoods Enterprise," *Canal History and Technology Proceedings* 8 (1989): 213–239.

25. Fining pig iron by hand was carried on in Sweden until 1964, and the skills needed have been recorded (Barbro Bursell, *The Clog Nobility* [Stockholm: Nordiska Museets, 1975]). A skilled hammerman could draw out a loup into a bar so uniform in cross section that it is very difficult to distinguish it from a rolled bar. Samples of Swedish bar iron made about 1866 and placed in the Metallurgical Museum of Yale College cannot easily be distinguished from rolled plate in their surface finish and uniformity.

26. This forge is described in Helen R. Schenck and Reed Knox, "Valley Forge: The Making of Iron in the Eighteenth Century," *Archaeology* 39 (1986): 27–33.

27. Robert B. Gordon, "Materials for Manufacturing: The Response of the Connecticut Iron Industry to Technological Change and Limited Resources," *Technology and Culture* 24 (1983): 602–634.

28. Cyril Stanley Smith, "Production de fer à la fenderie de Saugus aux alentours de 1660," *Revue d'histoire de la sidérurgie* 7 (1966): 7–15.

29. Kenneth T. Howell and Einer W. Carlson, *Men of Iron: Forbes & Adam* (Lakeville, Conn.: Pocketknife Press, 1980), pp. 43–92.

30. Harry Miller, "Potash from Wood Ashes: Frontier Technology in Canada and the United States," *Technology and Culture* 21 (1980): 187–208.

31. Thomas Turner, *The Metallurgy of Iron* (London: Griffin, 1900), p. 306.

32. Bruce Seely, *Adirondack Iron and Steel Company "New Furnace," 1849–1854*, HAER No. NY-123 (Washington, D.C.: Historic American Engineering Record, 1978), p. 78.

33. James M. Swank, *History of the Manufacture of Iron in All Ages*, 2d ed. (Philadelphia: American Iron and Steel Association, 1892), pp. 297–300.

34. Myron Stachiw, *Negro Cloth: Northern Industry and Southern Slavery* (Boston: Boston National Historical Park, 1981).

35. See, for example, a letter with negro-cloth samples sent to Rhode Island manufacturer R. G. Hazard on October 29, 1844, in the records of the Peacedale Manufacturing Company, box A, case 7, folder B, Baker Library, Harvard University.

36. Myron Stachiw, John Worrell, and Jack Larkin at Old Sturbridge Village have done a great deal of research on this topic. See Jack Larkin, *The Reshaping of Everyday Life, 1790–1840* (New York: Harper & Row, 1988), and Marcie Cohen, "The Journals of Joshua Whitman, Turner, Maine, 1809–1846," in *The Farm*, ed. Peter Barnes (Boston: Boston University Press, 1988), pp. 49–59.

37. Curators Sandra Norman and Priscilla Brewer acquired and moved the disassembled lathe to Slater Mill Historic Site. Brown University students Christopher Regan and Mark Strassman drew the parts with a computer-aided design program and reassembled them on the computer screen, thus ascertaining their function, fit, and spatial relationships. This computerized reassembly allowed careful study of the fragile machine without further damaging it. Some parts were warped, worn, or decayed; a few were missing.

38. Carolyn C. Cooper and Patrick M. Malone, "The Mechanical Woodworker in Early Nineteenth-Century New England as a Spin-Off from the Textile Industry" (Paper presented at Old Sturbridge Village Colloquium, 17 March 1990). For discussion of preindustrial work habits, see E. P. Thompson, "Time, Work-Discipline, and Industrial Capitalism," *Past and Present* 38 (1967): 56–97.

39. John Worrell, "Ceramic Production in the Exchange Network of an Agricultural Neighborhood," in *Domestic Pottery of the Northeastern United States, 1625–1850*, ed. Sarah Turnbaugh (New York: Academic Press, 1985), pp. 153–169, esp. 160–161; Worrell, "Hervey Brooks's Pottery," in *Unearthing New England's Past: The Ceramic Evidence*, ed. Susan Montgomery (Lexington, Mass.: Museum of Our National Heritage, 1984), pp. 57–62.

40. John Worrell, "Re-creating Ceramic Production and Tradition in a Living History Laboratory," in *Domestic Pottery of the Northeastern United States*, ed. Turnbaugh, p. 87.

41. Worrell, "Ceramic Production," pp. 87–88.

42. Recent documentary evidence from patents is presented in Kenneth L. Sokoloff and B. Z. Kahn, "The Democratization of Invention During Early Industrialization: Evidence from the U.S., 1790–1846," *Journal of Economic History* 50 (1990): 363–378.

7
Fuel and Materials

As American entrepreneurs enlarged their undertakings and began to shift them from waterpowered shops in the countryside to factories in the cities, they created a demand for new sources of energy and larger quantities of raw materials. The coal and, later, oil that they used to power their factories were brought to manufacturing centers on canals and railways and by coastal or river shipping. They used the wood and water resources of North America more heavily than ever, but they also created new kinds of workplaces. Their workplaces in the coal and oil fields, on canals and railways, in mills that made iron with mineral coal, and in the nonferrous-metal mines and mills were outside any previous experience of American artisans. Often, these workplaces were not adequately described or recorded before they were replaced. Material evidence helps us fill this gap in the historical record.

Coal

Anthracite Mining

In mining anthracite, both miners and mine operators faced a complex underground environment where there were few reliable clues to guide their work (Chapter 4). Geologists could help little, and, as anthracite was not much used elsewhere in the world, mining expertise could not be easily borrowed; instead, mining methods were developed through experience and error on the part of individual miners. The technological and social practices that endured in anthracite mining were largely established in the years between 1827 and 1834 by inexperienced adventurers whose aim was to obtain coal quickly and with the least trouble. Many of these practices were later adopted in underground bituminous mines.

We can reconstruct a picture of the work of anthracite miners from study of the remaining mines, artifacts, and accounts of mine operation. Each breast in a mine was worked by a miner, who was paid on piece rate. He directed and paid one or two helpers, for whom he provided the necessary tools and supplies. They reached the breast where they worked by walking through the haulage ways and gangways that were the common ground in the mine (Fig. 7.1). Once in their breast, the miner and helper were isolated from other miners and from supervisors; they worked as an independent team, but were dependent on others for hauling out the coal, providing adequate ventilation, and pumping water out of the mine. They could be

FIGURE 7.1. In this nineteenth-century anthracite mine in Pennsylvania, coal blasted out by miners working in breasts was hauled in carts pulled by mules through the timbered tunnel. This photograph by Bretz is one of the first to show the interior of an operating coal mine. The haulage way is higher and dryer than most, but the timbering and track are typical. Gangways leading to breasts opened off the haulage way. Ordinarily, the only light would be from candles attached to the miner's hats. (Courtesy of Hugh Moore Historical Park and Museums)

endangered by bad judgment or carelessness on the part of the mine operator; the above-ground staff handling the pumps, hoists, or fans; or almost anyone working underground in the mine. Other miners might, for example, block the ventilation system by bringing down coal or rock in ill-judged places, cause an explosion by using candles when safety lamps were called for, or cause a crush (collapse of the mine openings) by robbing too much coal from the pillars. Miners were dependent on the managers and owners of the mine for proper design of the ventilation and drainage systems, supervision of the operation of the mine as a whole, and accurate weighing of the coal they produced. Miners could be cheated by short weighing and endangered by inadvertently breaking into old, unmapped workings filled with gas or water because previous mine operators had failed to keep adequate records of their work. [1]

In the system of mining that evolved in Pennsylvania, there was little centralized supervision of the underground work. The "fire boss" inspected for explosive concentrations of fire damp (methane) before work began each day, and overall supervision of the underground work was the responsibility of the "inside boss," who might visit each breast once a day. [2] Immediate judgments about the working of a breast and about safety within it were in the hands of the individual miners.

MINING SKILLS

An important component of skill in mining is the capacity to carry on work with incomplete information available to guide decisions. The many geological complexities that gave few clues, the need for the miner to reach decisions without the presence of supervisors, and the likelihood of serious accident due to misjudgment meant that a miner needed real technical skills to survive physically and economically in the trade. [3] The work was also physically arduous. [4] The miner and helper had to climb to the working face in their breast through narrow manways carrying their tools and the heavy timbers needed to support the roof. They drilled holes for the powder charges and shifted the broken coal largely by hand, as few power-driven appliances or mining machines could be used in anthracite mines.

Miners had to discern local geological conditions and adapt general knowledge of mining methods to them. Since visible clues about the locations of coal veins were sparse, the geological characteristics of mines had to be discovered by experience underground. This knowledge was most valuable at the mine and its immediate environs and of limited value elsewhere. Coal-mining skills were unlike the skills acquired by nineteenth-century artisans in woodworking and metalworking, which were applicable to many different products made by numerous factories and could be applied wherever a new opportunity offered. Mechanics discovered the best way to accomplish tasks by personal experience and disseminated that information when they worked for different makers of a given product or for makers of different products. There were fewer opportunities for such improvement in anthracite mining. As miners and operators developed a set of underground workings, their knowledge of the mine became valuable intellectual property. This property was protected neither by ownership (there was no equivalent of a patent for miners) nor by a market that could value it. Lack of proprietary interest was a disincentive to both miner and operator to learn the geological complexities of a mine or to invest in the mine infrastructure needed for safe operation.

MINING ACCIDENTS

Using explosives to bring down coal in a confined underground space was inherently dangerous work. People can do hazardous things, such as flying in aircraft, with little risk when market forces and government regulation make operators devote substantial resources to necessary safety precautions. In anthracite mining, neither markets nor regulations had much influence on the safety of the work, and accident rates were high. We have reliable data on mine accidents only for the years after 1870.[5] In 1899, the annual death rate in anthracite mining was 1 in 305, and the injury rate was 1 in 136.[6] (For comparison, the death rate among workers on railroads in Pennsylvania was 1 in 434, but the injury rate was higher than in the anthracite mines.) Between 1870 and 1899, the death rate changed incrementally with the production rate;[7] no improvements in mine safety had been made. Even these data fail to reveal fully the risk faced by the underground miners. First, only about 50 percent of the mine labor force worked underground, where nearly 90 percent of the deaths occurred; second, deaths resulting from injuries were not counted; and, third, there was undercounting of accidents.[8] Anthropologist Anthony Wallace believes that all these factors together indicate a death rate for underground anthracite mining closer to 1 in 127 a year and that at some mines the rate was higher, approaching that of military losses in combat.[9] Mine operators might find work for injured miners among the boys cleaning coal in the breakers (Fig. 7.2); beyond that, they had to rely on whatever charity the community could provide.

Popular accounts of coal mining focus on disasters caused by gas explosions, but the principal cause of fatal accidents was roof falls that occurred close to the working faces in the breasts, the areas of the mine under the immediate control of the individual miners.[10] These incidents killed or injured a few individuals at a time, day in and day out, but did not attract the attention accorded the drama of gas explosions. Pennsylvania mine inspectors attributed the frequent roof falls to a combination of carelessness, poor judgment, and reluctance to take precautions because timbering was "dead

FIGURE 7.2. The breaker crew crushed the coal brought up from an anthracite mine and screened it for size. They then ran it down troughs in front of boys who picked out any slate that was mixed with the coal. A disabled miner working with the boys in the breaker has leaned his crutches on the coal trough. This photograph was taken about 1890 at a breaker on the Girard Estate in Pennsylvania. (Courtesy of the Smithsonian Institution)

time" (work for which there was no direct payment to the miner or mine operator).[11] The Pennsylvania system of mine organization and inspection provided neither effective enforcement of safety regulations nor sufficient inducements for miners to erect adequate roof support. In anthracite mines, and to an even greater extent in bituminous mines, there were actually financial incentives for miners to risk death or injury from roof falls by taking timber posts from areas that had been worked out. Mine operators regularly offered special payments for retrieving valuable posts during final mining operations (removal of supporting pillars of coal). When accidents resulted, inspectors and operators usually followed the tradition of blaming the miner for his carelessness or inexperience.[12]

Bituminous Mining

Mining with hand methods was particularly arduous in bituminous areas because seams of soft coal were usually level and not very thick. Unlike their contemporaries in the anthracite fields, the miners of this soft coal got little help from gravity. To drop the coal with an explosive charge, a miner first had to undercut it, a task that he usually performed by lying on his side and swinging a pick. Loading ton after ton of variable-size pieces of rock into mine cars from a level surface was literally backbreaking labor, much more physically demanding than the usual anthracite practice of loading from above, using a chute. All these difficulties were magnified in narrow seams, where low roofs made everyone stoop or crawl and where it was sometimes necessary to cut a trench in the stone floor to bring a car near the coal.[13]

Mine operators, as mentioned in Chapter 4, found it easier to adopt mechanized cutting and loading equipment in coal mines that had horizontal seams, but there were tradeoffs for the resulting alleviation of heavy labor and increase in productivity. Miners who had worked with the freedom of semiindependent contractors came under much tighter supervision and found themselves doing narrowly defined tasks, sometimes with greater risk of injury or occupational disease. Heavy machinery, and the electricity that powered much of it, was dangerous in a mine. This was particularly true during the transition period from the hand methods of the 1880s to the extensive mechanization and tighter safety regulation of the 1940s. Machinery injured workers by accidental contact and played its part in roof falls, explosions, and electrocutions. The clouds of dust kicked up by mechanized operations not only impaired vision in hazardous working areas, but also had the potential to ignite in the presence of a spark. Worst of all for the miners were the long-term health effects from breathing this dust; we now know that it causes miner's pneumoconiosis, or black lung.[14]

Mechanization of bituminous mining increased in the late 1880s as undercutting machinery began to replace hand picks. One form was the "pick," or punching machine, first patented as a pneumatic device by J. W. Harrison in 1877. It mimicked the action of the miner with his hand tool, but with much more force and rapidity. The Goodman Equipment Company has one of its early picks on display at its plant near Chicago, where workers still make very effective mine locomotives. This company and its precursors, which used many designs by the noted American inventor Elmer Sperry, had more success with chain cutters (a British idea) than with electrically driven versions of the punching machine. Chain cutters, various types of loaders and conveyors, and haulage equipment transformed the workplace and the jobs of most coal miners by the end of World War II. The terrible accident rate was declining. However, it would be another twenty years before workers suffering from black lung were declared legally eligible for compensation as victims of an occupational disease.[15]

The exhibit on coal mining at the Chicago Museum of Science and Industry cleverly re-creates the experience of traveling down a mine shaft, but it offers a sanitized and unrealistic version of the working areas in a mine. The mechanized mining equipment is too clean and unscarred, and there is no suggestion of the dust that this machinery would produce in operation. The emphasis in the interpretation is on safety practices and efficient production, as one might expect from an exhibit sponsored and supported by the very industry it describes. There seems to be a higher priority on public relations than on accurate depiction of working conditions.

Combustion Technology

A determined effort by many entrepreneurs was needed to convince Americans that anthracite was a useful fuel.[16] Until the early nineteenth century, it was not evident to most people that anthracite would burn at all: "The coal found was so different from any previously known, that it was deemed utterly valueless—more especially as no means could be found to ignite it."[17] Two properties of anthracite created difficulties when people first tried to use it. First, since anthracite is nearly pure carbon and contains little volatile matter, it had to be heated to a high temperature before it would burn; a cold draft of air would extinguish it. Second, anthracite burns with a very short flame, making it difficult to distribute the heat it generates over the surface of a boiler or furnace.

Professional scientists participated in the development of anthracite combustion technology, but the value of anthracite as a fuel was established primarily through experimentation over a thirty-year period during which artisans learned the skills they needed to use it. Since anthracite was not generally used in Europe or Britain, the techniques needed to burn it had to be invented in America. The three major applications of anthracite were heating homes and public buildings; firing boilers of stationary steam engines, steamboats, and locomotives; and smelting and refining iron. Jesse Fells began to experiment with grates in 1808,[18] and by the years 1828 to 1835, when a large number of patents for stoves were issued to Eliphalet Nott and others,[19] the technology of heating buildings with anthracite was well in hand. Inventors then turned to coal-fired boilers for stationary steam engines, thus increasing the attractiveness of steam as an alternative to water power for factories. Designing grates and fireboxes that would permit anthracite to be used in steamboats and locomotives was a more difficult problem that took longer to solve. Locomotive designers for the Baltimore and Ohio Railroad began to experiment with anthracite fuel in 1831 but suffered many problems with burned-out grate bars and fireboxes, in part because of the special skills needed to keep an anthracite fire burning properly. Twenty-five years later, a satisfactory locomotive firebox for anthracite was finally developed (for the Reading Railroad), and it was not until 1860 that raw bituminous coal was successfully used as locomotive fuel (on the Pennsylvania Railroad).[20] The development of combustion technology for anthracite is another example of the solution of technological problems by incremental innovation made largely by practitioners.

Railroads

Railway workers, like anthracite miners, established a social structure and work customs in the first years of railroad operation that endured for decades; some, for better or worse, are still with us. In coal mining, the potential for accidents was high and only partially under the control of individual workers. But the operation of a railway could be regulated by dispatchers with the aid of trackside signals (Fig. 7.3) and telegraphed instructions. Because of the control effected through signals, railway managers could attain traffic densities unmatched by any other method of transportation. Railroad officials were the first Americans to be able to extend centralized management over large areas of the continent. One of the social consequences of their efforts was the establishment of national standard times.[21] Managers who controlled distant train movements enlarged their organization to include control of distant business practices as well; they fully exploited this spin-off from technology.[22]

A simple way for a dispatcher to operate a single-track railway was to send a train from one terminal and await its arrival at the other end before starting a train in the reverse direction, leaving most of the track idle most of the time. Railway managers attained higher traffic densities by building passing places at intervals along the line and by placing signals to control train movements. They were able to move even more traffic when they invested in automatic block signals, which gave advance warning of the need to stop (Fig. 7.3). The engine driver could safely run at a speed well above that corresponding to the train crew's range of sight. Signals assured the crew that the track ahead was clear.

One of the most important characteristics of railway work, one that was new to the American industrial scene, was that safe operation depended on the faithful observance of every trackside signal by train crews. The signal system set precise bounds on the discretion that the train crew could exercise. Railway signals were an early, publicly visible means of centralized control of a technological system. But semaphore and light signals were discrete indicators placed at definite intervals along the line and did not provide the continual control of train movements that later became possible with radio communication. The train crew had full control of operations within the bounds set by the signals and had to decide how best to keep to the overall schedule. There were many opportunities to use planning skills and display personal style in railway work.

Anther novel aspect of railway work was that immediate control of the train was in the hands of individuals who could not always see or speak to

FIGURE 7.3. The Royal Blue of the Baltimore and Ohio Railroad on the line between Philadelphia and Baltimore has just crossed the Susquehanna River and is about to enter the next block of track. The lowered arm of the top semaphore (the home signal) shows the engine driver that the block is clear, but the raised arm of the lower semaphore (the distant signal) shows him that the next block is not clear and that he must be prepared to stop when he reaches it. A signalman operated the semaphores from a tower (not shown) by the rods visible in the foreground. These rods were notorious among railroaders for being at just the right height to trip over. The extra pair of rails inside the track on the bridge was intended to keep the train from going over the edge should it derail. (Courtesy of the Smithsonian Institution)

FIGURE 7.4. The visible parts of a diesel-electric locomotive give few indications of how the mechanism worked because the diesel engine, generator, and traction motors cannot be seen. Once inside, the engine crew is hardly visible to observers. (Photographed at the Valley Railroad, Essex, Connecticut)

one another or, frequently, see all of the train at one time. They depended on a system of communication that was universally understood by railroaders and, before the advent of portable radios, was based on whistle and hand signals. Each member of the train crew had to know the course of action that should follow each signal. The mutually shared understanding of signaling rules and customs helped create a fraternity among railroaders.

The limitations of whistle and hand signals, the lack of full visibility, and the time that it took for motion to be communicated through the slack between cars in a train combined to make work in switching yards dangerous. Workers could be injured by unexpected movement of the train as they stepped between cars to open or close couplers and to make hose connections; brakemen riding on the sides or tops of cars were at risk from trackside obstructions and passing trains.[23] Outside the yards, equipment failures such as broken rails and axles, bridge collapses, boiler explosions, and derailments caused many accidents in nineteenth-century railroading. Much ingenuity was expended on correcting these technological deficiencies through inventions such as the Westinghouse air brake, through learning proper designs and standardizing equipment, and through inspection systems such as the Sperry rail fault detector. But laws were often needed to force railway managers to adopt new technology that reduced the potential for injuries.

The steam locomotive was perhaps the most visible aspect of the character of the railroad. People like steam locomotives, and there is enough interest in them among casual riders and rail enthusiasts to support one or more steam-train, tourist-railway operation in almost every state and province in the United States and Canada. Nostalgia, the mechanics of the engine itself, the skill needed to drive it, and the reaction of train riders and trackside viewers all contribute to the enduring popularity of steam locomotives.[24]

A steam locomotive has a complex but comprehensible texture; when in steam, it smells of hot oil and coal smoke, and it makes animal-like sounds as it works. The diesel-electric locomotive, which replaced it, is covered up by an elegant shroud that obscures both the mechanism and the engine crew (Fig. 7.4); instead of rhythmically puffing, it simply roars at us. In American steam-locomotive design before the 1930s, the working parts of the engine and, to a large degree, the engine crew were exposed to view (Fig. 7.5).[25] The comprehensible complexity of the locomotive mechanism is seen

FIGURE 7.5. Until they were shrouded by industrial designers in the 1930s, nearly all the working parts of American steam locomotives were exposed to view. The cab afforded the driver and fireman some protection from the weather, but allowed persons on a station platform to watch their work. The locomotive driver controlled the engine with the throttle lever grasped in his left hand, the air brake (out of sight in this photograph), and the reversing lever (visible at the bottom of the cab window). The fireman had a seat on the left side of the cab to use when watching signals or not working the fire. Numerous valves, try cocks, and gauges required occasional attention. The steam whistle lanyard hung above the driver; the bell-pull, above the fireman. (Photographed at the Valley Railroad, Essex, Connecticut)

FIGURE 7.6. The power train of the steam locomotive consists of the piston and cylinder (at the lower left) that turn the four driving wheels (outlined in white) by means of a crank and connecting rods. Additional rods and cranks operate the valve that admits steam to the cylinder and an automatic lubricator. The boiler is mounted above the cast-iron frame of the engine; attached to its sides are two air compressors, needed to operate the brakes. The firebox is at the right. (Photographed at the Valley Railroad, Essex, Connecticut)

in the pistons, valve gear, driving wheels, and other parts of the engine (Fig. 7.6), conveying a sense of purpose and controlled power.[26] A picture cannot convey the fascination of many people with watching the parts in motion, movements that are intriguing because some of them are difficult to anticipate from the appearance of the mechanism at rest. Observers can satisfy their interest in the engine mechanism without feeling threatened because, as they stand nearby and watch a locomotive at work, they know that the machine's domain is precisely defined by the track. A locomotive can move along a crowded station platform quietly and on a clearly prescribed course in a way that is impossible for an aircraft, for example. Steam locomotives also attract our attention by making sounds suggestive of life. While the engine is stopped, there is the humming of the steam-turbine dynamo and the pumping of the air compressor. When the locomotive is in motion, the sound of the steam exhaust announces how hard the engine is working with gentle snorts or puffs of heavy breathing. The author of a book of instruction on locomotive driving describes his impressions:

> I love to see one of those huge creatures, with sinews of brass and muscles of
> iron strut forth from his stable and, saluting the train of cars with a dozen

sonorous puffs from his iron nostrils, fall back gently into his harness. There he stands champering and foaming upon the iron track, his great heart a furnace of glowing coals, his lymphatic blood boiling within his veins, the strength of a thousand horses nerving his sinews, he pants to be gone.[27]

The engine driver and the fireman worked as a team as they performed their special tasks. Firing a locomotive by hand may appear to be simply a matter of heaving coal into a firebox, but the job was far more complicated than that. The fireman had to maintain a uniform flame over the grate bars. He kept the fire ready to build up when more steam was needed to climb hills, and he cut it back on downgrades. Since the capacity of the boiler to store steam was limited and it took some time to increase the boiling rate, the fireman had to anticipate the engine driver's demand for steam; poor firing was evident on upgrades if the steam pressure dropped as the locomotive climbed or on downgrades or stopped if the safety valve lifted. The fireman also helped watch signals and looked backward to check the condition of the train when it was visible on curves. The driver of a steam locomotive had only the throttle, brake, and reversing lever to control the train. Practice and intelligence were needed to start a heavy train without slipping the driving wheels, to stop the train smoothly and at the right place, to keep to a schedule as the train passed varying grades and track conditions, and to maneuver the locomotive in coupling and uncoupling cars. Lack of skill in these operations was immediately apparent to the rest of the train crew, to the passengers, and to observers on station platforms or along the line.

The members of the crew of a steam locomotive had many opportunities to display their professional accomplishments and personal style. Until the 1870s, each locomotive was run by one assigned crew, who could decorate it to their taste and care for it as their own.[28] Emerging from the cab to oil the locomotive mechanism was part of the ritual in engine driving. The locomotive whistle provided another outlet for the display of style, since its tone could be varied according to the amount of steam admitted to it; drivers could produce distinctive sound signatures that announced their passage to the surrounding countryside. (The bell, with its somewhat more limited opportunities for personal expression, was the fireman's province.) Unlike conductors of passenger trains, airline pilots, and bus drivers, the locomotive crew always appeared without uniforms and in work clothes that could reflect individual preferences. For all these reasons, the steam locomotive created an unusually rich work environment. In diesel locomotives, some of this opportunity is lost; it is almost impossible to slip the wheels of a diesel-electric engine when starting a train, for example, and the engine crew is largely enclosed and invisible to the passengers or other observers. However, the adoption of diesel locomotives eliminated the unpleasant and unhealthful task of cleaning locomotive fireboxes, increased the reliability of railway motive power, reduced the dirt deposited along the lines, and made it easier to pull long trains.

As railroad managers pushed their industry to maturity in the United States, they created workplaces within organizations that were larger and more highly structured than any yet seen in North America. The system of control that regulated train movements by trackside signals was precise but sharply bounded. Within those bounds, control rested with the train crew, who could not be directly supervised by managers in offices. The railway became a part of every community through which it passed, interacting with it economically and symbolically.

Iron

Coal technology also had an effect on the iron industry. Pennsylvania black-smiths had used anthracite in the eighteenth century, but many more people learned about it when faced with the shortages of bituminous coal caused by the War of 1812; they adopted it for heating iron to be forged or rolled and for melting iron in foundries. Their work was changed little by adopting the new fuel. Ironmasters were able to make their blast furnaces much bigger by using powerful blowing engines and mineral coal in place of charcoal fuel. With coal fuel, they could also increase the size of their ironworks and place them in towns served by canals and railways rather than in remote wood-lands, where charcoal was abundant. A few years after 1840, large-scale production of pig and wrought iron with coal fuel was under way at inte-grated ironworks in Pennsylvania. Ironworkers lived in towns and worked in larger organizations than they had on iron plantations.

The work of charging and tapping a blast furnace was not changed much when coal fuel was substituted for charcoal, but the scale of operations increased after 1854 as ironmasters replaced pyramidal, stone furnace stacks with cupola furnaces, iron-sheathed cylinders with platforms on top for the charging crew. The ore, fuel, and flux were brought up to the crew by elevators and wheeled by hand to the charging doors. Charging the furnace was an arduous and potentially dangerous task until, after 1883, furnace designers introduced skip cars that emptied themselves and were manipu-lated from below.

Puddling Furnaces

When the proprietors of ironworks adopted coal fuel, they had to make wrought iron with puddling furnaces instead of finery hearths in order to avoid contaminating the metal with the sulfur in the coal. Before it became possible to make steel cheaply, in the last third of the nineteenth century, the wrought iron used for such purposes as rails, ship hulls, and bridges was made in batches of about 400 pounds by individual puddlers, who used their judgment skills to control the quality of the metal they made. The puddling furnace, a deceptively simple-looking apparatus, was a small reverberatory furnace with a firebox at one side and a stack fitted with a damper at the other (Fig. 7.7). The only control was the damper handle, which could be lowered to reduce the draft and thereby create a more reducing atmosphere over the hearth. About once a week, the puddler had to prepare the bottom

FIGURE 7.7. While his helper lifts the furnace door, the puddler in this historic photograph pulls a puddle ball out of the furnace with his long tongs. He uses the chain suspended from the roof above the furnace to carry part of the weight of the iron. Liquid slag is draining from the ball as the puddler moves it through the furnace door. The hearth for the coal fire is on the right side of the furnace, in front of the helper. The puddler keeps his tools in the water trough at the left, and a supply of pigs for the next heat is stacked next to the trough. (Courtesy of the Smithsonian Institution)

of the hearth. To do this, he brought the furnace to full heat and then covered the bottom with fettling, a mixture of mill and hammer scale (iron oxide broken off the hot metal as it passed through rolling mills or forge hammers), ore, and other sources of iron oxide that might be about the shop, selected according to the puddler's preference to have the desired fusion temperature. He repaired the fire bridge (the wall separating the firebox from the hearth) with clay as needed and adjusted the "monkey" to his liking. (The monkey was a small pile of brick on the fire bridge placed to control the distribution of heat on the hearth.) Then the puddler made up a ball of odd bits of scrap iron and pushed it over the bottom of the furnace to work the fused fettling into cracks and crevices.

To begin making iron, the puddler and his helper opened the charging door and placed about 400 pounds of iron pigs on the hearth, distributing them to facilitate melting. They raised the damper, closed the charging door, and did all further manipulation through a small aperture known as the stopper hole. The puddler controlled the process with the aid of indirect indications of what was happening on the hearth. He had to maintain close control of the temperature and the oxidizing power of the furnace atmosphere throughout the process. To do this, he placed a piece of coal in the stopper hole while the pig was melting; as it burned, the coal reduced the flow of oxygen into the furnace. Once the pig was melted, the puddler lowered the damper the amount he thought appropriate to prevent oxidation at too rapid a rate. The puddler and helper took turns of one to two minutes of rabbling, or stirring the iron with a paddle, an iron bar with a flattened end. During this stage of the process, first the silicon and then the carbon in the pig were oxidized, the melting temperature of the metal rose, the metal appeared to boil, solid iron began to form, and the physical labor of rabbling became very severe. The puddler manipulated the damper to keep the boil going at the desired rate; if it went too rapidly, metal would be lost. When the puddler judged that the boil was completed, he used the paddle to divide the iron into four quarters of about 100 pounds each. He then opened the furnace door, lifted the damper to keep the draft up, and removed the first ball. His helper took this ball to a hammer or squeezer while the puddler kept the remaining iron at welding temperature in the furnace by manipulating the damper and door. After the last ball was removed, he opened the damper and knocked the plug out of the tap hole to drain the slag from the hearth. He then plugged the tap hole with sand and made any needed repairs to the interior of the furnace with fettling before commencing the next heat.[29]

Puddling demanded heavy physical labor and the constant exercise of judgment skills, since the chemical reactions that converted pig into wrought iron were controlled on the basis of indirect clues about their progress, such as the feel of the iron as the puddler worked it with the paddle. The puddler had to work with varied materials available in the shop—mill scale, ore from various sources, sand, and clay—that were not analyzed and could not be counted on to have uniform composition. He selected among them on the basis of experience. Because of their variability, together with the lack of uniformity in the composition of the pig iron, frequent modification of the operating procedure was needed. Organizational skills were less important since there was only one helper, who could be given explicit instructions. The method of learning was through being a helper.

It was easy to make bad iron in a puddling furnace; iron that was hot short (brittle when hot) was detected quickly because it broke up in the hammer or rolls. The test for cold shortness (brittleness at room temperature caused by phosphorus in the iron) was to break a sample of the finished bar, but poor ductility due to excessive or badly distributed slag was more difficult to detect. Quantitative tests were little used, and iron was sold on the basis of the makers' reputations. Maintaining quality called for skilled workers and careful management techniques; the environment in which the puddlers worked must have been an important factor in this endeavor, but at present we do not know how quality control was attained in the wrought-iron industry. The extensive tests done in 1832 at the Franklin Institute during its study of the causes of steam-boiler explosions showed that American iron-workers did not always provide iron of the uniformly good quality that was needed for rail, machinery, and boiler plate.[30] The consequences of inadequate quality control could be disaster.

Rolling Mills

While puddling was always a task for an individual working with a helper, a team effort was needed in the subsequent rolling of iron into products such as rails, beams, and plates. These items were usually manufactured in the same works that housed the furnaces. The commonly used two-high rolling mill was operated by a team of up to seven artisans, depending on the product being made. The roll train for making bar or rail had several sets of rolls, each with a series of grooves cut in them to produce successive changes in the shape of the work. One or more heaters kept a supply of iron ready at the correct temperature. The person in charge of the overall operation, the roller, set up the mill and usually fed the iron into the rolls for the first few passes. The catcher grasped the emerging metal, placed it on the top roll to return to the roller for the next pass, and adjusted the gap between the rolls. After several passes through the rolls, the bar was handed over to a second and, in a large stand, a third roller–catcher pair. With six or more artisans handling three bars of red-hot iron at one roll stand, coordination and smooth, graceful work with tongs as well as physical strength were needed. When things went wrong, knowledge of how to respond rapidly to contingencies was essential. Rolling plate on a two-high mill was also demanding, since catchers standing on each side of the mill had to grasp with tongs the hot metal emerging from the mill and return it over the top of the rolls for the next pass.[31] Iron could be rolled in both directions when a three-high mill was used. In the rolling mill's most sophisticated form, the looping mill, the catcher grasped the iron emerging from one pass, looped it around himself, and inserted it in the next pass so that the bar was being rolled simultaneously in two or more passes (Fig. 7.8). Confident, coordinated handling of the hot iron was needed in this work.

Since the wrought iron had a tendency to split as it passed through the rolls, vigilance and frequent decisions were needed to keep a rolling mill in steady operation. Because the work presented constantly changing problems, required a team effort, and was physically arduous, it fully engaged the physical and mental strength of the rolling crew.

Change in the Social Setting of Work

At a finery forge, one person working at a hearth converted pig to wrought iron. There were usually two (as at Valley Forge) to four hearths in the finery building, and the peer group in which the finer carried on his work was small. Ironmasters gradually supplanted fining with puddling. An iron puddler worked one furnace, but also supervised the work of a helper, who was responsible for conducting part of the process and was usually learning the job. Rolling mills had as many as forty puddling furnaces in one works, so the puddlers and helpers carried on their work in the presence of a large number of co-workers, a peer group within which the skills of different individuals could be ascertained and appreciated and in which the best procedure could be discovered and agreed on. The rollers also worked in large groups and were afforded many opportunities for the display of skill in managing the mill. The social relationships within one of these ironworks involved many subtleties and complexities that are not easily captured in discourse framed simply in terms of "labor" and "management."

Another change in the social setting of work arose when ironmasters adopted mineral coal because almost all the anthracite-fired blast and puddling furnaces were located in towns or cities and used canals or railways to transport the raw materials needed to operate them. The communities in which the ironworkers lived were larger and, usually, more diversified than were the iron plantations and forges.

FIGURE 7.8. Rolling rod at the Washburn Wire Company in East Providence, Rhode Island, in 1980. Hot metal emerging from the rolls is grasped by the catcher with tongs, looped around, and inserted in the next pass of the rolls. Confident, accurate work with the tongs was needed to keep the hot metal flowing smoothly through the mill. The metal here is steel, but the technique is the same as that used earlier in rolling iron.

Steel

Wrought iron and crucible steel were made by individual artisans aided by a few helpers and specialists, such as the hammer driver in an ironworks or the melter and teemer in a crucible steelworks. They made their own judgments and relied on their physical strength to do the manipulations. Two new processes for making steel in tonnage lots—the Bessemer process, used

FIGURE 7.9. This pair of Bessemer converters at the Wheeling Steel Company is typical of the converter installations used in the nineteenth century. The converter on the left is upside down, and the crew is putting a new bottom on it. The converter on the right has just been blown and has been inverted to dump out any remaining slag and debris before it is turned upright to receive the next charge of liquid iron. A spare bottom sits at the right; converter bottoms had to be replaced frequently. The port for connecting the air blast can be seen on the left side of the spare bottom. (Courtesy of the Smithsonian Institution)

in the United States after 1865, and the open hearth, increasingly used after 1878—had to be carried out by the coordinated efforts of a team of artisans because the equipment was too large to be manipulated by individuals. When hot metal from a blast furnace was used to charge the Bessemer converters or the open hearths in an integrated steelworks, centralized management was needed to coordinate the movement of metal through the successive processes.

Bessemer Steel

To make steel with a Bessemer converter, a team of artisans had to move a ton or more of liquid metal through a sequence of operations rapidly and precisely. Mishaps in handling the hot metal or adjusting the blast pressure could amplify the already spectacular events that took place in the converter. W. F. Durfee recounted how a group of distinguished visitors to the first Bessemer shop in the United States was blown over by a steam explosion caused by an inexperienced operator;[32] similar events undoubtedly punctuated the process of learning this new technology in other shops. The basic equipment in a Bessemer shop included a furnace for melting pig (unless hot metal could be taken directly from an adjacent blast furnace), ladles or other apparatus for conveying the hot metal to the converter, the converter itself (Fig. 7.9) with its tilting apparatus and blowing engine, a furnace for melting the recarburizer, and a ladle for receiving the liquid steel. Since even the earliest converters used a ton of metal in a charge, cranes and other mechanical appliances were needed to move and tip the ladles and to tilt the converter.

Operating a Bessemer shop depended on the coordinated efforts of upward of a dozen men. The converter crew had to melt pig iron in a cupola (or bring it as liquid from a blast furnace), transfer it to the converter with a ladle and a crane, blow the converter, add the recarburizer, and pour the liquid steel into another ladle for teeming into ingots. In one important respect, Bessemer steelmaking was like iron puddling; there was no instrumentation, and control of the process rested with judgments based on visual and audible clues. The person in charge, the blower, judged the progress of the conversion of iron to steel from the color and size of the flame and from the sound of the converter; he controlled the process by altering the blast pressure, the injection of steam into the blast, and the tilt of the vessel. The primary tasks were to maintain the temperature needed to keep the charge in the converter from freezing and to terminate the blow at the moment at which conversion to steel was completed. The pace of work was fast, voice communication was difficult because of the high noise level in the shop, and each member of the converter crew had to know what to do without detailed instructions. There were few chances for correcting errors, and misjudgments might result in a spill of liquid iron or steel that could be spectacular, dangerous, and exceedingly difficult to clean up. However, the heavy, debilitating physical labor required of the puddler was eliminated. Since the converter blow took about ten minutes, the liquid-metal transfer, charging, and casting operations were repeated many times in one work shift. The converter crew worked with a sustained, coordinated effort to maintain steady production. In the transformation from iron puddling to Bessemer steelmaking, judgment skills were still required, but the crew also needed new skills in reacting quickly to contingencies and in organizing and coordinating the efforts of a dozen or more artisans.[33]

Open-Hearth Steel

In the open-hearth process, a crew of steelworkers converted more than 100 tons of iron to steel on the hearth of a large reverberatory furnace (Fig. 7.10) in an operation that took several hours to complete. At first, the furnaces were small and were worked entirely by hand labor, but when ironmasters brought in charging machines, they were able to increase the size of the furnaces and reduce the heaviest physical labor. As with the puddling furnace and the Bessemer converter, control of the process rested with the experience and judgment of the person in charge (the melter) and the furnace crew of three to five helpers. Success depended on control of the temperature of the hearth and the carbon content of the steel. Instruments and analyses were not used. Instead, the melter determined the temperature of the hearth by holding a steel bar in the liquid metal until its end melted off; he could accurately judge the temperature of the bath from the shape of the remaining end of the bar after it was withdrawn from the furnace. The melter determined the carbon content of the steel on the hearth by taking a sample with a small ladle and casting it into a bar. As soon as it was cool, he broke the bar with a sledge and estimated the percentage of carbon from the appearance of the fracture. Comparisons with chemical analyses have shown that these methods were reliable; they had the added advantage of avoiding the difficulties of handling delicate instruments in the shop. The melter's skills could not be learned in a classroom or from a book, nor could they be learned quickly; practice on the job was necessary. The open-hearth process did allow, however, the first intrusion of scientific methods into steelworks. As alloy steels came into use, rapidly made chemical analyses of samples sent to a laboratory in the works were needed to ensure correct composition. Because the liquid steel could be held in the furnace during laboratory work, the melter could make corrections to its composition before the charge was tapped, which could not be done with a Bessemer converter.

FIGURE 7.10. Even when mechanical charging machines were used at an open-hearth steel furnace, there was still much hand labor to be done. Here the melter and helpers repair the lining of a furnace in Birmingham, Alabama, before beginning a new heat. The members of the furnace crew in rapid succession aim and throw shovels of refractory cement onto a weakened spot within the furnace. (Courtesy of the Smithsonian Institution)

The melter had to organize the efforts of the furnace crew of four to six workers, deal with the inevitable contingencies (such as burnouts of the firebrick lining of the furnace), and coordinate the services provided by operators of the crane and charging machine. Much of the work was hot, heavy, and potentially dangerous, but little of it ever became routine.[34]

Survivals

Iron puddling and Bessemer and open-hearth steelmaking were among the most important American industrial experiences, but they are very poorly represented in our surviving industrial material culture. No puddling furnace is on public display in North America. The operation of a Bessemer converter or an open-hearth furnace would be beyond the means of any imaginable industrial museum. Probably the only museum in the world that will be able to show what it was like to work with hot metal on an industrial scale is the Blists Hill Museum near Ironbridge, England, which operates a puddling furnace, steam hammer, and roll train in full view of visitors. The museum staff also runs an iron foundry. There is no substitute for seeing equipment like this in operation to understand the work environment in the iron and steel industry.

Nonferrous Metals

Until the mid-nineteenth century, North Americans did relatively little extraction of nonferrous metals. Fortunately, the increased demand for products such as metallic cartridges and electrical equipment, which arose as Americans adopted new technologies, coincided with improved access to copper, lead, and zinc resources in the central and western states and Canadian provinces. The expansion of nonferrous mining and metallurgy after 1850 created opportunities for the application of established skills, such as hard-rock mining. It also created new kinds of workplaces, additional environmental hazards, and the need to master unfamiliar metallurgical processes.

The miners of Mississippi Valley lead–zinc ores and Michigan native copper first worked in small, surface pits and later used underground, hard-rock methods similar to those employed in tunneling. Miners made holes in the ore with hand-held steel drills and sledges (hand jacking), charged the holes with black powder, fired the shots, and mucked out the broken ore.[35] Unlike the builders of transportation tunnels, miners had to follow ore veins and in doing so often created complex, three-dimensional networks of cramped passages. The miners, many from Cornwall, followed their traditional technology and organization, including the tut system, in which miners organized themselves into teams to take contracts for working specific parts of a mine. They also brought milling and smelting methods with them, but adapting these procedures to American conditions often proved difficult.[36]

A railroad-construction project led to advances in the technology of metal mining. American inventors attempted to mechanize hard-rock drilling at the Hoosac Tunnel of the Greenfield and Troy Railroad, undertaken in 1851 to penetrate nearly 5 miles of rock in northwestern Massachusetts (Chapter 4). Early attempts to use a boring machine failed, and the tunnelers made little progress until after 1865. (The remains of this false start can still be seen on the side of the mountain.) Then the Burleigh Rock Drill Company of Fitchburg developed mechanical drills powered with compressed air, and George Mowbray set up a nitroglycerine works to supply the tunnel project.

Mowbray demonstrated that this dangerous explosive was particularly un-stable if it was not chemically pure. Another discovery came when a nitro-glycerine shipment dispatched over the mountain on a sled in winter over-turned but failed to detonate. The explosive had been accidentally frozen, which proved to be a relatively safe way of transporting it. Nevertheless, there were many injuries and deaths in the tunnel before the engineers learned how to make reliable fuses and the tunnelers understood the proper firing methods.[37]

Even before the Hoosac was finished in 1875, the proprietors of copper mines in northern Michigan tried Burleigh drills. They proved to be too large to use in the confined spaces of these mines, but more manageable drills introduced in 1880 were well adapted to the work. Copper miners accepted these two-man drills because their use was not required (hand methods persisted in parts of most mines) and because it was possible to increase individual earnings with the mechanized apparatus. The air ex-hausted from the drills improved ventilation in miners' workplaces, partially counteracting the increased dust caused by the higher rate of drilling. But in western precious-metal mines, the rock contained more quartz than did that in the Michigan copper mines, and there rock dust released by mechanical drilling caused such severe health problems that many miners refused to use pneumatic drills. In fact, some states sought to outlaw them. Then J. G. Leyner, who was looking for a more effective drilling technique in the 1890s, made a major safety improvement: he designed a drill in which water was pumped down a hole that ran the length of the drill. The water flushed chips from the bit, created mud that improved cutting action, drew off heat, and simultaneously reduced the release of dangerous dust. Leyner had turned to water flushing only after western miners wisely resisted his earlier attempt to use compressed air to blow dust out of the way. The successful drill is now credited to Leyner, but equal credit should go to the unnamed American machinists who devised a way to make a $\frac{1}{8}$-inch hole the length of a 6-foot drill bit.[38]

When the managers of Michigan mining companies tried to substitute smaller, one-man drills for team-operated machines in the early twentieth century, they ran into determined resistance. Miners disliked working alone for both social and safety reasons, and they thought that the drills were too much for a single person to handle. In addition, they accurately predicted a sharp drop in employment because of the new machines. Some even disliked the water-injection system because it made a wet mess as it kept the dust down. The Western Federation of Miners' strike in the Lake Superior dis-trict in 1913 was primarily over the forcing of the new drill on the miners. The managers went ahead with this technological change and reduced the size of the work force.[39]

Milling ore was an important part of mining enterprises (Chapter 5). At first, miners tried Cornish designs for the stamps and rolls that crushed the ore, but Americans soon changed to larger, more powerful machines with interchangeable parts. Because the ore at each mine presented different separation problems, there were many opportunities for the modification of existing methods and the invention of new ones. At times, it seemed as though everyone at the mining camps had ideas for new methods of milling. The most successful methods were developed by workers at individual mines through successive, incremental improvements. As was the case earlier with water-powered manufacturing in the East, mechanics could try out new ideas without large investments, and rapid communication between practitioners speeded the discovery of the best methods.

Smelting procedures based on English and German methods were often ineffective for American ores. Cornish milling techniques and the Welsh process for smelting copper with reverberatory furnaces failed at the Bruce Mine in Ontario because the grade of the ore was different from that processed in Britain. Because of widespread experimentation and the variation of ore between mining districts, widely used, standardized procedures for smelting nonferrous metals were established much later than those for smelting iron.[40] Teaching and research in metallurgy at universities began with the appointment of George J. Brush as professor of metallurgy at Yale in 1855 and the founding of the Columbia School of Mines in 1867, but there were few academically trained engineers in the mining districts until the twentieth century. Process metallurgy was a forerunner of chemical engineering and became an important source of growing American technological competence.

Underground nonferrous mining and anthracite mining were similar in a number of ways, but different in others. In both types of mining, men often worked in independent teams, confronted geological complexity, and needed technical skill. Because it was not easy to mechanize work in mines, the adoption of machinery to mine coal or metal was a drawn-out process marred by technical setbacks and worker resistance. It was particularly difficult to make effective use of underground machinery in the anthracite fields. Anthracite mining was confined to four basins in Pennsylvania, while metal mining was spread through many of the central and western states. The social setting of the anthracite communities was unlike that of western boomtowns and distinct from even the paternalistic copper towns of northern Michigan. Milling and smelting metal ores offered opportunities for innovation by artisans that did not exist in the production of coal. Metal-mining ventures were often short-lived, and miners frequently moved between mines and mining districts. There was far less mobility for anthracite miners, whose technical skills were not in as great demand a those of metal miners.

FIGURE 7.11. When zinc is smelted in retorts, the metal is formed as vapor that has to be condensed. A smelterman is preparing a rack of zinc condensers to receive vapor at a smelter in Pennsylvania. Zinc vapor causes the "spelter shakes" when inhaled. Smoke and dust are common in the work areas of a smelter; the smelterman's bandanna might provide some protection against breathing the dust. (Courtesy of the Smithsonian Institution)

Brass was one nonferrous metal that was not made in the United States until the second half of the nineteenth century. Until then, American makers of brass products used scrap and imported metal. With the opening of the mines in northern Michigan, there was enough American copper to satisfy the domestic demand and provide a surplus for export. Zinc, the other ingredient in brass, was not smelted in the United States until 1867.[41] As Americans began to make zinc and brass, they encountered unfamiliar technical problems and health hazards. Zinc was smelted in crucible furnaces that produced zinc vapor, which was collected in small condensers that had to be pulled from the furnace and emptied by hand. Zinc vapor causes the "spelter shakes" (spelter is another name for crude zinc) when inhaled, and workers at zinc smelters often had little protection as they emptied the condensers (Fig. 7.11). Fumes and smoke were released into the atmosphere. In Donora, Pennsylvania, they were a component of the poisonous smog that killed twenty residents during a severe atmospheric inversion in 1948.

Because the boiling temperature of zinc is below the melting point of copper, it is difficult to combine the two metals without losing some of the zinc through vaporization. Making brass to specified composition calls for ingenuity and care. Once made, liquid brass avidly dissolves gases from the fire in the melting furnace; as the brass solidifies in a mold, this gas boils out of the metal as bubbles that make the solidified casting porous. Brass founders needed experience and metallurgical knowledge to minimize gas absorption and dexterity to pour liquid brass into molds without letting the metal touch the sides of the molds so that they filled from the bottom to make sound ingots.[42] The work was unhealthy because adequate ventilation and new working methods that minimized exposure of workers to zinc vapor were only gradually introduced into the brass mills.

American artisans also needed new skills in the subsequent fabrication of brass products. Brass cartridge cases function properly only if they are finished with the correct temper. If too hard, they will split upon firing, releasing gas in the face of the shooter; if too soft, they will not spring back from the rifle chamber and cannot be extracted to allow reloading of the weapon. Artisans using craft skills and unaided by instrumentation were unable to cope with these problems, and the metallic ammunition they made sometimes failed to perform at critical moments.[43] The issue of soft metal was even more important with copper cartridges, some of which became stuck in the chambers of the army's Springfield carbines during the Battle of the Little Bighorn in 1876. Archaeologists have found cartridges with marks of extraction failure at positions held by Custer's Seventh Cavalry.[44] Difficulties with cartridge brass attracted attention again during World War I when inexperienced makers went into ammunition manufacture.

Because craft-skill methods were unequal to the increasingly stringent quality control demanded by brass customers, proprietors of brass mills were more forward in adopting new melting equipment and instrumentation and in requesting the services of metallurgists than were most American industrialists. This raises an interesting question about the work experience in brass mills, because some labor historians have interpreted the replacement of the nonquantitative, uninstrumented methods by electric furnaces fitted with pyrometers as a prime example of "de-skilling" undertaken to allow managers to wrest control of the shop floor from workers.[45] The brass industry had reached the limit of quality assurance that could be attained with craft methods unaided by instrumentation by the end of the nineteenth century and could not make reliable products without new methods. Introduction of these methods brought a need to learn new skills; it also resulted in the disappearance of some colorful characters in the shop. But because of the new technology, there were improvements such as better control of fumes, healthier working conditions, and more reliable products—points overlooked in the de-skilling arguments.

Work in the Oil Fields

Work in the oil fields had its own occupational variations, hierarchy, and culture.[46] Some jobs were created by the particular challenges of the new technology, but many skills were transferred from established fields of mining and manufacturing. Machinists, the high priests of mechanization, could usually find work making or repairing the equipment used in drilling, pumping, conveying, and refining petroleum. Because parts broke frequently and delays were costly, drillers put a high priority on rapid repairs. They also tried out new ideas and depended on machinists who could produce prototypes for testing. Al Hamill remembers: "Inventions then, they just kind of happened so. If you'd need a tool, you'd think about it, you'd rig it up and go to the machine shop and have it made. Never think anything about getting a patent on it."[47]

Artisans with experience in operating steam engines and tending boilers were also in demand, although the alarming frequency of steam accidents implies that qualifications and safety standards were relaxed in the frenzied environment of the oil patch. When employers were desperate to get their wells producing, they were likely to cut corners and take chances with individuals whose abilities were unproven. Workers were quick to leave declining fields and to seek employment in other regions where discoveries had opened up hundreds or thousands of jobs. For those with geographic mobility and technical aptitude, the oil industry offered opportunity.

Many of the special occupations in the petroleum industry required training on the job and the development of unique skills. Drillers and the "roughnecks" who worked on oil rigs under their supervision were essential figures during exploration and in the boom period of a producing field. Roughnecks would learn to handle one or more of the basic types of drilling equipment (portable spudder, cable-tool, or rotary rig) and might rise to the status of second or first driller after gaining experience. A cable-tool operator had to feel the correct impact of the bit with the percussion action of his rig when he was drilling through different strata (Fig. 7.12). Perceptive rotary drillers could judge progress and prospects of success by the mud brought up from the well. As one Texas veteran recalled, "That's what made a driller, was his ability to read his mud."[48]

In some of the first oil fields in Pennsylvania, workers "kicked down" a well, using their own body weight (or arm strength) and a spring pole to produce a hammering action by the drill bit in a hole. The later cable-tool rigs used a similar impact-drilling principle, but their mechanical application of steam power made an enormous difference in the human energy expended. To give a sense of the effort formerly required in kicking down and to stimulate hands-on participation in the technology of the oil fields,

FIGURE 7.12. A Pennsylvania cable-tool rig. The driller, in the center of this historic photograph, has just withdrawn the drill stem and bit from the well and is preparing to use the bailer suspended (and canted diagonally) at left center. Heavy wrenches for tightening and loosening joints are leaning against a corner post of the wooden derrick. Over the driller's head is the walking beam, which provides the up-and-down motion for percussion drilling. Behind him is the bull wheel, a windlass that he uses to move equipment within the rig and to raise or lower tools in the well. Everything is powered by a single steam engine, out of the picture to the right. It took a highly coordinated team effort to stop and start machinery by controlling the various rope drives, the steam-engine throttle, and the brake on the bull wheel. The driller had to be able to sense the way a drill was working far below the derrick floor. Work on a cable-tool rig demanded mechanical skills, strength, dexterity, speed, and good judgment. (Courtesy of Robert Vogel)

288

FIGURE 7.13. A "shooter" fills a torpedo with liquid nitroglycerine, a highly sensitive and very powerful explosive. He is pouring very carefully from one of his four cans. When a torpedo was lowered into a hole and set off underground, it might bring in a new well (make oil start to flow) or improve a producing one. The potential profits were so attractive that drillers took risks or hired others to do so. Working with nitroglycerine was probably the most dangerous task in American industry. (Courtesy of Robert Vogel)

the Drake Well Museum has set up a working spring-pole rig and invites visitors to try it out. No one stays at this educational exercise for very long.

"Shooters" learned to handle liquid nitroglycerine and to assess just how much of an explosion was needed to start or increase the flow of oil from a well (Fig. 7.13). One shooter commented on the unforgiving nature of the work, "You don't make but one mistake handling this stuff."[49] An advertisement for the services of another said that he had the "honor of being one of the oldest shooters and torpedo men engaged in the hazardous profession." One "moonlighter," who apparently filled torpedoes in his house to avoid patent-infringement charges from the Roberts Petroleum Torpedo Company, killed both himself and his wife with the sensitive liquid.[50] A nitroglycerine wagon on display at the Drake Well Museum is accompanied by a telling photograph of local youths studying a slight depression and some wagon fragments on a dirt road through the Pennsylvania oil fields, a small alteration of the industrial landscape marking the abrupt end of one shooter's trip.

The tall derricks that gave such a distinctive look to the landscape of the oil fields were usually built in a hurry and remained within the American tradition of wood construction into the 1920s, when steel frames became common. These wooden drilling rigs were rough, impermanent, yet sturdy and resilient structures (Figs. 5.19 and 5.20). Their erection (or dismantling) required specialized skills, usually learned on the job. Charlie Storms, a "rig builder" who began working in the oil fields of Oklahoma in 1915, described the demands of the job and the difficulty of transferring skills from normal carpentry:

> The way they'd build a rig in those days, the rig builders had to do everything. We dug the cellars, made the footing, sawed out the lumber for the rig, and then built it. . . . And carpenters weren't worth a damn in building those wooden rigs either. . . . A carpenter could be a rig builder, but he had to start from the ground up, from the beginning, and learn everything. He had to forget all he ever knew about finish work and learn how to do rough stuff; and he had to learn how to cut lumber in a different way from any he ever knowed.[51]

Oilmen gradually abandoned the wooden tanks they used for holding crude oil and refinery products, replacing them with tanks made of iron or steel. The skills required for constructing wood tanks bound with wrought-iron hoops were in some ways carryovers from the craft of coopering barrels (much oil was transported in barrels, and it is still measured by the barrel), but the size and design of oil-storage containers were closer to those of agricultural silos or the wooden cisterns that can still be seen on the rooftops of many New York City buildings. The first bulk carriers for rail transport of oil were modified flatcars developed in Pennsylvania in 1865; each carried two wooden tanks, similar in form to the larger stationary ones. By the 1880s, iron tank cars were common.[52]

The men who made oil tanks were called "tankies." "Corkers," who caulked wood storage tanks with oakum, got paid more than the regular builders, but a tankie reported that the pay differential was "not enough to make a man want to have to stoop over all day or get down on his knees for it." As steel holding tanks came into wide use in the second decade of the twentieth century, the tankie's occupation changed to a metalworking trade. Some men were versatile enough to adapt to that fundamental change: "I don't know which was the hardest, wood or steel, but I've put in many a day on both kinds." For many years, tankies continued to use wood construction for supporting framework until the metal roof of a large steel tank was completed.[53]

The last workers in many oil fields were members of salvage crews. Derricks might be pulled down soon after a well went into production; pipes, pumping apparatus, tanks, and shops were important only as long as the oil flowed. Equipment and materials of little use in a declining area were still valuable where a new boom was under way. The mechanization of salvage included the use of pipe-pulling equipment powered by horses, steam, or internal-combustion engines. Improved hydraulic jacks eventually made it possible to exert enormous force. Companies that specialized in recovering expensive casing pipes and other saleable equipment sent crews to far-flung sites and often erased much of the physical evidence of oil production.[54] At Pithole, Pennsylvania (Chapter 5), where little trace of oil activity remains, a long, shallow trench indicates past salvage activity along the world's first crude-oil pipeline.

Wood, water, and iron were widely available to artisans and entrepreneurs in North America. This was not true of coal, petroleum, and nonferrous metals, which were found only in those few places where they had been concentrated by ancient geological processes. Those who extracted these materials were often specialists living in isolated communities that produced only one product. The artisans who transformed nonferrous metals into finished goods were separated from the production of the natural resources they used. The economic context of their work was enlarged to include the distant, primary producers and the transportation systems that brought materials to the manufacturing site. Artisans and managers in a wide range of manufacturing industries came to depend on distant producers of coal, oil, and metals; on the smooth functioning of canals and railways; and on decisions made by capitalists in urban financial centers.

Accompanying these changes in the economic context were changes in the social context of the workplace. As managers organized larger work groups, they created more opportunities for artisans to display their skills to co-workers. But this grouping also reduced the public visibility of the individual artisan, whose accomplishments were often hidden from those outside. The community no longer understood what went on in its workplaces. In jobs such as rolling metals and making steel, men worked in highly organized teams that carried out specialized and very demanding tasks.

While it was still possible for many industrial artisans to participate in the creation of technology through shop-floor innovation, others felt stifled by restrictive regulations and managerial or union controls.

Skills and machinery from established industries, such as coal-mining and milling operations, were often adopted in newer ones, such as nonferrous metallurgy and petroleum production. However, working with different resources made many demands that older or borrowed technology could not satisfy. There were also problems because of variations in primary materials and in geological or topographical conditions. In fabricating brass, there were so few clues to guide artisans as they worked that traditional methods proved unreliable. Miners of coal and metal and drillers of oil wells found that their skills were not always adequate to cope with the complexity they sometimes encountered. Changes in equipment, processes, and work practices could solve technical problems and improve productivity, but workers often found it painful to give up traditional methods. Some lost the independence and status they had enjoyed on the job and encountered new threats to their physical and mental health in increasingly mechanized operations. Particular skills lost their value in a changing industrial economy, creating personal hardships for many. But a shifting assemblage of skills has remained essential over the years in every form of industrial extraction, production, and transportation. Artisans and the skills they practice will never disappear from the industrial workplace.

Notes

1. H. M. Chance, *Mining Methods and Appliances Used in the Anthracite Coal Fields* (Harrisburg, Pa.: Second Geological Survey, 1883), p. 293.

2. Ibid., pp. 169, 401.

3. J. R. Harris shows that coal mining in Britain was highly skilled work but was not so recognized outside the trade because the skills had developed gradually and little was written about them ("Skills, Coal, and British Industry in the Eighteenth Century," *History* 61 [1976]: 167–182).

4. See the description of the difficult, physically demanding tasks in Chance, *Mining Methods*, pp. 425–426.

5. Systematic collection of data on mine accidents began in response to the requirements of an act passed by the Pennsylvania legislature on April 5, 1870. The first data appear in "Reports of the Inspectors of Coal Mines of the Anthracite Regions of Pennsylvania for the Year 1870" (Harrisburg, Pa., 1871). Reports were issued annually thereafter.

6. Peter Roberts, *The Anthracite Coal Industry* (New York: Macmillan, 1901), p. 168.

7. Ibid., graph opposite p. 159.

8. Anthony Wallace, *St. Clair: A Nineteenth-Century Coal Town's Experience with a Disaster-Prone Industry* (New York: Knopf, 1987), pp. 249–253.

9. Ibid., p. 253.

10. Chance, *Mining Methods*, p. 409.

11. Ibid., p. 400.

12. Keith Dix, *Work Relations in the Coal Industry: The Hand-Loading Era, 1880–1930* (Morgantown: University of West Virginia Press, 1977), pp. 72–73. The value of posts rose as the Appalachian timber boom, lasting from the 1870s to the 1920s, depleted forest resources in coal-mining regions.

13. Ibid., pp. 8–12; Homer L. Morris, *The Plight of the Bituminous Coal Miner* (Philadelphia: University of Pennsylvania Press, 1934), pp. 64–69; Harry M. Caudill, *Night Comes to the Cumberlands* (Boston: Little, Brown, 1963), pp. 115–117.

14. Caudill, *Night Comes to the Cumberlands*, pp. 118–122; Keith Dix, *What's a Coal Miner to Do? The Mechanization of Coal Mining* (Pittsburgh: University of Pittsburgh Press, 1988), pp. 92–94, 99–107. There was also a risk of methane-gas explosion in some bituminous mines. The risk of roof falls, historically the greatest cause of fatalities in bituminous as in anthracite mining, was finally diminished after the adoption of metal roof bolts in the 1940s. From 1923 to 1948, roof falls caused 16,702 fatalities (54.9 percent of the total) in bituminous mines.

15. Dix, *What's a Miner to Do?*, pp. 28–32, 47–50, 77–106. We are also grateful to the Goodman Equipment Company for a fascinating plant tour and the opportunity to inspect both a punching machine and a locomotive.

16. There are many accounts of efforts made to gain acceptance of anthracite in the United States. Two comprehensive discussions are H. Benjamin Powell, *Philadelphia's First Fuel Crisis: Jacob Cist and the Developing Market for Pennsylvania Anthracite* (University Park: Pennsylvania State University Press, 1978), and Frederick M. Binder, *Coal Age Empire: Pennsylvania Coal and Its Utilization to 1860* (Harrisburg: Pennsylvania Historical and Museum Commission, 1974).

17. Ele Bowen, *The Coal Regions of Pennsylvania* (Pottsville, Pa.: Caravalho, 1848), p. 26.

18. Ibid., p. 18.

19. Binder, *Coal Age Empire*, chap. 1.

20. Ibid., chap. 6.

21. Carlene Stephens, "'Most Reliable Time': William Bond, the New England Railroads, and Time Awareness in 19th-Century America," *Technology and Culture* 30 (1989): 1–24.

22. The growth of management of railroads is discussed in Alfred D. Chandler, Jr., *The Visible Hand: The Managerial Revolution in American Business* (Cambridge, Mass.: Harvard University Press, 1977), chap. 3.

23. Walter Licht, *Working for the Railroad* (Princeton, N.J.: Princeton University Press, 1983), chap. 5.

24. Many of these emotions are illustrated in David Weitzman, *Superpower: The Making of a Steam Locomotive* (Boston: Godine, 1987). For the evolution of American locomotive design, see John H. White, Jr., *A History of the American Locomotive* (New York: Dover, 1979).

25. In the 1930s, owners of steam locomotives began to cover them with shrouds that suggested aircraft or automobiles. For a while this helped attract passengers

(Robert C. Reed, *The Streamline Era* [San Marino, Calif.: Golden West Books, 1975]).

26. These characteristics of the locomotive mechanism are also depicted in Charles Sheeler's painting *Rolling Power* (1939) (Susan Fillin-Yeh, "Charles Sheeler's *Rolling Power*," in *The Railroad in American Art*, ed. Susan Danly and Leo Marx [Cambridge, Mass.: MIT Press, 1988], pp. 145–163).

27. Quoted in Michael Reynolds, *Locomotive-Engine Driving* (London: Clowes, n.d.), p. 1.

28. Licht, *Working for the Railroad*, p. 162.

29. The sequence of operations in puddling was recorded in G. R. Morton and R. G. Brit, "The Present Day Production of Wrought Iron," *Journal of the Historical Metallurgy Society* 8 (1974): 96–102. For the technology of the process, see J. M. Camp and C. B. Francis, *The Making, Shaping and Treating of Steel*, 4th ed. (Pittsburgh: Carnegie Steel, 1919), pp. 214–243.

30. Robert B. Gordon, "Strength and Structure of Wrought Iron," *Archeomaterials* 2 (1988): 109–137.

31. The best accounts of the work at bar and plate mills lacking mechanized materials-handling equipment are for English mills: W.K.V. Gale, "The Rolling of Iron," *Transactions of the Newcomen Society* 37 (1964–1965): 35–46; Gale, *The Black Country Iron Industry* (London: Metals Society, 1979), appendix 15.

32. Jeanne McHugh, *Alexander Holley and the Makers of Steel* (Baltimore: Johns Hopkins University Press, 1980), p. 183.

33. The operation of a Bessemer converter is described in Camp and Francis, *Making, Shaping and Treating of Steel*, pp. 275–280.

34. Although there is an extensive technical and historical literature on the tonnage steelmaking processes, there are very few descriptions of the work environment that go beyond superficial exclamations about the heat, noise, and spectacular sights. Patrick McGeown has written a thoroughgoing account of the work of the melter, the person in charge of an open-hearth furnace, in the days before instrumentation introduced a degree of scientific control. He writes about Scottish and English steelworks, but the work would have been much the same in America (McGeown, *Heat the Furnaces Seven Times More* [London: Hutchinson, 1967]). There are concise descriptions of work at the open hearths in John Strohmeyer, *Crisis in Bethlehem: Big Steel's Struggle to Survive* (Bethesda, Md.: Adler and Adler, 1986), chap. 3, and Thomas E. Leary and Elizabeth C. Scholes, *From Fire to Rust* (Buffalo, N.Y.: Buffalo and Erie County Historical Society, 1987), pp. 34–41.

35. For a detailed description of work in underground mines, see Otis E. Young, Jr., *Black Powder and Hand Steel* (Norman: University of Oklahoma Press, 1975).

36. On the transfer of Cornish mining customs to America, see Arthur C. Todd, *The Cornish Miner in America* (Truro: Barton, 1967); for one example of the technical difficulties encountered, see Dianne Newell, *Technology on the Frontier: Mining in Old Ontario* (Vancouver: University of British Columbia Press, 1986), pp. 65–72.

37. Robert M. Vogel, "Tunnel Engineering," Paper No. 41, USM Bulletin No. 240, *Contributions from the Museum of History and Technology* (1964): 201–240; George M. Mowbray, *Tri-Nitro Glycerine as Applied in the Hoosac Tunnel, Submarine Building, Etc.* (North Adams, Mass.: J. T. Robinson, 1872).

38. Larry D. Lankton, "The Machine Under the Garden: Rock Drills Arrive at the Lake Superior Copper Mines, 1868–1883," *Technology and Culture* 24 (1983): 1–37; Otis E. Young, Jr., *Western Mining* (Norman: University of Oklahoma Press,

1970), pp. 209–210; Mark Wyman, *Hard Rock Epic: Western Miners and the Industrial Revolution, 1860–1910* (Berkeley: University of California Press, 1979), pp. 87–92.

39. Larry Lankton, *Cradle to Grave: Life, Work, and Death at the Lake Superior Copper Mines* (New York: Oxford University Press, 1991), pp. 103–109, 241.

40. For an excellent summary of the development of technology in mining, milling, and smelting, see Newell, *Technology on the Frontier,* chap. 2.

41. William G. Lathrop, *The Brass Industry in the United States,* rev. ed. (Mount Carmel, Conn.: Lathrop, 1926), p. 80.

42. For a description of the craft and metallurgical skills needed to cast brass ingots successfully, see Daniel R. Hull, *Casting of Brass and Bronze* (Cleveland: American Society for Metals, 1950).

43. Earl Naramore, *Principles and Practice of Loading Ammunition* (Georgetown, S.C.: Samworth, 1954), p. 52; E. C. Crossman, *The Book of the Springfield* (Marines, N.C.: Samworth, 1932), p. 356.

44. Douglas D. Scott and others, *Archaeological Perspectives on the Battle of the Little Bighorn* (Norman: University of Oklahoma Press, 1989), pp. 113–115, 178. Scott does not attribute Custer's defeat to problems with cartridges.

45. Jeremy Brecher, Jerry Lombardi, and Jan Stackhouse, *Brass City* (Philadelphia: Temple University Press, 1982), p. 67–71.

46. Paul Lambert and Kenny Franks, *Voices from the Oil Fields* (Norman: University of Oklahoma Press, 1984), pp. 3–7, 18–19, 29, 121, 128; Mody Boatright and William A. Owens, *Tales from the Derrick Floor: A People's History of the Oil Industry* (Lincoln: University of Nebraska Press, 1970), chap. 10.

47. Quoted in Boatright and Owens, *Tales from the Derrick Floor,* p. 199.

48. David Weitzman, *Traces of the Past: A Field Guide to Industrial Archaeology* (New York: Scribner's, 1980), pp. 183–193; Newell, *Technology on the Frontier,* pp. 122–124; Plummer M. Barfield, quoted in Boatright and Owens, *Tales from the Derrick Floor,* p. 200. We are also grateful to Professor Joseph Steim, who grew up in the Pennsylvania oil fields and shared with us his observations of skilled drillers at work.

49. Lambert and Franks, *Voices from the Oil Fields,* pp. 5, 9, 38, 56, 69. For the quoted interview with "Shorty" Moses, see pp. 102, 110.

50. *The Derrick's Hand Book of Petroleum* (Oil City, Pa.: Derrick Publishing, 1898), p. iii. The day-by-day listing of oil-field incidents since 1859 in this volume includes many accounts of death and injury from accidental nitroglycerine explosions. For grisly details, including the 1873 family example, see John T. McLaurin, *Sketches in Crude-Oil* (Harrisburg, Pa.: McLaurin, 1896), p. 343.

51. Lambert and Franks, *Voices from the Oil Fields,* pp. 22, 26–27.

52. Ernest C. Miller, *Pennsylvania's Oil Industry* (Gettysburg: Pennsylvania Historical Association, 1974), pp. 32, 36.

53. Lambert and Franks, *Voices from the Oil Fields,* pp. 175, 180–181, 187.

54. Ibid., pp. 240, 245, 251–252.

8
The Factory

With Samuel Slater's textile mill (1793, in Pawtucket, Rhode Island) and Eli Whitney's armory (1798, in Whitneyville, Connecticut), American entrepreneurs began to make in factories products that had formerly been made in homes or craft shops. Another new concept in manufacturing, the principle of uniformity (sometimes described as "interchangeability"), was also winning converts in America. Factories making uniform products increasingly used power-driven machinery in the production process. However, it is a mistake to conflate mechanization, factories, and uniformity. Mechanization was used in colonial craft shops as well as in nineteenth-century factories. Until the late nineteenth century, factory managers achieved uniformity primarily through improved handwork skills and gauging rather than with machinery. Chapter 9 will cover the mechanization of work in factories as well as efforts to achieve uniformity in machine parts.

Many of the best examples of early American factories are in New England, where there was a serendipitous combination of water power, entrepreneurial capital, and the artisanal skills necessary to build mills and machinery. The textile mills erected there had a powerful influence on the evolution of American factory architecture. As we look closely at a number of New England mills, remember that similar patterns of structural development can be found in other regions of the United States and that the basic forms of the textile factory were readily adapted for other types of industry, including the manufacture of wood, metal, and paper products.

Early Industrial Buildings

Shops and Manufactories

Factories were not the first industrial buildings in America, nor did they represent more capital expenditure than some of the early and costly iron-works. Two processes of textile manufacturing and finishing, the carding of fibers and the fulling of woven cloth, had been powered by waterwheels (and occasionally by draft animals) before the first successful factory was built in Pawtucket in 1793. Proprietors of shops and country mills usually operated their enterprises directly with little of the managerial hierarchy and division of labor that would appear in the full-blown factory system. Shops lacked the factory's sequential organization of powered machinery and its extensive mechanization through multiple stages of production. Their mode of operation did not fit Andrew Ure's classic definition of the British factory system: "the combined operation of many orders of work people . . . tending with assiduous skill a system of productive machines continuously impelled by a central power."[1]

The large, eighteenth-century textile shops in Philadelphia, New York, Boston, and Baltimore were sometimes called manufactories. The prefix of this archaic term is appropriate because the owners of these manufactories simply clustered manual equipment, primarily hand-operated looms or spinning wheels, in urban buildings and put workers under close supervision. A more advanced manufactory built in Beverly, Massachusetts, in 1788 had many of the characteristics of a small factory, but depended on manual power to run spinning jennies and looms. The only prime movers for machinery were a "handsome span of chestnuts." These horses walked in a circle in a separate building, turning a vertical shaft linked to the manufactory for running its carding machine. Joshua Herrick, who drove the team while a boy, said that he adjusted the speed of his team in response to orders shouted out the window of the brick factory building.[2]

Slater Mill: The First American Factory

Samuel Slater deserves the credit usually given him for bringing the British factory system to America and for erecting what is arguably the first true factory here. With the support of his American partners, most notably the Providence merchant and manufacturer Moses Brown, the recent immigrant began his mechanized textile spinning at Pawtucket Falls in a water-powered fulling mill. He paid local artisans to build some machines under his direction and repaired or modified others until he had a close approximation of the famous Arkwright process of mechanized cotton spinning in operation. This successful experiment in 1790 and 1791 gave Slater and his partners enough confidence to begin the construction of a dam and factory just upstream.[3]

For the first specially built American factory, the firm of Almy, Brown, and Slater erected a wood-framed building, using distinctively American construction techniques familiar to the housewrights and millwrights of the region. Completed in 1793, the Slater Mill was an unpretentious, functional structure only 43 feet by 29 feet in plan, with an attached shed over the waterwheel (Fig. 8.1). It copied the narrow width of British factories, but not their masonry construction. A plasterer's bill for the Slater Mill dated 1793 shows that the interior plastering and whitewash finish of the present restoration are accurate reproductions. The reflecting white walls help light from the windows reach the center of the work spaces.[4] To strengthen the mill's extensively fenestrated walls, the builders combined post-and-beam framing (two stories of original framing survive, as shown in Fig. 8.2) with nailed, vertical-plank siding (in place of studs), a vernacular design that simplified construction but, while making use of the abundant forests and sawmills of the region, created a strong demand for less abundant iron nails.[5]

Workers in a factory room could transport materials easily through the aisles between horizontal rows of machinery. The relatively unobstructed views in the work areas made it possible for managers to watch the efforts of many operatives at once. Professional management and continual supervision were key elements of the factory system;[6] overseers and foremen could detect problems quickly anywhere in the rooms of well-designed factories.

British industrialists preferred to build substantial factories of stone or brick, usually longer and taller than Slater's original two-story (or two and a half, since the evidence for attic windows is inconclusive) wooden structure in Pawtucket. Most textile mills built in this country after 1810 had fire-resistant masonry walls. The Slater Mill was a tentative, cautious step toward heavily capitalized industrialization. Although the 1793 mill may have had a small belfry to call workers, the proud Neoclassical cupola that stands on the restored mill today was added later, after the economic and political power of factory owners was more clearly established.[7]

Physical Evidence of Building Technology and Design

Industrial archaeologists have encouraged the physical examination of surviving factory structures as a way to test the assumptions of architectural and technological historians and to provide new insights on industrial development. Because we have few architectural plans, building specifications,

FIGURE 8.1. The Slater Mill, built in 1793 and expanded many times, has been partially restored to approximate its form in the mid-1830s. The first addition to the main body of the mill was in 1801, at the far end. Another addition extended the building toward the river between 1818 and 1820. Carpenters framed the projecting tower between 1828 and 1832.

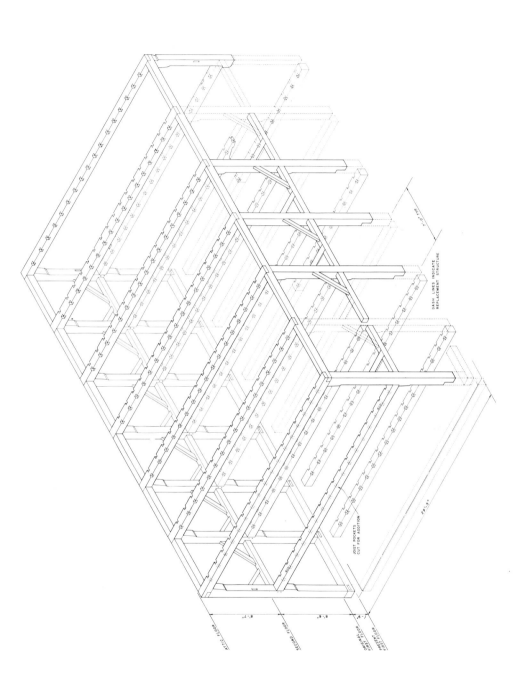

FIGURE 8.2. An axonometric drawing of the timber framing in the original (middle) section of the present Slater Mill. Note the joist pockets cut into the floor beams. Dotted lines indicate replacement parts. (Drawing by Robert Giebner. Courtesy of the Historic American Engineering Record)

detailed illustrations, or clearly written descriptions of early factories, material evidence is particularly important for study of the antebellum period. It is also a valuable and sometimes essential complement to documentary and graphical evidence of more recent developments.

Building Safety

One important innovation in building techniques of early factories was slow-burning construction. Material evidence has been essential in explaining the introduction and diffusion of this technique, an important structural development in factory architecture. Through the first quarter of the nineteenth century, millwrights used joists, carried by heavier beams, to support thin floorboards. But the exposed corners of the projecting joists were easily ignited (Fig. 8.3). During a fire, the floorboards burned through, creating drafts that increased combustion. Joists then failed quickly under the load of textile machinery as consuming flames reduced their effective cross section.

Slow-burning construction was primarily a response to the vulnerability of early mills with joisted floors. It consisted of a continuous floor of splined or tongue-and-grooved planks at least 3 inches thick, covered with a layer of replaceable wearing boards. The flat bottom surface of this floor rested on beams of very large section, spaced 8 to 12 feet apart. There were few edges to catch fire, less surface area for combustion, and nothing that could burn through quickly. Except in the worst conflagrations, heavy timber beams tended to char on the surface but resist deeper penetration, thus allowing time to put out a fire before a mill was destroyed.[8] Many factories have beams that continue to carry their loads despite surface scarring from past fires.

It was once assumed that Zachariah Allen installed the first American slow-burning floor when he built his stone-walled mill at Allendale, Rhode Island, in 1822.[9] Allen was already a gifted student of mill engineering by that time and was soon to become the founder of Manufacturer's Mutual Fire Insurance Company and a leading proponent of fire-retardent factory construction.[10] Thick plank floors, built without the floor joists found in all earlier American factories, were even visible in part of this Rhode Island mill. That evidence turned out to be misleading; physical examination and documentary research by Richard Candee and other industrial archaeologists have proved that Allen did not use this form of slow-burning construction when he first erected the building.[11]

Allen lengthened his Allendale Mill in 1839, and it is only in the later section of the building that the new type of flooring appears. Hidden for many years behind a lowered ceiling, an original joisted floor of the 1822 factory was recently exposed (Fig. 8.4). A project to adapt the building for

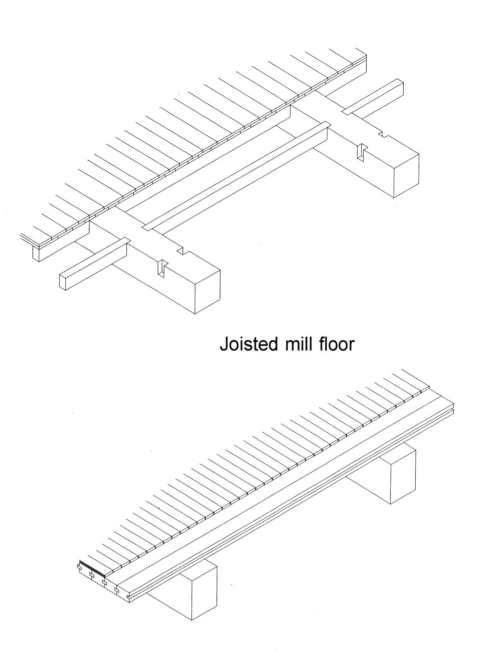

Joisted mill floor

Slow-burning mill floor

FIGURE 8.3. Joisted and slow-burning floors. The joisted form is much more vulnerable to fire than the slow-burning construction. In the drawing of the slow-burning floor, gaps between the thick planks are blocked by inserted splines; tongue-and-groove joints can perform the same function.

FIGURE 8.4. The joisted floor exposed in the 1822 section of the Allendale Mill. This is conclusive material evidence that Zachariah Allen did not build his first factory with slow-burning construction. However, he later became the principal advocate of effective fire-prevention and -retardation practices in mill engineering. (Photograph by Warren Jagger. Courtesy of the Rhode Island Historical Preservation Commission)

reuse has provided unusual opportunities to study and photograph construction details.[12]

The earliest known, and still surviving, example of slow-burning construction is in the stone-walled mill built in 1827 by Rhode Island's Woonsocket Manufacturing Company. Apparently a number of mill designers began to change their construction methods soon after the 1826 republication in the *American Mechanics Magazine* of a British article describing thick plank floors in several mills in Manchester. Actually, most British mill builders, lacking access to cheap timber, depended on cast-iron and masonry structural systems to reduce fire hazards; it was Americans who found this wood-intensive framing ideal for their needs and quickly adopted it.[13]

The fire-resistant nature of the thick wood floors was only one of a number of factors that explain their acceptance in America. The strength and stiffness of these floors were advantages in mills that housed heavy, vibrating machinery. Spilled oil did not seep through them to soil products on lower levels, and there was less water damage if workers had to extinguish a blaze. In 1831, a junior manager in a Lowell mill, Robert Israel, reported that corporations had recently eliminated joisted flooring in their brick factories because of problems with falling plaster. According to him, company agents in the great textile center had originally put plaster ceilings under the joists (for appearance, light reflection, or fire prevention), but vibration had fractured the plaster and caused pieces to drop onto the textile machines below. A flat, planed surface of thick planks solved that problem.[14]

In time, and with effective promotional efforts by insurance companies, the new framing system became known as slow-burning construction or factory construction. It was widely used in American industrial buildings by 1850 and, with refinements, remained a popular construction technique through the 1920s. Combined with sprinkler systems, pumps, hoses, fire doors, isolated tower stairways, and many other preventive measures, it helped to reduce the frequency and the extent of fire damage in industries, such as cotton-textile manufacturing, that processed flammable materials.

Insurance companies, particularly the mutual firms that provided most of the coverage for manufacturers, had a great influence on the design of industrial buildings. Insurers assessed the risks of fire and the potential for loss in the buildings they covered, raising rates or canceling policies when unusual danger was apparent. Mill engineers frequently adopted the standard forms of factory construction favored by insurance companies. Pressure from insurers in the last quarter of the nineteenth century largely ended the construction of factories with an attic story, including the Mansard-roofed forms that had proved to be so combustible in the Great Boston Fire of 1872 (Fig. 8.5).[15]

Many factories were altered, raised one story, and given an almost flat roof, a safer form because there were fewer members that might ignite and not as many sheltered or inaccessible spaces for fire to develop. A different window style at the top floor is often evidence of this modification. As an associated benefit, mill owners gained more manufacturing floor space and solved the clearance problems of the old attics. The insurance companies had simply promoted the adoption of existing structural forms and stressed the capabilities of roofing materials that made these forms practical.

Columns or posts in mills underwent scrutiny as well. Americans were slow to adopt the cast-iron columns that had been used in many British mills since the late eighteenth century. Strong and relatively inexpensive wood columns (usually made of longleaf yellow pine, with a hole in their center to prevent checking and dry rot) remained part of the design of most "slow-burning" mills. Although cast iron would not ignite and was often praised for its fire-resistant qualities, engineers were worried that it might fracture when sprayed with water in a fire or that it might deform when hot (an

FIGURE 8.5. An 1870s Mansard-roofed building in the Methuen Mill complex in Massachusetts. The attached toilet tower extends from the attic story all the way down the side of the building to the river. The arched openings in its base are vivid reminders of a time when people were little concerned about pollution of river waters by human wastes.

exaggerated threat). A noted engineer identified other problems after the Pemberton Mill collapsed in 1860, causing great loss of life and property: James B. Francis placed most of the blame on poor casting and placement of its hollow iron columns. The present Pemberton Mill, erected on the same site by 1863, has wooden columns spaced closer than the iron columns were. Although Francis published tables and technical advice for safe installation of iron columns, he could not restore full confidence in them. Further engineering study of columns, much of it done for mutual insurance companies, established a preference for wood over cast iron. By the 1880s, the mutual insurance companies that defined safe mill construction, and rewarded it with lower premiums, were recommending wood posts and columns.[16]

Roof Trusses

Columns, posts, and load-bearing interior walls took up space and restricted the maximum size and arrangement of manufacturing equipment.[17] They also interfered with the movement of materials. In all but the narrowest multistory buildings, some type of interior support for floors was unavoidable, but it was possible to span a considerable distance with roof trusses, structural forms that took advantage of the rigidity of triangular shapes. The use of trusses could leave a large interior area free of any obstruction. American builders since the early nineteenth century have excelled in the design and construction of wood, wood and metal, or metal trusses. Although bridges were the most spectacular demonstration of the capabilities of this technology, the use of trusses in roofs and as strengthening devices for long-span beams had a significant impact on the industrial workplace.

Designers put iron tension members in wooden trusses for railroad buildings to shelter wider areas of track. The train shed of the Central of Georgia Railroad in Savannah, built about 1855, represents an early use of long-span trusses. This type of structural progress opened up possibilities in many types of industrial architecture and increased the confidence of builders.[18]

Rolling mills in the iron and brass industries were usually much wider than textile mills. Managers of these plants needed large open areas for their engines, boilers, heavy machinery, and heating furnaces. Trusses spanning interior spaces allowed much greater flexibility in the placement of equipment, and they could support overhead hoisting equipment. An article in the Baltimore *American* on November 17, 1842, described the work under way at the Mount Savage Coal and Iron Works: "They are at present constructing a rolling mill, of great extent, and with a self-supporting roof, not surpassed by any roof of the kind in the country." In nearby Cumberland, Maryland, two recently demolished industrial buildings had long-span roofs: the first was the Baltimore and Ohio Railroad Rail Rolling Mill, built between 1869 and 1871, with wood and iron composite roof trusses (Fig. 8.6). The second was the Baltimore and Ohio's Bolt and Forge Shop, constructed in 1873, with iron Fink trusses.[19]

Prime Movers and Mechanical-Power Transmission in Factories

Before the widespread adoption of individual electric-motor drive in the twentieth century, power in factories was transmitted mechanically from waterwheels, turbines, or steam engines to production machines by gears, shafts, pulleys, belts, or ropes. As factory steam engines have already been mentioned in Chapter 4, this discussion will focus on waterwheels and turbines.

FIGURE 8.6. The Baltimore and Ohio Railroad Rail Rolling Mill, erected in Cumberland, Maryland, in 1869 to 1871. This mill had no interior posts to obstruct process flow or restrict machinery placement; roof trusses made of wood and wrought iron spanned the building. The monitored roof let in light and provided ventilation for the wide working area below. The roll trains were being removed at the time this picture was taken. (Courtesy of the Smithsonian Institution)

Waterwheels

To harness water power, a factory owner usually needed a canal or headrace to deliver water to his factory, a gate to control the flow, a pit for a water-wheel or turbine, and a tailrace to return the water to the river. Although the waterwheels in early factories are usually gone, masonry arches in foundation walls may show where races entered and exited (Fig. 3.15). Sometimes, as in the Wilkinson Mill, wheel pits were later covered over, leaving important features in place. When excavated, the wooden floor of the Wilkinson pit was still intact, complete with a curved breast that once fit close to the face of the missing waterwheel. The breast helped to keep water from spilling out of the buckets until the bottom point of rotation (Fig. 1.3). By measuring it, archaeologists determined the dimensions of the waterwheel and estimated its power.[20]

The breast wheel was the principle means of driving water-powered textile mills during the first half of the nineteenth century.[21] Like the overshot wheel, a breast wheel rotated because of the weight of water in its buckets, but it turned in the opposite direction, toward the incoming water. This gave the wheel an advantage in moderate backwater, because it helped to push water out of the wheel pit. In good conditions, breast wheels were almost as efficient as overshot wheels, capturing more than 60 percent of the potential energy in the flow of water. Experience with the reconstructed wheel in the Wilkinson Mill has confirmed that efficiency declines sharply if water rises more than 2 feet in the pit.

By the mid-1820s, progressive textile mills had flyball (centrifugal) governors that automatically regulated the flow of water to their wheels, thus keeping the machinery running at nearly constant speed. A governor sensed any departure from normal wheel speed caused by changes in the power demands of operating machinery (turning machines on or off), in the level of the millpond, or in backwater conditions. This automatic "feedback control" can be compared with the shouted instructions to the horse driver at the Beverly Manufactory. Discovery of a waterwheel governor (the only one known to have survived in America) in the Moffitt Machine Shop in Lincoln, Rhode Island, answered many questions about construction details and linkage techniques that were not provided by written sources and drawings (Fig. 8.7). The governor's elegant clutch mechanism, for instance, was much more sophisticated than anyone had expected.[22]

Turbines

Water turbines had become an attractive alternative to breast wheels by the mid-1840s (Fig. 8.8). Factory designers could soon choose from many different turbines. Testing by James Francis, James Emerson, and others demonstrated the superiority of turbines over waterwheels and compared the performance of various models.[23] The Pawtucket Gatehouse in Lowell, site of some of Francis's turbine experiments, is one of our nation's earliest industrial-research laboratories. The first "Francis" turbine, installed in 1847, is still in place in the gate house, where there are masonry chambers and measuring devices designed for hydraulic experimentation.[24] Park guides in Lowell conduct tours of the building. At the nearby Suffolk Mill and at the Hagley Museum in Delaware, visitors can see later versions of the Francis turbine in operation. There is much artifactual evidence on turbine installation at water-power sites all over North America.

In addition to being smaller, faster, more efficient (75 to 85 percent was

FIGURE 8.7. Historical architect Charles Parrott measuring the mid-nineteenth-century flyball governor in the Moffitt Machine Shop in Lincoln, Rhode Island. This is the only waterwheel governor known to have survived in the United States. It is now in the collections of the Slater Mill Historic Site. The shop owner preserved this automatic feedback device after replacing his waterwheel with a turbine. The machine shop, which was built around 1810, has also served as a wheelwright shop and as a small braiding mill.

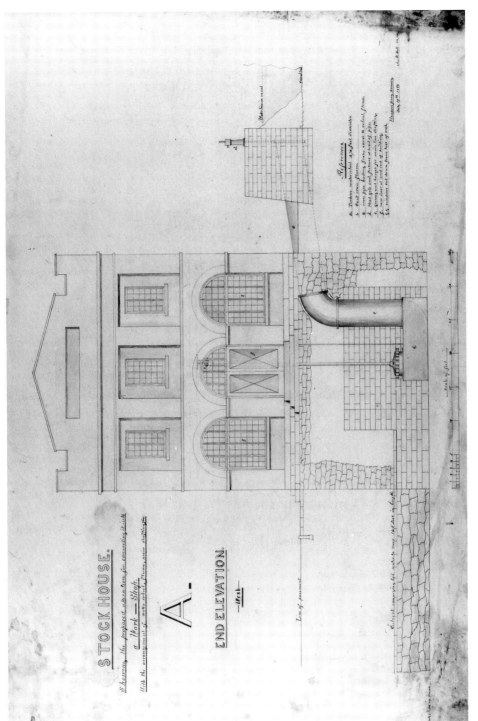

FIGURE 8.8. A turbine installed in a workshop (converted from a storehouse) at the U.S. Armory in Harpers Ferry, Virginia, in 1858. A canal at the right supplies water through a metal penstock to the turbine pit. Water, under pressure, enters the Boyden/Fourneyron turbine from below, sets in motion a bladed runner on a vertical shaft, and then discharges outward. In theory, there would be little energy left in the water at that point. The vertical shaft delivers power to the work area above. (Drawing by A. M. Ball at Harpers Ferry, 1858. Courtesy of Harpers Ferry National Historical Park)

common), and more durable than vertical waterwheels, most turbines ran well when they were submerged and were thus much better in wheel pits that were subject to frequent flooding. At Lowell, where engineers recorded an average of 127 "working days of backwater" each year between 1875 and 1893, this consideration was important. Turbines had other advantages as well. They could handle a range of heads and were unaffected by minor fluctuations in the level of a millpond. They were more readily governed than waterwheels, thus providing relatively constant speeds under the varying loads that were typical of many manufacturing operations. They also ran at much higher speeds, which could mean simpler, more efficient transmission systems and savings in the cost of gears and pulleys.[25]

Gears, Shafts, and Belts

Bolt holes and other marks of attachment on original beams and columns provide the best evidence of the exact placement of early shafting in many factories, including the Slater Mill.[26] At the 1810 Wilkinson Mill next door to Slater's factory, a restoration team found a wooden bearing block behind the plastering of an end wall on the first floor. Much of the evidence for the development of mechanical-power transmission in the United States has come from the examination of discarded or *in situ* components.[27]

Millwrights soon favored cast iron over wood for its strength and wear resistance in gears and shafts, even though it was brittle. Archaeological evidence of breakage of cast iron at the Wilkinson Mill includes a fractured vertical shaft reused as a lintel over a wheel-pit opening and a discarded horizontal shaft that failed at a turned bearing point. Wrought-iron shafting was tougher and could stand higher rotational speeds and torsional loads, but it was not generally available until the 1840s. Higher speeds increased the effectiveness of an important American development in power transmission: main belt drive, the practice of driving the horizontal line shafts in a factory with large leather belts.

The first American installation of a leather-belt main drive was in the Appleton Manufacturing Company in Lowell in 1828. By the 1840s, factory managers favored multiple belts running from the prime mover to line shafts on various floors or between shafts on adjacent floors. Although some American and most British mills clung to vertical shafts with geared connections for the line shafts on each floor, the advantages of leather belts were hard to deny. Most of all, American mill owners feared disruption of their operations by broken gearing that was both slow and costly to replace. Belt repairs took far less time. In addition, belting systems could be rearranged more easily than cumbersome sets of shafts and gears, an important consideration in flexible manufacturing environments.[28]

Nevertheless, the British expressed a clear preference for gears. Even James Montgomery, who reported the American achievements with leather-belt drives to his countrymen in 1840, took pride in the "neat manner in which Factories are geared in Great Britain."[29] Perhaps this preference reflected the early superiority of British iron-founding practice, which may have produced smoother running, more durable gears. A re-created 1826 vertical shaft system in the Wilkinson Mill has unintentionally reproduced some of the historic problems with American bevel gears. When one compares those noisy gears with the main belt system driven by a turbine at the Lowell National Historical Park, it is not difficult to understand why leather-belt drives became popular in America.

Whatever prime mover drove the line shafts, leather belts of relatively narrow width provided most of the connections to machines on the factory floor. Connections could be either downward, from an overhead shaft, or upward, through the floor from a shaft in the room below. In many old factories, floors are still perforated with slanted holes that indicate machinery driven by belts from below. This practice made it easier for fires to spread from floor to floor and was discouraged by insurance companies. There was a profusion of belts and belt-shifting levers in machine-filled rooms with overhead shafting (Fig. 8.9). The dangers of exposed leather belts for those who worked among them were serious. Many women were injured when their long hair was caught by a belt. Fourteen-year-old mill operative Camela Teolli, testifying before Congress in 1912, described her accident, which "pulled the scalp off." Some workers lost their lives in moving parts of manufacturing systems. A Massachusetts gravestone records the sad fate of nineteen-year-old Asenath Townsley: she "was suddenly killed by being caught in the machinery of a Factory in Southbridge, June 3, 1829."[30]

Although laws were passed in many states in the late nineteenth century to require the shielding of dangerous parts (such as gearing) in machines, they were not well enforced and usually did not specify guards for belting from overhead shafts. An analysis by historian Carl Gersuny of accident records from the Lyman Mills, a cotton manufacturer in Holyoke, Massachusetts, shows a high proportion of injuries from moving machinery and belts. Of the 814 injuries for which causes were listed between 1895 and 1916, 513 (63 percent) were caused by workers becoming caught in moving machinery (an additional 76 accidents were due to "flying shuttles and falling objects"). Gersuny concludes that "the extent of injury resulting from machinery reflects the hazards entailed by a technology relying on belts connected to shafting which was in turn geared to a central power source."[31]

The survival of mechanical drive systems (including rope drives) well into the age of electricity, despite safety legislation, acknowledged dangers, frictional power losses, and heavy maintenance requirements, may seem sur-

FIGURE 8.9. Machinery, belting, and shafting in the Wheeler and Wilson factory for the manufacture of sewing machines, around 1880. The drawing shows the crowded environment of this work space for machine tools and their operators. The workers would have had to take care to avoid being caught by an exposed belt. (From Charles Fitch, "Report on the Manufacture of Interchangeable Mechanisms," in Bureau of the Census, *Report on the Manufactures of the United States at the Tenth Census* [Washington, D.C.: Census Office, 1883], vol. 2, p. 650)

prising. Belting and shafting is still in use in some small shops, although an electric motor is almost always driving the transmission system. In some cases, this survival represents managerial inertia. but it can also testify to the effectiveness of mechanical transmission and the cumulative improvements made by generations of ingenious millwrights and engineers.[32]

It is incorrect to assume that the use of shafting and belting limited factory and shop layout to a few simple, linear patterns. There were other reasons besides ease of power transmission for lining up machines in the long rows we associate with factory production. Many managers liked the orderly and disciplined look of a linear arrangement. Aisles between rows enabled movement of materials and people, and they provided clear lines of sight for floor managers. Architectural constraints also played a part in this arrangement; the best solution for placing large machines in spaces that were divided by lines of supporting columns was usually a linear plan.

Rows of machines parallel to the long axis of a rectangular factory were the most common pattern, but there were other variations in mechanically driven plants. The size, weight, operating characteristics, or power consumption of particular machine types could influence their positioning. Manufacturing equipment might cause excessive floor vibrations when aligned in one direction but be relatively stable when rotated 90 degrees. If a worker ran a number of machines, they might be grouped for easy access. Similarly, automatic transfer of work from one machine to another might necessitate unusual layouts.

Many factories were not designed with a rectangular floor plan, and additions or expansions could complicate mechanical-power delivery. Industrial archaeologists frequently encounter transmission systems that turn corners and stretch into almost inaccessible spaces. A tour through the basement floor of the Hanford Mills, a woodworking factory in East Meredith, New York (now operating as a museum), provides a vivid lesson in the versatility of mechanical transmission. Belts slap, pulleys spin, shafts turn, and power seems to reach out in every direction, driving machines in different rooms on the floor above.

Mechanical-power systems, which performed adequately over moderate distances, were a proven, mature technology when promoters of electrical equipment began to suggest motors for driving production machinery in the 1880s. The many factory owners and mill engineers who were slow to adopt motor drive were not necessarily obstinate opponents of electrification. Often, they were simply hesitant to make a substantial investment in electrical equipment until it was proved effective for their particular needs.

Electricity in Factories

Electric Lighting

Electrical lighting systems were easier to sell to industry than were motors. Managers had not entirely eliminated fire dangers, smoke, and fumes when they switched from candles or whale-oil lamps to kerosene lamps and gaslights in the mid-nineteenth century. In hot, poorly ventilated rooms, burning gas or kerosene contributed to workers' discomfort and provided barely adequate illumination on dark days or in the evenings. The Waltham Watch Company found that gaslights adversely affected the workers in its Massachusetts factory:

> The peculiar requirements of the factory demand a separate light for nearly every person, and with the large number of persons employed in single rooms the inevitable result was the rapid consumption of the oxygen and consequent vitiation of the air, causing headaches, uneasiness, and a general indisposition to work.[33]

The production of intricate timepieces required more light than most industrial operations, but any factory work suffered when employees lacked adequate lighting. A major objective of mill design was to maximize the amount of natural light in work spaces. Weaving mills reported that the quality of fabric declined in the winter months when gaslighting was needed for at least a part of every day. The problem was more than seasonal in the growing number of plants that had begun to run at night.[34]

The need for better industrial illumination led to the installation of electric-arc lamps in factory spaces months before they were used on city streets. Unfortunately, a fire in 1990 destroyed the Riverside Worsted Mill in Olneyville, Rhode Island, where electric lighting was first used in a textile factory, in 1879. There, with a Brush dynamo supplying direct current, an electric arc between the carbon points in each lamp produced intense light.[35] Many factories had arc lighting by the mid-1880s, but the harsh glare and deep shadows were a serious handicap.[36] John Bowditch, a curator at the Henry Ford Museum, has an operable arc light in his dining room. His enthusiastic demonstrations temporarily blind his guests but are instructive experiences for those who may not appreciate fully the blessings of incandescent (glowing filament in a bulb) lighting.

Textile mills in New York and Massachusetts purchased Edison incandescent-lighting equipment in 1881. The Wamsutta Mills in New Bedford attracted widespread attention when no gas lines were installed during the construction of the new No. 6 mill in 1882; engineers provided power for all the artificial illumination with three 250-light Edison dynamos.[37] Incandescent lighting was a great boon for factory managers and, with some exceptions, for workers as well. Air quality and fire safety improved dramatically. There were fewer accidents in well-lighted spaces, and fewer workers suffered deterioration of vision from constant eyestrain. Improved illumination reduced errors and promoted accurate work, thereby improving both quality and productivity. In jobs requiring judgments based on subtle color distinctions, a properly placed electric lamp could be a great asset. In 1882, J. C. Ludlum noted that electric lighting "was very valuable" at the Merrimack Manufacturing Company in places "where it is very important that we should be able to distinguish shades of color and note any variations."[38]

There were some social costs associated with the introduction of incandescent-lighting systems in factories. Because electricity made it practical for many companies to add an extra shift and run all night, some workers had to make difficult alterations in their daily schedules. Also workers could be assigned to isolated or windowless spaces that might not have been usable without electric lamps. Electricity was beneficial in many ways, but it was also a potentially destructive force that had to be carefully controlled. Although miners, electricians, and linemen were more exposed than most factory employees, shocks, electrical burns, and electrocutions were soon high on the list of industrial hazards.

Once electric lighting was installed in a factory, other applications for electric energy soon appeared (if they were not already in place). The Waltham Watch Factory began to replace its gaslights in 1883, and within five years had 2,700 incandescent lamps. By then it also had an extensive collection of electrical equipment: an arc light for photo printing, apparatus for plating and gilding, an "electric time signal" for its astronomical clocks, signal connections between manufacturing spaces and the engine room, indicators for water tanks in the mill towers, a telephone system, a watchman's clock, gongs in every department to announce the start and end of work, and fire alarms.[39]

The industrial use of electricity actually began long before electric lighting. It is said by some to have begun in 1831 with the ore separator at Ironville, New York (Chapter 4). The silver-plating process perfected by the Rogers brothers in 1847 introduced electrical manufacturing technology, and electrochemical processes were well established before incandescent lighting appeared. However, electrical-equipment manufacturers would not have a significant impact on most American factories until they developed practical motors driven by electrical current.

Electric-Motor Drive

Electrical manufacturers steadily improved electric motors and adapted them for a variety of industrial purposes. Mill engineers were quick to recognize the advantages of electricity in providing light, but most were initially skeptical about driving production machinery with the same type of power. The first use of an electric motor in a textile mill was usually to run an elevator. Although many textile mills still depended on exterior hoists and doorway entrances through towers, freight elevators had become common in the years since Elisha Otis's demonstration of his safety brake at the New

York World's Fair in 1853.[40] Electrical drive for elevators proved to be superior to steam or hydraulics before the turn of the century, and many factories still have components of this electrical equipment.

There were good reasons for moving cautiously in adopting electric motors for driving textile machinery before 1905. Although Dunnell Printworks in Pawtucket, Rhode Island, achieved early progress with direct-current (DC) motors for its calico printing, beginning in 1891, a similar approach would not necessarily be successful with weaving or spinning. First, DC motors sparked, a great liability in mills with flammable fibers floating in the air. There were also different power and speed requirements for particular processes. Direct-current motors equipped with rheostat controls at Dunnell had handled the high start-up loads of the heavy printing machines and met their need for speed variation, but most textile processes demanded constant speed. Powerful alternating-current (AC) induction motors had to be developed to provide constant speed even under variable loads.[41]

A great deal of incremental improvement of electric motors was necessary before conservative textile manufacturers were convinced of their value.[42] The Henry Ford Museum and the Western Museum of Mining and Industry have extensive collections of American electric motors and control apparatus. Other places in which to examine the development of this type of equipment include mill-supply warehouses and machinery-salvage firms.

The boom in construction of mills in the South during the 1890s was in many ways a response to the opportunities presented by electrification. It was also a powerful argument for the adoption of electrical-drive systems in older northern factories. The decision to adopt new technology was easier to make if owners did not have an investment in an existing system that was already doing the job.

The Columbia Mills in South Carolina built the first cotton factory to have all its machinery driven by electric motors. General Electric installed motors on the ceilings of that mill (now the state museum) in 1893; they were belted to shafting that drove groups of textile machines. Group drive with a few large motors was more common than individual drive (one small motor per machine) until after World War I. At first, small motors were costly to purchase and inefficient in operations requiring frequent stopping and starting. In many older mills, mill engineers could install group-drive systems with only modest alteration of existing shafting arrangements.[43]

The Pawtucket Gatehouse in Lowell, although not a factory, is a good place to see physical evidence of the same power systems that were tried in nearby textile mills. It has a main leather-belt drive from its abandoned turbine to a line shaft that once drove ten gate-hoisting mechanisms. Experiments with electric-motor drive took place in the gate house in 1891, when

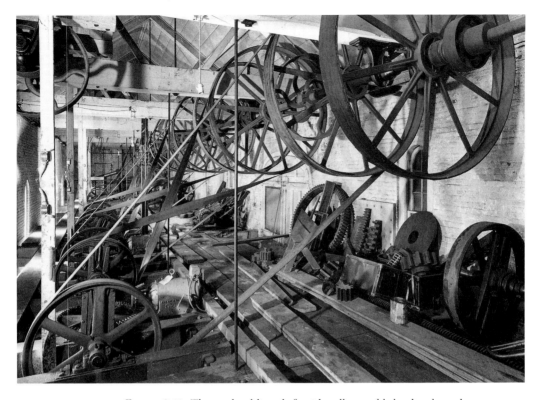

FIGURE 8.10. The overhead line shaft with pulleys and belts that drove the ten gates (left and below) in the 1847 Pawtucket Gatehouse. A main belt drive from James Francis's first hydraulic turbine (still in place) drove the shaft until electric motors took over. Wooden patterns for casting gears in the gate machinery are stored against the wall. (Photograph by Jack Boucher for the Historic American Engineering Record. Courtesy of the Library of Congress)

first two and then three motors drove sections of the line shaft (and thus groups of gates). These early motors did not perform well, and the water-power company reluctantly went back to belt drive from the turbine. Drawings and documents show that engineers continued to plan for electrical drive. In 1923, the company installed the large single motor that is still there, but it and the entire line shaft (Fig. 8.10) were idled by a final change to the individual motors that now control each gate directly.[44]

Northern mill owners who resisted complete conversion to electrical drive into the 1920s either were satisfied with their mechanical-drive systems or did not want to make a substantial investment when much of the textile industry was moving to the South. In Lowell, in 1918, the ten large companies on the canal system used less than two-thirds of their total steam and water-power capacity to generate electricity. All generated some electricity, but the Lawrence Mills produced only a tiny amount, probably for lighting and for elevators. A report in 1923 said that "the individual mills are only partially electrified" and that the Lawrence Mills still had no electrification of manufacturing. One of the giant pulleys from the mechanical-drive systems of that company is now an outdoor exhibit in Lowell.[45]

Individual motor drive eventually proved advantageous in almost all factories, not just those in the textile industry. The availability of reasonably priced motors helped to spread powered manufacturing to small establishments that could not afford the capital costs of water-power systems or steam engines. Companies that did not generate their own power could often purchase it from a central station. Within an industrial plant, there were substantial energy savings from elimination of shaft drives, with their friction and need for lubrication and adjustment. Managers had more flexibility in choosing the best positions for particular machines in a production process. When their machines were powered with small, portable electric motors, they could change a plant layout quickly and inexpensively. Mill engineers, freed from the restrictions imposed by shafts and belts, had a wider range of architectural options when they designed new plants. Designers made electric motors integral parts of many machines soon after the turn of the century. These motors gave machine-tool operators more choice of cutting speeds and feeds just when high-speed tool steel was creating a demand for more powerful and better controlled machinery.[46]

Factories in Motion

Machinery, particularly power looms with their repetitive and violent beating motions, shook the frames and masonry walls of factories. Vibration caused structural damage to the buildings that housed the looms and was unpleasant and unhealthy for workers. It also damaged the machines that were causing the problem. Factory floors that were no longer level because of building movement could put the machinery out of alignment and cause bearings to overheat. As production machinery grew heavier and operated at higher speeds, these problems increased.[47]

The Boott Cotton Mills, in Lowell, had a long record of structural problems from machine vibrations. Physical inspection of the complex today confirms the damaging effects. In the twentieth century, the mills' managers had to run machines at less than their full speed and, in one case, were forced to limit the number of modern looms they could install because "our experience was so disastrous on the building."[48] It is appropriate that the Boott Mills are now the site of an operating weave room, part of a National Park Service exhibit in the complex. Visitors can feel the vibrations and hear the incredible noise of eighty-eight looms in motion. Every student of American industrial history should have this sensory experience.

Millwrights and engineers developed ways to reduce much of the vibration from machines and mechanical-power-transmission systems. They isolated gearing for waterwheels in its own energy-absorbing heavy timber frame, independent of the mill's framing or the outer walls. A reconstructed frame of this type can be seen in the wheel pit of the Wilkinson Mill. Placement, orientation, and even starting sequence of machines could be important factors. Before the Civil War, manufacturers often placed looms on an upper floor in a textile mill, usually the third floor in the Lowell pattern. This practice caused severe problems because walls at upper levels were thinner than at lower levels, and the factory structure was not rigid enough to withstand the actions of weaving transmitted through the floor beams. By the end of the century, mill engineers had succeeded in moving looms down to the first or second floor in most mills or even to a separate weave shed. The re-created weave room in the Boott Mills exhibit area is, appropriately, on the first floor of an 1871 building in the complex.

Industrialists needed larger factories, and both the weight and the speed of machinery increased. In these wider buildings, several rows of columns were required to support beams, and larger windows were needed to light the interior (Fig. 8.11). To provide structural strength and allow more window area, many companies adopted pilaster or pier construction, reinforcing load-bearing sections of the brick wall between each window bay (see Fig. 8.17). You can see one of the first applications of these brick piers at the White Rock Mill in Westerly, Rhode Island. The noted mill engineer David Whitman supervised the construction of this factory in 1849. He and other engineers worked to stiffen the framing of mills, to improve ventilation and humidification, and to introduce systematic and rational planning procedures for new construction.[49]

In the 1880s, companies began to construct large, one-story buildings with work spaces illuminated by extensive window surfaces in saw-tooth roofs. These roofs, with their multiple ridge lines, could cover enormous floor areas. American factory designers improved on the British saw-tooth concept to reduce leakage from the ice and snow buildup that was inevitable in most American manufacturing regions. Mill engineer Charles T. Main remarked in 1886, with considerable exaggeration, that "the old style of high and narrow mills has gone out of use." While admitting the higher cost per square foot for single-story construction, he noted that the "particular advantages" of these structures were "less vibration, which is conducive to better work, and more light, which tends towards the same end." He also pointed out that older mills with many small rooms had to have more overseers. Many textile manufacturers preferred to put their looms in one-story weave sheds under saw-tooth roofs.[50]

The adoption of standardized designs became common because of their obvious utility; also, mutual insurance companies by this time had become

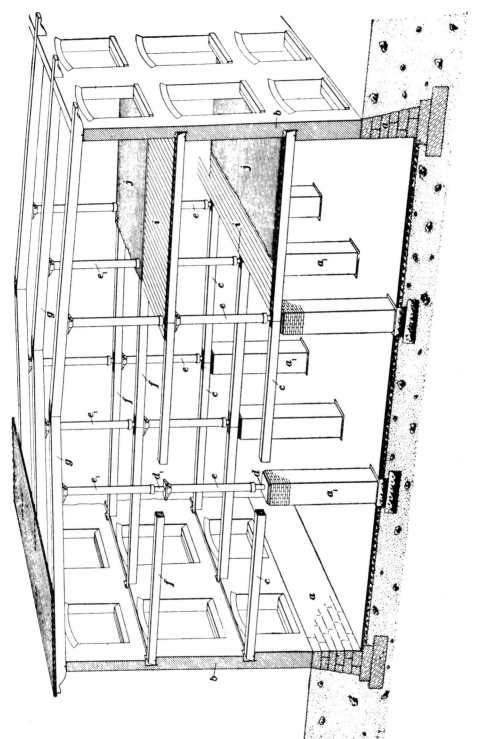

FIGURE 8.11. One example of mill construction, around 1905: a cutaway view of a factory with slow-burning flooring and two rows of round wood columns. The masonry building has a wide, almost flat roof and windows with segmental arches. The walls are thinner at higher levels. The mill lacks strengthening piers, or pilasters, that would allow larger windows (and thus wider, naturally lighted floors). The letters on the drawing refer to elements described in a correspondence course. (From *Yarns, Cloth Rooms, and Mill Engineering* [Scranton, Pa.: International Textbook, 1924], p. 56)

powerful, and they favored certain proven forms. Mill engineers designed factories to fit the particular needs of a manufacturer, but they were much more likely to produce a customized alteration of a standard design than a radical departure. Readily available manuals and journal articles disseminated the approved technology. Not surprisingly, builders of mills in the South were likely to incorporate advances in mill engineering, while older mills in the North fell behind. Also southern sites usually offered plenty of space for wide factories or multibuilding complexes of the latest design.[51]

Faced with obsolescence in their buildings, power and lighting systems, and production machinery, many northern textile companies recognized the need to modernize their entire plants. An increasingly tempting option for those considering the construction of factories was to move operations to the South, rebuilding in a region that offered low taxes, minimal business regulation, compliant workers, hydroelectric power, steam coal deposits, space for future expansion, and (for cotton textile manufacturers) close proximity to cotton fields. Industrial development in the South, much of it financed by local investors, had been accelerating since the 1880s. Aggressive promotional efforts by southern boosters were highly effective in attracting new or transplanted manufacturing enterprises. Mill-engineering and machinery firms with New England roots were active participants in this radical alteration of America's industrial landscape. By the mid-1920s, the South had passed the North in cotton-textile production, was making inroads in woolens, and was beginning to move into the promising field of synthetics.[52]

Variations in Factory Design

Textile mills had an overwhelming influence on factory design in the nineteenth century, but some types of manufacturing adopted variations or distinctive forms that were more suitable for their particular needs. Many printworks that applied patterns to cloth used very tall machines that required higher rooms. Bleacheries and dyeworks had to have buildings that could handle liquid spills and prevent excessive condensation of vapors. Foundry operators, needing effective ventilation for smoke, favored monitor roof forms with large venting windows. Managers of machine shops that handled heavy materials or erected large mechanisms such as steam engines installed craneways in wide bays with high vertical clearance.

Metalworking factories of the nineteenth century were often quite similar to textile-mill buildings (Fig. 8.12). Long, open rooms and linear arrangement of shafting and machinery fit the needs of much of American industry, including many firms that shaped metal with machine tools. While textile companies were building wider mills, however, some metalworking

FIGURE 8.12. The Robbins and Lawrence Rifle Works in Windsor, Vermont, built in 1846. This water-powered factory is very similar to many brick textile mills of the same period. Manufacturers struggled to admit enough light into half-story attic spaces to make them functional work areas. The trapdoor monitor in this building is simply a raised section of the pitched roof. Other ways of illuminating mill attics with windows included dormers, skylights, and clerestory monitors—vertical breaks in the roofline that ran the length of a building. This building now houses the American Precision Museum. (Photograph by Matthew Roth)

firms developed different ways to increase floor area. They added wings and built factories in L, E, H, U, or hollow-square patterns.[53] The Colt Armory of 1855 (rebuilt in 1865) in Hartford, Connecticut, is an early and influential example of the H plan.[54]

In these expanded variations on the basic multistory, narrow factory form, most rooms were relatively small; this promoted close supervision of precision tasks. The buildings also retained adequate natural lighting and ventilation from windows. For particularly delicate work, manufacturers placed as many employees as possible at benches directly in front of the windows (Fig. 8.13). At the Colt Armory, filers of precision parts sat by the windows, while machine operators worked in the center of a room. Extremely narrow mills, with more windows than was customary in most factories, became common in the watch industry and in the manufacture of

FIGURE 8.13. Watch assemblers at the Waltham Clock Company work at benches in front of large, multiple windows. The assemblers select from sorted batches of slightly varying parts and do a great deal of hand fitting. Only a few watches are made each day in part of a factory that was once famous for mass-production. However, this company keeps alive proud traditions of craftsmanship, precision, and accuracy that distinguished the old Waltham Watch Company.

costume jewelry. The factory complex of the Waltham Watch Company, altered and enlarged many times between 1854 and 1914, is a striking example (Fig. 8.14). It has closely spaced windows in its numerous wings and projections, some of which create H and hollow-square plans.[55]

An H pattern could be repeated over and over in a factory plan. When Remington built a new military-rifle factory in Bridgeport, Connecticut, in 1915, *American Machinist* commented on this plant, made up of

> a number [13] of multiple story main building units placed side by side in a row, with equal spacing between them and joined together in the middle by connecting wings [Fig. 8.15]. This is probably the most flexible plan that can be devised for a manufacturing plant. Any number of units can be built at the start, and future growth is provided for by the addition of more units without disrupting manufacturing operations.

The factory offered 1.5 million square feet of floor area; the original Slater Mill had 3,500.[56]

FIGURE 8.14. The Waltham Watch Company's factory in Waltham, Massachusetts. The evolution of this expanded and much altered complex can be traced with the use of plans, drawings, photographs, business records, stylistic evidence, and structural forms. The buildings date from 1854 to 1914. Individual structures and development patterns show a strong concern for letting natural light into work spaces. This view shows the narrow width of most buildings in the complex.

The "Mill Doctors"

Mill engineers naturally favored the construction of mills that incorporated the latest advances in their field. After 1870, these industrial consultants were likely to be university-trained specialists, although millwright traditions continued to influence their work. They dealt with both structural imperatives and aesthetic possibilities; the building had to stand up, but an attractive façade could enhance the prestige of the company. Engineers became increasingly involved not only in the design of buildings and the delivery of power to various rooms, but also in the rational layout of machinery for the intended products and the efficient transfer of materials between each stage of manufacture. They could site and design large mills (or carefully integrated sets of industrial buildings) to meet the particular needs of a manufacturer, while still allowing flexibility for later changes.

Lockwood, Greene and Company offered a full range of mill-engineering services. This advertisement suggests the type of contract they preferred, although such business was difficult to get: "We will *plan* the undertaking, *design* the plant, layout of machinery and equipment in detail, let the building contract, *superintend* the construction—and turn the plant over to you *complete* and *ready to run*."[57]

The popular name applied to mill engineers is an obvious indication that new construction was only a part of their professional practice. They were called "mill doctors." Like medical doctors, they spent a great deal of their time getting people to change bad habits and repairing damaged components of complex systems.[58]

Most historic industrial plants have been extensively altered, enlarged, and repaired over time. Expansion or replacement of individual buildings, construction of multiple additions, and linking of structures with connecting buildings or with bridges were normal paths of development. At the Boott Cotton Mills in Lowell, buildings and connectors date from the 1830s to the early twentieth century. Inclined ramps were necessary at numerous junctions because floor levels in different mills did not match. Industrial archaeologist Laurence Gross used reports from engineering consultants, managerial complaints, and his own examination of ramps, steps, and floor levels to refute the popular assumption that early Boott managers planned for the future connection of their four original brick mills. Later construc-

FIGURE 8.15. The Remington Rifle Factory in Bridgeport, Connecticut, is perhaps the ultimate factory built in an H pattern. Thirteen buildings were constructed side by side in 1915 and linked by central connecting wings. The plan allowed for the possibility of expansion on the same pattern. The building is now used by the General Electric Company.

tion in the complex could not solve previous alignment problems and sometimes created new ones.[59]

Original factory construction was often hidden inside expanded complexes or incorporated into larger buildings. It takes a practiced eye to discern the outlines of the Boston Manufacturing Company's 1813 and 1816 brick mills in the extended wall of the present structure in Waltham, Massachusetts.[60] Repairs and jury-rigged improvements hold together the worn fabric at many sites, and "temporary" solutions to structural or mechanical problems have often outlasted their creators. In some cases, owners could not afford appropriate changes in marginal plants, but there is also a disturbing pattern of seeking immediate returns while avoiding costly capital improvements that might bring future success. Running mills "into the ground" was not unusual, particularly in declining industrial regions such as twentieth-century New England.[61]

Many complexes eventually became too inefficient to function competitively in one manufacturing sector and were transferred to another or adaptively reused for nonindustrial purposes. Others stand vacant or exist only as ruins. Companies have ordered factories to be demolished simply to avoid paying taxes on the empty buildings. Sayles Finishing Company, having lost most of the tenants in its Valley Falls Mill complex in Cumberland, Rhode Island, contracted with wreckers to tear it down. They were "to have the roofs off all the buildings prior to the Fifteenth of June, 1934." That happened to be the first day of the new tax year, and buildings without roofs were not taxed. After decades of abandonment, the foundations and open raceways are now being transformed into a riverside park for the community.[62]

Reading the Factory Interior

It is not easy to imagine the way a factory room was used when equipment, materials, and productive employees are absent, but there are usually a number of clues. A close look at the vacant space should detect marks left by machines, power systems, and workers. It is always advisable, of course, to learn as much as possible about the history of an inactive factory and its production technology before attempting to read the material evidence inside.

A factory that still has historic machinery and furnishings in place is a physical record of manufacturing technology and labor activities that, even if incomplete, can offer insights missing from documentary descriptions and expand our understanding of workers' experiences. Watkins Mill near Kansas City, Missouri, is a rarity; it is a woolen factory preserved much as it was when it closed at the turn of the century. The manufacturing spaces are crowded with machinery and evocative of another time. People who spent their working days in this mill left traces behind them that tell us about their mechanical skills, the occupational hazards they faced, and the ways they performed particular jobs. The wooden floors are surprisingly revealing; there are wear marks that explain the foot-treadle operation of a yarn hanker and indicate the paths taken by mule spinners walking back and forth with the moving carriages of their machines.[63]

At the Atwood-Crawford Bobbin Factory in Pawtucket, Rhode Island, workers hung a pair of crutches on a wall as a testimonial to a disabled artisan who died after many years of shaping wood. Next to these senti-mental relics of shop culture were two badly bent drills, crossed like sabers—reminders to one embarrassed worker (and to every aspiring crafts-man in the factory) that it was one thing to ruin a single tool but something else to ruin two in one day. On the same wall, a photograph of a stern-faced individual stared down from within a well-worn toilet seat. The meaning of this particular framing arrangement was not difficult to understand. The unpopular employee had left, but his sins were not forgiven.[64]

An empty box on the end wall of a pulping mill at Val Jalbert, Quebec, once sheltered a religious statue (Fig. 8.16). The French-Canadian employ-ees could see it from their positions as they fed short logs into the turbine-driven grinders that occasionally snatched someone's hand. Perhaps the presence of the crucifix made it easier for them to accept the perils of their work. The mill and surrounding company town are now part of an extensive historical site in which the role of religion in the workplace and the indus-trial community is a powerful interpretive theme.[65]

Twentieth-Century Changes

Manufacturing structures had to support greater floor loads and withstand more vibration in the twentieth century. They also needed larger windows to light wider floor spaces. Standard multistory factories with load-bearing brick walls, slow-burning floors, and wood columns now seemed to lack sufficient strength and rigidity for many applications, including weaving. In addition, there was the danger of rot when shortages of longleaf yellow pine forced buildings to accept substitute timbers or when wet processes created damp environments. Even the most conservative mill engineer could not ignore the structural potential of newly available materials such as steel and concrete. Yet change did not come quickly.

FIGURE 8.16. A pulping mill at Val Jalbert, Quebec. The roof and most of the window sash are gone from this former work area, but it still has its metal roof trusses and several pulping machines connected to water turbines. On the wall at left center, a gabled box once held a crucifix. Platforms have been added for visitors to this interpreted site.

Steel Framing

Steel framing, revolutionary in its implications for tall commercial buildings, had only a modest effect on factory architecture before the 1920s.[66] There was little question about the strength of steel or its effectiveness in stiffening factory floors, but its high cost compared with that of other structural materials and concern about its vulnerability to distortion in the heat of fires delayed its broad acceptance for industrial buildings. Unless there was little danger of fire, steel had to be carefully shielded with brick, tile, or concrete.[67]

Until the late nineteenth century, most American steel was produced to make rails. Engineers used steel in a few bridges before the 1890s, most notably the Eads Bridge across the Mississippi River at St. Louis, Missouri, built in 1874; the Glasgow Bridge, built at Glasgow, Missouri, over the Missouri River in 1879; and the Brooklyn Bridge, spanning the East River, in 1883.[68] The availability of structural steel had little effect on American

architecture until 1885, when engineer William LeBaron Jenney introduced
it in the frame of the Home Insurance Building in Chicago. Designers of
tall, skeletal-framed buildings soon made increasing use of steel, as producers began to apply improved rolling technology to a wide variety of structural forms.

The costs of shielding steel structural members were not excessive for
builders of commercial structures because most architects already intended
to apply ornamental sheathing and interior finishes over the steel for aesthetic purposes. In industrial structures, however, covering the interior columns, beams, and girders with fireproof materials could be a significant
expense.[69] In manufacturing plants where fire was not a threat, exposed
steel (covered with paint for corrosion resistance) became increasingly common. As we will see later in this chapter, steel eventually became the
standard framing material for one-story automobile plants.

Reinforced Concrete

In the last quarter of the nineteenth century, engineers and architects began
building industrial structures with reinforced concrete, a fireproof building
material that has great strength in compression and, to a lesser extent, in
tension as well. They gradually accepted the fact that reinforcing elements
of iron or steel (imbedded beams, bars, rods, or wire mesh) can add the
tensile strength and toughness that plain concrete lacks. Concrete of several
types had been known since the Hellenistic period. Used conservatively in
bridges and buildings by the Romans but rarely applied again until the mid-
eighteenth century, concrete is a mixture of cement, water, sand, and sometimes an aggregate of crushed stone or gravel. While still in a viscous state,
concrete can be poured into forms at a construction site and allowed to set in
the desired shape.[70]

Americans used an imported hydraulic cement in a flight of masonry
locks on the Middlesex Canal in the 1790s and processed cement stone near
Chittenango, New York, for use in Erie Canal structures in the 1820s.
James Francis installed a waterproof wall of plain concrete at the entrance of
his 1847 Northern Canal, now part of the Lowell National Historical Park.
However, it was Ernest Ransome in the 1880s who first demonstrated the
potential of reinforced concrete in factory construction.[71]

The Pacific Coast Borax Plant, in Bayonne, New Jersey, built in two
phases (1897–1898 and 1903), is the most influential example of Ransome's
work. The California builder had tested reinforced concrete in both bridges
and factories, but the borax plant was his first project on the east coast and
probably the first factory in the region with a complete structural system of
reinforced concrete. A terrible fire in this factory in 1902 presented a dra-

FIGURE 8.17. The Pennsylvania Woven Carpet Mills. This brick mill was built in Philadelphia in 1899. Its wall at the left is a good example of pier, or pilaster, construction. The owners added the reinforced-concrete mill on the right in 1937. The difference in window size is dramatic; thin concrete piers can carry more load than the much wider brick piers.

matic demonstration of the qualities of concrete. The heat left heavy steel equipment in twisted piles, but the reinforced concrete of the outer walls, floors, and columns survived the inferno. Ransome and other proponents of concrete construction pointed with justifiable pride to the survival of this concrete structure and went on to develop the "true daylight factory," in which large windows spanned wide bays between external concrete columns (Fig. 8.17).[72]

The best-known applications of concrete construction in factory design were in the twentieth-century plants of the emerging automobile industry (Fig. 8.18).[73] Architect Albert Kahn created an international reputation with his work for Packard and Ford.[74] In 1905, after building nine conventional factories for the Packard Motor Company, he and his brother designed Building 10 with a reinforced-concrete frame that pushes the limits of functional, minimalist design. It was the first multistoried automobile factory to be constructed with this structural material. The narrow framing members in the outer walls of Building 10 form an open grid that seems almost too delicate to have survived the weight and vibration of more than half a century of automobile manufacturing. In a pattern repeated in factories for many other industries, large windows and thin brick spandrel walls fill the spaces between verticals and horizontals of concrete.[75]

Kahn's work for Ford Motor Company included much of the Highland Park Plant, famous as the site of the introduction of the automobile assembly line in 1913. A tiny fraction of the 1909 plant is still intact but derelict today; the company demolished most of the earliest buildings in 1959 and has sold the property. The four-story, concrete-framed "Old Shop" made good use of gravity chutes for materials, but it was not well suited for the largely horizontal layout of assembly lines. Single-story factories at other sites would be appropriate to this method of manufacturing in years to come, but first Ford added more multistory buildings at Highland Park.[76]

With the later buildings at the complex, Kahn and the Ford engineers tried to ease Henry Ford's increasing concern for efficient movement of parts and materials both within and between buildings. The new phase of construction, coming soon after the 1913 development of assembly-line methods, included long craneways linking parallel buildings. Industrial engineers were trying to find building designs that matched the specific needs of production, and they concentrated on the critical problem of materials handling. Highland Park's craneways were part of a growing system of mechanized transport for heavy raw materials, machine parts, and subassemblies.[77] Ample natural light for manufacturing entered through their glass

FIGURE 8.18. A Fisher Body Plant in Detroit. The strength of reinforced-concrete framing is apparent in this multistoried factory complex. Most of the wall area is glass, for letting in a maximum amount of daylight.

roofs and through very large factory windows set in strong steel sash. Ford said, "You know, when you have lots of light, you can put the machines close together."[78] He saved space and minimized transfer time with closely packed machines, but the crowded and noisy environment could not have been pleasant for the workers.

Many of the great concrete factories from the first decades of the twentieth century house operating industries today; their durability is a testament to the combined accomplishments of American architects, engineers, builders, and material producers. The evolution of concrete construction techniques and of concrete chemistry has continued. As engineers became more confident of reinforcing techniques, they substituted flat slabs for the deep beams cast into the floors of most early factories (Fig. 9.25). Designers no longer tried to mimic in concrete what had been proved sound in timber. C.A.P. Turner of Minneapolis pioneered the combination of a flat slab cast with supporting mushroom-shaped columns in 1905 and 1906. Even the flaring tops of Turner's columns (and countless variations thereon) were eventually seen as unnecessary to support most floor slabs; straight columns cast integral with the floor and linked to it by patterns of reinforcing bars were sufficient in all but the heaviest loading situations.[79]

The best way to increase one's appreciation for the capabilities of reinforced concrete is to watch an attempt to demolish it. High explosives, which can sever steel columns in an instant and can bring metal skeletal frames crashing down in controlled "implosions," sometimes have almost no destructive effect on reinforced-concrete structures. A radio talk show recently covered the impending removal of a multistoried concrete building in Rhode Island. The guest, a demolition engineer, claimed that his company would "blow that thing down at 7 a.m. . . . We'll start removing debris before coffee break!" A local concrete worker named Mario replied:

> You can huff . . . and puff . . . and blow all you want . . . but that building is not going to come down with your puny firecrackers. You can use an A-bomb tomorrow, and that building will still stand. . . . Even if you use a Z-bomb, it still won't matter, because I built that building and I tied iron rod in it thicker than your thumb. In the old days we didn't use that chicken-wire-reinforced cement you clowns in New York are used to blowing up.[80]

Neither the morning blast nor a second attempt caused anything more than cracks and thick clouds of annoying dust. Demolition required months of battering with a wrecking ball. Mario and his reinforced concrete were vindicated.

Modern European architects, including many of the founders of the International style, were strongly influenced by the practical but visually striking designs of American factories, warehouses, and grain elevators built with concrete. Architectural historians have begun to recognize that American contributions to the development of reinforced-concrete construction technology deserve a high rating for their significance to architecture and engineering. These contributions were made primarily in industrial settings, often at considerable geographic and cultural distance from the established centers of architectural innovation in Chicago and New York.[81]

Single-Story Factories at River Rouge

By 1917 Americans were making more than 1.7 million vehicles a year in multistory factories. Plants in metropolitan Detroit turned out 1 million of those automobiles.[82] As we have seen, however, multiple floors were becoming a handicap for the new automobile assembly lines. Unfortunately for the city, new factories with all their operations on one or two floors required more land for the same amount of manufacturing space. It was usually difficult, and sometimes impossible, to expand existing industrial complexes in a congested urban area. When auto manufacturers chose to build additional plants with expansive floor plans, they favored locations in the outlying suburbs or the countryside, a pattern that persists in many parts of the nation. Land is usually cheaper, taxes are lower, and highway connections are easier outside the industrial cities.

When Henry Ford, in 1918, began to construct manufacturing plants at the River Rouge site south of Detroit, he switched to single-story construction and steel framing. More efficient assembly was possible on one floor, and there was little need for all the fireproofing, corrosion resistance, and vibration damping that made reinforced concrete so valuable in tall buildings. Steel framing was strong and easy to erect, and it took up less space than concrete. The wide roof trusses that could be built with steel allowed manufacturers to dispense with supporting columns, thus allowing more flexibility in equipment layout.[83]

Albert Kahn already had experience in single-story industrial construction before his firm designed a series of great factories for Ford at "the Rouge." In 1906, Kahn and the New England mill-engineering firm of Lockwood, Greene and Company had designed a plant, primarily of single-story form, for the George N. Pierce Company of Buffalo, New York, which was soon to be well known for its Pierce Arrow automobiles. It seems likely that Lockwood, Greene shared with Kahn the fruits of its wide experience in textile-mill architecture;[84] the similarity between single-story weave sheds (with saw-tooth roofs) and buildings in the Pierce complex is striking.

The Rouge still has most of its Kahn structures, including Building B, "Kahn's first monumental steel-framed manufacturing building, measuring 100 feet high, 300 feet wide, and 1,700 feet long." It was originally used to make Eagle Boats (submarine chasers) in World War I and later to manufacture automobile parts and assemble automobiles and tractors. The single-story building, unusually tall because of Eagle Boat requirements, has been altered and enlarged,[85] but it is one of Kahn's most influential buildings. Today the single-story factory with steel frame (often prefabricated) is a ubiquitous feature of American industrial parks.

Henry Ford integrated many types of manufacturing operations in his new complex of unprecedented scale on the Rouge River. On this 2,000-acre tract, his architects were free to build single-story factories that would eliminate the movement of parts and materials between floors. In 1927, Ford gave the Rouge primary responsibility for the production of the Model A Ford, the company's replacement for the obsolete Model T. The complex then had almost 100 structures, 53,000 machine tools, and 75,000 workers. It had become one of the largest industrial plants in the world, the central element in an ambitious effort at vertical integration.[86]

Ford had been trying for years to free himself from heavy dependence on outside suppliers of parts and materials. Ironically, one of the advantages of the Detroit area for most automobile manufacturers was its concentration of suppliers. Ford sought more control than the other manufacturers: he wanted the capability to make most of the parts that went into his cars. He even wanted to control the extraction of natural resources and the processing of important raw materials.[87]

The vertical integration at Ford eventually reached all the way to Brazil, where the company bought rubber plantations in the 1930s. Ford ships brought iron ore from the company's mines in Michigan and Minnesota, across the Great Lakes, up the Detroit and Rouge rivers, and right to the docks at the Rouge complex. Lumber came from Ford forests in Michigan. Coal miners in Kentucky and West Virginia were Ford employees, as were glassworkers in Pennsylvania and Minnesota, and woodworkers in Michigan lumber areas. The company even owned rail lines, including the 90 miles of track that criss-crossed the Rouge site and connected its various structures.[88]

The Rouge had blast furnaces, coke ovens, a complete steel mill, a production foundry, a jobbing foundry, a glass plant, a by-products plant, a tire plant, a cement factory, a locomotive shop, motor and final assembly buildings, and two coal-fired powerhouses. At its boat slip, gigantic bridge cranes and Hewlett unloaders could transfer thousands of tons of coal, iron ore, limestone, and other materials to storage bins, rail cars, or skips (Fig. 8.19). Although Ford wanted as little inventory as possible (he was an early proponent of what has recently become known as "just-in-time" manufacturing), he did have to store some materials, such as iron ore during the months when the Great Lakes were frozen.[89] Waterways, railways, and an expand-

FIGURE 8.19. The vast River Rouge complex from an aerial perspective in 1927. A movable bridge over the Rouge River channel is at the lower right, and vessels are in the boat slip at the center. The glass plant, cement plant, and single-story assembly buildings are beyond and to the right of the boat slip. Smoke rises from the blast and electric furnaces, the production foundry, and the multiple stacks of the power house. Steel mill buildings are to the left. (From the collections of Henry Ford Museum and Greenfield Village, negative number 833.48955)

ing national highway system tied together the integrated empire of the Ford Motor Company.

It is, however, an exaggeration to say that Henry Ford made everything that went into his automobiles or that he stopped all dealings with suppliers of parts that he did make. His vertical integration was extensive but incomplete. He was never close to being self-sufficient, not even in steel production. For example, one often forgets how many textile products went into a car, not only for upholstering, but also for such items as woven tire fabric and braided covering on wires. The Ford Motor Company did not buy or build its own textile mills. Among other products that Ford had to buy were the copper for electrical wiring and for radiators.

Ford was pragmatic enough to accept the need for some outside supply, and his production heads saw genuine advantages in such contractual arrangements. Charles Sorenson and A. M. Wibel realized that outside suppliers could enable the company to boost production of the popular Model A while minimizing expenditures for more tooling. The company's own resources and manufacturing capabilities remained valuable as a hedge against the shutoff of contracted supplies and as a way to force down the costs or to improve the quality of outside purchases. When the Great Depression set in, the Ford Motor Company increased its links to outside suppliers.[90]

The centralization of so much of Ford's manufacturing capacity at the Rouge did not continue for long. From 1928 to 1931, the company expanded its production of the Model A by turning to branch assembly plants. This was in many ways a return to the regional assembly plan adopted for the Model T in 1910. In 1917, approximately 90 percent of Ford motor vehicles had been assembled in the company's twenty-nine branch plants. Between 1928 and 1931, the Ford Motor Company converted or replaced its old assembly plants and added six new ones to the branch system. All the new plants were built by Albert Kahn, the architect of the Rouge, and all but one shared its access to deep-water vessels. The two-story Edgewater Assembly Plant in New Jersey has been called "the largest above-ground structure ever erected on the waterfront in the port of New York."[91]

Movable bridges spanning the narrow Rouge River still open for the occasional passage of ore carriers and other freighters. The arrival of ships and trains at the Rouge was more frequent in the 1920s and 1930s, when Charles Sheeler recorded the dramatic geometric forms of its industrial landscape in his series of renowned photographs and paintings.[92] The scale of the site is as astounding as ever, but it is no longer the integrated complex that Henry Ford created. Automobile manufacturing continues in the now enlarged factory where Model A Fords were first assembled.[93] Appropriately enough, the best view of the Rouge (unless you have an airplane) is from the modern multilane highway that crosses the river at a high elevation. Highways are among the most visible features of a national landscape and a culture transformed by the factory production of automobiles.

Factories and Mechanization

The factory system brought new levels of organization and mechanization to manufacturing industries. It spurred American productivity and, as part of the cost, put many workers in stressful or boring jobs. Seen from the managerial viewpoint, the factory building was a critical component in a system of rationalized production, a stationary frame on which to support the sinews of dynamic operations. To be effective, it had to allow or, better yet, promote profitable enterprise. It had to distribute power to and firmly support operating machinery, allow for easy movement of materials, resist combustion, retard the spread of fires, and provide adequate light, heat, and air for workers. The look of the factory was also important, for appearances helped to shape the public conception of the company. The cover illustration of the *Lowell Offering*, an 1830s magazine written by women workers but subsidized by manufacturing interests, includes a handsome factory. The cover also shows a Lowell mill girl standing next to a beehive. The symbolism is obvious: when Lowell's industrialists dreamed of the perfect factory and work force, they envisioned a hive buzzing with intense, purposeful activity.

Notes

1. Anthony Ure, *The Philosophy of Manufactures* (London: Charles Knight, 1835), p. 13; Gary Kulik, "A Factory System of Wood," in *Material Culture of the Wooden Age*, ed. Brooke Hindle (Tarrytown, N.Y.: Sleepy Hollow Press, 1981), pp. 307–312.

2. William R. Bagnall, *The Textile Industries of the United States* (New York: Augustus Kelley, 1971), vol. 1, pp. 98–99.

3. Paul Rivard, *Samuel Slater: Father of American Manufactures* (Pawtucket, R.I.: Slater Mill Historic Site, 1974); James L. Conrad, "The Making of a Hero: Samuel Slater and the Arkwright Frames," *Rhode Island History* 45 (1986): 3–13; Kulik, "Factory System of Wood," pp. 300–304; David Jeremy, *Transatlantic Industrial Revolution: The Diffusion of Textile Technologies Between Britain and America, 1790–1830s* (Cambridge, Mass.: MIT Press, 1981), pp. 83–86.

4. Bill, Benjamin Kingsley to Almy and Brown, 1793, entry 1531, Almy and Brown Papers, Rhode Island Historical Society, Providence; *Factory* 19 (August 1917): 397; William L. Case, *The Factory Buildings* (New York: Industrial Extension Institute, 1919), p. 272; C.J.H. Woodbury, "Electric Lighting in Mills," *Proceedings of the N.E. Cotton Manufacturers Association* 33 (1883): 20–21. The practical benefit of white walls was still promoted heavily in the painting advertisements in *Factory* magazine in the twentieth century.

5. Kulik, "Factory System of Wood," pp. 309–310. David Macaulay used the Slater Mill as the model for the fictional "Yellow Mill" in his beautifully illustrated book *Mill* (Boston: Houghton Mifflin, 1983). The Slater Mill is now the subject of a recording project by the Historic American Engineering Record. The authors appreciate access to the HAER drawings in progress and to a draft of the historical narrative by Emma Dyson and Louis P. Hutchins.

6. Daniel Nelson, *Managers and Workers: Origins of the New Factory System in the United States, 1880–1920* (Madison: University of Wisconsin Press, 1975), pp. ix, 3–4.

7. Kulik, "Factory System of Wood," pp. 316–318; William H. Pierson, Jr., *American Buildings and Their Architects: Technology and the Picturesque* (Garden City, N.Y.: Doubleday, 1978), pp. 33–42; Theodore Sande, "The Textile Factory in Pre–Civil War Rhode Island," *Old Time New England* 66 (1975): 13–18; Louis Hutchins and Emma Dyson, Historic American Engineering Record, report on Slater Mill, 1991.

8. *Yarns, Cloth Rooms, and Mill Engineering*, International Library of Technology, vol. 78, no. 87 (Scranton, Pa.: International Textbook, 1924), pp. 54–55.

9. See, for instance, *The Factory Mutuals, 1835–1935* (Providence, R.I.: Manufacturer's Mutual Fire Insurance Company, 1935), pp. 31–32.

10. For a brief but accurate look at Allen and some of his many achievements, see Richard Greenwood, "Zachariah Allen and the Architecture of Industrial Paternalism," *Rhode Island History* 46 (1988): 117–135. Greenwood is now completing a doctoral dissertation on Allen at Brown University.

11. Richard Candee, "The 1822 Allendale Mill and Slow-Burning Construction," *IA, Journal of the Society for Industrial Archeology* 25 (1989): 21–32.

12. The Rhode Island Historical Preservation Commission, with contributions from the National Trust for Historic Preservation, is preparing an exhibition, "The Bare Bones of Industry," that will examine the adaptive reuse of industrial buildings. Part of this project has involved photographic documentation at a number of mills, including Allendale, which has just undergone adaptation for housing.

13. Candee, "Allendale Mill," pp. 21–32. The owners of the Bernon Manufacturing Company were apparently not sure about the value of this new floor form: they built Bernon Mill No. 2 with joisted floors in 1833. Examination of one floor of that mill reveals that the joists were heavy and given additional protection by a thick plaster ceiling.

14. Robert Israel to Uncle Lewis, 9 August 1831, Collections of the Historical Society of Pennsylvania, Philadelphia. We are grateful to Steven Lubar, now at the Smithsonian Institution, for discovering this letter.

15. *Factory Mutuals*, pp. 76–77; *Report of the Commissioners . . . The Great Fire in Boston* (Boston, 1873), pp. 20–23; Samuel B. Lincoln, *Lockwood Greene: The History of an Engineering Business, 1832–1958* (Brattleboro, Vt.: Stephen Greene, 1960), pp. 90–93; Nelson, *Managers and Workers*, pp. 12–14. For information on one of the first textile mills with a very shallow gable roof (recorded by the Historic American Buildings Survey in 1968), see Richard Borden, "Manufacturing Company, Mill #1 (1873)," in *The New England Textile Mill Survey* (Washington, D.C.: Historic American Buildings Survey, 1971), pp. 3–9. The mill, despite its fire-resistant roof form, was destroyed by a conflagration in the 1980s.

16. James B. Francis, "Fall of the Pemberton Mill," *Journal of the Franklin Institute* 39 (1860): 242–250. See also Betsy Bahr, "New England Mill Engineering:

Rationalization and Reform in Textile Mill Design, 1790–1920" (Ph.D. diss., University of Delaware, 1987), pp. 27, 70–77, 134, 176–181, and C.J.H. Woodbury, *The Fire Protection of Mills and Construction of Mill Floors: Containing Tests of Full Size Wood Columns* (New York: Wiley, 1882), pp. 109–114.

17. Case, *Factory Buildings,* pp. 305, 339.

18. Carl W. Condit, *American Building* (Chicago: University of Chicago Press, 1968), pp. 46–47, 131–133; Historic American Engineering Record, documentation and recording of the Savannah Shed and Station, file GA-2, Library of Congress; David Weitzman, *Traces of the Past: A Field Guide to Industrial Archaeology* (New York: Scribner's, 1980), pp. 123–130.

19. The authors are grateful to John McGrain and Dennis Zembala for information about the Mount Savage Mill. For the two Cumberland buildings, see Historic American Engineering Record, files MD-2A and MD-2B, Library of Congress. Architect Charles Parrott, HAER recorder of the Bolt and Forge Shop, shared his ideas on truss development with the authors. He points out that there were also impressive roof trusses in industrial buildings at U.S. Army arsenals and that a new rolling mill in Phoenixville, Pennsylvania, in 1874 was 938 feet by 290 feet, with a free span of 90 feet created by an all-metal truss. See Margaret Schiffer, *Survey of Chester County, Pennsylvania, Architecture* (Exton, Pa.: Schiffer, 1976).

20. Industrial archaeologists involved in the Wilkinson Mill excavations and analysis included Albert Bartovics, Paul Rivard, Patrick Malone, Charles Parrott, Bruce Cavin, Richard Greenwood, Gary Kulik, Sandra Norman, Lisa Jensen, and many others. The maximum power of the first wheel (two were indicated by archaeological evidence and later confirmed with key documents found by Harold Kemble and John Johnson), less than 10 horsepower, was clearly insufficient to run all the machinery in a three-and-a-half-story factory. This conclusion, plus anthracite pieces and cinders found in the pit, lent credence to the claim by Edward Wilkinson, who worked there as a boy, that the mill also had a steam engine when it opened in 1810.

21. Terry S. Reynolds, *Stronger Than a Hundred Men: A History of the Vertical Water Wheel* (Baltimore: Johns Hopkins University Press, 1983); Reynolds, "The Emergence of the Breast Wheel and Its Adoption in the United States," in *The World of the Industrial Revolution: Comparative and International Aspects of Industrialization,* ed. Robert Weible (North Andover, Mass.: Museum of American Textile History, 1986), pp. 55–88. Reynolds studied the working re-creation of the Wilkinson Mill waterwheel and interviewed its builders-operators as part of his research on breast wheels. This section also draws on pilot educational materials written by Patrick Malone, Stephen Kasierski, Beth Parkhurst, Mark McDonough, and Robert Macieski (all of Slater Mill Historic Site) for the Blackstone River Valley National Heritage Corridor in 1988.

22. The governor, now in the collections of the Slater Mill Historic Site, was discovered by Gary Kulik during an HAER inventory project and recorded in place by teams under the direction of Patrick Malone and Charles Parrott.

23. See, for example, James Emerson, *Treatise Relative to the Testing of Water-Wheels and Machinery,* 4th ed. (Williamanset, Mass.: Emerson, 1892).

24. Patrick M. Malone, "James B. Francis and the Northern Canal," in *Boston's Water Resource Development: Past, Present, and Future,* ed. Jonathan B. French (New York: American Society of Civil Engineers, 1986), pp. 12–16. Francis did not include his tests of the 1847 wheel in his famous study, *Lowell Hydraulic Experiments* (Boston: Little, Brown, 1855), but voluminous data in his journals and physical evidence in

the gate house reveal an extensive program of experimentation. In 1974, Patrick Malone opened the sealed wheel pit and did an underwater exploration for the National Park Service to prove that the submerged turbine was identical to the one in engineering drawings from 1847. For an evaluation of Francis as an industrial researcher, see Edwin T. Layton, "Scientific Technology, 1845–1900: The Hydraulic Turbine and the Origins of American Industrial Research," *Technology and Culture* 20 (1979): 64–89.

25. "Table showing the number of days of backwater for each year from 1875 . . . ," Papers of the Proprietors of Locks and Canals, ND-1, Baker Library, Harvard University; Malone, "James B. Francis and the Northern Canal," p. 14; Louis C. Hunter, *A History of Industrial Power in the United States, 1780–1930*, vol. 1, *Waterpower* (Charlottesville: University Press of Virginia, 1979), pp. 330–331. There is an obvious transfer of governing technology from waterwheels to turbines, but improvements in gate and governor design produced faster turbine response to changing loads.

26. In 1991, an HAER team carefully recorded the original frame and the location of all holes, mortises, and patches on framing members.

27. Albert Bartovics, working for Directors Paul Rivard and Patrick Malone, conducted the first phase of excavations at the Wilkinson Mill. Theodore Z. Penn researched and presented theories of power system evolution in New England mills ("The Development of the Leather Belt Main Drive," *IA, Journal of the Society for Industrial Archeology* 7 [1981]: 1–14).

28. Penn, "Development of the Leather Belt Main Drive." In tracing the evolution of early power-transmission systems, Penn depends heavily on material evidence gathered at New England sites.

29. James Montgomery, *A Practical Detail of the Cotton Manufacture of the United States of America* (Glasgow: John Niven, 1840), p. 21. See also David J. Jeremy, *Technology and Power in the Early American Cotton Industry* (Philadelphia: American Philosophical Society, 1990).

30. Gary Kulik, Roger Parks, and Theodore Z. Penn, eds., *The New England Mill Village, 1790–1860* (Cambridge, Mass.: MIT Press, 1982), pp. 429–430, 435; U.S. Congress, House, *House Documents*, vol. 138, 62d Congress, 2d sess., 4 December 1911–26 August 1912 (Washington, D.C.: Government Printing Office, 1912), p. 170. We are indebted to teacher Michael Hughes for sharing his research on factory accidents.

31. Carl Gersuny, *Work Hazards and Industrial Conflict* (Hanover, N.H.: University Press of New England, 1981), pp. 55–56. Gersuny notes that Massachusetts passed a law in 1877 requiring covers for moving parts.

32. Dianne Newell and Ralph Greenhill, *Survivals: Aspects of the Industrial Archaeology of Ontario* (Erin, Ont: Boston Mills Press, 1989). The chapter on power transmission uses a great deal of physical evidence from Ontario factories and shops.

33. "The American Waltham Watch Factory," *Electrical Review,* 17 November 1888, p. 2. The authors thank Michael Brewster Folsom for providing a copy of this illustrated article. Timepieces of a slightly different form (for aircraft use) are still made in the factory at Waltham. Unfortunately, Folsom died shortly after guiding one of the authors on a tour of the plant. He was a pioneer in the field of industrial archaeology.

34. Woodbury, "Electric Lighting in Mills," pp. 18–19, 21.

35. "General Electric in the Development of the Textile Industry" (advertise-

ment/article in *Index to the Transactions of the National Association of Cotton Manufacturers,* 1926).

36. C. E. Clewell, "What It Pays to Know About Factory Lighting, III," *Factory* 19 (1917): 537–540; Woodbury, "Electric Lighting in Mills," p. 16.

37. Harold C. Passer, *The Electrical Manufacturers, 1875–1900* (Cambridge, Mass.: Harvard University Press, 1953), pp. 78–104; "General Electric."

38. J. C. Ludlum, quoted in discussion following Woodbury, "Electric Lighting in Mills," pp. 45–47; Clewell, "Factory Lighting," p. 187. Where it was available, some managers still preferred natural light for judging true colors, because incandescent bulbs could cause changes in visual perception of certain hues.

39. "American Waltham Watch Factory," p. 2.

40. *The Electric Century, 1874–1974,* reprints from *Electrical World* (New York: McGraw-Hill, 1974), pp. 31–32.

41. For a thorough discussion of the adoption of electric motor drive by textile manufacturers, see Julia C. Bonham, "Cotton Textile Technology in America: Three Centuries of Evolutionary Change" (Ph.D. diss., Brown University, 1979), chap. 4. Unusually high rooms in buildings of the Dunnell Printworks (now the site of mixed industrial operations) testify to the massive size of its printing machinery.

42. There is a rich literature of on electrification in the industrial journals and popular scientific press of the period. See, for example, the discussion in "Electrical Transmission," *New England Cotton Textile Manufacturers Association Transactions* 76 (1904): 201–206, and W. B. Woodhouse, "The Electrical Driving of Textile Machinery," *Cassier's Magazine* 38 (1910): 24–38.

43. "Driving Cotton Mills by Electricity," *Engineering News* 31 (1894): 369; Louis Bell, "Electricity in Textile Manufacturing," *Cassier's Magazine* 7 (1895): 275–284; Sidney Paine, "Electrical Driving of Textile Establishments," *New England Cotton Manufacturers Association Transactions* 58 (1895): 216–241; Bonham, "Cotton Textile Technology in America," pp. 309–314; "General Electric."

44. Patrick M. Malone and Robert Weibel, *Lowell Water Power System: Pawtucket Gatehouse Hydraulic Turbine* (Lowell, Mass.: American Society of Mechanical Engineers, 1985). See also site research by Ann Booth.

45. Arthur Safford, chief engineer, to C. P. Baker, 7 May 1918, Proprietors of Locks and Canals Business Records, DG-8, Baker Library, Harvard University. We are indebted to Alan Steiner for finding this letter and its tabulated data. His Brown University seminar paper, "The Electrification of Mills on the Lowell Canal System," has been very helpful. See also "Merrimack River Survey," 1 August 1927, in "Water Power" (notebook, Boott Mills/Proprietors of Locks and Canals).

46. Richard B. DuBoff, "The Introduction of Electrical Power in American Manufacturing," *Economic History Review* 20 (1967): 509–518; Norbert Weiner, *The Human Use of Human Beings: Cybernetics and Society* (New York: Avon, 1954), pp. 193–195; W. E. Hall, "Direct Electric-Driven Machines," *Cassier's Magazine* 7 (1895): 314–320; *Metalworking: Yesterday and Tomorrow* (New York: American Machinist, 1978), p. 63. Conversations with Matthew Roth were also helpful on this topic.

47. Laurence Gross, "Building on Success: Lowell Mill Construction and Its Results," *IA, Journal of the Society for Industrial Archeology* 14 (1988): 29–30; Case, *Factory Buildings,* pp. 337–340.

48. Quoted from stenographic records in Gross, "Building on Success," p. 32.

49. Bahr, "New England Mill Engineering," pp. 206–251, 290–293. For discussion of the effectiveness of pier construction, see Reyner Banham, *A Concrete Atlantis* (Cambridge, Mass.: MIT Press, 1989), pp. 45–49. On Whitman the "mill doctor," see Lincoln, *Lockwood Greene,* pp. 11–17.

50. Charles T. Main, *Notes on Mill Construction* (Boston: Massachusetts Institute of Technology, 1886), p. 5. See also Bahr, "New England Mill Engineering," pp. 218–221, 228–229.

51. Frank E. Kidder, *The Architect's and Builder's Pocket-Book,* 14th ed. (New York: Wiley, 1905), pp. 687–785; Edward Atkinson, "Slow-Burning Construction," *Century Magazine* 37 (1889): 566–579; Lincoln, *Lockwood Greene,* pp. 142–144, 172–174; John Stilgoe, *Metropolitan Corridor: Railroads and the American Scene* (New Haven, Conn.: Yale University Press, 1983), pp. 81–88; Woodbury, *Fire Protection of Mills,* pp. 105–117; Bahr, "New England Mill Engineering," pp. 224–232.

52. For an example of southern promotional literature, see *Industrial Georgia: Cotton Manufactures* (Georgia Railway & Power Company, 1923). See also Patrick Hearden, *Independence and Empire: The New South's Cotton Mill Campaign, 1865–1901* (DeKalb: Northern Illinois University Press, 1982); Case, *Factory Buildings,* pp. 61–63; and Charles T. Main, *Industrial Plants* (Boston: Main, 1911).

53. Nelson, *Managers and Workers,* pp. 20–21.

54. Matthew Roth, *Connecticut: An Inventory of Historic Engineering and Industrial Sites* (Washington, D.C.: Society for Industrial Archeology, 1981), p. 50.

55. We are grateful to the late Michael Folsom, who provided plans (based on his thorough research) showing the evolution of the Waltham Watch Company factory and led a guided tour of the complex.

56. "Plants of the Remington Arms Co. . . . , I," *American Machinist* 45 (1916): 881–886. The plant is still in use, occupied by General Electric.

57. Advertisement, *Factory* 19 (November 1917): 734.

58. For early use of the term "mill doctor," see Bahr, "New England Mill Engineering," pp. 77–79, 206–234, and Lincoln, *Lockwood Greene,* pp. 9–10.

59. Gross, "Building on Success," pp. 23–34.

60. Pierson, *American Buildings and Their Architects,* pp. 59–62.

61. Gross, "Building on Success," pp. 29, 32–34.

62. Patrick M. Malone, Michael S. Raber, and Beth Parkhurst, "Historical and Archaeological Assessment: Valley Falls Heritage Park" (Report for the Town of Cumberland, Rhode Island, 1991), pp. 21–22; Contract with United Building Wrecking Company, Cumberland Record of Deeds, 83:350.

63. Lawrence F. Gross, "The Importance of Research Outside the Library: Watkins Mill, A Case Study," *IA, Journal of the Society for Industrial Archeology* 7 (1981): 22. Gross also describes incremental changes in the mill's machinery and walls scarred by misdirected shuttles, topics to be covered in Chapter 9.

64. The crutches are now in the collections of the Slater Mill Historic Site. George McComiskey, a second-generation wood turner and long-time employee at the factory, provided an interpretation of the various wall hangings. The building burned soon after the staff at the historic site had accepted the donation of a large number of artifacts.

65. A letter on exhibit discusses the loss of a worker's arm in the machinery at Val Jalbert. For an examination of the role of religion in an American industrial community, see Anthony Wallace, *Rockdale* (New York: Knopf, 1978).

66. Bahr, "New England Mill Engineering," pp. 134, 186, 219.

67. Lincoln, *Lockwood Greene,* pp. 296–297.

68. David Plowden, *Bridges: The Spans of North America* (New York: Viking Press, 1974), pp. 125–137.

69. Banham, *Concrete Atlantis,* p. 63; Kidder, *Architect's and Builder's Pocket-Book,* pp. 736–747; Lincoln, *Lockwood Green,* p. 297.

70. Emory L. Kemp, "Structural Evaluation of Historic Concrete Bridges," in *Proceedings of the 3rd Historic Bridges Conference,* ed. David Simmons and Robert Sierakowski (Columbus: Ohio Historical Society, 1990), pp. 8–13; Robert W. Lesley, ed., *Concrete Factories* (New York: Cement Age Company, ca. 1907).

71. Banham, *Concrete Atlantis,* p. 32.

72. Ibid. pp. 33, 64–65, 72–80, 106–107. Two of Ransome's bridges, built in 1886 and 1887 at Golden Gate Park in San Francisco, are the first reinforced-concrete bridges in this country. Only one wall from his original building phase in Bayonne has survived a modern rebuilding program.

73. For discussion of the development of the automobile plant in America, see Lindy Biggs, "Industry's Master Machine: Factory Planning and Design in the Age of Mass Production, 1900–1930" (Ph.D. diss., Massachusetts Institute of Technology, 1987).

74. For coverage of Kahn's career and architectural achievements, see Grant Hildebrand, *Designing for Industry: The Architecture of Albert Kahn* (Cambridge, Mass.: MIT Press, 1974).

75. Banham, *Concrete Atlantis,* pp. 84–86; Hildebrand, *Designing for Industry,* pp. 28–31; Charles K. Hyde, *Detroit: An Industrial History Guide* (Detroit: Detroit Historical Society, 1980), p. 21, site 8. We are grateful to Professor Hyde, who is the authority on the industrial archaeology not only of Detroit but also of Michigan, for giving a personal tour of all the Detroit sites discussed in this book.

76. Charles K. Hyde, *The Lower Peninsula of Michigan: An Inventory of Historic Engineering and Industrial Sites* (Washington, D.C.: Historic American Engineering Record, 1976), pp. 62–63; Hildebrand, *Designing for Industry,* pp. 45–51.

77. Lindy Biggs, "The Engineered Factory" (Paper presented at the annual conference of the Society for the History of Technology, Madison, Wisconsin, 1 November 1991). We thank Biggs for generously sharing her ideas before publication. See also Hildebrand, *Designing for Industry,* pp. 52–53; Allen Nevins and Frank E. Hill, *Ford: The Times, the Man, and the Company* (New York: Scribner's, 1954), pp. 453–456; and Horace Arnold and Fay L. Faurote, *Ford Methods and the Ford Shops* (New York: Engineering Magazine, 1915).

78. Quoted in Hildebrande, *Designing for Industry,* pp. 52–53.

79. Condit, *American Building,* pp. 243–244, fig. 89; Lesley, *Concrete Factories.*

80. Greg Coppa, "Mario the Master Builder Had the Last Laugh," *Providence Sunday Journal,* 26 May 1991, p. E–2.

81. Banham, using techniques of industrial archaeology, has led the way in drawing attention to the American achievements in reinforced concrete (see *Concrete Atlantis*). For a discussion of grain elevators, see also Robert Frame, "Grain Storage and the Development of the Elevator," in *A Guide to the Industrial Archeology of the Twin Cities,* ed. Nicholas Westbrook (Washington, D.C.: Society for Industrial Archaeology, 1983), pp. 62–66.

82. Hyde, *Detroit,* p. 20.

83. Hildebrand, *Designing for Industry*, pp. 91–92.

84. Ibid., pp. 33–43; Banham, *Concrete Atlantis*, pp. 86–87; Lincoln, *Lockwood Greene*, pp. 142, 249–261, 295. Single-story construction was becoming common in textile-mill design by the turn of the century, and Lockwood Greene was very experienced in this type of construction. The Pierce complex is now a successful industrial "park."

85. Hyde, *Detroit*, site 45.

86. Ibid.; May Jane Jacob and Linda Downs, *The Rouge: The Image of Industry in the Art of Charles Sheeler and Diego Rivera* (Detroit: Detroit Institute of Arts, 1978), p. 7.

87. James J. Flink, *The Automobile Age* (Cambridge, Mass.: MIT Press, 1988), pp. 57–59.

88. Jacob and Downs, *Rouge*, p. 7; Flink, *Automobile Age*, pp. 58–59; Nevins and Hill, *Ford;* discussions with Charles K. Hyde.

89. Hyde, *Detroit*, site 45; Jacob and Downs, *Rouge*, pp. 7–42; photographs in the Archives and Library, Henry Ford Museum, Dearborn, Michigan.

90. David Hounshell, *From the American System to Mass Production* (Baltimore: Johns Hopkins University Press, 1984), p. 300; discussions with Hyde.

91. Michael S. Raber, *Ford Motor Company Edgewater Assembly Plant: Assembly Building*, HAER No. NJ-53-A (Washington, D.C.: Historic American Engineering Record, 1990), pp. 1, 4, 9; Gerald T. Bloomfield, "Coils of the Commercial Serpent: A Geography of the Ford Branch Distribution System, 1904–1933," in *Roadside America: The Automobile in Design and Culture*, ed. Jan Jennings (Ames: Iowa State University Press, 1990), pp. 40–51.

92. Jacob and Downs, *Rouge*, pp. 11–45.

93. We are indebted to Charles K. Hyde for his Historic American Engineering Record inventory work at the Rouge, for *Detroit*, as well as for personal tours and communications.

9

Work in Factories

Factories, and the factory system, are at the heart of the American industrial experience. Since the 1790s, Americans have developed many different types of factories and varieties of work within each of them. It is a terrible mistake to think of factory workers as simply automatons who do some type of mindless, repetitive task, day in and day out. The average American has never been in a factory and knows very little about what actually goes on there. Typically, there are dozens of employee classifications in one of these highly organized and hierarchical workplaces. A person employed in a factory might be a sweeper, vatman, machine operator, machine fixer, machinist, toolmaker, millwright, stockroom supplier, shipper, overseer, foreman, draftsman, electrician, or engineer. Machine operation, only one form of factory work, requires widely varying levels of skill, depending on the type of machine and the pace of production. Some jobs are routine and undemanding, but others challenge the intellect and manual dexterity of even the most skilled and experienced employees. There are tasks to be performed by one person as well as group activities that require extensive social interaction. The work culture of the factory is, and has always been, far more complex and dynamic than an organizational chart would imply.

Although factory work frequently included operations done by hand and processes that did not require any motive power, all true factories used some power-driven machinery. Mechanization was a key element in the development of the factory system. Additionally, the owners of many factories followed the principle of uniformity, aiming to make standardized products from parts that were, to some degree, interchangeable. The first American factories, as we have seen in Chapter 8, were textile mills; but soon after

Americans began to make yarn in places like the Slater Mill, they were also shifting the manufacture of products such as clocks, firearms, and edge tools from craft shops to factories.

In the 1790s, Samuel Slater's youthful operatives tended a sequence of special-purpose machines powered by a waterwheel. He regarded the manufacturing process in textile mills as a mechanized system, with a continual flow of material through successive stages of production, and he believed that this process could be achieved only with rigid work discipline.[1] In the new cotton factories, the pace of work was controlled by the speed of the machinery and was enforced by overseers. A slowing of production at any point in the system affected the entire process, for one set of machines fed the next and had to provide a steady flow of material. Other types of factories could be just as demanding of workers and managers.[2]

The factory system was based on the concept of division of labor. Managers tried to divide the process of manufacture into a series of simple, preferably mechanized operations. This was a significant departure from traditional craft practices in which one artisan drew on a number of discrete skills to make an entire article. However, it was easier to divide work than to simplify every task in a factory. Even with extensive mechanization, it was seldom possible to eliminate the need for skilled workers at some stage of production. Hand skills, such as filing metal parts, persisted into the twentieth century; and running some machines, such as the spinning mule, was never a simple job. Even machines that were easy to operate when they ran correctly might be extremely difficult to set up and require frequent adjustment. When mechanization did reduce the level of skill required to perform a particular operation, it usually created needs for skilled machine builders and maintenance specialists.

There were, and still are, differences of opinion on the best way to group machine tools in a factory. The Brown and Sharpe Company, Rhode Island's most successful manufacturer of machine tools and measuring devices, grouped its equipment by basic function or machining process. Its large factory complex had departments for milling, for grinding, and the like. Foremen in such departments were experts in the machining processes they supervised. An alternative approach was to arrange machines in a sequence that closely matched the actual steps of manufacture for a particular part. The latter procedure, most effective when production flow was highly predictable and unlikely to change, avoided many of the routing difficulties involved in shuffling parts back and forth between departments.[3]

Business historians have concentrated on entrepreneurial and managerial aspects of factory production, such as capitalization and profitability of manufacturing companies, supervision of workers, and centralized control of the flow of materials through manufacturing processes.[4] Traditional labor historians have focused on union activities and conflicts between managers and workers; only recently have "new labor historians" turned to the broader subjects of "changing work habits and the culture of work."[5] Industrial archaeologists have much to contribute to this expanding study of factory work. They are well placed to learn about mechanized processes, skills, and innovation on the shop floor; and they are eager to test historical conclusions with information that is not available in documentary sources.

Machinery as a Research Tool

Historic machines are wonderful sources of information for any student of industrial history. We sometimes find them in operation in museums, historic sites, personal workshops, or "old-fashioned" factories. Occasionally, curators will permit cautious imitative experiments with machines in their collections or will build a replica that can withstand rigorous testing. If we do nothing more than visually inspect a stationary machine, we still benefit from the opportunity to see the actual artifact in three dimensions.

When Richard Hills tested the capabilities of an Arkwright cotton-spinning frame that dated from around 1775 by running it briefly at what is now the Greater Manchester Museum of Science and Industry in the 1970s, he sent a vicarious thrill through the hearts of many industrial archaeologists, curators, and historians of technology. He also alarmed those who feared for the survival of ancient mechanisms. There have always been differences of opinion about when it is appropriate to operate historic machinery as part of exhibition, filming, or research programs.[6] Obviously, museum directors and curators must weigh the interpretive and scholarly benefits of operation against the risks of permanently damaging a particular artifact. Nevertheless, limited and carefully controlled operation is often possible for all but the rarest or most fragile machines, and there is much to be learned from studying a machine performing its function.

From observations of yarn spun in his imitative experiment, Hills concluded that this spinning frame could produce only a hard-twisted yarn "suitable for the warp of the coarser types of cloth." The drawing rollers did little to smooth out unevenness in the rovings that were fed into the machine, and yarn that was "too fine or too lightly twisted" would break during the winding process.[7] Eighteenth-century descriptions of Arkwright machinery in England or America (Slater used machines of the Arkwright type) do not provide this kind of critical, detailed evaluation. Hills also confirmed that, unlike the spinning jenny and the spinning mule, operation of a water frame required minimal skill.[8]

While a fellow at the National Museum of American History, one of the

FIGURE 9.1. Peter Liebhold and Carolyn Cooper, with advice from Martin Burke, are setting up a Lincoln milling machine for an experimental study of nineteenth-century machining technology. Liebhold is using the hand wheel under the machine to adjust the height of the spindle. After making the adjustment, he will tighten the two screws at the top to hold the spindle in place. He will use the large hand wheel to retract the table after each cut is completed. (Photographed at the National Museum of American History)

authors decided to see what was actually involved in making interchangeable precision parts using a common, nineteenth-century Lincoln milling machine (Fig. 9.1). He benefited from the assistance of a skilled machinist on the Smithsonian staff, who made a replica of an early cutter in the museum collection. In a factory, toolmakers with years of experience would have had to provide this essential support for most milling-machine operators. Adjusting the correct vertical position of the cutter on the historic machine proved to be more difficult than expected. Once set up, the miller cut metal much faster than a hand-filer could, but wear on the cutting tool (made of metal approximating the physical characteristics of the plain carbon steel used in the mid-nineteenth century) was a problem. In re-creating a production operation, the experimenters found that to achieve accuracy comparable to that which could be attained by hand-filing, they had to adjust the machine for cutter wear every forty-five minutes. As much as 25 percent of the operator's time in this experiment was spent making such adjustments. However, roughing cuts were possible with less frequent adjustment. The experiment showed why hand-filing continued to be used to attain precision long after milling machines came into use. The operation of a milling machine in a factory would not require years of training, but it was far from foolproof, and it could not produce parts of complex shape without cutters made by skilled toolmakers. In practice, it would make sense to mill parts until they were close to interchangeable tolerances, and then have filers work them to gauge.[9]

Unlike the sturdy Lincoln milling machine, some historic machines are too fragile, incomplete, or badly damaged to be operated even briefly. The Blanchard copying lathe at the Springfield Armory National Historic Site (see Fig. 9.9) is not a good candidate for powered demonstrations, but a replica at the National Museum of American History can turn a wooden blank into the rough, external shape of a gunstock with startling efficiency. This accurate replica is perfect for both scholarly experiments and regular public demonstrations. The operating principles of a Blanchard lathe will be explained later in this chapter.[10]

When an artifact of great technological significance no longer exists, written descriptions or drawings of the vanished machine may allow the manufacture of a model that closely approximates the form and operating characteristics of the original. Researcher Theodore Penn and a group of technicians at Old Sturbridge Village proved that it was possible to build a working, full-scale replica of a typical 1820s cotton-drawing frame. The new machine was a tour de force of mechanical re-creation (Fig. 9.2). However, their dream of equipping a restored factory with a complete set of operating replica textile machines was shelved by museum administrators who were concerned about the high costs of such an ambitious plan.[11]

In most cases, industrial archaeologists are forced to analyze machine operation and skill requirements without either running a historic machine or building a working replica. Simply thinking through the steps that would have to be taken to accomplish a task on a machine can be a valuable exercise.[12] The spatial arrangement of controls and adjustment points can provide clues about the operator's positioning, body movements, and visual perceptions. Close examination of the entire machine and any associated tools or spare parts is essential. Older artifacts are often worn and show signs of damage or replacement of parts. This physical evidence helps us to discover some of the problems with which factory artisans had to contend in their everyday lives.

By studying the characteristics of a mechanical artifact, we can shed light on its capabilities and gain a sense of the skills required to make and operate it. Individual machines sometimes had flaws or peculiarities that could affect their performance. Measurements of the tabletop and sliding ways of a metal planer made by John Gage between 1845 and 1851 revealed a tilt

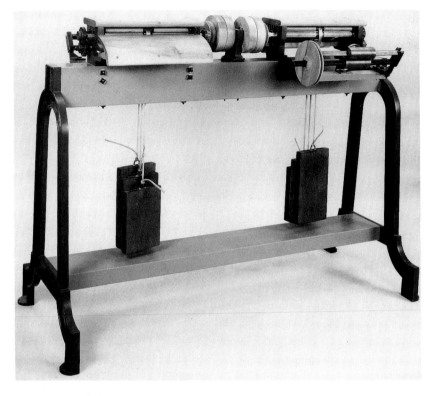

FIGURE 9.2. A full-size, operating replica of a drawing frame. This machine was constructed for Old Sturbridge Village under the direction of researcher Theodore Z. Penn. It is now on display at the Charles River Museum of Industry in Waltham, Massachusetts. (Courtesy of Old Sturbridge Village)

error that would have made it difficult to plane parallel surfaces. Others had inadvertently degraded the inherent accuracy of Gage's planer when they remachined its table, sometime after it left his shop. A machinist would have had to pack up the work on the table carefully to compensate for this tilt error. The precision that could be attained in operating the planer would depend on the skill and judgment of the operator in overcoming the faults of the machine; in good hands, this planer could make surfaces flat and parallel to within about four-thousandths of an inch. Another problem appears in the quality of castings that Gage used. The founders of cast-iron parts for this machine apparently had difficulty eliminating porosity in their products, a common foundry problem in the United States in the 1840s. However, in casting the planer's table, it appears that they designed their mold so that any porosity caused by failure to vent gases during solidification of the iron would be on the bottom side, out of sight and where it was unlikely to cause uneven wear patterns. The several zones of porosity found on the machine did not seriously impair its function.[13]

Mechanized Production

Shaping Mechanisms

Artisans used shaping mechanisms to make things that could not be produced by hand, as in turning a truly round surface with a lathe. These machines could be as useful in a craft shop as in a factory, but in a factory they were more likely to be driven by external power and to be part of a carefully planned sequence of production.

A wood turner could use a foot-treadle-driven lathe to rotate a workpiece while manipulating a cutting tool supported on a steady rest, but needed foot and hand dexterity to keep the work spinning while simultaneously guiding the cutter. With external power to spin the lathe (Fig. 9.3), it was easier to give full attention to shaping the work with the hand-held cutting tools. Experienced artisans turned wood rapidly and precisely on these powered machines.

Eli Terry produced 3,000 clocks in 1809 by assembling interchangeable wooden parts made for him by contractors. Historian Donald Hoke has

FIGURE 9.3. This lathe has a wooden bed and metal head and tail stocks. It is driven by a waterwheel in the basement of the shop through shafts and a belt. The turner grasped the cutting tool with both hands, supported one end on the steady rest, and manipulated it against the rotating workpiece to form the desired shape. (Photographed at the Log Village Grist Mill Museum, East Hartford, New York)

reconstructed the production methods used by Terry and his contractors. By studying clocks, unused clock parts, and surviving machines now in museums, he found that Terry's artisans had hand-controlled lathes (probably like the one in Fig. 9.3), drill presses, and circular saws to cut the parts to shapes specified by gauges.[14] These machines could have been human-powered, but nineteenth-century makers of wooden clocks usually worked in small factories that had water power.

Mechanized woodworking processes speeded the manufacture of parts in many industries. Some of the American machines for making gunstocks, such as the Blanchard lathe, drew international acclaim. The gunsmith's task of letting the lock into the stock had been a tedious job when chisels and gouges were used. Two examples of inletting machines made by the Ames Manufacturing Company of Chicopee, Massachusetts, in 1854 for the British Enfield Armory are preserved in museums.[15] Examination of these machines shows us that the armorer cut the lock recess in the stock by moving a rapidly rotating, powered router up and down and side to side with one lever while shifting the work back and forth with a second lever. A steel model of the recess to be cut was attached to the table that carried the stock, and a tracer pin was attached to the frame that carried the spindle. The armorer traced the pin around the model by manipulating the two levers, thereby forming the recess. The speed and pattern of cutting (within the limits set by the model) was left to the armorer's judgment, aided by sight, sound, and the feel of the cutter sensed through the operating levers. To complete the lock recess, the armorer moved five different routers successively into position by rotating the head of the machine; an experienced armorer could finish the job in less than a minute. Gunstocks inletted with this machine can be recognized by the characteristic marks left by the cutters (Fig. 1.5).

A person manipulating this type of hand-controlled machine had to tend it continuously; ill-judged movements could wreck the work or damage the cutters. The operator had full control of the pace at which the machine worked and could study the physical characteristics of the workpiece while shaping it. With experience using hand tools, an artisan would know something about the properties of different woods and the way grain orientation affects wood strength. That kind of knowledge would help in guiding the cutter. The artisan's work might be repetitious or varied, fast paced or slow, but it always demanded full attention.

Applied Power

An artisan using a power-driven machine could often avoid much of the physical labor in a task without changing the basic way the work was done. Armorers at the Springfield Armory made musket barrels from flat,

FIGURE 9.4. A tilt hammer produced a rapid succession of blows of uniform strength. The large shaft was turned by a waterwheel located just outside the wall of the shop. The iron pawls tilted the end of the hammer beam down and then released it, allowing the hammer head to fall. The smith sat in front of the anvil block, held the workpiece in tongs, and manipulated it under the hammer head to make the desired shape. (Courtesy of the Smithsonian Institution)

wrought-iron plates that were bent into cylinders and then welded to make a tube. Using hand methods, an armorer and two strikers wielding sledges made six barrels a day, welding them shut inch by inch. They found the heavy labor in the extreme heat of the forge shop debilitating. When a tilt hammer was introduced in 1815, an armorer with one helper made sixteen barrels in the same time, made better welds, and found the work healthier. At Springfield, armorers and managers were generally able to agree on new rates of pay for mechanized work without serious strife.[16]

A tilt hammer driven by a waterwheel gave a rapid succession of hammer blows of uniform strength at a rate set by the speed of the wheel (Fig. 9.4). By holding the work in tongs, a smith could use both hands to manipulate it under the hammer while judging the developing shape of the product by eye. Smiths found tilt hammers particularly useful in shaping metal into thin tools, such as knives, scythe blades, and spades.

EDGE TOOLS

Edge tools, particularly axes and scythes, were in great demand in nineteenth-century North America. A smith faced much arduous hammering in shaping an axe or a scythe and welding on the cutting edge (Chapter 6). To avoid this, entrepreneurs like Simeon North set up water-powered shops (Chapter 3) to mechanize the production of edge tools with tilt hammers. The task and methods were the same in an edge-tool factory, but smiths worked in company with many peers, making it easy to exchange ideas about improved methods. Even though the pace of work was still controlled by the individual smiths, the noise, fumes, and heat could make axe and scythe factories less attractive places to work than shops with one or two hammers.

After axes and scythes were forged to shape, other artisans ground them to their final form and finish. Workers at the Forestdale Scythe Factory in Rhode Island wore out 1 pound of grindstone in making a scythe blade that contained 4 pounds of metal.[17] These artisans were constantly breathing silica particles from the grindstones, making the work very unhealthful. As the detrimental effects of the work became known, proprietors of edge-tool works found it difficult to hire grinders. When immigrant workers were first employed at Forestdale, they were assigned to the grinding room.[18] Additionally, whenever business was brisk, artisans skilled at tilt-hammer work often took more attractive jobs elsewhere. Some scythe and axe makers found that they could attract and retain workers by carrying mechanization further.

A group of ingenious mechanics who joined the Collins Company shortly after its founding in 1826 later transformed the production of axes by replacing much of the forging and grinding by alternative techniques that went beyond reproducing a smith's handwork methods with powered machinery. The documentary record of their new production methods is poor, but artifacts enable us to reconstruct them.[19] Formerly, a smith working at a tilt hammer made an axe poll by forming, bending, and welding an iron plate (Fig. 9.5). In the new system of the 1840s, artisans formed the poll from a solid piece of iron with steady pressure and, in place of grinding, shaved the axe to final form (Fig. 9.6). An individual did most of these tasks at a series of work stations on a single machine. First, he heated a bar of iron white hot and cut it to length with a cam-activated chisel. Next he formed the hole that would become the eye of the poll with a pair of steel punches driven toward each other by the action of two lever-operated cams; he placed the hot iron between the punches where it was supported laterally by two transverse guides activated by the machine and, by stepping on a foot pedal, set the machine in motion. He knocked out the residual metal left where the two punches did not quite meet by forcing an "eye pin" entirely through the poll

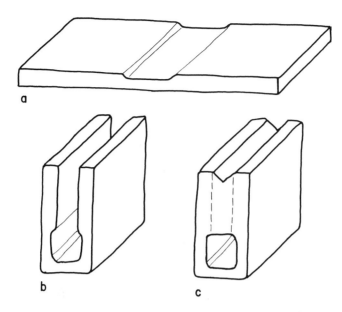

FIGURE 9.5. To form an axe poll by the method known as "plating out," a smith hammered a plate of iron to the shape shown in (a), and then bent it around a pin (b). Next, the smith inserted and welded an iron block (c). (From R. B. Gordon, "Material Evidence of the Development of Metal Working Technology at the Collins Axe Factory," IA, *Journal of the Society for Industrial Archeology* 9 [1983]: 20)

FIGURE 9.6. Study of the surficial markings on this partially completed axe poll shows how solid iron was formed into an axe shape in dies and rolls rather than by forging. Forming technology was developed at the Collins Axe Company when it proved difficult to recruit enough artisans willing to work in the company's forge shop. The steel bit is in place ready to be welded on. (Specimen from the Metallurgical Museum of Yale College. Photograph by William Sacco)

with the aid of a pair of small plattens operated by the same pair of cams. The artisan left the poll on the eye pin and passed it through a series of dies attached to rolls that moved through a partial turn forward and then reversed to release the work. After the poll was cool, machinists cut it to final form on shaving machines. In 1846, Samuel Collins set up sixteen forming machines and twenty-six shaving machines in a newly built building with waterwheels at each end to provide the mechanical power needed.

A smith and helper who made 12 polls a day working at a tilt hammer could make about 100 polls with the forming machine.[20] This machine was self-acting to only a limited degree. Some stations on the machine had stops and guides to help position the workpiece, but the operator had to transfer the work between stations, properly insert it, and then set the machine in motion for each step. Because each machine had a series of stations at which one operator could carry out all the steps required to form a poll, use of this equipment did not increase the division of labor. In this sense, Collins retained important elements of a craft production system in his factory. He eliminated the noise of the tilt hammers and much of the debilitating work of grinding. Artisans still needed some of the skills used in forging an axe with hammers, in addition to new skills. They did not have to judge the shape of the axe by eye because it was determined by the punches, dies, and patterns in the forming and shaping machines. But they did have to ascertain when the metal was at the right temperature and place the work in the forming rolls in the proper orientation and in proper registry with the die cavities. They could not make a correction once the machine was set in motion, whereas in forging under a tilt hammer the results of a few badly placed blows could be corrected with subsequent hammer strokes. Successful welding of the steel bit under the tilt hammer still depended on experience and judgment of temperature. The new forming machines helped Collins attract and retain skilled artisans. The quality of the product was much improved by the elimination of the weld in the poll, the place where handmade axes often failed. Collins axes commanded premium prices because most of them were sold to skilled users of edge tools who could discern a superior product and who were willing to pay extra for it.

DROP FORGING

Some forging tasks could be done with one hammer blow by placing the metal between dies containing a cavity that was the shape of the desired part and striking the dies with a sledge to cause the metal to fill out the cavity. French mechanician Honoré Blanc used die forging in 1778,[21] and, beginning with John Hall at the Harpers Ferry Armory in the early 1820s, many Americans experimented with the application of mechanical power to Blanc's technique. In the drop hammer, power from overhead shafting turned rollers at the top of the machine to lift a wooden plank with an attached hammerhead; the operator could disengage the rollers at any time to drop the hammer on the dies with the desired force. Guides on the side of the frame held the dies in alignment. Because of the accurate alignment and the high force applied (which caused the metal to flow into the finest detail of the die cavities), artisans could make very precise forgings with a drop hammer. The forge operator had to heat the metal to the right temperature, place it accurately between the dies, and know the correct height from which to drop the hammer. The level of skill needed was comparable to that in hand-forging with a sledge. The operator retained control of the pace of work, but worked alone rather than with a striker; this procedure may have increased the risk of injury from inattention, particularly when a long run of forgings of a given part was to be made at a high production rate. The violence of the blows struck by a drop hammer was hard on the machinery and dies and made a noisy, dangerous work environment. As we have seen, tool designers at the Collins axe works in the 1840s overcame these problems by substituting pressing and rolling technology for forging.

Self-Acting Machines

When entrepreneurs mechanized production with self-acting machines, they created new changes in the workplace because, in theory, at least, this machinery could be set in motion and left at work, unattended, until a job was completed. There were some automatic features in early sawmills and gristmills, but textile factories were probably the first plants in which workers made extensive use of self-acting equipment. Manufacturers introduced machinery with similar capability in woodworking and metalworking factories in the 1820s.

TEXTILE MANUFACTURING

Most textile machines did not need continual intervention, but things did go wrong. At first, operatives had to watch their machines very closely, looking for even minor problems and stopping any machine that developed trouble. No matter how alert they were or how keen their peripheral vision, they could not keep track of work on more than a few machines at once. It is not surprising that mill owners and machine builders in the early nineteenth century sought mechanical ways to reduce the need for constant oversight of textile machinery. They turned increasingly to automatic fault detection and stop motions. Paul Moody included these types of mechanical feedback controls on many early machines at Waltham; by 1818, he was using mechanical devices to sense breaks, to measure lengths of yarn, and to halt spinning frames when bobbins were full.[22]

FIGURE 9.7. Automatic fault detection and stop-motion devices on an early twisting frame. A long, thin metal weight hangs from each strand of yarn being drawn from the spools at the top of the machine. The machine can detect a break in any strand (sets of four are being twisted into single threads) because the broken yarn will release its attached metal weight. The falling weight then causes a chain of mechanical actions that stops the machine. (Photographed at Slater Mill Historic Site)

A sixteen-spindle twisting frame (a machine for twisting two or more yarns together) at the Slater Mill Historic Site has mechanisms that cut off power to the machine if any yarn breaks (Fig. 9.7). The Lowell Machine Shop made this frame, apparently before 1850. A small weight hangs from each strand of yarn feeding the twister spindles. Any release of tension from a break in the yarn causes one of the weights to drop, and as it falls to a lower position, it interferes with the constant motion of a rocker bar and stops the machine. The mechanical fault detection is always sensitive to every yarn, and its stopping action is faster than the hand of any operative.

Devices that made machines more nearly self-acting could significantly increase labor productivity, particularly when they allowed an operative to tend more machines. This type of mechanical improvement won wide approval by managers of American textile mills; William Burke, superintendent of Boott Mills in Lowell, recognized the cumulative value of the "many important inventions and attachments to save labor and perfect work."[23] The resistance of workers to these technological changes (and to the wage cuts, stretch outs, and speed ups that often accompanied them) was less effective in America than in Britain. After the adoption of self-acting temples by most American mills by the 1820s, weavers no longer had to stop their looms frequently to adjust the mechanisms that held the sides of the fabric and stretched it across the loom. It has been estimated that weavers spent ten minutes of every hour resetting the manual temples on power looms at the Boston Manufacturing Company before the change to self-acting forms. British weavers, fearing cuts in the piece rates (payments) for yards woven, resisted the use of these labor-saving devices until almost 1850.[24]

The adoption of self-acting machinery did not always result in setbacks for labor. Managers were disappointed to find that the self-acting mule did not give them more control over male mule spinners, who demanded high piece rates for the superior yarns their machines produced. Machine builders in both Britain and America had been working since the 1820s to perfect a cotton-spinning mule with enough automatic features to be run by unskilled workers. Despite widespread diffusion of "self-actor mules" in the United States during the 1840s and later, mule spinners remained a relatively privileged elite in many textile mills until well into the twentieth century. Improved ring spinning machines ultimately eliminated the need for mules and mule spinners. The technical complexity of self-acting mules is readily apparent to anyone who examines one in a museum collection. Because it was difficult to keep them in proper adjustment, only skilled workers could operate them. Self-acting features could increase the productivity of a mule without loss of yarn quality, but they also presented a significant mental challenge for the operator. The militant mule spinners of the nineteenth century made sure that they were paid well for their essential knowledge of machine technology and their manual dexterity.[25]

WOODWORKING

Finishing large boards with hand planes was heavy physical labor. Carpenters were quick to adopt lumber made by self-acting planing machines that converted rough-sawn timber into planks with uniform dimensions and a good finish. Designers of wood planers in the first half of the nineteenth century incorporated into their machines a power-driven cutter, a device to grip the timber, and a feed mechanism to produce a steady advance of the timber. These mechanically inclined inventors created and patented many different planing-machine mechanisms; one of these, the Daniels planer (Fig. 9.8), can be studied at Slater Mill Historic Site. Sharp blades on horizontal arms are rotated at high speed by a vertical shaft. The operator engages a power-driven feed to move the timber into the whirling cutter, which produces a plane surface with characteristic circular marks.

Machines brought drastic changes to planing work. The manual skills of manipulating hand planes were no longer needed; instead, cutters had to be sharpened and properly set into their holders (with carbon-steel cutters, this had to be done rather often), and the operator had to select the feed and speed to match the characteristics of the wood being cut. Care and experience were needed to get the timber properly secured on the table. There was risk of injury in working one of these machines because the moving parts were fully exposed, and any loose material picked up with the chips or a cutter blade that became detached could be thrown violently out of the machine. The docents who demonstrate the Daniels planer at Slater Mill stand where a vertical post of the frame provides some protection. For-

FIGURE 9.8. With a Daniels planer, a carpenter no longer had to prepare timbers with adze and hand planes. The operator clamps the rough timber on the table of the machine, sets the cutters in motion by engaging a belt from overhead shafting, and starts the automatic feed. With the hand crank at the side of the center post, the operator can adjust the depth of the cut at any time. This machine was originally in a water-powered machine shop at the Crown and Eagle Mills, North Uxbridge, Massachusetts. (Photographed at Slater Mill Historic Site)

362

FIGURE 9.9. This gunstock lathe was probably built by Thomas Blanchard at the Springfield Armory in 1826 to replace the original lathe, which had been destroyed by fire. The gear train (left background) rotates the stock and the model in synchronism while the cutter is guided by the tracer wheel following the model (right background). The iron carriage traverses the cutter and follower along the length of the workpiece. Once the operator sets the machine in motion, it continues cutting until the task is done and then shuts off automatically. (Photographed at the Springfield Armory National Historic Site)

tunately, this is a perfect position from which to manipulate the control levers; the designers must have understood the dangers and placed the controls accordingly.

One of the best-known self-acting woodworking machines is the irregular lathe invented by Thomas Blanchard in 1819 for turning objects that were not figures of revolution, such as axe handles. Blanchard mounted the workpiece and a model of the object to be made on horizontal spindles geared together to turn in synchronism. He placed a rapidly rotating cutter wheel on a frame that moved in and out as the follower wheel rolled over the model. As both work and model slowly revolved, the cutter reproduced the form of the model on the workpiece. The Blanchard lathe made in 1826 and now preserved at the Springfield Armory National Historic Site was used to rough out the butt ends of gunstocks (Fig. 9.9). Like most American machinery of this period, it has a heavy wooden frame, cast-iron gears, wooden pulleys, and leather belts. The operator clamped the roughly sawn stock

FIGURE 9.10. This hand grip for a modern Bren gun was turned on one of the Blanchard lathes made by the Ames Company of Chicopee, Massachusetts, for the Enfield Armory in England in 1854. These machines remained in service for over 100 years. The rapidly rotating cutter advancing along the slowly revolving workpiece made the spiral pattern of tool marks.

blank in place, shifted the carriage so the tracer wheel was at one end of the model, and set the lathe in motion. In principle, the operator could leave the machine unattended, since an automatic stop disengaged the feed when the carriage reached the other end of the model. All this artisan had to do was insert the stock, start the machine, and, later, remove the product. When we study the surviving machine and the working replica at the National Museum of American History, we find that dexterity and judgment were needed to place the workpiece in the machine correctly and to deal with irregularities in the wood. The operator needed mechanical experience to sharpen and adjust the cutters, to compensate for stretching of the belts, and to keep a complex, imperfectly made mechanism operating. Since the

Blanchard lathe did only rough shaping (Fig. 9.10), skilled armorers working with hand tools had to complete the stocks.

METALWORKING

The oldest surviving example of an American self-acting, metal-cutting machine is the miller that Eli Whitney III found in the barn of the Whitney Armory (Fig. 9.11). Edwin Battison describes it as the type of machine used at John Hall's rifle works at Harpers Ferry and suggests that it may have been made about 1827 in Connecticut.[26] When we look at this machine closely, we see that it has a substantial cast-iron frame and was probably made by artisans working from a drawing with calipers. These men had an engine lathe capable of cutting threads and holding dimensions to a few thousandths of an inch, but the fact that all the flat surfaces were filed by hand shows either that they had no milling or planing machine or, if they did, it was not capable of achieving the accuracy they wanted. The turning, threading, dovetailing, and fitting of the parts were done in a professional manner, showing that the builders were thoroughly proficient in their work. Several essential parts are now missing from the machine. The milling

FIGURE 9.11. Robert Vogel, curator emeritus of engineering at the Smithsonian Institution, is measuring the "Whitneyville" milling machine at the New Haven Colony Historical Society. The drive pulley, table, and cutter had been lost when the machine was recovered from Eli Whitney's barn in the early twentieth century. The makers of this machine took more care with its appearance and construction than Blanchard did with his lathe (Fig. 9.9), made just a few years earlier. (Photographed at the New Haven Colony Historical Society)

cutter would have been mounted on the end of the spindle, and there would have been a pulley on the other end for the drive belt. A table to carry the workpiece would have been fitted into the dovetail ways.

The Whitneyville miller was convenient to use once it was set up for a specific job. The operator stood in front with all the controls at hand, clamped the work on the table, set the cutter in motion by shifting the overhead belt with a handle that would have been placed just above the machine, and engaged the power feed by lifting up the pivoted feed shaft with the handle provided on its end. Theoretically, the machine could then be left unattended until it shut itself off at the end of the cut. The operator then unclamped the work and retracted the table by spinning the hand crank and was ready for the next piece. The work could be routine if all went well, but when we use similar machines today, we find that this could not be counted on. The operator had to apply coolant or cutting oil to the cutter more or less continually and adjust the speed and feed to compensate for wear of the cutter and for inhomogeneities in the metal stock used.

The common assertion that the adoption of self-acting machines like the Whitneyville miller eliminated artisans' handwork skills in making metal parts for mechanisms such as firearms is not correct. Throughout the nineteenth century, artisans working with files and gauges routinely attained higher levels of dimensional accuracy than could be reached with machine tools. Most of the fine work needed to meet ever-increasing standards of precision remained in these artisans' skilled hands.[27] The use of self-acting machines also created a need for new skills. Artisans had to make the cutters used in those machines, heat treat them to the proper hardness, and then sharpen them frequently. They had to design and make fixtures to hold the work and had to set up machines for each new job. As proprietors adopted self-acting woodworking and metalworking machinery, they reduced the physical labor that mechanics expended on cutting and shaping, but they could not eliminate all the tasks that required both skilled hands and a good mind.

PROGRAMMABILITY AND AUTOMATIC SELECTION

Programmed control of machine operation, which has become so crucial in modern industrial engineering, owes a major debt to such textile innovations as Jacquard, chain-pattern, and Dobby-head looms. These programmable adaptations of the basic loom allowed wide variation in woven patterns. William Crompton, who had immigrated to Massachusetts from Britain, invented a system using a pattern chain for automatic selection of loom harnesses in his first loom in 1837. The harnesses were used to raise or lower sets of warp threads in a programmed sequence.[28] By the late 1850s, the competing fancy looms developed by George Crompton (William's son)

FIGURE 9.12. This Furbush loom, built around 1870, can be programmed to weave fancy patterns. Its drop boxes hold three shuttles, each of which can carry weft of a different color. Here the loom is weaving a plaid fabric. The electric motor drive is a recent addition. (Photographed at the Museum of American Textile History)

and by Lucius Knowles included drop boxes for automatic shuttle selection. These boxes (magazines holding several shuttles) made inevitable the demise of American industrial hand weavers, who had continued to dominate the production of fancy woven goods long after the introduction of the basic power loom. An operating Furbush drop-box fancy loom of around 1870 at the Museum of American Textile History uses a roller chain to select harnesses and another, in conjunction with cams, to operate its three drop boxes (Fig. 9.12). The loom automatically chooses shuttles carrying particular colors of weft and raises or lowers appropriate sets of warp threads for each pass, or pick, of a chosen shuttle.[29]

Perhaps the most impressive engineering achievement of textile-machinery builders was the solution of the problem of changing bobbins in the shuttles of high-speed looms. Weavers were stopping looms up to a hundred times a day to replace the empty weft bobbins by hand. A loom could hold miles of warp on its beam, but relatively little weft on the bobbin carried by its shuttle. Continual, mechanized production, with interruption only to halt damage to machine, product, or worker, was a long-desired goal; but the flying shuttle of a power loom seemed inaccessible unless the loom was stopped. Eventually, a transplanted Englishman named James H. Northrop developed the key features for an automatic loom while working for the Draper Company in Hopedale, Massachusetts. The Northrop loom, known as the Model A Draper, was perfected with American engineering assistance by 1894, and it greatly speeded the weaving of cloth.[30] The rare early example at the Slater Mill Historic Site has automatic bobbin changing while the loom is in operation, warp and weft stop motions (to halt the loom if a warp or weft yarn breaks), and smash protection (to prevent damage from a shuttle being trapped in the "shed" of the warp). With machines like this in their mills, textile managers moved to increase the number of looms that a weaver operated; production soared on these automatic machines. The strain on weavers (and loom fixers), now responsible for far more machines, was a negative side effect seldom considered in an industry dedicated to mass-production. However, the new looms did eliminate the need for workers to use their mouths to suck filling yarn (weft) through a hole in the older "kiss of death" shuttle. Mechanized rethreading, which was part of the automatic bobbin-changing process, was thought to reduce the spread of tuberculosis in factories. Actually, it was more effective in reducing the risk of other diseases, including byssinosis, the "brown lung" illness caused by inhalation of cotton dust; we now know that tuberculosis was not likely to be transmitted through shuttle kissing.[31]

Transfer Machines

Transfer machines automatically shifted work or tools between successive operations either within a shop or within a machine. In the system of flour milling designed by Oliver Evans in 1786, the miller received grain at one end of a gristmill and dispatched flour from the other end without any shifting of materials by hand. Bucket elevators lifted grain and flour from floor to floor, and screw conveyors moved it at each level. Mechanical devices spread the grain for cooling and drying before passing it to the bolters. Evans used familiar mechanisms; the novelty of his design was more in the concept of continuous production than in the means for accomplishing it. American millers were adopting Evans's system within a few years of the completion of his first automated mill.[32]

The first American textile factory also incorporated mechanical methods for conveying materials during manufacturing processes. Slater's spinning frames unwound cotton roving from spools, drew it through a series of rollers, spun it with a revolving flyer, and then wound the spun yarn on a bobbin. Industrial archaeologists who examine textile mills and machinery

FIGURE 9.13. An Apperly feed for a wool-carding machine. A continuous rope of wool is being transferred from one machine and fed into the next in the production process. (Photographed at Upper Canada Village)

have determined that the method of moving materials on, off, or between machines was a critical part of the nineteenth-century manufacturing system. John Goulding of Massachusetts invented a condenser in 1826 that drew a continuous sliver of wool from a carding machine. After mid-century, the imported Apperly feed allowed the mechanical transfer of wool from one carding machine to another without human intervention (Fig. 9.13).[33] Variations on both these devices are in operation for the public at the nineteenth-century woolen mill of Upper Canada Village, near Morrisburg, Ontario.

The important textile antecedents to the conveyor systems used in automobile assembly lines have received less attention from historians of technology than they deserve. Proprietors of both cotton and woolen mills cut labor costs and increased production with machinery that moved, measured, and carefully "handled" fiber materials at various stages of manufacture. The need for efficient transfer of materials (through tubes, chutes, elevators, passageways, and towers) also influenced the design of new mills and caused frequent alteration of older ones.

Where manufacturers wanted to make large numbers of standardized objects, such as nails or pins, by a sequence of forming or cutting operations, they adopted mechanical transfer of the work between steps to eliminate the need for highly repetitive hand movements. Americans needed large quantities of nails. They made them by casting from molten iron, hand-forging from rod, cutting strips from plates, or forming from wire. The cast nails used in the late eighteenth and early nineteenth centuries were malleablized cast iron; carpenters chose them when they wanted a nail shape that could not be made easily by forging.[34] Cast nails can usually be recognized by the flash retained at the parting line of the mold in which they were cast. Smiths made hand-forged nails out of nail rod cut from plates in a slitting mill (as at the Saugus ironworks [Chapter 3]). The nailer heated the end of the rod to forging temperature, tapered it with hammer blows on an anvil, cut it, dropped it into a die, and headed it by hammering over the exposed end. About twenty-five hammer strokes completed a nail. An old nail that is not badly rusted can be identified as handmade from the traces of the hammer marks on it; if rusted, its internal structure may distinguish it.

Beginning about 1790, many American inventors devised machines that would cut nails out of cold iron plate; Thomas Jefferson bought one in 1796. Some were hand-operated; the nailer placed the iron plate on a die block fitted with a hold-down mechanisms and sheared off the nails with a knife driven by turning a high-pitch screw. Since cut nails are tapered, the operator had to either wiggle the plate or turn it over between cuts. The nailer formed the head in a separate machine by clamping the cut blank in a die block and striking one blow with a lever-operated hammer. It was relatively

FIGURE 9.14. This nailer is cutting large nails off a steel plate that he manipulates by hand. He has to position the plate for the next cut each time the knife blade is opened by the mechanism. The belt drive in the rear powers the machine. (Photographed at the Tremont Nail Works, Wareham, Massachusetts)

easy to apply power to drive the knife of a nail-cutting machine. By the 1830s, inventors had devised automatic headers, but they did not work out an automatic feed that would eliminate the need to manipulate the nail plate between knife strokes until late in the nineteenth century.[35] Artisans made cut nails from plates whose width equaled the length of the nail until about 1840; the length of the nail therefore fell in the transverse direction of the plate. When wrought iron was used, the fiber of the iron was transverse to the length of the nail. Since wrought iron has a lower strength and ductility in the direction transverse to its fiber, cut nails made this way lacked ductility and could not be "clinched" (the ends bent over to prevent withdrawal).

When ironmasters acquired rolling mills that could make iron plate wide enough, strips with a width equal to the length of the nails could be cut off crosswise. The nails made from these strips had the fiber of the iron parallel to the length of the nail. Making cut nails by hand on a powered machine was repetitive work; the operator was expected to rotate (flip) the plate through a half-turn after each cut and insert the plate under the knife in time to catch the next downstroke (Fig. 9.14). Proprietors of nail factories automated the work by building transfer machines that rotated the plate between cuts and shifted the nail to a header die, where the end was struck by a punch to form the head. Instead of standing at one machine, the nailer fed stock into a number of machines, a task that took less manual skill.

Manufacturers in the New York area began to make wire nails in the 1850s. Most customers preferred them because of their relatively low cost. The shape, surficial markings, and internal structure of a nail can sometimes be used to place limits on its date of manufacture.[36] David Wilkinson, owner of a Pawtucket slitting mill, bought a nail-cutting machine about 1816. Archaeologists used the different kinds of nails found in the floorboards of the wheel pit of his mill to date its successive rebuildings (Chapters 2 and 8).[37]

An automatic pin-making machine had to cut wire to the desired length, upset one end to make the head, and point the other end. Making a mechanism that could handle the small, delicate pins as they passed through the successive stages of fabrication was a challenge that intrigued American mechanicians, and, starting with Moses Morse in 1814, they patented a succession of designs. John Howe's machine, based on his patent of 1841, was probably used in the 1850s and is now at the National Museum of American History (Fig. 9.15).[38] The devices that produce the motions of the machine (gears, cams, and levers) and the tools that make the pins (shears, upsetting dies, rotary files, and abrasive belts) were all common mechanical elements in 1842, and the principal novelty in Howe's design was his method of handling the pins, particularly the difficult task of turning them end for

FIGURE 9.15. A Howe pin machine, viewed from above. In order to reverse the pins after they have been headed, they are transferred between chucks mounted on the two rotating heads. The rotation of these heads passes the pins through a series of work stations; the chucks themselves rotate to form the circular section of the pins. (Courtesy of the Smithsonian Institution)

end after the heads were formed so that the points could be made. In Howe's transfer mechanism, chucks on the small diameter wheel grip cut lengths of wire for transfer to the header. They were then picked up by other chucks on the large diameter wheel, thereby reversing them so that the points could be passed over a succession of rotary files and abrasive belts arranged around the periphery of the large circle. The mechanism is exposed to full view in the machine and adds to the interest of watching it in operation. The Smithsonian curators who ran Howe's machine found that the mechanician who set it up and got it operating in steady production faced a formidable task in adjusting the components so that all the motions functioned as intended; effecting the transfer of the pins between the two circles was particularly difficult. The widespread use of machines such as this in the 1850s shows that many artisans had acquired mechanical skills that would have been almost nonexistent in the United States two decades earlier. As entrepreneurs adopted transfer machines, they released many people from the tedious, repetitive labor of making products such as pins and nails by hand, while creating a need for mechanicians capable of setting up and maintaining the machinery.

Standardization and Uniformity

French officers serving in the newly established U.S. Army in the early days of the republic were strong advocates of the principle of uniformity in manufactured products. Their ideal was that the parts of any weapon should be interchangeable with the corresponding parts of any other weapon of the same kind. Most mechanicians agreed that a degree of uniformity was useful—military supply was simpler and more reliable if every musket used the same size ball—but the notion of uniformity became an obsession in the Ordnance Department that was carried far beyond operational needs. The department made it the primary goal for the national armories and private contractors, without much regard for cost or benefits. During the nineteenth century, the principle of uniformity was usually adopted in the civilian sector only to the degree that it was economically useful in the production process.[39] Three new factors created an increased demand for uniformity in the twentieth century. First, perfect interchangeability was needed for products made on an assembly line because there was no time for fitting. Second, the expanded interpretation of manufacturers' liability for product performance required that every item be produced to be a duplicate of its mates. Third, consumers and most providers of repair services were no longer expected to do more than substitute replacement parts. With this deskilling of consumers, new parts had to function without adjustment.

Gauges

Under the principle of uniformity, an artisan could no longer shape the components of a mechanism to his own taste. Designers transmitted their specifications to artisans by gauges that specified the size and shape of each component of a mechanism. The centralized control that managers and designers intended to exercise over these artisans' work was expressed through gauges. It is still widely believed that this control was as complete as nineteenth-century writers claimed. New archaeological evidence now shows that this notion is incorrect.[40]

When a product such as a rifle was made entirely by one armorer, each part could be individually shaped according to that individual's preference, provided only that the finished product performed as desired. In a craft shop, the artisan's discretion might be curtailed if the master prescribed a specific method of working or if strict division of labor was practiced. As the principle of uniformity was gradually adopted by manufacturers from 1798 onward, artisans had to make products that conformed to design specifications chosen by others and expressed in tangible form by gauges and inspection procedures. The skill of making a set of parts to function as a whole was replaced by that of judging compliance to a gauge or, later, to dimensions specified numerically. The adoption of gauges in the nineteenth century, and of dimensional tolerances in the twentieth, along with the specification of chemical and physical properties of materials, diminished the discretion that individual artisans could exercise in some aspects of their work and, at the same time, increased the demand for new skills and methods of attaining higher standards of precision.

Through the first two-thirds of the nineteenth century, drawings, dimensions, and numerical measurements had little place in artisans' work. The designer's intentions were expressed in a prototype that was to be duplicated by the mechanic. Since piece-by-piece comparison with the prototype was impractical in a shop of any size, managers introduced gauges to facilitate the comparisons. The underlying principle of mechanical gauging is illustrated in Figure 9.16. Each dimension of the wooden spool is shown by the

FIGURE 9.16. The principle of gauging developed in the nineteenth century is illustrated by this metal gauge for wooden spools. The different slots and grooves in the gauge show the dimensions to which the spool is to be made. How closely the finished spool fits the gauge is a matter of judgment. (Photographed at Slater Mill Historic Site)

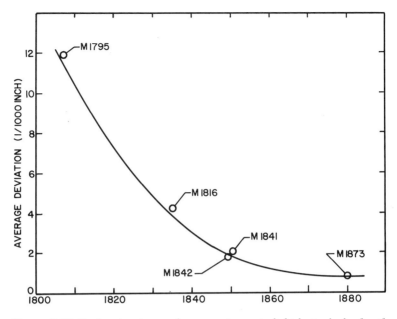

FIGURE 9.17. During the nineteenth century, increasingly high standards of uniformity were achieved in making parts for the small arms used by the U.S. Army. Until 1892, the basic design of the lock mechanism used for muskets and, later, rifles changed very little. The graph shows the average deviation in thousandths of an inch among examples of one lock part, the tumbler, made at the national armories and by private contractors. Throughout this time period, artisans filed the machined parts by hand to meet dimensions specified by gauges. The different models of weapons are designated by the years in which they were introduced. (From R. B. Gordon, "Who Turned the Mechanical Ideal into Mechanical Reality?" *Technology and Culture* 29 [1988]: 762)

size of one of the slots cut in the metal gauge. This gauge is not an absolute standard because the closeness of the fit of any one spool to the gauge remained a matter of judgment. Hence, to use this kind of gauge, artisans and inspectors had to reach an understanding on how close a fit was acceptable. Such understandings could easily be upset by new managers or changes in personnel in the shop.

As managers put more gauges in factories, they created a need for gauge-making, a new kind of exacting work. Through much of the nineteenth century, gauge-makers worked with hand tools. They had to bring each pair of gauging surfaces to the required dimension by repeated trials on the prototype, and a single file stroke could ruin an entire gauge. The increase in the standards of quality for mechanical work can be seen by examining successive generations of small arms made for the Ordnance Department. The improvement in dimensional uniformity has the form of a learning curve (Fig. 9.17). By the 1870s, the gauge-maker's art was expressed in elaborate, beautifully made symbols of standardization and precision, such

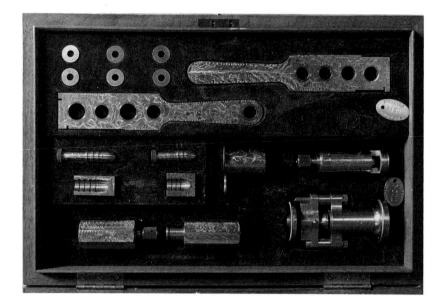

FIGURE 9.18. Standard gauges for the .45 caliber rifle and revolver cartridges used by the U.S. Army in 1877. There are three distinct types of gauges in the set. As in the early gauge sets, there are models of the cartridge cases and bullets as well as groove gauges to show their lengths. The receiving gauges have holes that specify the maximum and minimum diameters for the front and back ends of the cartridge cases. The gauge for measuring the thickness of the head of the cartridge case for the rifle works on the micrometer principle; the dial shows the number of thousandths of an inch that the thickness is above or below standard. These gauges are not hardened (to achieve greatest accuracy) and were intended for checking production gauges. Decorative finish has been applied to the nongauging surfaces. (Photographed at the Springfield Armory National Historic Site)

as the master gauges for the .45 caliber military cartridges (Fig. 9.18). Companies such as Pratt and Whitney made similar gauges for the private sector.

The uncertainties of judgment and discretion in inspection could be reduced by a gauging system that specified tolerances, the acceptable range of size and shape in a product. A "go/no-go" (limit) gauge has openings that specify the greatest and least acceptable size for each dimension to be gauged; the part had to fit into one opening but not the other. The designer had to decide on the range allowed for each dimension by balancing the costs and benefits of working to closer tolerances. This was a difficult determination to make for a mechanism containing more than two or three parts, and it was usually carried out by trial and error until the advent of computer-aided design procedures. Few gauges used in the nineteenth century specified tolerances. Engineers worked out practical tolerances and inspection procedures in the early years of large-scale production of automobiles. In principle, the introduction of limit gauges could simplify the relationship between artisans and inspectors by reducing discretion in judging how well a part conformed to a gauge. By giving artisans definite standards to work to, limit gauges protected them from arbitrary judgments by inspectors and managers. But these standards also diminished opportunities for artisans to exercise judgment skills.

Numerical Methods

As early as the 1850s, European engineers were discussing the specification of dimensions on drawings as an alternative to a model that represented the designer's intentions.[41] However, the lack of measuring instruments suitable for shop use slowed adoption of numerical methods. American manufacturers took the lead in producing instruments that artisans could use in their daily work beginning with the manufacture of steel vernier calipers by Brown and Sharpe in 1851 and the introduction of gauges based on the pivot indicator at the Waltham Watch Company in the early 1860s.[42] The most important step toward numerical control of mechanical work was the manufacture of micrometer calipers on a production basis started by Brown and Sharpe in 1867 and subsequently taken up by Starrett, Slocomb, and others. Slocomb, in particular, aimed to produce micrometer calipers at a low enough cost that every mechanic could own one. Artisans had to learn new skills as designers began to put numerical dimensions on mechanical drawings in the 1870s.[43] At the same time, an important obstacle to incremental improvement of products was removed because engineers could alter a design by changing a drawing instead of ordering a new set of gauges. Machinists simply set their micrometers to the new dimensions. These artisans also changed the way they worked at machines. A machinist measured the size of a workpiece, calculated the amount of metal that had to be removed, and set the machine accordingly. The relatively rapid adoption of these techniques in the United States, particularly as compared with Britain, may reflect the higher level of education attained by American artisans as well as their greater willingness to accept new methods. These factors were important in bringing the United States to world leadership in manufacturing technology.[44]

Jigs, Fixtures, Cutters, and Dies

Because many of the machine tools used to make uniform parts were general-purpose machines, artisans equipped them with special combinations of jigs, fixtures, cutters, and dies for particular operations. Fixtures are attached to machines and hold workpieces in position, while jigs are

FIGURE 9.19. This Pratt and Whitney Lincoln-type milling machine has been set up with a cutter shaped to form the curved surface of a part for a shotgun. The cutter is mounted on an arbor supported at each end and is rotated by the belt and gears at the left. The workpiece is clamped in the special fixture beneath the cutter; the pipe above drips coolant on the cutter while the machine is operating. (Photographed at the former Winchester Repeating Arms Company factory, New Haven, Connecticut)

usually attached to the workpieces and guide cutting tools.[45] Jigs and fixtures were important components of the production systems for wooden clocks developed by Eli Terry and his successors,[46] and for metal mechanisms developed by John Hall and others. Astute managers found that artisans working on the shop floor often devised the best designs for jigs and fixtures. When arranged so that finished work could be quickly released and new work inserted, they allowed machine operators to spend most of their time shaping metal rather than setting up work.[47]

To mill an irregular surface, a machinist used a cutter shaped to the desired curve (Fig. 9.19). Elite machinists (often called toolmakers), who had learned their art through experience, designed and built cutters. The rate at which wood or metal could be cut was usually limited by the endurance of the cutter rather than by the power of the machine. As shown in the experiments described at the beginning of this chapter, a worn cutter made parts of the wrong shape, and the machine operator had to judge when to resharpen or replace it. Experienced machinists took pride in sharpening and setting their own cutting tools, but in shops where production machines were tended by less skilled operators, worn cutters were resharpened by specialists. Machinists had to learn new metallurgical skills to harden cutters properly after they were formed to the desired shape. In the hands of the inexperienced, a cutter made with the expenditure of many hours of labor could easily be cracked in heat treatment (Fig. 9.20). Good judgment was needed to attain the correct balance between hardness and toughness. As machine tools came into common use, many artisans had to learn the techniques of making and hardening cutting tools.

Through most of the nineteenth century, artisans made cutters out of carbon steel, which would take a fine, hard edge but would not retain that edge well under heavy use. Machinists raised the limitation on machining rates set by the carbon-steel cutters when they adopted "high-speed steel," an alloy that, if properly heat-treated, would retain a sharp edge at the temperatures generated by machine tools running at high speed. Robert Mushet made the first high-speed steel in 1868, but machinists made little use of these alloys until Frederick W. Taylor and others completed systematic tests in the early twentieth century to find alloy compositions, heat-treating procedures, and cutting fluids that produced the best results. To take advantage of the new tool steel, machine-shop proprietors had to replace a whole generation of tools with much heavier machines that could hold

FIGURE 9.20. This nineteenth-century milling cutter found at the site of the machine shop of the Carolina Mills in Rhode Island has cracked because of stresses created in it during hardening. To successfully harden a carbon-steel cutter, it must be heated red hot and then quenched in water or oil. The teeth at the rim cool faster than the thicker interior. When the interior does reach low temperature, the rim is already hard; as the interior transforms to the hard constituent in steel (martensite), it expands and places the rim under tension. A crack has run in from the rim of this cutter through the tension zone and then branched as it reached the interior. The outside diameter of the cutter is 2.34 inches, and it has ninety teeth. (Courtesy of the Smithsonian Institution)

correct dimensions under the high forces developed at increased cutting rates.[48] Taylor subsequently exploited the reputation he gained from his metallurgical accomplishments to advance his social theories about organization and control of the workplace.[49]

In mechanized manufacturing, toolmakers made the jigs, fixtures, and cutters used in production. In forge shops, die sinkers worked like sculptors with hand tools to shape steel dies that were then hardened to a temper that could withstand the shocks of prolonged use, itself a specialized art. Toolmakers and die sinkers, together with the pattern makers discussed in Chapter 6, were a triumvirate of highly skilled artisans essential to the production of metal products. Each had to use abstract concepts that would have been uncommon in mechanics' work before the advent of factories. The die sinker made a negative image of the part to be forged. The pattern maker worked with a positive image created in wood and made oversize by an amount just large enough to compensate for the shrinkage of the metal during solidification. Toolmakers created three-dimensional objects to precise size and shape and often had to work with drawings based on projections of the finished product. All these tasks called for mental as well as manual agility.

Incremental Innovation on the Shop Floor

Historians of manufacturing technology have focused on particular machine innovations and, to a lesser extent, on system developments that had a major impact on industrial production. In so doing, they have largely ignored the incremental changes that, taken together, may have been much more important. Engineering drawings and documentation of small modifications in machinery or technical processes were less likely to be saved than were the records of great inventions. Incremental innovations by workers on the shop floor were so common in many industries that they received little notice. Few of these modest improvements were ever patented, and many were made directly from the mental conceptions of their inventors without sketches or written specifications.[51]

Nathan Rosenberg has called attention to the stultifying effects of what he labeled "Schumpeterian blight," the prevailing historical emphasis on technological leadership and on "the more dramatic and discontinuous aspects of innovation." He urged historians to study "the cumulative impact of relatively small innovations (which were of great importance in the design, development, and adaptation of machines)." Rosenberg has praised those who see the normal pattern of technological progress as "steady accretion of innumerable minor improvements and modifications, with only very infrequent major innovations."[52] Recently, Philip Scranton noted the importance of Rosenberg's insights for labor historians and bemoaned the absence of scholarship on the technical development that takes place on the shop floor: "The history of workers' role in incremental technical change remains as opaque today as the general history of the workplace was two decades ago."[53]

Old manufacturing machinery is seldom found in the exact form described by original patent records, company advertisements, and contemporary technical publications. Physical evidence of technological change is usually apparent upon examination of this machinery; it ranges from long lists of dated patents on machine frames to altered parts and added features. Sometimes a machine is a hybrid form made up of components from several other machines and special-purpose devices made in the user's shop. At the Dudley Shuttle Company in Wilkinsonville, Massachusetts, retired foreman Harold Swenson pointed out a number of machines that he had designed and built to answer the particular needs of shuttle manufacturing. Inspection of his machines in the factory proved that he frequently cannibalized broken or spare machines for parts.[54]

Some changes were intended as short-term solutions to problems in limited production runs.[55] Many historic machines have mysterious components seemingly unrelated to their last known use. Industrial archaeologists look for the marks of previous attachments on a machine and for the bin of old fixtures or cutting tools that may reveal past functions and capabilities. Creative adaptation was also a very good way for managers to take advantage of technical ideas and suggestions from company employees.

Managers who contributed directly to the technical development of machines and production systems were far more common in past generations than they are today. By the end of the nineteenth century, the engineering staffs in many large firms had taken responsibility for innovation and production improvements, but technical ideas continued to flow back and forth between all levels in the company hierarchy. Staffing charts and written statements of roles and responsibilities seldom give an accurate picture of the way technical ideas are actually generated and put into practice in a manufacturing company.

The textile industry is a good place to study incremental innovation on the shop floor because it is a highly diversified industry that is subject to sudden changes in market demands and public tastes. Textile mills that depended on "batch" manufacturing rather than long runs of standardized products needed technical flexibility. Mill operatives, loom fixers (Fig. 9.21), overseers, machinists, and foremen made many of the improvements and modifications in textile machinery. George Draper credited much of his success as a machinery manufacturer to ideas that were developed in the textile mills: "Many of the important improvements originate in small, out of

FIGURE 9.21. A loom fixer in a Pennsylvania carpet mill. This job has always required a great deal of skill. Fixers not only set up, adjust, and repair complex looms, but also modify them for particular applications. Many incremental improvements in weaving technology have come from the creative minds of these artisans.

the way mills." Acknowledging the value of shop-floor innovations in general, Draper reported that by 1872 he "had distributed over $225,000 in cash among inventors. This amount had been paid mainly to overseers and others who were men of moderate circumstances." A. G. Cumnock, a textile manufacture in Lowell, agreed: "Our mechanics and overseers are mostly poor men, and most of the inventions of any value have come from them."[56]

Looms were complex products of the cumulative efforts of many individuals and firms. George Hutchins, who worked in loom development from 1873 to 1928, said that "the Knowles Loom was not invented at any one time, but came into existence through a long series of inventions."[57] The same could be said of all the well-known Draper automatic looms. One Model E Draper loom at the Museum of American Textile History carries a manufacturer's plate listing 134 applicable patents dating from 1912 to 1927; the obvious debt to designers from the nineteenth century and earlier is not mentioned.

Major inventions in the textile industry always incorporate preexisting elements or ideas, and "new" machines are seldom successful without further refinement. Evolutionary changes were far more common than revolutionary developments. Few of these modifications, which were often conceived and implemented by anonymous artisans in factories, were ever patented. Laurence Gross has commented on the diversity of power-loom designs represented in the surviving machinery at the Watkins Mill in Lawton, Missouri (Fig. 9.22). Without the material evidence in that factory, "these alternative efforts, would otherwise have remained unknown, lost amid the plethora of patented inventions."[58]

Weavers and other machine operators whose jobs we might consider repetitive and boring were often keen observers of mechanical functions and excellent analysts of machine problems. They had a lot of time to study their machines in operation, and if they were being paid by the piece, they could profit (at least for a while) from improving the capability of their machines. Suggestions and complaints from women operatives led to many mechanical improvements, but they were seldom allowed to do more than pass their ideas on to men who could have a new part or an assembly made in the mill's shop.[59] They could, however, be involved once again in later stages of the development process. Machine operators played an important role in the testing and evaluating of new technology; feedback from them often led to further refinement and improvement of experimental devices by textile mills or machinery manufacturers.[60]

Many alterations might have lasting value in the factory where they were implemented but limited application in other plants. An untold number of brilliant ideas went unrecognized outside the factory door, and few were ever recorded in drawings. Even when an incremental improvement had the

FIGURE 9.22. Looms in the Watkins Mill, Lawton, Missouri. Many of these looms are modifications of standard designs. They provide material evidence of technical solutions by anonymous artisans whose ideas were never patented. (Photograph by Jet Lowe. Courtesy of the Historic American Engineering Record)

potential for widespread adoption, a manufacturing firm might try to retain a competitive advantage by keeping it instead of trying to patent and market it. For these reasons, artifactual evidence and oral history may offer the best opportunities for examining the normal process of technological change.[61]

The Transformation of Work

Jobs in a Textile Mill

Much, but not all, work in textile mills demanded only modest levels of skill and was both monotonous and uncomfortable to perform. A great deal of the average operative's working day involved observation of machinery and constant attention to the same process, hour after hour. A roving would break and have to be pieced together, bobbins would fill and require replacement, a belt would begin to slip and need dressing. Most workers stayed on their feet all day, walking miles within a small area. There were multiple machines to watch, and a problem might arise at any minute. Flaws in the product could mean penalties, reduced pay for pieceworkers, or even dismissal. In some rooms, the floors vibrated violently, and noise levels were deafening; in others, dust and loose fibers filled the air, festooned the machinery with gossamer strands, and clogged the lungs of long-time workers, who had to strain for adequate oxygen with every breath. High humidity, good for spinning and weaving, was maintained (sometimes with jets of steam) even in the heat of summer.[62]

It was possible for some workers to acquire impressive skills in a mill, to rise in the occupational hierarchy, and to gain employment on interesting equipment or in the more pleasant work spaces. Opportunities were not always equal, however. The best-paid jobs (mule spinner, loom fixer, wool carder, overseer) were open only to men. Ethnic and racial discrimination existed in many regions, and family influence or connections sometimes counted more than ability and effort in determining where a worker was placed. If employees were injured or suffered serious occupational illnesses, compensation was often minimal or nonexistent. Byssinosis has sapped the strength and shortened the lives of many cotton-mill workers.[63] When asked about the debilitating lung disease, a manager in a Georgia mill told one of the authors that it did not exist, adding as an aside that some workers are "allergic to cotton."

Visiting some of America's older operating textile mills is a valuable research exercise that can broaden a scholar's understanding of a historic working environment and of the jobs performed by workers long ago. The sound and vibration of weave rooms are a shock for the uninitiated. Pit marks in the walls and dented safety screens (relatively recent concessions to safety) testify to the danger of deflected shuttles, one of which flew out of a loom during a tour of a carpet mill for the preparation of this book. Conditions are far from ideal in many mills, but the air is generally cleaner than it was in the past, and obvious safety hazards are fewer. Individual motor drives on textile machines have eliminated the need for overhead shafting and the maze of leather belts that sometimes caught and maimed unwary operatives. Despite the absence of line shafts and belts, one still finds the machines in most rooms arranged in rows. It takes some imagination to stand in a mill today and picture the same scene in the nineteenth century, but less than you might expect.

Constraints on Factory Labor

Factory managers tried, not always with complete success, to convince their employees to give up the irregular work habits that were common in craft shops, homes, and farms. E. P. Thompson describes the traditional routine as "alternative bouts of intense labor and idleness" and regards factory labor as more disciplined and "time-oriented." Machine tenders were expected to work at a steady pace for long periods, starting and stopping their labor only at the signal of a foreman or the sound of the factory bell. There was little seasonal variation in the length of the factory day. The power system and the capabilities of the machinery established the pace of work, and they could be relentless taskmasters.[64] When production was organized in a sequence of steps, it was essential to keep the entire system in balance. A worker who was late when the shafting began to turn or who failed to perform his or her task at an acceptable rate would soon create a serious problem and draw the attention of managers. Small inequalities in work rates could be managed by providing storage reservoirs for partially completed work that could be drawn on or filled as needed, but their capacity could provide only temporary relief for imbalance in the production line.

The culture of work in a factory could promote or suppress innovation. In some workplaces, there was easy communication between employees and opportunities to compare ways of doing a job. The best managers enforced standards of uniformity in their products and maintained high rates of production while still encouraging experimentation in manufacturing technology and rewarding good ideas from the shop floor. If, however, workers perceived that their superiors did not appreciate their contributions or that their peer group resented efforts to display individual ambition and initiative, they might refrain from exercising their full abilities. There were also factories where the pace of work was so demanding that both machine operators and fixers had no time to do anything but concentrate on their immediate tasks.

Effects of the Uniformity Principle on Work

One of the greatest transformations of the work done in factories was the introduction of new standards of precision and workmanship, not for just a few elite artisans, but for average workers carrying out rapid, large-scale production. Collections of successive generations of a product made over a period of years are the best evidence of this change. Examples of such products can be found in the extensive arms collection at the Springfield Armory National Historic Site. The parts in early-nineteenth-century gun locks, such as the tumbler in Figure 9.23, show much evidence of indifferent workmanship. By 1828, John Hall, working in Virginia, and Simeon North, working in Connecticut, had succeeded in making the parts of the model 1819 flintlock rifle interchangeable regardless of which armory they were made in. Additionally, their artisans achieved a standard of workmanship not seen before in large-scale production of metal mechanisms. This

FIGURE 9.23. A tumbler from the lock of a model 1812 U.S. Army musket made at the Whitney Armory about 1820. It is rather crudely shaped, and facets from individual file strokes are visible at many places. The crack is the result of improper hardening. Parts of this model musket do not interchange. (Photograph by William Sacco)

FIGURE 9.24. A tumbler from the lock of a model 1841 U.S. Army rifle made at the Whitney Armory in 1851. Study of surficial markings on the tumbler shows that, except for the two cylindrical surfaces, it has been hand-filed to its final shape. The improvement in the standard of workmanship over the tumbler made in 1820 is evident. Parts of this model rifle, which was made at five different armories, interchange. (Photograph by William Sacco)

achievement was accomplished not with precision built into machines, but with the combined skills of artisans who knew how to set up and adjust machinery, how to make accurate gauges, and how to file machined parts until they fit those gauges. As American artisans gained experience, they produced finished gun parts that we can hardly distinguish from the work of modern machine tools (Fig. 9.24). A broad spectrum of factory workers, dividing complex manufacturing processes into a series of distinct operations, jointly acquired the skills that had formerly been the property of a few. And, at the same time, they raised the quality level of their products. The same type of transformation took place more gradually, but just as impressively, in industries that applied the uniformity principle to such civilian products as sewing machines and accurate watches.

In the second decade of the twentieth century, another transformation in factory production left thousands of factory workers without any opportunity to exercise their personal skills and subjected them to a high level of stress on the job. Very fine division of labor, strict application of the principle of uniformity, and rigorous, mechanical pacing of work were characteristic of automobile assembly lines.

Assembly-Line Production

The automobile assembly line introduced at the Ford Motor Company in 1913 was a clever synthesis of technological concepts that were already part of the American manufacturing experience. Henry Ford and his industrial engineers used interchangeable parts in combination with moving conveyors, and they divided assembly work into a series of relatively simple tasks that could be accomplished quickly by workers with minimal training.[65] No longer was interchangeability just an obsession of military officers or a conceit of mechanical engineers and toolmakers; now it was essential to the success of the assembly process and to the reliability of the product. On the moving assembly line (and most subassembly lines), there was no time for hand-fitting with file or whetstone and no time for selecting from a range of sized parts to find one that would fit (Fig. 9.25).[66]

To understand the dynamics of the automobile assembly line, it is best to see one in operation. Documentary films provide some sense of the repetitive nature of work on the line and show the steady movement of the conveyor systems. Workers' memoirs, sociological studies, fictional accounts of time "on the line," and Diego Rivera's powerful murals give indications of the stress created by this type of labor. Cinema productions from *Modern Times* to *Blue Collar* have been even more negative, presenting images of madness and social pathology. Few forms of production have been so controversial and so much in the public eye. With free tours of automobile plants available in

FIGURE 9.25. Final assembly line at the Highland Park Plant of the Ford Motor Company around 1914. This photograph shows the moving line, the large windows, and the flat slab floor that identify the factory as recently constructed. The first Highland Park assembly building had cast beams. (From the collections of Henry Ford Museum and Greenfield Village, negative number 833.994)

many regions of the country, it is unfortunate that most Americans have no direct experience with the manufacturing technology that provides their most cherished means of personal transportation.

The technical and economic efficiencies of the moving line for many types of mass-production are difficult to deny, but worker dissatisfaction has been one of the costs. Mental stress and physical ailments from repetitive motions were already a problem by the 1920s, when Robert and Helen Lynd studied the installation of a conveyor belt in the packing room of a midwestern glass factory. One company official acknowledged that there had been "several nervous breakdowns" among the women who packed glass jars. Another said, "This system may be good for the plant, but it certainly isn't good for the girls."[67] Today, even with high wages, rotation of tasks, and increased emphasis on teamwork, many assembly-line workers find their jobs boring and their pace of work barely tolerable.

It is instructive to walk along a final assembly line in an automobile plant, observing the hundreds of manual, machine-assisted, and robotic operations. But it is also important to stand at one station and watch one worker for an extended period. There is no surprise in the movement of the car being assembled, but the movements of the worker are somehow unexpected. The job must be done while the car is traveling down the line and must be completed in a specific interval of both time and space. In *Modern Times*, Charlie Chaplin's character is supposed to stay in place and do his simple tightening of bolts as the unidentified work-in-progress passes by him on a conveyor. When he falls behind, he has to run to keep up with the line, disrupting other workers who are standing at stations ahead of him. On an automobile final assembly line, the workers are almost always in motion. Some step aboard the line to perform a task as the conveyor carries them and the product forward. Some walk beside the line, working while they try to match its pace. A few walk in a trench under the moving vehicles to perform tasks from below. All have to finish their operations and return to their starting point in time to meet the next partially assembled car entering their station. The workers surge back and forth like the tide, but the cycle is much faster—a minute (sixty cars an hour) is not unusual. In a single shift, an automobile assembly worker may repeat this process more than 500 times.

Behind the capability to assemble cars at this rate are the casting, stamping, forging, and machining operations that are needed to create interchangeable parts. The essential elements of mass-production have not changed a great deal since the days of the Model T, although the level of automation is now much higher. Jigs, fixtures, and gauges have remained key elements of the production machinery that supports the assembly process, as they were in all the nineteenth-century industries that adopted "armory practice," with its emphasis on uniformity. The Ford Motor Company was making extensive use of these devices by 1907. A Ford plant superintendent called them "farmers' tools" because they made it possible to teach young men right off the farm to make precision parts.[68]

Jigs and fixtures became even more important when the company finally switched from the Model T to the Model A in 1927. Retooling for the new car taught company engineers the limitations of their special-purpose machine tools, many of which could not be converted to perform operations on parts for the new automobile. The type of "flexible mass-production" that became necessary to compete with the annual model changes at General Motors put a premium on versatile machinery.[69] Jigs and fixtures were not just a way to de-skill part of the work force; they also made it possible to alter general-purpose machinery rapidly and inexpensively. Using these devices, manufacturers could change the tooling and production capabilities without having to purchase specialized machines. The managers at the Springfield Armory had used this technique with the fixtures for their highly adaptable

Lincoln milling machines when the army adopted a different form of service rifle (a bolt-action) in 1892.[70]

The automobile industry borrowed many of the procedures used by armories, but not their hand processes for fitting hardened parts.[71] Most steel parts had to be hardened by heat-treating processes to ensure their durability in internal-combustion engines and drive trains. Unfortunately, that heat treatment could deform them and change critical dimensions. With bench assembly of small mechanisms, a whetstone might solve problems of minor distortion; but hand-fitting was not possible at assembly-line speeds, nor was it effective on the cylindrical surfaces of parts such as crankshafts. As had the makers of sewing machines and bicycles before them, the automobile manufacturers turned to grinding machines, which could cut hardened steel to tight tolerances and produce superior surface finishes. Applications for grinding machines proliferated as production engineers devised ways to eliminate many of the turning or milling operations traditionally done on "soft" parts before they were hardened. Grinding in automobile plants soon became not just a finishing or surfacing process, but also a means of heavy machining.[72]

The mass-production of automobiles that the average American could afford was a technical and managerial triumph. Assembly-line methods played an essential role in that achievement, but automobile workers are still paying part of the cost for that technology and for the personal mobility we enjoy.

The Transformation of Products

Factory production reduced the price and increased both the availability and the reliability of American manufactured goods. Reliability was particularly important to nineteenth-century Americans because it was slow and costly to ship replacements and because the failure of a product such as a rifle or an axe could have life-threatening consequences. In such a market, manufacturers of high-quality, reliable products—such as the Collins axe, the Winchester rifle, and the Colt revolver—could succeed, even though their products sold at premium prices. These makers stamped their names into their products deeply enough to remain visible throughout their working lives. Uniformity was an essential component of their marketing strategy because a few bad items could ruin the firm's reputation.

The superior design and reliability of American manufactured products earned an international reputation that enabled their makers to displace established European competitors from world markets. The author of an 1831 English treatise on metalworking observed:

We have seen in the last few days an axe, from an extensive manufactory in Connecticut, which was not only made of excellent materials, but was formed and finished with a degree of perfection that must have convinced any person in the least acquainted with such matters, that the maker of such a tool had nothing to learn in his business, and little to fear from the competition.[73]

Some years later, a Sheffield agent reported:

But it was not the mere fact of [Americans] manufacturing those [tools] that so much caused uneasiness as that, from the first, there was a superior intelligence brought to bear upon the design, shape and finish of the articles manufactured. If, for instance, it was an axe brought under our notice, we observed that it had been constructed with a scientific regard to the purpose for which it would be used.[74]

English makers of edge tools, on the contrary, offered the American market, "a vast mass of patterns, meretricious and gaudy design, absurdly numerous in variety, and all but useless in quality and strength."[75]

The replacement of craft products by factory-manufactured goods is described by some critics as the displacement of the skill of the artisan's hand by the impersonal work of a machine. An alternative view is that mechanized production allowed persons of limited means to benefit from the craftsmanship of designers, toolmakers, die sinkers, and other skilled artisans just as, three centuries before, printing presses had allowed more people to own the products of authors, bookbinders, and type designers. Woodsmen admired the balance and graceful shape of Collins axes, even though they were made in a factory. Part of the satisfaction in using such tools resides in knowledge of their uniformity and, hence, reliability, and in their unseen but important intrinsic qualities, such as the homogeneity and temper of the steel. These characteristics may be of little interest to collectors or art historians who do not use the tools, but they were important to the original owner and contributed to the pleasure of working with well-made tools. There is, indeed, something very satisfying and democratic about affordable factory products that meet the highest standards of craftsmanship.

Notes

1. James L. Conrad, "The Making of a Hero: Samuel Slater and the Arkwright Frames," *Rhode Island History* 45 (1986): 3–13; Gary Kulik, "The Beginnings of the Industrial Revolution in America: Pawtucket, Rhode Island, 1672–1829" (Ph.D. diss., Brown University, 1980) chap. 2; Paul Rivard, "Textile Experiments in Rhode Island, 1788–1789," *Rhode Island History* 33 (1974): 33–45.

2. C. J. Brickett, *The Cotton Textile Workers' Handbook* (Scranton, Pa.: International Textbook, 1925), pp. 300–301.

3. *Rhode Island Industries Catalogued and Illustrated* (Providence: Chamber of Commerce, 1904), p. 27; Daniel Nelson, *Managers and Workers: Origins of the New Factory System in the United States, 1880–1920* (Madison: University of Wisconsin Press, 1975), pp. 20–21. After 1872, Brown and Sharpe built one of the best factory complexes in the nation, using a hollow square pattern on a site in Providence. The company, which now concentrates on metrology, has moved to a new suburban location and is no longer manufacturing machine tools. Most of its former factory is being turned into a multiuse development with a misleading name, The Foundry.

4. See, particularly, Alfred Chandler, Jr., *The Visible Hand: The Managerial Revolution in American Business* (Cambridge, Mass.: Harvard University Press, 1977); John Chamberlain, *The Enterprising Americans: A Business History of the United States* (New York: Harper & Row, 1963); and Thomas C. Cochran, *Frontiers of Change: Early Industrialism in America* (New York: Oxford University Press, 1981).

5. Herbert Gutman, *Work, Culture, & Society in Industrializing America* (New York: Vintage Books, 1977), pp. 9–12. See also Philip Scranton, "The Workplace, Technology, and Theory in American Labor History," *International Labor and Working Class History* 35 (1989): 3–19; David Montgomery, *Workers' Control in America: Studies in the History of Work, Technology, and Labor Struggles* (Cambridge: Cambridge University Press, 1979); and David Noble, *Forces of Production: A Social History of Industrial Automation* (New York: Knopf, 1984).

6. For discussion of the value of operating both original artifacts and replicas, see Richard L. Hills, "Museums, History and Working Machines," in *History of Technology*, 2d annual volume, ed. A. Rupert Hall and Norman Smith (London: Mansell, 1977), pp. 157–167, and *Risks and Rewards: Perspectives on Operating Mechanical Artifacts* (Greenville, Del.: Hagley Museum and Library, 1991). John H. White, Jr., curator of transportation in the National Museum of American History, raised concerns about operating historic machinery in "The Railway Museum: Past, Present, and Future," *Technology and Culture* 14 (1973): 599–613. Then, in 1981, he decided to run (and film) the museum's John Bull, a steam locomotive built in England in 1831 and imported for the Camden and Amboy Railroad, whose engineers modified it for steeper and more curving American tracks. Steven Lubar later described it as "the world's oldest operable locomotive" in *Engines of Change* (exhibition catalog) (Washington, D.C.: National Museum of American History, 1986), p. 46. Ralph H. Lewis suggests using "reproduced objects" for demonstrations, often not an economically feasible alternative with complex machinery (*Manual for Museums* [Washington, D.C.: National Park Service, 1976], p. 119).

7. Richard L. Hills, *Cotton Spinning* (Manchester: North Western Museum of Science & Industry, n.d.), pp. 12–13.

8. Hills, "Museums, History and Working Machines," pp. 164–165.

9. William Worthington made the replica cutter, and Peter Liebhold played the role of machinist. Both are with the Division of Engineering and Industry at the National Museum of American History, Smithsonian Institution. Robert Vogel and Carolyn Cooper contributed technical advice.

10. For discussion of the Blanchard copying lathe, see Carolyn C. Cooper, *Shaping Invention: Thomas Blanchard's Machinery and Patent Management in Nineteenth-Century America* (New York: Columbia University Press, 1991).

11. Theodore Z. Penn, "A Brand-New 150 Year Old Drawing Frame," *Bulletin of the Association for Preservation Technology* 12 (1980): 49–54.

12. Laurence Gross used this technique with other methods of industrial archaeology, including imitative experiment and observation of skilled workers, to argue that managers and machine designers were not able to eliminate the need for skilled carders in woolen factories ("Wool Carding: A Study of Skills and Technology," *Technology and Culture* 28 [1987]: 804–827).

13. Robert B. Gordon, "Machine Archeology: The John Gage Planer," *IA, Journal of the Society for Industrial Archeology* 17 (1991): 3–14. Gordon was assisted in the analysis of this machine by Carolyn Cooper, Peter Liebhold, and Robert Vogel.

14. Donald Hoke, *Ingenious Yankees: The Rise of the American System of Manufactures in the Private Sector* (New York: Columbia University Press, 1990), chap. 2.

15. The surviving machines are in the American Precision Museum, Windsor, Vermont, and the Science Museum, London. See K. R. Gilbert, "The Ames Recessing Machine: A Survivor of the Original Enfield Rifle Machinery," *Technology and Culture* 4 (1963): 207–211.

16. Felicia J. Deyrup, *Arms Makers of the Connecticut Valley* (Northampton, Mass.: Smith College, 1948), p. 95; Michael S. Raber and others, "Conservative Innovators and Military Small Arms: An Industrial History of the Springfield Armory, 1794–1968" (Report for the National Park Service, 1989), pp. 132, 174–175.

17. Patrick M. Malone and others, "Phase III Archaeological Investigation at Forestdale Scythe Works, North Smithfield, Rhode Island" (Brown University Public Archaeology Laboratory for North Smithfield Sewer Commission, 1979).

18. Ibid.

19. Hoke, *Ingenious Yankees*, chap. 3; Robert B. Gordon, "Material Evidence of the Development of Metal Working Technology at the Collins Axe Factory," *IA, Journal of the Society for Industrial Archeology* 9 (1983): 19–28; Paul Uselding, "Elisha Root, Forging, and the 'American System,'" *Technology and Culture* 15 (1974): 543–568. The artifactual evidence leads to a different interpretation of the metal-forming system developed at the Collins works from that advanced by Uselding.

20. Uselding, "Elisha Root," pp. 543–568.

21. H. Blanc, superintendent of the Royal Manufactory of Arms in France, began to develop new methods of making lock parts for the model 1777 musket in about 1778 (W. F. Durfee, "The First Systematic Attempt at Interchangeability in Firearms," *Cassier's Magazine* 5 [1893–1894]: 469–477).

22. David J. Jeremy, *Transatlantic Industrial Revolution: The Diffusion of Textile Technologies Between Britain and America, 1790–1830s* (Cambridge, Mass.: MIT Press, 1981), pp. 192–198.

23. William Burke, "Statistics Relating to the Cost of Manufacturing Drillings and Standard Sheetings in 1838 and 1876," *New England Cotton Manufacturers Association Proceedings* 21 (1876): 12.

24. Jeremy, *Transatlantic Industrial Revolution*, p. 198; C. B. Kidwell and M. C. Christman, *Suiting Everyone: The Democratization of Clothing in America* (Washington, D.C.: Smithsonian Institution Press, 1978), p. 68.

25. Harold Catling, *The Spinning Mule* (Newton Abbot: David & Charles, 1970), pp. 147–148; David Montgomery, *The Fall of the House of Labor* (New York: Cambridge University Press, 1987), pp. 124, 157–165; William Lazonick, "Factor Costs and the Diffusion of Ring Spinning in Britain Prior to World War I," *Quarterly Journal of Economics* (February 1981): 90–109.

26. The history of this artifact is discussed in Edwin A. Battison, "Eli Whitney and the Milling Machine," *Smithsonian Journal of History* 1 (1966): 9–34, and Bat-

tison, "A New Look at the 'Whitney' Milling Machine," *Technology and Culture* 14 (1973): 592–598.

27. Evidence of the continued reliance on handwork to make interchangeable parts after mechanization became common in armories is presented in Robert B. Gordon, "Who Turned the Mechanical Ideal into Mechanical Reality?" *Technology and Culture* 29 (1988): 744–788, and Gordon, "Simeon North, John Hall, and Mechanized Manufacturing," *Technology and Culture* 30 (1989): 179–188.

28. A. H. Cole, *The American Wool Manufacture* (Cambridge, Mass.: Harvard University Press, 1926), vol. 1, pp. 307–308, 313–314.

29. "History of Weaving Machinery as Applied to Crompton & Knowles Loom Works," file of unpublished company histories, Crompton & Knowles Development Board Records, 1917–1954, 26 vols., Museum of American Textile History, North Andover, Massachusetts. In particular, see George Hutchins, "History of the Knowles Loom." We are indebted to curator Laurence Gross for information on the Furbush loom, which he helped to restore to operating condition.

30. M. T. Copeland, *The Cotton Manufacturing Industry of the United States* (New York: Kelley, 1966), pp. 86–88; William H. Chase, *Five Generations of Loom Builders* (Hopedale, Mass.: Draper, 1950), pp. 13–19; William Mass, "Mechanical and Organizational Innovation: The Drapers and the Automatic Loom," *Business History Review* 63 (1989): 876–929.

31. William Mass and Charles Levenstein, "Labor Relations, Technology, and Occupational Disease: Banning the Suck Shuttle in Massachusetts, 1911" (Paper presented at the Business History Conference, Hartford, Conn., March 1984). Mass and Levenstein use modern theories of disease transmission to argue that the suck shuttle was "unrelated to the transmission of tuberculosis."

32. Eugene S. Ferguson, *Oliver Evans: Inventive Genius and the American Industrial Revolution* (Greenville, Del.: Hagley Museum, 1980).

33. Jeremy, *Transatlantic Industrial Revolution*, pp. 235–238; Cole, *American Wool Manufacture*, vol. 1, pp. 353–356; Gross, "Wool Carding," pp. 811–815.

34. E. J. Lenik, "A Study of Cast Iron Nails," *Historical Archaeology* 11 (1977): 45–47.

35. Amos J. Loveday, Jr., *The Rise and Decline of the American Cut Nail Industry* (Westport, Conn.: Greenwood Press, 1983).

36. Based on Lee H. Nelson, "Nail Chronology as an Aid to Dating Old Buildings," *History News* 24 (1968). [American Association for State and Local History Technical Leaflet No. 48]

37. A 1979 research report on the nails by a Brown University undergraduate is in the files at Slater Mill Historic Site (Keith Freeman, "An Analysis of the Nails from the Wilkinson Mill").

38. The historical background and a description of this machine are in Steven Lubar, "Culture and Technological Design in the 19th-Century Pin Industry: John Howe and the Howe Manufacturing Company," *Technology and Culture* 28 (1987): 253–282.

39. David A. Hounshell, *From the American System to Mass Production, 1800–1932* (Baltimore: Johns Hopkins University Press, 1984), chaps. 1, 2; Hoke, *Ingenious Yankees*.

40. Robert B. Gordon, "Gaging, Measurement and the Control of Artificers' Work in Manufacturing," *Polhem* 6 (1988): 159–172; Paul Uselding, "Measuring Techniques and Manufacturing Practice," in *Yankee Enterprise,* ed. Otto Mayr and

Robert C. Post (Washington, D.C.: Smithsonian Institution Press, 1981), pp. 103–126.

41. Peter J. Booker, *A History of Engineering Drawing* (London: Chatto and Windus, 1963), p. 188.

42. Gordon, "Gaging," pp. 159–172; Hoke, *Ingenious Yankees,* p. 336.

43. The comprehensive text on machine drawing edited by W. E. Worthen (*Appleton's Cyclopedia of Drawing* [New York: Appleton, 1869]) does not show numerical dimensions on the drawings; ten years later, in C. W. MacCord, *Lessons in Mechanical Drawing* (New York: Munn, 1879), they are shown on all detailed drawings.

44. Gordon, "Gaging," pp. 159–172. Despite the versatility of micrometers, fixed gages continued to be important in factory production because workers could use them quickly and were less likely to make errors with them.

45. Franklin D. Jones, *Jig and Fixture Design* (New York: Industrial Press, 1920), pp. 3–6, 9–11, 211.

46. The use of fixtures in making wooden-works clocks is described in Hoke, *Ingenious Yankees,* chap. 2.

47. Patrick M. Malone, "Little Kinks and Devices at Springfield Armory, 1892–1918," *IA, Journal of the Society for Industrial Archeology* 14 (1988): 23–35, 59–76.

48. Geoffrey Tweedale, *Sheffield Steel and America: A Century of Commercial and Technological Interdependence, 1830–1930* (Cambridge: Cambridge University Press, 1987), chap. 5.

49. Daniel Nelson, *Frederick W. Taylor and the Rise of Scientific Management* (Madison: University of Wisconsin Press, 1980); Sudhir Kakar, *Frederick Taylor: A Study in Personality and Innovation* (Cambridge, Mass.: MIT Press, 1970), pp. 170–176; Charles D. Wrege and Ronald Greenwood, *Frederick W. Taylor, the Father of Scientific Management: Myths and Reality* (Homewood, Ill.: Business One Irwin, 1991), p. 42.

50. Nathan Rosenberg, *Perspectives on Technology* (Cambridge: Cambridge University Press, 1976), p. 292. See also Malone, "Little Kinks and Devices," pp. 63–65.

51. Eugene Ferguson, "The Mind's Eye: Nonverbal Thought in Technology," *Science* 197 (1977): 827–836.

52. Rosenberg, *Perspectives on Technology,* p. 292n; Nathan Rosenberg, *Inside the Black Box: Technology and Economics* (Cambridge: Cambridge University Press, 1982), pp. 6–7.

53. Scranton, "Workplace, Technology, and Theory in American Labor History," p. 10. For recognition of the importance of incremental innovation and evolutionary development in the textile industry, see Thomas R. Navin, "Innovation and Management Policies—The Textile Machinery Industry: Influence of the Market on Management," *Bulletin of the Business Historical Society* 25 (1951): 15–30, and Julia C. Bonham, "Cotton Textile Technology in America: Three Centuries of Evolutionary Change" (Ph.D. diss., Brown University, 1979), pp. 1–4, 174–178, 283. Bonham offers extensive evidence of "the cotton textile industry's time-honored tradition of piecemeal, incremental change." For coverage of early textile machinery and modification of imported British technology, see Jeremy, *Transatlantic Industrial Revolution.*

54. Carolyn C. Cooper, "Making Shuttles by Machine at Wilkinsonville, 1825–1984" (Report for the Blackstone River Valley National Heritage Corridor, 1989), pp. 2–3, 12–13, 17. See also the transcribed interview conducted by Paul Hudon and the videotape taken by Laurence Gross. The entire study, which includes a business history, was done for the Blackstone River Valley National Heritage Corridor. It

complements an earlier HAER survey and interviews conducted in 1966 at the Dudley Shuttle Company. Patrick Malone toured the company's mill in the 1970s, before it closed, and took slides of the work process. Swenson, who is now deceased, never patented any of the machinery he made or modified in the factory. Cooper concludes from a study of patent records that special-purpose shuttle-making machines "seem to have evolved from anonymous shop practice."

55. At a jewel-case manufacturing plant in Providence, Rhode Island, most of the machinery has been either altered or built entirely by company employees. The extent of modification generally reflects the length of anticipated production runs; products with continuing demand justify extensive automation and fixture development, while short runs are done with basic machines and more manual involvement by the operators.

56. Philip Scranton, *Figured Tapestry: Production, Markets, and Power in Philadelphia Textiles, 1885–1941* (New York: Cambridge University Press, 1989), pp. 1–2, 8–10, 13; George Draper and A. G. Cumnock, quoted in a discussion in *New England Cotton Manufacturers Association Proceedings* 13 (1872): 8.

57. Hutchins, "History of the Knowles Loom."

58. Laurence Gross, "The Importance of Research Outside the Library: Watkins Mill, a Case Study," *IA, Journal of the Society for Industrial Archeology* 7 (1981): 20.

59. Julia Bonham provides an example of innovation by a nineteenth-century woman, Lucy Johnson of Coventry, Rhode Island, who altered her loom to improve her weaving of coverlets ("Cotton Textile Technology in America," p. 31). Specific examples of women innovators in the textile industry are hard to find in the documentary record, but there are numerous reference to ideas from weavers in periods when most of them were female operatives. Oral history appears to be the best way to examine the often neglected role of women in incremental change.

60. The Crompton & Knowles Development Board Records show frequent trials in mills and effects of feedback from operators.

61. A retired loom fixer interviewed at Slater Mill Historic Site by Patrick Malone and Robert Macieski said that mills were sometimes secretive if they had figured out a way to make a fabric that no one else could make, but he acknowledged that nothing remained confidential very long in the textile industry. People would sometimes hire him because he knew how to make a difficult product—another example of the ancient practice of acquiring new technology by bringing in a worker with the right skills. The loom fixer prefers to remain anonymous, but allowed the museum to file notes of his interview in 1990. Tom Rockwell, a former carding-machine erector for Davis and Furber, says that managers in each textile mill he visited thought they were doing something unusual. Occasionally, they would warn him about keeping their secrets, or they would try to prevent him from seeing new devices (Tom Rockwell, taped interview with Patrick Malone, 18 January 1990, on file at Museum of American Textile History, North Andover, Massachusetts).

62. Carl Gersuny, *Work Hazards and Industrial Conflict* (Hanover, N.H.: University Press of New England, 1981), pp. 20–21; Betsy Bahr, "New England Mill Engineering: Rationalization and Reform in Textile Mill Design, 1790–1920" (Ph.D. diss., University of Delaware, 1987), pp. 249–250.

63. Gersuny, *Work Hazards and Industrial Conflict*, pp. 55–67; Edward Beardsley, *A History of Neglect: Health Care for Blacks and Mill Workers in the Twentieth-Century South* (Knoxville: University of Tennessee Press, 1987), pp. 229–242; Richard Guarasci, "Death by Cotton Dust," in *Corporate Violence*, ed. Stuart Hills (Totowa, N.J.: Rowman and Littlefield, 1987), pp. 76–92.

64. E. P. Thompson, "Time, Work-Discipline, and Industrial Capitalism," *Past and Present* 38 (1967): 56–97; Gutman, *Work, Culture & Society,* pp. 19–27, 32–39. Gutman notes that later immigrants from rural cultures or craft backgrounds had many of the same "irregular work habits" as early-nineteenth-century American artisans who were being introduced to factory labor for the first time.

65. For coverage of the origins of the assembly line, see Hounshell, *From the American System to Mass Production,* pp. 238–256. Hounshell discusses earlier conveyors in flour mills (dating back to the 1790s mills of Oliver Evans), breweries, canneries, meat-packing plants, and the Westinghouse Foundry. He does not, however, describe the textile industry's long involvement with mechanical conveying of materials between machines. Although there is no evidence of direct influence on Ford or his production men, textile mechanization was at a high level by the early twentieth century and had received a great deal of attention in engineering and industrial journals.

66. Hand fitting is a part of the assembly of revolvers and many other precise mechanisms. It was standard practice during rifle assembly at Springfield Armory until World War II. At the Waltham Watch Company, matching of watch parts involved careful selection instead of hand fitting with a whetstone. Assemblers chose watch components "from the right boxes or jars." These finished components had been presorted and placed in containers according to very precise distinctions in size, weight, or strength (Malone, "Little Kinks and Devices," pp. 65–66, 71, 76; David Landes, *Revolution in Time* [Cambridge, Mass.: Harvard University Press, 1983], pp. 314–316; "The Building of a Watch," *Scientific American,* 4 March 1899, p. 132).

67. Robert Lynd and Helen Lynd, *Middletown: A Study in American Culture* (New York: Harcourt, Brace & World, 1956), pp. 69–70. The Lynds also reported localized physical ailments resulting from repetitive movements by a few small muscles.

68. Max Wollering, quoted in Hounshell, *From the American System to Mass Production,* pp. 221, 230–232. A veteran Indiana machinist who mentions Ford and job specialization also gives credit to improved metal cutting tools for reducing the level of skill required to make parts: "You had to know how to use the old carbon steel to keep it from gettin' hot and spoilin' the edge. But this 'high speed steel' and this new 'stelite' [Stellite, a nonferrous alloy of cobalt, tungsten, chromium, and carbon] don't absorb the heat and are harder than carbon steel. You can take a boy fresh from the farm and in three days he can manage a machine as well as I can, and I've been at it twenty seven years" (Lynd and Lynd, *Middletown,* p. 74).

69. Hounshell, *From the American System to Mass Production,* p. 294. "Flexible mass production" was a phrase used by Henry Ford's ghostwriter.

70. The custom shop of the former Winchester Repeating Arms Company is still using Lincoln millers and still changing its fixtures for different models of weapons.

71. Firearms parts were usually too small and complex in shape for effective grinding. They were brought to gauge dimensions by other machining or filing processes, and then hardened by heat treating. Unfortunately, that heat treating could cause distortion of the metal part. In final assembly of closely fitting rifle or revolver parts, it was often necessary to apply a few strokes with a whetstone.

72. Rosenberg, *Perspectives on Technology,* pp. 26–27.

73. Dionysius Lardner, *Manufactures in Metal,* vol. 1, *Iron and Steel* (London: Longman, 1831), p. 319.

74. Tweedale, *Sheffield Steel and America,* p. 144.

75. "How Sheffield Lost the American Trade," *Sheffield Independent,* 17 June 1875, quoted in ibid., p. 133.

Bibliography

Albion, Robert, and others, *New England and the Sea*. Mystic, Conn.: Mystic Seaport, 1972.

Allen, R. F., and others, "An Archeological Survey of Bloomery Forges in the Adirondacks." *IA, Journal of the Society for Industrial Archeology* 16 (1991): 3–20.

Allen, Richard S. *Separation and Inspiration*. Historical Publication No. 1. Ironville, N.Y.: Penfield Foundation, 1967.

Allen, Zachariah. *The Science of Mechanics*. Providence, R.I.: Hutchens & Cory, 1829.

"The American Waltham Watch Factory." *Electrical Review*, 17 November 1888, p. 2.

Anderson, Jay. *Time Machines: The World of Living History*. Nashville, Tenn.: American Association of State and Local History, 1984.

Arnold, Horace, and Fay L. Faurote. *Ford Methods and the Ford Shops*. New York: Engineering Magazine, 1915.

Asher, Robert. *Connecticut Workers and Technological Change*. Storrs: Center for Oral History, University of Connecticut, 1983.

Atkinson, Edward. "Slow-Burning Construction." *Century Magazine* 37 (1889): 566–579.

Bagnall, William R. *The Textile Industries of the United States*. Vol. 1. New York: Augustus Kelley, 1971.

Bahr, Betsy. "New England Mill Engineering: Rationalization and Reform in Textile Mill Design, 1790–1920." Ph.D. diss., University of Delaware, 1987.

Banham, Reyner. *A Concrete Atlantis*. Cambridge, Mass.: MIT Press, 1989.

Barker, Elmer E. *The Story of Crown Point Iron*. Historical Publication No. 3. Ironville, N.Y.: Penfield Foundation, 1969.

Bartholomew, Craig L. "William M. Weaver—Superintendent of the Macungie Furnace." *Canal History and Technology Proceedings* 5 (1986): 151.

Bartholomew, Craig L., and Lance E. Metz. *The Anthracite Iron Industry of the Lehigh Valley*. Easton, Pa.: Center for Canal History and Technology, 1988.

Basalla, George. "Museums and Technological Utopianism." In *Technological Innovation and the Decorative Arts*, edited by Ian M. G. Quimby and Polly A. Earl, pp. 355–371. Charlottesville: University Press of Virginia, 1973.

————. *The Evolution of Technology*. New York: Cambridge University Press, 1988.

Battison, Edwin A. "Eli Whitney and the Milling Machine." *Smithsonian Journal of History* 1 (1966): 9–34.

————. "A New Look at the 'Whitney' Milling Machine." *Technology and Culture* 14 (1973): 592–598.

Battle, J. H., ed. *History of Columbia and Montour Counties*. Chicago: Warner, 1887.

Beardsley, Edward. *A History of Neglect: Health Care for Blacks and Mill Workers in the Twentieth-Century South*. Knoxville: University of Tennessee Press, 1987.

Bell, I. Lothian. *Principles of the Manufacture of Iron and Steel*. London: Routledge, 1884.

Bell, Louis, "Electricity in Textile Manufacturing." *Cassier's Magazine* 7 (1895): 275–284.

Billington, David P. *The Tower and the Bridge*. New York: Basic Books, 1983.

Biggs, Lindy. "Industry's Master Machine: Factory Planning and Design in the Age of Mass Production, 1900–1930." Ph.D. diss., Massachusetts Institute of Technology, 1987.

Binder, Frederick M. *Coal Age Empire: Pennsylvania Coal and Its Utilization to 1860*. Harrisburg: Pennsylvania Historical and Museum Commission, 1974.

Bishop, J. Leander. *A History of American Manufacturers from 1608 to 1860*. Philadelphia: Young, 1868.

Bloomfield, Gerald T. "Coils of the Commercial Serpent: A Geography of the Ford Branch Distribution System, 1904–1933." In *Roadside America: The Automobile in Design and Culture*, edited by Jan Jennings, pp. 40–51. Ames: Iowa State University Press, 1990.

Boatright, Mody, and William A. Owens. *Tales from the Derrick Floor: A People's History of the Oil Industry*. Lincoln: University of Nebraska Press, 1970.

Bodnar, John. *Anthracite People: Families, Unions and Work, 1900–1940*. Harrisburg: Pennsylvania Museum and Historical Commission, 1983.

Bonham, Julia C. "Cotton Textile Technology in America: Three Centuries of Evolutionary Change." Ph.D. diss., Brown University, 1979.

Booker, Peter J. *A History of Engineering Drawing*. London: Chatto and Windus, 1963.

Borgmann, Albert. *Technology and the Character of Contemporary Life*. Chicago: University of Chicago Press, 1984.

Botiggi, Sally A. "An Iron Experiment: The Livingston Ironworks and the Colonial Iron Industry, 1743–1790." In *The Livingston Legacy: Three Centuries of American History*, edited by Richard C. Wiles and Andrea K. Zimmerman, pp. 283–298. Annandale-on-Hudson, N.Y.: Bard College, 1987.

Boucher, Jack W. *Of Batsto and Bog Iron*. Batsto, N.J.: Batsto Citizens Committee, 1980.

Bowditch, John. "The Big, the Bad, and the Ugly: Collecting Industrial Artifacts for History Museums." *Pittsburgh History* 72 (1989): 88–95.

Bowen, Ele. *The Coal Regions of Pennsylvania*. Pottsville, Pa.: Carvalho, 1848.

Bracegirdle, Brian. *The Archaeology of the Industrial Revolution*. London: Heinemann, 1973.

Bradford, William. *Of Plymouth Plantation, 1620–1647*. Edited by Samuel E. Morison. New York: Modern Library, 1967.

Brecher, Jeremy, Jerry Lombardi, and Jan Stackhouse. *Brass City*. Philadelphia: Temple University Press, 1982.

Brewer, James W. *Jerome*. Tucson: Southwest Parks and Monuments Association, 1987.

Brickett, C. J. *The Cotton Textile Workers' Handbook.* Scranton, Pa.: International Textbook, 1925.

Brodeur, Paul. *Currents of Death.* New York: Simon and Schuster, 1989.

Brough, Joseph. *Wrought Iron: The End of an Era at Atlas Forge.* Bolton: Bolton Metropolitan Arts Department, n.d.

Brown, Sharon. "The Cambria Iron Company of Johnstown, Pennsylvania." *Canal History and Technology Proceedings* 7 (1988): 19–46.

Bucki, Cecelia, and others. *Metal, Minds, and Machines: Waterbury at Work.* Waterbury, Conn.: Mattatuck Historical Society, 1980.

Bureau of the Census. Tenth Census. *Reports on the Water-Power of the United States.* Vols. 16 and 17. Washington, D.C.: Census Office, 1885, 1887.

Burke, William. "Statistics Relating to the Costs of Manufacturing Drillings and Standard Sheetings in 1838 and 1876." *New England Cotton Manufacturers Association Proceedings* 21 (1876): 6–13.

Bursell, Barbro. *The Clog Nobility.* Stockholm: Nordiska Museets, 1975.

Calhoun, Daniel H. *The American Civil Engineer: Origins and Conflict.* Cambridge, Mass.: MIT Press, 1960.

Camp, J. M., and C. B. Francis. *The Making, Shaping and Treating of Steel.* 4th ed. Pittsburgh: Carnegie Steel, 1919.

Candee, Richard M. "Merchant and Millwright: The Water Powered Sawmills of the Piscataqua." *Old Time New England* 60 (1970): 131–149.

———. "The 1822 Allendale Mill and Slow-Burning Construction." *IA, Journal of the Society for Industrial Archeology* 25 (1989): 21–32.

Carrell, Toni, James Bradford, and W. L. Rusho. *Submerged Cultural Resources Site Report: Charles H. Spencer's Mining Operation and Paddle Wheel Steamboat.* Southwest Cultural Resources Center Professional Papers No. 13. Santa Fe, N.M.: Southwest Cultural Resources Center, 1987.

Carroll, Charles F. *The Timber Economy of Puritan New England.* Providence, R.I.: Brown University Press, 1973.

Case, Willard L. *The Factory Buildings.* New York: Industrial Extension Institute, 1919.

Catling, Harold. *The Spinning Mule.* Newton Abbot: David & Charles, 1970.

Caudill, Harry M. *Night Comes to the Cumberlands.* Boston: Little, Brown, 1963.

Chamberlain, John. *The Enterprising Americans: A Business History of the United States.* New York: Harper & Row, 1963.

———. *Frontiers of Change: Early Industrialism in America.* New York: Oxford University Press, 1981.

Chance, H. M. *Mining Methods and Appliances Used in the Anthracite Coal Fields.* Harrisburg, Pa.: Second Geological Survey, 1883.

Chandler, Alfred, Jr. "Anthracite Coal and the Beginnings of the Industrial Revolution in the United States." *Business History Review* 46 (1972): 141–181.

———. *The Visible Hand: The Managerial Revolution in American Business.* Cambridge, Mass.: Harvard University Press, 1977.

Chase, William H. *Five Generations of Loom Builders.* Hopedale, Mass.: Draper, 1950.

Clark, C. M. "Trouble at t'Mill: Industry Archaeology in the 1980s." *Antiquity* 61 (1987): 169–179.

Clark, James J., and Michael Halbouty. *Spindletop.* Houston: Gulf Publishing, 1952.

Clewell, C. E. "What It Pays to Know About Factory Lighting, III." *Factory* 19 (1917): 537–540.

Coal and Your Environment. Washington, D.C.: National Coal Association, n.d.

Cochran, Thomas C. *Frontiers of Change: Early Industrialism in America.* New York: Oxford University Press, 1981.

Cohen, Marcie. "The Journals of Joshua Whitman, Turner, Maine, 1809–1846." In *The Farm,* edited by Peter Barnes, pp. 49–59. Boston: Boston University Press, 1988.

Cohen, Stan. *King Coal: A Pictorial Heritage of West Virginia Coal Mining.* Charleston, W.Va.: Pictorial Histories, 1984.

Cole, A. H. *The American Wool Manufacture.* Vol. 1. Cambridge, Mass.: Harvard University Press, 1926.

Coles, John. *Experimental Archaeology.* London: Academic Press, 1979.

Colvin, Fred H. *Sixty Years with Men and Machines.* New York: Whittlesey House, 1947.

Condit, Carl W. *American Building.* Chicago: University of Chicago Press, 1968.

Conrad, James L. "The Making of a Hero: Samuel Slater and the Arkwright Frames." *Rhode Island History* 45 (1986): 3–13.

Conzen, Michael P., ed. *The Making of the American Landscape.* Boston: Unwin Hyman, 1990.

Coolidge, John. *Mill and Mansion.* New York: Russell and Russell, 1967.

Cooper, Carolyn C. "The Production Line at the Portsmouth Blockmill." *Industrial Archaeology Review* 6 (1981–1982): 28–44.

―――. "The Portsmouth System of Manufacture." *Technology and Culture* 25 (1984): 182–225.

―――. "The Evolution of American Patent Management: The Blanchard Lathe as a Case Study." *Prologue* 19 (1987): 245–259.

―――. "'A Whole Battalion of Stockers': Thomas Blanchard's Production Line and Hand Labor at Springfield Armory." *IA, Journal of the Society for Industrial Archaeology* 14 (1988): 37–57.

―――. "Making Shuttles by Machine at Wilkinsonville, 1825–1984." Report by the Museum of American Textile History for the Blackstone River Valley National Heritage Corridor, 1989.

―――. *Shaping Invention: Thomas Blanchard's Machinery and Patent Management in Nineteenth-Century America.* New York: Columbia University Press, 1991.

Cooper, Carolyn C., R. B. Gordon, and H. V. Merrick. "Archeological Evidence of Metallurgical Innovation at the Eli Whitney Armory." *IA, Journal of the Society for Industrial Archeology* 8 (1982): 1–12.

Cooper, Carolyn C., and Patrick M. Malone. "The Mechanical Woodworker in Early Nineteenth-Century New England as a Spin-Off from Textile Industrialization." Paper presented at Old Sturbridge Village Colloquium, 17 March 1990.

Copeland, M. T. *The Cotton Manufacturing Industry of the United States.* New York: Kelley, 1966.

Corbin, William H. *Edward Clinton Terry, Ph. B.* Hartford, Conn.: Louise E. Terry, 1943.

Cossons, Neil. *The B P Book of Industrial Archaeology.* Newton Abbott: David & Charles, 1975.

Cowley, Charles. *Illustrated History of Lowell.* Boston: Lee and Shepard, 1868.

Crompton & Knowles Development Board Records, 1917–1954. 26 vols. Museum of American Textile History, North Andover, Massachusetts.

Cronon, William. *Changes in the Land.* New York: Hill and Wang, 1983.

Crossley, David. *The Bewl Valley Ironworks.* London: Royal Archaeological Institute, 1975.

Crossman, E. C. *The Book of the Springfield.* Marines, N.C.: Samworth, 1932.

Cummings, William J. *Iron Mountain's Cornish Pumping Engine and the Mines It Dewatered.* Iron Mountain, Mich.: Cornish Pumping Engine and Mining Museum, 1984.

Darrah, William C. *Pithole: The Vanished City.* Gettysburg, Pa.: Darrah, 1972.

Danly, Susan, and Leo Marx, eds. *The Railroad in American Art.* Cambridge, Mass.: MIT Press, 1988.

Davis, James J. *The Iron Puddler.* Indianapolis: Bobbs-Merrill, 1922.

DeKok, David. *Unseen Danger: A Tragedy of People, Government, and the Centralia Mine Fire.* Philadelphia: University of Pennsylvania Press, 1986.

Dent, Richard J. "On the Archaeology of Early Canals: Research on the Patowmack Canal in Great Falls, Virginia." *Historical Archaeology* 20 (1986): 50–62.

The Derrick's Hand Book of Petroleum. Oil City, Pa.: Derrick Publishing, 1898.

Dew, Charles B. *Ironmaker to the Confederacy: Joseph R. Anderson and the Tredegar Iron Works.* New Haven, Conn.: Yale University Press, 1966.

Deyrup, Felicia J. *Arms Makers of the Connecticut Valley.* Northampton, Mass.: Smith College, 1948.

Dix, Keith. *Work Relations in the Coal Industry: The Hand-Loading Era, 1880–1930.* Morgantown: West Virginia University Press, 1977.

———. *What's A Coal Miner to Do? The Mechanization of Coal Mining.* Pittsburgh: University of Pittsburgh Press, 1988.

Documents Relative to the Manufactures in the United States [Louis McLane report]. 1833. Reprint. New York: Burt Franklin, 1969.

Dougherty, Janet W. D., and Charles M. Keller. "Taskonomy: A Practical Approach to Knowledge Structures." In *Directions in Cognitive Anthropology,* edited by Janet W. D. Doughtery, pp. 161–174. Urbana: University of Illinois Press, 1985.

Drake Well. Titusville: Pennsylvania Historical and Museum Commission, n.d.

Drier, Roy, and Octave du Temple, eds. *Prehistoric Copper Mining in the Lake Superior Region.* Calumet, Mich.: Privately printed, 1961.

"Driving Cotton Mills by Electricity." *Engineering News* 31 (1894): 369.

DuBoff, Richard B. "The Introduction of Electric Power in American Manufacturing." *Economic History Review* 20 (1967): 509–518.

Ducoff-Barone, Deborah. "Marketing and Manufacturing: A Study of Domestic Cast Iron Articles Produced at Colebrookdale Furnace, Berks County, Pennsylvania, 1735–1751." *Pennsylvania History* 50 (1983): 20–37.

Dupree, A. Hunter. *Science and the Federal Government.* Cambridge, Mass.: Harvard University Press, 1957.

———. "The Role of Technology in Society and the Need for Historical Research." *Technology and Culture* 10 (1969): 528–534.

Durfee, W. F. "The First Systematic Attempt at Interchangeability in Firearms." *Cassier's Magazine* 5 (1893–1894): 469–477.

Eavenson, Howard N. *The First Century and Quarter of American Coal Industry.* Pittsburgh: Eavenson, 1942.

Elder, Ken, ed. *Site Guide for the SIA Study Tour of the Yukon and Alaska.* Ottawa: Society for Industrial Archaeology, 1990.

The Electric Century, 1874–1974. Reprints from *Electrical World.* New York: McGraw-Hill, 1974.

"Electrical Transmission." *New England Cotton Textile Manufacturers Association Transactions* 76 (1904): 201–206.

Elliott, D. O. *The Improvement of the Lower Mississippi River for Flood Control and Navigation.* Vicksburg, Miss.: U.S. Waterways Experiment Station, 1932.

Emerson, James. *Treatise Relative to the Testing of Water-Wheels and Machinery.* 4th ed. Willimanset, Mass.: Emerson, 1892.

Englund, John. "Sawmills of Worcester County." File report, Old Sturbridge Village, 1982.

Erikson, Kai T. *Everything in Its Path: Destruction of Community in the Buffalo Creek Flood.* New York: Simon and Schuster, 1976.

Evans, Oliver. *The Young Mill-Wright and Miller's Guide.* 13th ed. Philadelphia: Lea & Blanchard, 1850. Reprint. New York: Arno Press, 1972.

Eves, Jamie. "'Shrunk to a Comparative Rivulet': Deforestation, Stream Flow and Rural Milling in 19th-Century Maine." *Technology and Culture* 33 (1992): 38–65.

Ezell, Edward C. *The AK47 Story.* Harrisburg, Pa.: Stackpole, 1986.

The Factory Mutuals, 1835–1935. Providence, R.I.: Manufacturer's Mutual Fire Insurance Company, 1935.

Fell, James E. *Ores to Metals: The Rocky Mountain Smelting Industry.* Lincoln: University of Nebraska Press, 1979.

Ferguson, Eugene S. "The Mind's Eye: Nonverbal Thought in Technology." *Science* 197 (1977): 827–836.

————. *Oliver Evans: Inventive Genius of the American Industrial Revolution.* Greenville, Del.: Hagley Museum, 1980.

Ferraro, William M. "Biography of a Morris Canal Village: Bowerstown, Washington Township, Warren County, New Jersey, 1820–1940." *Canal History and Technology Proceedings* 8 (1989): 3–74.

Fillin-Yeh, Susan. "Charles Sheeler's *Rolling Power.*" In *The Railroad in American Art,* edited by Susan Danly and Leo Marx, pp. 145–163. Cambridge, Mass.: MIT Press, 1988.

The First Hundred Years of the New Jersey Zinc Company. New York: New Jersey Zinc Company, 1948.

Fitch, Charles H. "Report on the Manufactures of Interchangeable Mechanisms." In Bureau of the Census. *Report on the Manufactures of the United States at the Tenth Census.* Vol. 2, pp. 611–725. Washington, D.C.: Census Office, 1883.

————. "The Rise of a Mechanical Ideal." *Magazine of American History* 11 (1884): 516–527.

Fitzsimmons, Neal, ed. *The Reminiscences of John B. Jervis.* Syracuse, N.Y.: Syracuse University Press, 1971.

Flink, James J. *The Automobile Age.* Cambridge, Mass.: MIT Press, 1988.

Foley, Vernard, and others. "Leonardo, the Wheel Lock, and the Milling Machine." *Technology and Culture* 24 (1983): 399–427.

Forman, Benno M. "Mill Sawing in Seventeenth-Century Massachusetts." *Old Time New England* 60 (1970): 110–130.

Forty, Gerald. "Sources of Latitude Error in English 16th Century Navigation." *Journal of the Institute of Navigation* 36 (1983): 388–403.

————. "The Backstaff and the Determination of Latitude at Sea in the 17th Century." *Journal of the Institute of Navigation* 39 (1986): 259.

Fram, Mark, ed. *Niagara: A Selective Guide to Industrial Archaeology in Niagara Peninsula.* Toronto: Ontario Society for Industrial Archaeology, 1984.

Frame, Robert. "Grain Storage and the Development of the Elevator." In *A Guide to the Industrial Archeology of the Twin Cities,* edited by Nicholas Westbrook, pp. 62–66. Washington, D.C.: Society for Industrial Archeology, 1983.

Francaviglia, Richard. *Hard Places: Reading the Landscape of America's Historic Mining Districts.* Iowa City: University of Iowa Press, 1991.

Francis, James B. *Lowell Hydraulic Experiments.* Boston: Little, Brown, 1855.

————. "Fall of the Pemberton Mill." *Journal of the Franklin Institute* 39 (1860): 242–250.

Frank, Stuart M. "The Legacy of Stranded Whales." *Whalewatcher: Journal of the American Cetacean Society* 20 (1986): 3–9.

Freedley, Edwin T., ed. *A Treatise on the Principal Trades and Manufactures of the United States.* Philadelphia: Young, 1856.

Freeman, Keith. "An Analysis of the Nails from the Wilkinson Mill." 1979. Manuscript at Slater Mill Historic Site, Pawtucket, Rhode Island.

Fries, Russell. "European vs. American Engineering: Pierre Charles L'Enfant and the Water Power System of Paterson, N.J." *Northeast Historical Archaeology* 4 (1975): 68–96.

Fritz, John. *The Autobiography of John Fritz.* New York: Wiley, 1912.

Frye, Susan W., and Dennis E. Frye. *Maryland Heights Archaeological and Historical Resources Study.* Occasional Report No. 2, Regional Archaeology Program, National Capital Region. Washington, D.C.: National Park Service, 1989.

Gale, W.K.V. "Wrought Iron: A Valediction." *Transactions of the Newcomen Society* 36 (1963–1964): 1–11.

————. "The Rolling of Iron," *Transactions of the Newcomen Society* 37 (1964–1965): 35–46.

————. *The Black Country Iron Industry.* London: Metals Society, 1979.

"General Electric in the Development of the Textile Industry." Advertisement/article in *Index to the Transactions of the National Association of Cotton Manufacturers*, 1926.

Gersuny, Carl. *Work Hazards and Industrial Conflict.* Hanover, N.H.: University Press of New England, 1981.

Gibbon, Guy. *Explanation in Archaeology.* Oxford: Blackwell, 1989.

Gilbert, David T. *Where Industry Failed: Water-Powered Mills at Harpers Ferry, W.V.* Charleston, W.Va.: Pictorial Histories, 1984.

Gilbert, K. R. "The Ames Recessing Machine: A Survivor of the Original Enfield Rifle Machinery." *Technology and Culture* 4 (1963): 207–211.

Glass, Brent. *North Carolina: An Inventory of Historic Engineering and Industrial Sites.* Washington, D.C.: Historic American Engineering Record, 1976.

Gnudi, Martha T., trans. *The Various and Ingenious Machines of Agostino Ramelli.* 1588. Reprint. New York: Dover, 1976.

Gordon, Robert B. "The Metallurgical Museum of Yale College and Nineteenth Century Ferrous Metallurgy in New England." *Journal of Metals* 34 (1982): 102–110.

————. "Cost and Use of Water Power During Industrialization in New England and Great Britain: A Geological Interpretation." *Economic History Review* 36 (1983): 240–259.

————. "English Iron for American Arms: Laboratory Evidence on the Source of Iron Used at the Springfield Armory in 1860." *Journal of the Historical Metallurgical Society* 17 (1983): 91–98.

————. "History of Sea Level Changes Along the Connecticut Shore." In *Connecticut Archaeology: Past, Present, and Future*, Occasional Papers in Anthropology, edited by R. E. Dewar, K. L. Feder, and D. A. Poirier, pp. 61–78. Storrs: Department of Anthropology, University of Connecticut. 1983.

————. "Material Evidence of the Development of Metal Working Technology at the Collins Axe Factory." *IA, Journal of the Society for Industrial Archeology* 9 (1983): 19–28.

————. "Materials for Manufacturing: The Response of the Connecticut Iron Industry to Technological Change and Limited Resources." *Technology and Culture* 24 (1983): 602–634.

———. "Hydrological Science and the Development of Water Power for Manufacturing." *Technology and Culture* 26 (1985): 204–235.

———. "Laboratory Evidence of the Use of Metal Tools in Machu Picchu and Environs." *Journal of Archaeological Science* 12 (1985): 311–327.

———. "Sixteenth-Century Metalworking Technology Used in the Manufacture of Two German Astrolabes." *Annals of Science* 44 (1987): 71–84.

———. "Gaging, Measurement and the Control of Artificer's Work in Manufacturing." *Polhem* 6 (1988): 159–172.

———. "Material Evidence of the Manufacturing Methods Used in 'Armory Practice.'" *IA, Journal of the Society for Industrial Archeology* 14 (1988): 23–25.

———. "Strength and Structure of Wrought Iron." *Archeomaterials* 2 (1988): 109–137.

———. "Who Turned the Mechanical Ideal into Mechanical Reality?" *Technology and Culture* 29 (1988): 744–778.

———. "Simeon North, John Hall, and Mechanized Manufacturing." *Technology and Culture* 30 (1989): 179–188.

———. "Machine Archeology: The John Gage Planner." *IA, Journal of the Society for Industrial Archeology* 17 (1991): 3–14.

Gordon, Robert B., and M. S. Raber. "An Early American Integrated Steel Works." *IA, Journal of the Society for Industrial Archeology* 10 (1984): 17–34.

Gordon, Robert B., and T. S. Reynolds. "Medieval Iron in Society." *Technology and Culture* 27 (1986): 110–117.

Gordon, Robert B., and Geoffrey Tweedale. "Pioneering in Steelmaking at the Collins Axe Factory." *Journal of the Historical Metallurgy Society* 24 (1990): 1–11.

Gordon, Robert B., and N. J. van der Merwe. "Metallographic Study of Iron Artifacts from the Eastern Transvaal, South Africa." *Archaeometry* 26 (1984): 108–127.

Gordon, Robert B., and others. *Toward a New Iron Age? Quantitative Modeling of Resource Exhaustion.* Cambridge, Mass.: Harvard University Press, 1987.

Gracy, David, II. "Moses Austin and the Development of the Missouri Lead Industry." *Gateway Heritage* 1 (1981): 42–48.

Green, Lewis. *The Gold Hustlers.* Anchorage: Alaska Northwest, 1977.

Greenhill, Ralph. *Engineer's Witness.* Boston: Godine, 1985.

Greenleaf, James L. "Report on the Mississippi River and Some of Its Tributaries." In Bureau of the Census, Tenth Census. *Reports on the Water-Power of the United States.* Vol. 17, pp. 119–276. Washington, D.C.: Census Office, 1887.

Greenwood, Richard. "A History of the Blackstone Canal, 1825–1849." Report for the Rhode Island Historical Preservation Commission, 1984.

———. "Zachariah Allen and the Architecture of Industrial Paternalism." *Rhode Island History* 46 (1988): 117–135.

———. "Natural Run and Artificial Falls: Waterpower and the Blackstone Canal." *Rhode Island History* 49 (1991): 51–62.

Gross, Laurence. "The Importance of Research Outside the Library: Watkins Mill, A Case Study." *IA, Journal of the Society for Industrial Archeology* 7 (1981): 15–26.

———. "Wool Carding: A Study of Skills and Technology." *Technology and Culture* 28 (1987): 804–827.

———. "Building on Success: Lowell Mill Construction and Its Results." *IA, Journal of the Society for Industrial Archeology* 14 (1988): 29–30.

Guarasci, Richard. "Death by Cotton Dust." In *Corporate Violence,* edited by Stuart Hills, pp. 76–92. Totowa, N.J.: Towman and Littlefield, 1987.

Gundrum, Paul T. "The Charcoal Iron Industry in Eighteenth Century America: An Expression of Regional Economic Variation." Master's thesis, University of Wisconsin, 1974.

Gutman, Herbert. *Work, Culture, & Society in Industrializing America*. New York: Vintage Books, 1977.

Hall, W. E. "Direct Electric-Driven Machines." *Cassier's Magazine* 7 (1895): 314–320.

Hallet, M. M. "A Note on Slag from the First American Blast Furnace." *Bulletin of the Historical Metallurgy Group* 7 (1973): 6.

Hambourg, Serge. *Mills and Factories of New England*. New York: Abrams, 1988.

Hamilton, Alice. *Exploring the Dangerous Trades*. Boston: Little, Brown, 1943.

Hamilton, T. M. "Some Gun Parts from 17th Century Seneca Sites." In *Indian Trade Guns*, edited by T. M. Hamilton. *Missouri Archeologist* 22 (1960): 101–107.

Hardesty, Donald L. "The Archaeological Significance of Mining Districts." In *Proceedings of the Workshop on Historic Mining Resources*, edited by Jeff Beuchler, pp. 77–90. Vermillion, S.D.: State Historical Preservation Center, 1987.

———. *The Archaeology of Mining and Miners: A View from the Silver State*. Special Publication No. 6. N.p.: Society for Historical Archaeology, 1988.

Harrington, J. C. *Glassmaking at Jamestown*. Richmond, Va.: Dietz Press, ca. 1952.

Harris, J. R. "Skills, Coal, and British Industry in the Eighteenth Century." *History* 61 (1976): 167–182.

Harrison, J. L. *The Great Bore*. North Adams, Mass.: Advance Job Print Works, 1891.

Harte, Charles R. "Some Engineering Features of the Old Northampton Canal." *Proceedings of the Connecticut Society of Civil Engineers* 49 (1933): 21–53.

———. "Connecticut's Canals." *Proceeding of the Connecticut Society of Civil Engineers* 54 (1938): 118–179.

Hartenberg, Richard, S. *National Historic Mechanical Engineering Landmarks*. New York: American Society of Mechanical Engineers, 1979.

Hartley, E. N. *Ironworks on the Saugus*. Norman: University of Oklahoma Press, 1957.

Harvey, David. "Reconstructing the American Bloomery Process." *Historic Trades Annual* 1 (1988): 19–37.

Hatcher, Harlan. *A Century of Iron and Men*. Indianapolis: Bobbs-Merrill, 1950.

Hayden, Brian, ed. *Lithic Use-Wear Analysis*. New York: Academic Press, 1979.

Hazen, M. H., and R. M. Hazen. *Wealth Inexhaustible*. New York: Van Nostrand Reinhold, 1985.

Headrick, Daniel R. *The Tools of Empire*. New York: Oxford University Press, 1981.

Heald, Sarah P., ed. *Fayette County, Pennsylvania: An Inventory of Historic Engineering Sites*. Washington, D.C.: National Park Service, 1990.

Heardon, Patrick. *Independence and Empire: The New South's Cotton Mill Campaign, 1865–1901*. DeKalb: Northern Illinois University Press, 1982.

Hemmerlin, Samuel G. *Report About the Mines in the United States of America*. Translated by Amandus Johnson. 1783. Reprint. Philadelphia: John Morton Library, 1931.

Hewison, Robert. *The Heritage Industry*. London: Methuen, 1987.

Hildebrand, Grant. *Designing for Industry: The Architecture of Albert Kahn*. Cambridge, Mass.: MIT Press, 1974.

Hills, Richard L. "Museums, History and Working Machines." In *History of Technology*, edited by A. Rupert Hall and Norman Smith, pp. 157–167. 2d annual volume. London: Mansell, 1977.

————. *Cotton Spinning*. Manchester: North Western Museum of Science & Industry, n.d.

Hindle, Brooke. "The American Industrial Revolution Through Its Survivals." In *Science and Society in Early America*, edited by R. S. Klein, pp. 271–310. Philadelphia: American Philosophical Society, 1986.

————, ed. *America's Wooden Age: Aspects of Its Early Technology*. Tarrytown, N.Y.: Sleepy Hollow Restorations, 1975.

————. *Material Culture in the Wooden Age*. Tarrytown, N.Y.: Sleepy Hollow Press, 1981.

Hindle, Brooke, and Steven Lubar. *Engines of Change: The American Industrial Revolution, 1790–1860*. Washington, D.C.: Smithsonian Institution Press, 1986.

Hoadley, R. Bruce. *Understanding Wood*. Newtown, Conn.: Taunton Press, 1980.

Hochschild, Harold K. *Lumberjacks and Rivermen in the Central Adirondacks, 1850–1950*. Blue Mountain Lake, N.Y.: Adirondack Museum, 1962.

Hodder, Ian. *Reading the Past: Current Approaches to Interpretation in Archaeology*. Cambridge: Cambridge University Press, 1986.

Hodgen, M. T. "Domesday Water Mills." *Antiquity* 13 (1939): 261–279.

Hoerr, John P. *And the Wolf Finally Came: The Decline of the American Steel Industry*. Pittsburgh: University of Pittsburgh Press, 1988.

Hoke, Donald. *Ingenious Yankees: The Rise of the American System of Manufactures in the Private Sector*. New York: Columbia University Press, 1990.

Hole, Frank. "Changing Directions in Archaeological Thought." In *Ancient South Americans*, edited by J. D. Jennings, pp. 1–23. San Francisco: Freeman, 1983.

Holland, Max. *When the Machine Stopped*. Boston: Harvard Business School Press, 1989.

Hopewell Furnace: A Guide to Hopewell Village National Historic Site. National Park Handbook No. 34. Washington, D.C.: Department of the Interior, 1983.

Horn, James P. "'The Bare Necessities': Standards of Living in England and the Chesapeake, 1650–1700." *Historical Archaeology* 22 (1988): 74–91.

Howell, Charles. "Colonial Watermills in the Wooden Age." In *America's Wooden Age: Aspects of Its Early Technology*, edited by Brooke Hindle, pp. 120–159. Tarrytown, N.Y.: Sleepy Hollow Restorations, 1975.

Howell, Kenneth T., and Einar W. Carlson. *Men of Iron: Forbes & Adam*. Lakeville, Conn.: Pocketknife Press, 1980.

Hounshell, David. *From the American System to Mass Production, 1800–1932*. Baltimore: Johns Hopkins University Press, 1984.

Hubbard, Guy. "Development of Machine Tools in New England." *American Machinist* 59 (1923): 1–4, 139–142, 241–244, 311–315, 389–392, 463–467, 541–544, 579–581, 919–922; 60 (1924): 129–132, 171–173, 205–209, 255–258, 271–274, 437–441, 617–620, 875–878, 951–954; 61 (1924): 65–69, 195–198, 269–272, 313–316, 453–455.

Hubbert, M. King. "Energy Resources." In Committee on Resources and Man of the National Academy of Sciences. *Resources and Man*. San Francisco: Freeman, 1969.

Hudon, Paul. Interview with Harold Swenson, 1989. Transcription at Museum of American Textile History, North Andover, Massachusetts.

Hull, Daniel R. *Casting of Brass and Bronze*. Cleveland: American Society for Metals, 1950.

Hunter, Louis C. *A History of Industrial Power in the United States, 1780–1930*. Vol. 1, *Waterpower*. Charlottesville: University Press of Virginia, 1979.

————. *A History of Industrial Power in the United States*. Vol. 2, *Steam Power*. Charlottesville: University Press of Virginia, 1985.

Hunter, Louis C., and Lynwood Bryant. *A History of Industrial Power in the United States, 1780–1930.* Vol. 3, *The Transmission of Power.* Cambridge, Mass.: MIT Press, 1991.

Hutchins, George. "History of the Knowles Loom." In file labeled "History of Weaving Machinery as Applied to Crompton & Knowles Loom Works." Crompton & Knowles Development Board Records, 1917–1954. 26 vols. Museum of American Textile History, North Andover, Massachusetts.

Hyde, Charles K. *The Lower Peninsula of Michigan: An Inventory of Historic Engineering and Industrial Sites.* Washington, D.C.: Historic American Engineering Record, 1976.

———. *The Upper Peninsula of Michigan: An Inventory of Historic Engineering and Industrial Sites.* Washington, D.C.: Historic American Engineering Record, 1978.

———. *Detroit: An Industrial History Guide.* Detroit: Detroit Historical Society, 1980.

Jackle, John A. "Landscapes Redesigned for the Automobile." In *The Making of the American Landscape,* edited by Michael P. Conzen. Boston: Unwin Hyman, 1990.

Jacob, May Jane, and Linda Downs. *The Rouge: The Image of Industry in the Art of Charles Sheeler and Diego Rivera.* Detroit: Detroit Institute of Arts, 1978.

Jacobs, Renee. *Slow Burn: A Photodocument of Centralia, Pennsylvania.* Philadelphia: University of Pennsylvania Press, 1986.

Jeremy, David J. *Transatlantic Industrial Revolution: The Diffusion of Textile Technologies Between Britain and America, 1790–1830s.* Cambridge, Mass.: MIT Press, 1981.

———. *Technology and Power in the Early American Cotton Industry.* Philadelphia: American Philosophical Society, 1990.

Jewett, L. C. "What the Molder Has to Do." *American Machinist* 23 (1900): 323.

Jochim, Michael. "Optimization Models in Context." In *Archaeological Hammers and Theories,* edited by James A. Moore and Arthur S. Keene, pp. 157–172. New York: Academic Press, 1983.

Johnson, Leland R. *The Falls City: A History of the Louisville District, Corps of Engineers, U.S. Army.* Louisville, Ky.: U.S. Army Corps of Engineers, 1975.

Johnson, Walter R. *Notes on the Use of Anthracite in the Manufacture of Iron.* Boston: Little, Brown, 1841.

Jones, Franklin D. *Jig and Fixture Design.* New York: Industrial Press, 1920.

Jones, P. D., and K. R. Briffa. "Riverflow Reconstruction from Tree Rings in Southern Britain." *Journal of Climatology* 4 (1984): 461–472.

Joyce, Patrick, ed. *The Historical Meanings of Work.* Cambridge: Cambridge University Press, 1987.

Kakar, Sudhir. *Frederick Taylor: A Study in Personality and Innovation.* Cambridge, Mass.: MIT Press, 1970.

Kasierski, Steven. "Giving Out the Psalm." Honors thesis, Stanford University, 1988.

Kasson, John F. *Civilizing the Machine.* New York: Grossman, 1976.

Keene, Arthur S. "Biology, Behavior and Borrowing: A Critical Examination of Optimal Foraging Theory in Archaeology." In *Archaeological Hammers and Theories,* edited by James A. Moore and Arthur S. Keene, pp. 135–155. New York: Academic Press, 1983.

Keller, Charles M., and Paul Benson. "Ignatius Streibich, Blacksmith." *Chronicle of the Early American Industries Association* 42 (1989): 47–49.

Keller, Charles M., and Janet Keller. *Thinking and Acting with Iron.* Cognitive Science Technical Report CS-91-08, Learning Series. Urbana–Champaign: Beckman Institute for Advanced Science and Technology, University of Illinois, 1991.

Kelley, Robert L. *Gold vs. Grain: The Hydraulic Mining Controversy in California's Sacramento Valley.* Glendale, Calif.: Arthur Clark, 1959.

Kemp, Emory L. "Structural Evaluation of Historic Concrete Bridges." In *Proceedings of the 3rd Historic Bridges Conference,* edited by David Simmons and Robert Sierakowski, pp. 8–13. Columbus: Ohio Historical Society, 1990.

Kemper, Jackson, III. *American Charcoal Making.* Hopwell Village, Pa.: Eastern National Park and Monument Association, n.d.

Kent, William. *The Mechanical Engineer's Pocket Book.* New York: Wiley, 1903.

Kidder, Frank E. *The Architect's and Builder's Pocket-Book.* 14th ed. New York: Wiley, 1905.

Kidney, Walter C. *The Three Rivers.* Pittsburgh: History and Landmarks Foundation, 1982.

Kidwell, C. B., and M. C. Christman. *Suiting Everyone: The Democratization of Clothing in America.* Washington, D.C.: Smithsonian Institution Press, 1978.

Killick, David J. "Technology in Its Social Setting: Bloomery Iron Smelting at Kasungu, Malawi, 1860–1940." Ph.D. diss., Yale University, 1990.

Kouwenhoven, John A. "The Designing of the Eads Bridge." *Technology and Culture* 23 (1982): 535–568.

Kraner, Hobart M. "Ceramics in the Saugus Blast Furnace Circa 1650." *Ceramic Bulletin* 37 (1960): 354–358.

Kulik, Gary. "Birmingham: Old Iron Furnaces Still Central Element of Industrial City's Skyline." *American Preservation* (February–March 1978): 20–23.

———. "The Beginnings of the Industrial Revolution in America: Pawtucket, Rhode Island, 1672–1829." Ph.D. diss., Brown University, 1980.

———. "A Factory System of Wood." In *Material Culture of the Wooden Age,* edited by Brooke Hindle, pp. 307–312. Tarrytown, N.Y.: Sleepy Hollow Press, 1981.

———. "Dams, Fish, and Farmers: The Defense of Public Rights in Eighteenth-Century Rhode Island." In *The New England Working Class and the New Labor History,* edited by H. G. Gutman and H. Ball, pp. 187–213. Urbana: University of Illinois Press, 1987.

Kulik, Gary, and Julia C. Bonham. *Rhode Island: An Inventory of Historic and Engineering Sites.* Washington, D.C.: Government Printing Office, 1978.

Kulik, Gary, and Patrick M. Malone. *The Wilkinson Mill.* Landmark Dedication Program. Pawtucket, R.I.: American Society of Mechanical Engineers, 1977.

Kulik, Gary, Roger Parks, and Theodore Z. Penn, eds. *The New England Mill Village, 1790–1860.* Cambridge, Mass.: MIT Press, 1982.

LaFayette, Kenneth D. *Flaming Brands.* Marquette, Mich.: LaFayette, 1990.

LaLande, Jeffrey. "Sojourners in Search of Gold: Hydraulic Mining Techniques of the Chinese on the Oregon Frontier." *IA, Journal of the Society for Industrial Archeology* 11 (1985): 39–41.

Lamar, Howard R., ed. *The Reader's Encyclopedia of the American West.* New York: Crowell, 1977.

Lambert, Paul, and Kenny Franks. *Voices from the Oil Fields.* Norman: University of Oklahoma Press, 1984.

Landes, David. *Revolution in Time.* Cambridge, Mass.: Harvard University Press, 1983.

Langbein, W. B. *Hydrology and Environmental Aspects of Erie Canal (1817–99).* U.S. Geological Survey Water Supply Paper No. 2038. Washington, D.C.: Government Printing Office, 1976.

Lankford, William T., and others, eds. *The Making, Shaping and Treating of Steel.* 10th ed. Pittsburgh: United States Steel, 1985.

Lankton, Larry D. "The Machine Under the Garden: Rock Drills Arrive at the Lake Superior Copper Mines, 1868–1883." *Technology and Culture* 24 (1983): 1–37.

———. *Cradle to Grave: Life, Work, and Death at the Lake Superior Copper Mines.* New York: Oxford University Press, 1991.

Lankton, Larry D., and Charles K. Hyde. *Old Reliable: An Illustrated History of the Quincy Mining Company.* Hancock, Mich.: Quincy Mine Hoist Association, 1982.

Lardner, Dionysius. *Manufactures in Metal.* Vol. 1, *Iron and Steel.* London: Longman, 1831.

Larkin, Jack. *The Reshaping of Everyday Life, 1790–1840.* New York: Harper & Row, 1988.

Lathrop, William G. *The Brass Industry in the United States.* Rev. ed. Mount Carmel, Conn.: Lathrop, 1926.

Layton, Edwin T., Jr. "Technology as Knowledge." *Technology and Culture* 15 (1974): 31–41.

———. " 'Scientific Technology,' 1845–1900: The Hydraulic Turbine and the Origins of American Industrial Research." *Technology and Culture* 20 (1979): 64–89.

Lazonick, William. "Factor Costs and the Diffusion of Ring Spinning in Britain Prior to World War I." *Quarterly Journal of Economics* (February 1981): 90–109.

Leary, Thomas E. "The Labor Process in an Early Textile Machine Shop: Workers at the Davis and Furber Company of North Andover, Massachusetts, 1830–1860." Ph.D. diss., Brown University, 1985.

———. "Shadows in the Cave: Industrial Ecology and Museum Practice." *Public Historian* 11 (1989): 39–60.

Leary, Thomas E., and Elizabeth C. Sholes. *From Fire to Rust.* Buffalo, N.Y.: Buffalo and Erie County Historical Society, 1987.

Lechtman, Heather. "Andean Value Systems and the Development of Prehistoric Metallurgy." *Technology and Culture* 25 (1984): 1–36.

Lee, James. *The Morris Canal: A Photographic History.* Easton, Pa.: Delaware Press, ca. 1979, 1988.

Leffel, James, *Construction of Mill Dams.* Springfield, Ohio: Leffel, 1881.

Leitner, Paul S. "The Oxford Furnace: Some Surprising Firsts in a Backwoods Enterprise." *Canal History and Technology Proceedings* 8 (1989): 213–239.

Lenihan, Daniel, ed. *Submerged Cultural Resources Study: Isle Royale National Park.* Southwest Cultural Resources Center Professional Papers No. 6. Santa Fe, N.M.: Southwest Cultural Resources Center, 1987.

Lenik, E. J. "A Study of Cast Iron Nails." *Historical Archaeology* 11 (1977): 45–47.

Lesley, J. P. *The Iron Manufacturer's Guide.* New York: Wiley, 1859.

Lesley, Robert W., ed. *Concrete Factories.* New York: Cement Age Company, ca. 1907.

Lewis, Pierce, F. "Small Town in Pennsylvania." *Annals of the Association of American Geographers* 62 (1972): 323–351.

Lewis, Ralph H. *Manual for Museums.* Washington, D.C.: National Park Service, 1976.

Lewis, W. David. "The Early History of the Lackwanna Iron and Coal Company." *Pennsylvania Magazine of History and Biography* 96 (1972): 424–468.

Licht, Walter. *Working for the Railroad.* Princeton, N.J.: Princeton University Press, 1983.

Light, John D. "The Archeological Investigation of Blacksmith Shops." *IA, Journal of the Society for Industrial Archeology* 10 (1984): 55–68.

Light, John D., and Henry Unglik. *A Frontier Fur Trade Blacksmith Shop, 1796–1812.* Rev. ed. Ottawa: Environment Canada, 1987.

Lincoln, Samuel B. *Lockwood Greene: The History of an Engineering Business, 1832–1958.* Brattleboro, Vt.: Stephen Greene, 1960.

Lindqvist, Svante. *Technology on Trial: The Introduction of Steam Power Technology into Sweden, 1715–1736.* Uppsala: Almqvist & Wiksell International, 1984.

Litchfield, Carter, and others. *The Bethlehem Oil Mill, 1745–1934.* Kemblesville, Pa.: Olarius Editions, 1984.

Loveday, Amos J., Jr. *The Rise and Decline of the American Cut Nail Industry.* Westport, Conn.: Greenwood Press, 1983.

Lowe, Jet, and others. *Industrial Eye.* Washington, D.C.: Preservation Press, 1986.

Lubar, Steven. *Engines of Change.* Washington, D.C.: National Museum of American History, 1986.

———. "Culture and Technological Design in the 19th-Century Pin Industry: John Howe and the Howe Manufacturing Company." *Technology and Culture* 28 (1987): 253–282.

Lynd, Robert, and Helen Lynd. *Middletown: A Study in American Culture.* New York: Harcourt, Brace & World, 1956.

Macaulay, David. *Mill.* Boston: Houghton Mifflin, 1983.

MacCord, C. W. *Lessons in Mechanical Drawing.* New York: Munn, 1879.

McFarland, W.H.S. "Dredging Operations of the Yukon Consolidated." *The Miner,* November 1939, pp. 44–48.

McGaw, Judith. "Accounting for Innovation: Technological Change and Business Practice in the Berkshire County Paper Industry." *Technology and Culture* 26 (1985): 703–725.

———. *Most Wonderful Machine: Mechanization and Social Change in Berkshire Paper Making, 1801–1885.* Princeton, N.J.: Princeton University Press, 1987.

McGeown, Patrick. *Heat the Furnace Seven Times More.* London: Hutchinson, 1967.

McGregor, Robert K. "Changing Technologies and Forest Consumption in the Upper Delaware Valley, 1790–1880." *Journal of Forest History* 32 (1988): 69–81.

McHugh, Jeanne. *Alexander Holley and the Makers of Steel.* Baltimore: Johns Hopkins University Press, 1980.

Macieski, Robert. "Samuel Slater and the Cotton Bicentennial." *Slater Mill Historic Site Newsletter* 20 (1990): 1–3.

McLaren, D. J., and B. J. Skinner, eds. *Resources and World Development.* New York: Wiley, 1987.

McLaurin, John T. *Sketches in Crude-Oil.* Harrisburg, Pa.: McLaurin, 1896.

Magaziner, Henry J. "The Rebirth of an Engineering Landmark." *APT Bulletin* 18 (1986): 52–64.

Main, Charles T. *Notes on Mill Construction.* Boston: Massachusetts Institute of Technology, 1886.

———. *Industrial Plants.* Boston: Main, 1911.

Malone, Michael P. *The Battle for Butte: Mining and Politics on the Northern Frontier, 1864–1906.* Seattle: University of Washington Press, 1981.

Malone, Patrick M. "Changing Military Technology Among the Indians of Southern New England, 1600–1677." *American Quarterly* 25 (1973): 48–63.

———. *Canals and Industry.* Lowell, Mass.: Lowell Museum, 1983.

———. "Museums and the History of Technology." *The Weaver of Information and Perspectives on Technological Literacy* 3, no. 1 (1984): 1–3.

———. "James B. Francis and the Northern Canal." In *Boston's Water Resource Development: Past, Present, and Future,* edited by Jonathan B. French, pp. 12–16. New York: American Society of Civil Engineers, 1986.

————. "Little Kinks and Devices at Springfield Armory, 1892–1918." *IA, Journal of the Society for Industrial Archeology* 14 (1988): 23–35, 59–76.

————. Taped interview with Tom Rockwell, 18 January 1990. Transcription at Museum of American Textile History, North Andover, Massachusetts.

————. "Standard Oil Refinery." In *Rhode Island: An Inventory of Historic Engineering and Industrial Sites,* edited by Gary Kulik and Julia C. Bonham, p. 81. Providence: Rhode Island Department of Transportation, 1990.

————. *The Skulking Way of War: Technology and Tactics Among the Indians of Southern New England, 1600–1677.* Lanham, Md.: Madison Books, 1991.

Malone, Patrick M., Michael S. Raber, and Beth Parkhurst. "Historical and Archaeological Assessment: Valley Falls Heritage Park." Report for the Town of Cumberland, Rhode Island, 1991.

Malone, Patrick M., and Robert Weibel. *Lowell Water Power System: Pawtucket Gatehouse Hydraulic Turbine.* Lowell, Mass.: American Society of Mechanical Engineers, 1985.

Malone, Patrick M., and others. "Phase III Archaeological Investigation at Forestdale Scythe Works, North Smithfield, Rhode Island." Brown University Public Archaeology Laboratory for North Smithfield Sewer Commission, 1979.

Marcosson, Isaac F. *Anaconda.* New York: Dodd, Mead, 1957.

Martin, Patrick. "The Perspective of the Historical Archaeologist." In *Proceedings of the Workshop on Historic Mining Resources,* edited by Jeff Beuchler, pp. 91–107. Vermillion, S.D.: State Historical Preservation Center, 1987.

————. "Mining on Minong: Copper Mining on Isle Royale." *Michigan History* 74 (1990): 19–25.

————. "An Archaeological Perspective on Nineteenth Century Copper Mining Communities in Upper Michigan, USA." In *Toward a Social History of Mining,* edited by Klaus Tenfelde, pp. 199–214. Munich: Beck, 1992.

Mass, William. "Mechanical and Organizational Innovation: The Drapers and the Automatic Loom." *Business History Review* 63 (1989): 876–929.

Mass, William, and Charles Levenstein. "Labor Relations, Technology, and Occupational Disease: Banning the Suck Shuttle in Massachusetts, 1911." Paper presented at the Business History Conference, Hartford, Conn., March 1984.

Mead, Daniel. *Water Power Engineering.* New York: McGraw-Hill, 1920.

Meadows, H. D., and others. *The Limits of Growth: A Report for the Club of Rome's Project on the Predicament of Mankind.* New York: New American Library, 1970.

Meeks, Carroll L. V. *The Railroad Station: An Architectural History.* New Haven, Conn.: Yale University Press, 1956.

Metalworking: Yesterday and Tomorrow. New York: American Machinist, 1978.

Miller, Ernest C. *Pennsylvania's Oil Industry.* Gettysburg: Pennsylvania Historical Association, 1974.

Miller, Harry. "Potash from Wood Ashes: Frontier Technology in Canada and the United States." *Technology and Culture* 21 (1980): 187–208.

Mills, A. P. "The Old Essex–Merrimack Suspension Bridge at Newburyport, Massachusetts, and Tests of Its Wrought Iron Links after 100 Years' Service." *Engineering News* 66 (1911): 129–132.

Mills, C. E. "Ground Movement and Subsidence at the United Verde Mine." *Transactions of the American Institute of Mining and Metallurgical Engineers* 109 (1934): 153–172.

Minter, Roy. *The White Pass: Gateway to the Klondike.* Toronto: McClelland and Stewart, 1987.

Mirsky, Jeanette, and Allan Nevins. *The World of Eli Whitney.* New York: Macmillan, 1952.

Mokyr, Joel. *The Lever of Riches: Technology, Creativity and Economic Progress.* New York: Oxford University Press, 1990.

Molloy, Peter. "Technical Education and the Young Republic: West Point as America's Ecole Polytechnique, 1802–1833." Ph.D. diss., Brown University, 1975.

———. *History of Metal Mining and Metallurgy: An Annotated Bibliography.* New York: Garland, 1986.

Montgomery, David. *Workers' Control in America: Studies in the History of Work, Technology, and Labor Struggles.* New York: Cambridge University Press, 1979.

———. *The Fall of the House of Labor.* New York: Cambridge University Press, 1987.

Montgomery, James. *A Practical Detail of the Cotton Manufacture of the United States of America.* Glasgow: John Niven, 1840.

Moore, James A., and Arthur S. Keene, eds. *Archaeological Hammers and Theories.* New York: Academic Press, 1983.

More, Charles. *Skill and the English Working Class, 1870–1914.* London: Croom Helm, 1980.

Morris, Homer L. *The Plight of the Bituminous Coal Miner.* Philadelphia: University of Pennsylvania Press, 1934.

Morton, G. R., and R. G. Brit. "The Present Day Production of Wrought Iron." *Journal of the Historical Metallurgy Society* 8 (1974): 96–102.

Mowbray, George M. *Tri-Nitro Glycerine as Applied in the Hoosac Tunnel, Submarine Building, Etc.* North Adams, Mass.: J. T. Robinson, 1872.

Mulholland, James A. *A History of Metals in Colonial America.* University: University of Alabama Press, 1981.

Multhauf, Robert P. "Potash." In *Material Culture of the Wooden Age,* edited by Brooke Hindle, pp. 227–240. Tarrytown, N.Y.: Sleepy Hollow Press, 1981.

Naramore, Earl. *Principles and Practice of Loading Ammunition.* Georgetown, S.C.: Samworth, 1954.

Nash, Roderick. *Wilderness and the American Mind.* New Haven, Conn.: Yale University Press, 1967.

The National Atlas of the United States of America. Washington, D.C.: U.S. Geological Survey, 1970.

Navin, Thomas R. "Innovation and Management Policies—The Textile Machinery Industry: Influence of the Market on Management." *Bulletin of the Business Historical Society* 25 (1951): 15–30.

Nelson, Daniel. *Managers and Workers: Origins of the New Factory System in the United States, 1880–1920.* Madison: University of Wisconsin Press, 1975.

———. *Frederick W. Taylor and the Rise of Scientific Management.* Madison: University of Wisconsin Press, 1980.

Nelson, Lee H. "Nail Chronology as an Aid to Dating Old Buildings." *History News* 24 (1968). [American Association for State and Local History Technical Leaflet No. 48]

Nevins, Allen, and Frank E. Hill. *Ford: The Times, the Man, and the Company.* New York: Scribner's, 1954.

The New England Textile Mill Survey. Washington, D.C.: Historic American Buildings Survey, 1971.

Newell, Dianne. "Industrial Archeology as a Scholarly Discipline." In *Industrial Archeology and the Human Sciences,* edited by Dianne Newell, pp. 2–4. Washington, D.C.: Society for Industrial Archeology, 1978.

———. *Technology on the Frontier: Mining in Old Ontario.* Vancouver: University of British Columbia Press, 1986.

————, ed. *Industrial Archeology and the Human Sciences*. Occasional Publication No. 3. Washington, D.C.: Society for Industrial Archeology, 1978.

Newell, Dianne, and Ralph Greenhill. *Survivals: Aspects of Industrial Archaeology in Ontario*. Erin, Ont.: Boston Mills Press, 1989.

Nichols, Francis H. "Children of the Coal Shadow." *McClure's*, February 1903, pp. 437–444.

Nixon, Scott. "A History of Metal Inputs to Narragansett Bay." Report for the Narragansett Bay Project (preliminary draft), 1990.

Noble, David. *Forces of Production: A Social History of Industrial Automation*. New York: Knopf, 1984.

Norris, Frank. "The Tramway Story." Paper presented to the Society for Industrial Archeology—Yukon Study Tour, 1990.

North, S.D.N., and R. H. North. *Simeon North: First Official Pistol Maker of the U.S.* Concord, N.H.: Rumford Press, 1913.

Osborn, H. S. *The Metallurgy of Iron and Steel*. Philadelphia: Baird, 1869.

Overman, Frederick. *The Manufacture of Iron*. Philadelphia: Baird, 1850.

Paine, Sidney. "Electrical Driving of Textile Establishments." *New England Cotton Manufacturers Association Transactions* 58 (1895): 216–241.

Paley Commission [U. S. President's Materials Policy Commission]. *Resources for Freedom*. Washington, D.C.: Government Printing Office, 1952.

Palmer, Marilyn. "Industrial Archaeology as Historical Archaeology." *AIA Bulletin* 15 (1988): 1–3.

Parton, W. Julian. *The Death of the Great Company: Reflections on the Decline and Fall of the Lehigh Coal and Navigation Company*. Easton, Pa.: Center for Canal History and Technology, 1986.

Passer, Harold C. *The Electrical Manufacturers, 1875–1900*. Cambridge, Mass.: Harvard University Press, 1953.

Patric, J. H., and R. G. Reinhart. "Hydrologic Effects of Deforesting in Two Mountain Watersheds of West Virginia." *Water Resources Research* 7 (1971): 1182–1188.

Paul, Rodman. *Mining Frontiers of the Far West, 1848–1880*. Albuquerque: University of New Mexico Press, 1963.

Pelto, Pertti. *The Snowmobile Revolution: Technology and Social Change in the Arctic*. Menlo Park, Calif.: Cummings, 1973.

Penn, Theodore Z. "Archeological Evidence and the Study of Historical Industry." In *Industrial Archeology and the Human Sciences*, edited by Dianne Newell, pp. 6–8. Washington, D.C.: Society for Industrial Archeology, 1978.

————. "A Brand-New 150 Year Old Drawing Frame." *Bulletin of the Association for Preservation Technology* 12 (1980): 49–54.

————. "The Development of the Leather Belt Main Drive." *IA, Journal of the Society for Industrial Archeology* 7 (1981): 1–14.

Penn, Theodore Z., and Roger Parks. "The Nichols-Colby Sawmill in Bow, New Hampshire." *IA, Journal of the Society for Industrial Archeology* 1 (1975): 1–12.

Pierson, William H., Jr. *American Buildings and Their Architects: Technology and the Picturesque*. Garden City, N.Y.: Doubleday, 1978.

Pithole: A Brief History. Titusville, Pa.: Titusville Herald, 1962.

"Plants of the Remington Arms Co. . . . , I." *American Machinist* 45 (1916): 881–886.

Platt, Franklin. *Causes, Kinds, and Amount of Waste in Mining Anthracite*. Harrisburg, Pa.: Second Geological Survey, 1881.

Plowden, David. *Bridges: The Spans of North America*. New York: Viking Press, 1974.

Pool, J. Lawrence, and Angeline Pool. *America's Valley Forges and Valley Furnaces*. West Cornwall, Conn.: Pool, 1982.

Powell, H. Benjamin. *Philadelphia's First Fuel Crisis: Jacob Cist and the Developing Market for Pennsylvania Anthracite.* University Park: Pennsylvania State University Press, 1978.

Pressey, Henry A. *Water Powers of the State of Maine.* Water Supply Paper No. 69. Washington, D.C.: Government Printing Office, 1902.

Prolix, Peregrine [Philip Nicklin]. *Journal Through Pennsylvania—1835, by Canal, Rail and Stage Coach.* York, Pa.: American Canal and Transportation Center, 1978.

Pumpelly, R., J. E. Wolf, and T. N. Dale. *Geology of the Green Mountains in Massachusetts.* U.S. Geological Survey Monograph No. 23. Washington, D.C.: Government Printing Office, 1894.

Pursell, Carroll W., Jr. *Early Stationary Steam Engines in America.* Washington, D.C.: Smithsonian Institution Press, 1969.

Raber, Michael S. *Ford Motor Company Edgewater Assembly Plant: Assembly Building.* HAER No. NJ-53-A. Washington, D.C.: Historic American Engineering Record, 1990.

Raber, Michael S., and Patrick M. Malone. "Historical Documentation, River Canal Feasibility Study and Master Plan, Windsor Locks Canal Heritage State Park." Report for the Connecticut Department of Environmental Protection, 1991.

Raber, Michael S., P. M. Malone, and R. B. Gordon. "Historical and Archeological Assessment of the Tredegar Iron Works Site, Richmond, Virginia." Report for the Valentine Museum and the Ethyl Corporation, 1992.

Raber, Michael S., Patrick M. Malone, and Charles Parrott. "Muskingum River and Dam Study, Ohio Department of Natural Resources: Historical Significance." Report for Woolpert Consultants, 1991.

Raber, Michael S., and others. "Conservative Innovators and Military Small Arms: An Industrial History of the Springfield Armory, 1794–1968." Report for the National Park Service, 1989.

———. "Preliminary Cultural Resources Assessment, New York State Barge Canal Study." Report for the New York District, U.S. Army Corps of Engineers, 1983.

Rackham, Oliver. *Trees and Woodland in the British Landscape.* London: Dent, 1976.

Ransom, James M. *Vanishing Ironworks of the Ramapos.* New Brunswick, N.J.: Rutgers University Press, 1966.

Rao, Y. K. *Stoichiometry and Thermodynamics of Metallurgical Processes.* Cambridge: Cambridge University Press, 1985.

Rahtz, P. A. "Medieval Milling." In *Medieval Industry,* edited by David Crossley, pp. 1–15. Council for British Archaeology Research Report No. 40. London: Council for British Archaeology, 1981.

Reader, W. J. *Macadam: The McAdam Family and the Turnpike Roads, 1798–1861.* London: Heinemann, 1980.

Reed, Robert C. *The Streamline Era.* San Marino, Calif.: Golden West Books, 1975.

Report of the Commissioners . . . The Great Fire in Boston. Boston, 1873.

Reuss, Martin. "Andrew A. Humphreys and the Development of Hydraulic Engineering: Politics and Technology in the Army Corps of Engineers, 1850–1850." *Technology and Culture* 26 (1985): 1–33.

Reynolds, Michael. *Locomotive-Engine Driving.* London: Clowes, n.d.

Reynolds, Peter. *Iron Age Farm—The Butser Experiment.* London: British Museum, 1979.

Reynolds, Terry S. *Sault Ste. Marie: A Project Report.* Washington, D.C.: Government Printing Office, 1982.

———. "The Soo Hydro: A Case Study of the Influence of Managerial and Topographical Constraints on Engineering Design." *IA, Journal of the Society for Industrial Archeology* 8 (1982): 37–56.

———. *Stronger Than a Hundred Men: A History of the Vertical Water Wheel.* Baltimore: Johns Hopkins University Press, 1983.

———. "The Emergence of the Breast Wheel and Its Adoption in the United States." In *The World of the Industrial Revolution: Comparative and International Aspects of Industrialization,* edited by Robert Weible, pp. 55–88. North Andover, Mass.: Museum of American Textile History, 1986.

Rickard, Thomas A. *The Stamp Milling of Gold Ores.* New York: Scientific Publishing, 1901.

———. *Journeys of Observation Part II: Across the San Juan Mountains.* San Francisco: Dewey, 1907.

Risks and Rewards: Perspectives on Operating Mechanical Artifacts. Greenville, Del.: Hagley Museum and Library, 1991.

Rivard, Paul. *Samuel Slater: Father of American Manufactures.* Pawtucket, R.I.: Slater Mill Historic Site, 1974.

———. "Textile Experiments in Rhode Island, 1788–1789." *Rhode Island History* 33 (1974): 35–45.

Roberts, Ellis W. *The Breaker Whistle Blows.* Scranton, Pa.: Anthracite Museum Press, 1984.

Roberts, Peter. *The Anthracite Coal Industry.* New York: Macmillan, 1901.

Robinson, Paul, Marc Kelly, and Patricia Rubertone. "Preliminary Biocultural Interpretations from a Seventeenth-Century Narragansett Indian Cemetery in Rhode Island." In *Cultures in Contact: The European Impact on Native Cultural Institutions in Eastern North America, A.D. 1000–1800,* edited by William Fitzhugh, pp. 106–131. Washington, D.C.: Smithsonian Institution Press, 1985.

Roe, Joseph W. *English and American Tool Builders.* New Haven, Conn.: Yale University Press, 1916.

Rolt, L.T.C. *Navigable Waterways.* London: Longman, 1969.

———. *Tools for the Job.* Rev. ed. London: HMSO, 1986.

Rose, Joshua. *Modern Machine-Shop Practice.* 2 vols. New York: Scribner's, 1888.

Rose, Stephen J. *Workers on Edge: Work, Leisure, and Politics in Industrializing Cincinnati, 1788–1890.* New York: Columbia University Press, 1985.

Rosenberg, Nathan. *The American System of Manufactures.* Edinburgh: Edinburgh University Press, 1969.

———. *Perspectives on Technology.* Cambridge: Cambridge University Press, 1976.

———. *Inside the Black Box: Technology and Economics.* Cambridge: Cambridge University Press, 1982.

Rosenberg, Nathan, and L. E. Birdzell, Jr. *How the West Grew Rich.* New York: Basic Books, 1986.

Roth, Matthew. *Connecticut: An Inventory of Historic Engineering and Industrial Sites.* Washington, D.C.: Society for Industrial Archeology, 1981.

Roth, Matthew, and Bruce Clouette. *Historic Highway Bridges of Rhode Island.* Providence: Rhode Island Department of Transportation, 1990.

Rowe, Frank H. *The History of Iron and Steel in Scioto County.* Columbus: Ohio State Archaeological and Historical Society, 1938.

Rowe, John. *The Hard Rock Men: Cornish Immigrants and the North American Mining Frontier.* New York: Barnes & Noble, 1974.

Rutledge, J. W., and R. B. Gordon. "The Work of Metallurgical Artificers at Machu Picchu." *American Antiquity* 52 (1987): 578–594.

Saint Anthony Falls Rediscovered. Minneapolis: Minneapolis Riverfront Development Coordination Board, 1980.

Salay, David L., ed. *Hard Coal, Hard Times: Ethnicity and Labor in the Anthracite Region.* Scranton, Pa.: Anthracite Museum Press, 1983.

Salmon, John S. *The Washington Ironworks of Franklin County, Virginia, 1773–1850.* Richmond: Virginia State Library, 1986.

Saltonstall, Nathaniel. "A New and Further Narrative." In *Narratives of the Indian Wars*, edited by Charles H. Lincoln, pp. 75–98. New York: Barnes & Noble, 1959.

Sande, Theodore A. "The Textile Factory in Pre–Civil War Rhode Island." *Old Time New England* 66 (1975): 13–31.

————. *Industrial Archeology: A New Look at the American Heritage.* New York: Penguin, 1978.

Satterfield, Archie. *Chilkoot Pass.* Anchorage: Alaska Northwest, 1983.

Sayenga, Donald. "The Ohio Mississippi Waterway." *Canal History and Technology Proceedings* 7 (1988): 73–123.

Schenck, Helen R., and Reed Knox. "Wrought Iron Manufacture at Valley Forge." *MASCA Journal* 3 (1985): 132–141.

————. "Valley Forge: The Making of Iron in the Eighteenth Century." *Archaeology* 39 (1986): 27–33.

Schiffer, Margaret. *Survey of Chester County, Pennsylvania, Architecture.* Exton, Pa.: Schiffer, 1976.

Schivelbusch, Wolfgang. *The Railway Journal.* Translated by Anslem Hollo. New York: Urizen Books, 1977.

Schubert, H. R. *History of the British Iron and Steel Industry from c. 450 B.C. to A.D. 1775.* London: Routledge and Kegan Paul, 1957.

Scott, Douglas D., and others. *Archaeological Perspectives on the Battle of the Little Bighorn.* Norman: University of Oklahoma Press, 1989.

Scranton, Philip. *Figured Tapestry: Production, Markets, and Power in Philadelphia Textiles, 1885–1941.* New York: Cambridge University Press, 1989.

————. "The Workplace, Technology, and Theory in American Labor History." *International Labor and Working Class History* 35 (1989): 3–22.

Seely, Bruce. *Adirondack Iron and Steel Company "New Furnace," 1849–1854.* HAER No. NY-123. Washington, D.C.: Historic American Engineering Record, 1978.

Sellers, P. J., and J. G. Lockwood. "A Numerical Simulation of the Effects of Changing Vegetation Type on Surface Hydroclimatology." *Climatic Change* 3 (1981): 121–136.

Sellmer, George P. "Windham Forge Revisited." *New Jersey Highlander* 20 (1984): 3–33.

Shallat, Todd. "Building Waterways, 1802–1861: Science and the United States Army in Early Public Works." *Technology and Culture* 31 (1990): 18–50.

Shanks, M., and C. Tilley. *Re-Constructing Archaeology: Theory and Practice.* Cambridge: Cambridge University Press, 1987.

Sharp, M. B., and W. H. Thomas. *A Guide to the Old Stone Blast Furnaces in Western Pennsylvania.* Pittsburgh: Historical Society of Western Pennsylvania, 1966.

Sinclair, Bruce. *Philadelphia's Philosopher Mechanics: A History of the Franklin Institute, 1824–65.* Baltimore: Johns Hopkins University Press, 1974.

Sloane, Howard, and Lucille Sloane. *Pictorial History of American Mining.* New York: Crown, 1970.

Smith, Cyril Stanley. *A History of Metallography.* Chicago: University of Chicago Press, 1960.

————. "Production de fer à la fenderie de Saugus aux alentours de 1660." *Revue d'histoire de la sidérurgie* 7 (1966): 7–15.

————. *A Search for Structure.* Cambridge, Mass.: MIT Press, 1981.

Smith, Duane. *Mining America: The Industry and the Environment*. Lawrence: University Press of Kansas, 1987.

Smith, Grant H. *The History of the Comstock Lode, 1850–1920*. University of Nevada Bulletin, vol. 37, no. 3. Reno: Nevada Bureau of Mines and Geology, 1943.

Smith, Merritt Roe. "John H. Hall, Simeon North, and the Milling Machine: The Nature of Innovation Among Antebellum Arms Makers." *Technology and Culture* 14 (1973): 573–591.

———. *Harpers Ferry Armory and the New Technology*. Ithaca, N.Y.: Cornell University Press, 1977.

———. "Military Entrepreneurship." In *Yankee Enterprise*, edited by Otto Mayr and R. C. Post, pp. 63–102. Washington, D.C.: Smithsonian Institution Press, 1981.

———, ed. *Military Enterprise and Technological Change*. Cambridge, Mass.: MIT Press, 1985.

Snell, J. B. *Mechanical Engineering: Railways*. London: Longman, 1971.

Sokoloff, Kenneth L., and B. Z. Kahn. "The Democratization of Invention During Early Industrialization: Evidence from the U.S., 1790–1846." *Journal of Economic History* 50 (1990): 363–378.

Some of Pennsylvania's Child Workers. Pittsburgh: Pennsylvania Child Labor Association, 1913.

Spude, Robert L. S. "Mining Technology and Historic Preservation with Special Reference to the Black Hills." In *Proceedings of the Workshop on Historic Mining Resources*, edited by Jeff Buechler, pp. 45–58. Vermillion, S.D.: State Historical Preservation Center, 1987.

Spude, Robert L. S., and Sandra McDermott Faulkner. *Kennecott, Alaska*. Anchorage: National Park Service, Alaska Region, 1987.

Stachiw, Myron. *Negro Cloth: Northern Industry and Southern Slavery*. Boston: Boston National Historical Park, 1981.

Stackpole, Edouard A. *The Charles W. Morgan: The Last Wooden Whaleship*. New York: Meredith Press, 1967.

Stanton, Francis L. "The Use of Niagara Power." *Cassier's Magazine* 8 (1895): 173–192.

Stapleton, Darwin H. *The Transfer of Early Industrial Technologies to America*. Philadelphia: American Philosophical Society, 1987.

———, ed. *The Engineering Drawings of Benjamin Henry Latorbe*. New Haven, Conn.: Yale University Press, 1980.

Starbuck, David R. "The New England Glassworks." *New Hampshire Archaeologist* 27 (1986).

———. "The Shaker Mills in Canterbury, New Hampshire." *IA, Journal of the Society for Industrial Archeology* 12 (1986): 11–37.

State of Colorado Bureau of Mines Annual Report for the Year 1930. Denver: State of Colorado Bureau of Mines, 1931.

Steinberg, Theodore. *Nature Incorporated: Industrialization and the Waters of New England*. New York: Cambridge University Press, 1991.

Stephens, Carlene. "'Most Reliable Time': William Bond, the New England Railroads, and Time Awareness in 19th-Century America." *Technology and Culture* 30 (1989): 1–24.

Stetson, Francis L. "The Use of Niagara Water Power." *Cassier's Magazine* 8 (1895): 173–192.

Stilgoe, John R. *Metropolitan Corridor: Railroads and the American Scene*. New Haven, Conn.: Yale University Press, 1983.

Strohmeyer, John. *Crisis in Bethlehem: Big Steel's Struggle to Survive*. Bethesda, Md.: Adler and Adler, 1986.

Surface Water Supply of the United States, 1966–70. Part 1, *North Atlantic Slope Basins.* Vol. 1, *Basins from Maine to Connecticut.* U.S. Geological Survey Water Supply Paper No. 2101. Washington, D.C.: Government Printing Office, 1975.

Swain, George F. "Report on the Water Power of the Streams of Eastern New England." In Bureau of the Census, Tenth Census. *Reports on the Water-Power of the United States.* Vol. 16, pp. 39–160. Washington, D.C.: Census Office, 1885.

Swank, James M. *History of the Manufacture of Iron in All Ages.* 2d ed. Philadelphia: American Iron and Steel Association, 1892.

Swift, L. W., and others. "Simulation of Evapotranspiration and Drainage from Mature and Clear-cut Deciduous Forests and Young Pine Plantations." *Water Resources Research* 11 (1975): 667–673.

Temin, Peter. *Iron and Steel in Nineteenth-Century America: An Economic Inquiry.* Cambridge, Mass.: MIT Press, 1964.

"The Building of a Watch." *Scientific American,* 4 March 1899, p. 132.

Thompson, E. P. "Time, Work-Discipline, and Industrial Capitalism." *Past and Present* 38 (1967): 56–97.

Thompson, Kenneth. "Forest and Climate Change in America: Some Early Views." *Climatic Change* 3 (1980): 47–64.

Thompson, Michael D. *The Iron Industry of Western Maryland.* Morgantown, W.Va., 1976.

Thoreau, Henry David. *The Concord and the Merrimack.* New York: Bramhall House, 1954.

Tite, M. S. *Methods of Physical Examination in Archaeology.* London: Seminar Press, 1972.

Todd, Arthur C. *The Cornish Miner in America.* Truro: Barton, 1967.

Tomlinson, Charles. *Cyclopedia of Useful Arts, Mechanical and Chemical, Manufactures, Mining, and Engineering.* London: George Virtue, 1854.

Trachtenberg, Alan. *Reading American Photographs.* New York: Hill and Wang, 1989.

Trinder, Barrie. *The Making of the Industrial Landscape.* London: Dent, 1982.

Trout, W. E., III. *A Guide to the Works of the James River & Kanawha Canal from the City of Richmond to the Ohio River.* N.p.: Virginia Canals and Navigation Society, 1988.

Turner, Thomas. *The Metallurgy of Iron.* London: Griffin, 1900.

Twain, Mark. *Life on the Mississippi.* New York: Bantam, 1963.

———. *Roughing It.* New York: Penguin, 1983.

Tweedale, Geoffrey. *Sheffield Steel and America: A Century of Commercial and Technological Interdependence, 1830–1930.* Cambridge: Cambridge University Press, 1987.

———. "Science, Innovation and the 'Rule of Thumb': The Development of British Metallurgy in 1945." In *The Challenge of New Technology,* edited by Jonathan Liebenau, pp. 58–82. Aldershot: Gower, 1988.

Tweet, Roald. *A History of the Rock Island District, U.S. Army Corps of Engineers, 1866–1983.* Rock Island, Ill.: U.S. Army Engineer District, 1984.

Tylecote, Ronald F. *A History of Metallurgy.* London: Metals Society, 1976.

———. *The Prehistory of Metallurgy in the British Isles.* London: Institute of Metals, 1986.

Tylecote, Ronald F., and J. Cherry. "The 17th Century Bloomery at Muncaster Head." *Transactions of the Cumberland and Westmorland Antiquarian and Archaeological Society* 70 (1970): 69–109.

Underhill, Roy. *The Woodwright's Companion.* Chapel Hill: University of North Carolina Press, 1983.

U.S. Congress. House. *House Documents.* Vol. 138, 62d Congress, 2d sess., 4 December 1911–26 August 1912. Washington, D.C.: Government Printing Office, 1912.

Unrau, Harlan D. *Historic Structure Report (Historic Data Section): The Delaware Aqueduct.* Denver: National Park Service Center, 1983.

Ure, Andrew. *The Philosophy of Manufacture.* London: Charles Knight, 1835.

Uselding, Paul. "Elisha Root, Forging, and the 'American System.'" *Technology and Culture* 15 (1974): 543–568.

————. "Measuring Techniques and Manufacturing Practice." In *Yankee Enterprise,* edited by Otto Mayr and Robert C. Post, pp. 103–126. Washington, D.C.: Smithsonian Institution Press, 1981.

Vance, Stanley. *Industrial Structure and Policy.* Englewood Cliffs, N.J.: Prentice-Hall, 1961.

Vander Voort, George F. *Metallography Principles and Practice.* New York: McGraw-Hill, 1984.

————, ed. *Applied Metallography.* New York: Van Nostrand Reinhold, 1986.

Vandiver, Pamela. "The Implications of Variation in Ceramic Technology: The Forming of Neolithic Storage Vessels in China and the Near East." *Archeomaterials* 2 (1988): 130–174.

Vecchio, K. S., and A. R. Marder. "An Analytical Determination of a Saugus Pig." In *Microbeam Analysis-1984,* edited by A. D. Romig, Jr., and J. I. Goldstein, p. 247. San Francisco: San Francisco Press, 1984.

Vincenti, Walter P. "Technological Knowledge Without Science: The Invention of Flush Riveting in American Airplanes, ca. 1930–ca. 1950." *Technology and Culture* 26 (1984): 540–576.

Vogel, Robert M. "Tunnel Engineering." Paper No. 41, USM Bulletin No. 240. *Contributions from the Museum of History and Technology* (1964): 201–240.

————. *Roebling's Delaware and Hudson Canal Aqueducts.* Smithsonian Studies in History and Technology No. 10. Washington, D.C.: Smithsonian Institution Press, 1971.

————, ed. *Some Industrial Archeology of the Monumental City & Environs.* Washington, D.C.: Society for Industrial Archeology, 1975.

Walker, Joseph E. *Hopewell Village.* Philadelphia: University of Pennsylvania Press, 1966.

Wallace, Anthony. *Rockdale.* New York: Knopf, 1978.

————. *St. Clair: A Nineteenth-Century Coal Town's Experience with a Disaster-Prone Industry.* New York: Knopf, 1987.

Wegmann, Edward. *The Design and Construction of Dams.* New York: Wiley, 1922.

Weigley, Russell F., ed. *Philadelphia: A 300-Year History.* New York: Norton, 1982.

Weinburg, Arthur, ed. *Attorney for the Damned.* New York: Simon and Schuster, 1957.

Weiner, Norbert. *The Human Use of Human Beings: Cybernetics and Society.* New York: Avon, 1954.

Weiss, Harry B., and Grace M. Weiss. *The Early Sawmills of New Jersey.* Trenton: New Jersey Agricultural Society, 1968.

Weitzman, David. *Traces of the Past: A Field Guide to Industrial Archaeology.* New York: Scribner's, 1980.

————. *Superpower: The Making of a Steam Locomotive.* Boston: Godine, 1987.

Wells, Walter. *The Water Power of Maine.* Augusta, 1869.

White, John H., Jr. "The Railway Museum: Past, Present, and Future." *Technology and Culture* 14 (1973): 599–613.

————. "Tracks and Timber." *IA, Journal of the Society for Industrial Archeology* 2 (1976): 35–46.

————. *A History of the American Locomotive.* New York: Dover, 1979.

Williams, John H. *A Great and Shining Path.* New York: Times Books, 1989.

Williams, Michael. "Industrial Impacts on the Forests of the United States, 1860–1920." *Journal of Forest History* 31 (1987): 108–121.

————. *Americans and Their Forests.* New York: Cambridge University Press, 1989.

————. "The Clearing of the Forests." In *The Making of the American Landscape,* edited by Michael P. Conzen, pp. 146–168. Boston: Unwin Hyman, 1990.

Williamson, Harold F., and others. *The American Petroleum Industry: The Age of Energy, 1899–1959.* Evanston, Ill.: Northwestern University Press, 1963.

Wilson, Budd. "The Batsto Window Light Factory Excavation." *Bulletin of the Archeological Society of New Jersey,* no. 27 (1971): 11–18; no. 29 (1972): 28–31.

Wilson, John S. "Upper Factory Brook Sawmill." *IA, Journal of the Society of Industrial Archeology* 3 (1977): 43–52.

Winner, Langdon. *Autonomous Technology: Technics-out-of-Control as a Theme in Political Thought.* Cambridge, Mass.: MIT Press, 1977.

Wohl, Anthony S. *Endangered Lives, Public Health in Victorian Britain.* London: Dent, 1983.

Woodbury, C.J.H. *The Fire Protection of Mills and Construction of Mill Floors: Containing Tests of Full Size Wood Columns.* New York: Wiley, 1882.

————. "Electric Lighting in Mills." *Proceedings of the N. E. Cotton Manufacturers Association* 33 (1883): 14–58.

Woodbury, Robert S. "The Legend of Eli Whitney and Interchangeable Parts." *Technology and Culture* 1 (1960): 235–253.

————. *Studies in the History of Machine Tools.* Cambridge, Mass.: MIT Press, 1972.

Woodhouse, W. B. "The Electrical Driving of Textile Machinery." *Cassier's Magazine* 38 (1910): 24–38.

Working Water: A Guide to the Historic Landscape of the Blackstone River Valley. Providence: Rhode Island Department of Environmental Management, 1987.

Worrell, John. "Hervey Brooks's Pottery." In *Unearthing New England's Past: The Ceramic Evidence,* edited by Susan Montgomery, pp. 57–62. Lexington, Mass.: Museum of Our National Heritage, 1984.

————. "Ceramic Production in the Exchange Network of an Agricultural Neighborhood." In *Domestic Pottery of the Northeastern United States, 1625–1850,* edited by Sarah P. Turnbaugh, pp. 153–169. New York: Academic Press, 1985.

————. "Re-creating Ceramic Production and Tradition in a Living History Laboratory." In *Domestic Pottery of the Northeastern United States, 1625–1850,* edited by Sarah P. Turnbaugh, pp. 81–97. New York: Academic Press, 1985.

Worrell, John, and Ted Penn. "Of Ice and Men." *Old Sturbridge Visitor* 23 (1983): 6–7.

Worthen, W. E., ed. *Appleton's Cyclopedia of Drawing.* New York: Appleton, 1869.

Wrege, Charles D., and Ronald Greenwood. *Frederick W. Taylor, The Father of Scientific Management: Myths and Reality.* Homewood, Ill.: Business One Irwin, 1991.

Wyman, Mark. *Hard Rock Epic: Western Miners and the Industrial Revolution, 1860–1910.* Berkeley: University of California Press, 1979.

Yarns, Cloth Rooms, and Mill Engineering. Scranton, Pa.: International Textbook, 1924.

Yates, W. Ross. "Discovering the Process for Making Anthracite Iron." *Pennsylvania Magazine of History and Biography* 98 (1974): 206–223.

Young, Herbert V. *They Came to Jerome*. Jerome, Ariz.: Jerome Historical Society, 1972.

Young, Otis E., Jr. *Western Mining*. Norman: University of Oklahoma Press, 1970.

————. *Black Powder and Hand Steel*. Norman: University of Oklahoma Press, 1975.

Zimiles, Martha, and Murray Zimiles. *Early American Mills*. New York: Potter, 1973.

Zimmerman, Albright G. "The First Years of the Delaware Division Canal." *Canal History and Technology Proceedings* 8 (1989): 161–211.

Place and
Site Index

Numbers in italics refer to pages on which illustrations appear.

Subject Index

Numbers in italics refer to pages on which illustrations appear.

433

THE TEXTURE
OF INDUSTRY

*An Archaeological View
of the Industrialization
of North America*

Robert B. Gordon

Patrick M. Malone

New York   Oxford • Oxford University Press • 1994

Oxford University Press

Oxford   New York   Toronto
Delhi   Bombay   Calcutta   Madras   Karachi
Kuala Lumpur   Singapore   Hong Kong   Tokyo
Nairobi   Dar es Salaam   Cape Town
Melbourne   Auckland   Madrid

and associated companies in
Berlin   Ibadan

Published by Oxford University Press, Inc.,
200 Madison Avenue, New York, New York 10016

Library of Congress Cataloging-in-Publication Data
Gordon, Robert B. (Robert Boyd), 1929–
The texture of industry : an archaeological view of the industrialization
of North America / Robert B. Gordon, Patrick M. Malone.
p. cm.
Includes bibliographical references and index.
ISBN 0-19-505885-2
1. Industrial archaeology—North America.
2. Industrialization—North America.
I. Malone, Patrick M.   II. Title.
T21.G67 1994   609.7—dc20
92-17396

9 8 7 6 5 4 3 2 1

Printed in the United States of America
on acid-free paper